Peasant Violence and Antisemitism in Early Twentieth-Century Eastern Europe

Irina Marin

Peasant Violence and Antisemitism in Early Twentieth-Century Eastern Europe

palgrave
macmillan

Irina Marin
Augsburg University
Augsburg, Germany

ISBN 978-3-319-76068-1   ISBN 978-3-319-76069-8   (eBook)
https://doi.org/10.1007/978-3-319-76069-8

Library of Congress Control Number: 2018940694

Cover illustration: A cavalry patrol watching the burning of farmhouses by the rioters near
Bujeu. Samuel Begg, based on sketches sketches by Rook Carnegie in The Illustrated
London News (1907). Cover design by Tjaša Krivec

Printed on acid-free paper

This Palgrave Macmillan imprint is published by the registered company Springer Nature
Switzerland AG
The registered company address is: Gewerbestrasse 11, 6330 Cham, Switzerland

For Louisa, my beloved daughter

NOTE ON ARCHIVES AND ARCHIVAL RESEARCH

ANR = Arhivele Naţionale Istorice Centrale, Bucureşti, România.
PAAA = Politisches Archiv des Auswärtiges Amts, Berlin, Germany.
HHStA = Haus-, Hof- und Staatsarchiv, Vienna, Austria.
MOL = Magyar Országos Levéltár, Budapest, Hungary.
Covasna National Archives, Romania
Cluj National Archives, Romania
Bistriţa-Năsăud National Archives, Romania
Arhiva Istorică a Ministerului de Externe, Bucureşti, România.
Okhrana Archives, Hoover Institution Archives, Stanford University
Arhivele Naţionale Chişinău, Republica Moldova.
The National Archives, London, UK.

In this book I use archival material pertaining to all the provinces form-ing the triple frontier in addition to secondary sources and newspaper coverage in German, Romanian, Hungarian and Russian. The research has been anything but a smooth process primarily because of the atomized state of the relevant archives, destruction and dislocation through two world wars and bureaucratic obstruction. Take for instance the Archive of the Hungarian Ministry of the Interior between 1868 and 1918. The archive, which was originally located in Budapest, was partly destroyed during the wars, and partly removed and transferred to the Successor States after the First World War. The part of the archive relative to the ter-ritories that attached to Romania was taken by the Romanian army in 1919 and is currently divided between the Cluj and Bucharest archives.

The Romanian splinter of this archive has never been opened to the general public since 1919, was dipped in and out of by Communist Party historians and is currently fragmented: part of it is included in the Communist Party Archive in Bucharest, the bulk of it is in the Cluj archives, off-limits for the general public as it is uncatalogued. For the purposes of this book I only had access to the Bucharest archive, which means that, if/when the Cluj archive becomes available, the conclusions of the present study will have to be revisited in light of the new archival evidence. The full half of the glass in this story of archival inaccessibility is the philosophical consideration that, given the damage sustained during the war by the Hungarian archives in Budapest, the fact that part of the archive ended up in Romania is, even if off-limits for more than a hundred years and with no immediate prospects of that changing, nevertheless a blessing in admittedly very cunning disguise. The same fate befell the Habsburg archives in Czernowitz pertaining to the government of Bukovina under Austrian rule. They were removed by the Romanian authorities in 1918 and finished in the Bucharest National Archives in a holding labelled 'Guvernământul Bucovinei', which is currently only partly catalogued.

USE OF PLACE NAMES

In the present book I have opted for using historical place names rather than current ones where there does not exist an English version.

Beltsi / Bălţi
Brassó / Braşov
Czernowitz / Cernăuţi
Hermannstadt / Nagyszeben / Sibiu
Khotyn / Hotin
Kishinev / Chişinău
Kolozsvár / Cluj
Orsova / Orşova
Suczawa / Suceava
Temesvár / Timişoara

Acknowledgements

This book would never have been possible without the generous support of the Leverhulme Trust Foundation in the UK, who offered me a three-year Early-Career Fellowship between 2013 and 2016. This major grant gave me the necessary funding, time and peace of mind to conduct this study. I also owe a great debt of gratitude to the Vienna Wiesenthal Institute for Holocaust Studies, whose trustees awarded me a research fellowship, which enabled me to finish the final manuscript of the book.

A special place in my list of thanks goes to Trevor Thomas, for unstinting moral and academic support throughout the years and for delightful conversations about the topic of this book and a thousand other things as well as brilliant quotes and *mots*. I would of course never have embarked on this project and completed it without constant help, in every possible way, and timely prodding from my loving husband Daniel Brett.

A lot of friends and colleagues have also helped me with advice, bibliographic suggestions, sourcing material, feedback, constructive criticism and encouragement: Manuela Marin, Andrei Cușco, Ágoston Berecz, Daniela Sechel, Bálint Varga, Kati Prajda, Tom Lorman, Botond Nagy, Gábor Egry, Adrian Onofreiu, Alexander Korb, Steve King, Keith Snell, Rosemary Sweet, Joanna Story, Raul Cârstocea, Abigail Green, David Rechter, Patrick J. Bourne, Phil Barker, Vlad Popovici, Diana Covaci, Călin Goina, Mariann Nagy, Maria Mihaela Irimia, James Simpson, Juan Carmona, Socrates Petmezas, Valer Simion Cosma and the 2016 Telciu Summer Conference participants, Ulf Brunnbauer, Adrian-Bogdan Ceobanu, Cornel Micu, Béla Rásky and Éva Kovacs, Mark Lewis, Sarah Cramsey, Dimitrios Varvaritis, Ernst Langthaler, James Frunzetti, Adriana

Oprea, Andrei Sorescu, David Hopkin, Virgil Ţârău, Maren Johansen, Jeroen von Drunen, Natalya Lazar, Ceri Jones and Serena Iervolino, Karina Fernandez, Amy Samuelson and Jason Vaughn, Alexandru Săvescu, Pippa Sherriff and Maureen Duke.

I am particularly grateful to Maren Röger and Gregor Weber at the University of Augsburg for their patience and understanding while I was trying to balance out writing, teaching and child care. Warm thanks are also due to friends at Indiana University who helped: Alex Tipei and Jason Vincz who organized the Romanian Salon and provided me with the opportunity to present an early version of the project; Regina Smyth, Mark Roseman, Roberta Pergher, Ben Eklof, Maria Bucur, Padraic Kenney, Hiroaki Kuromiya and Julia Roos for their intellectual and social hospitality.

Special thanks are due to Dennis Deletant, Martyn Rady and Keith Snell for moral support and writing endless letters of recommendation long after I left the institutions they were affiliated with or, in the case of Dennis Deletant, long after he retired.

I would also like to thank Valerie Holman, Hilda Reed, Hetty and Martin Sookias, for being such wonderful neighbours while I lived in Charlbury, where I wrote the best part of the book manuscript. Gardening and apple tree wassailing provided therapeutic amusement as well as a welcome connection with rural worlds gone by.

Family support has always been forthcoming and generous and without it I would not have been able to finalize this project. Many thanks therefore are due to Christine Brett, Jenny Serra, John Brett, Elaine Brett, Adriana Marin and Sorin Marin.

The good things about the present book are the compounded result of help received from all of the above. Any shortcomings and failings are of my own making and, in part, caused by extraneous circumstances such as the vagaries of academia and the precarity of early-career researchers' everyday life. The final touches to this book were applied throughout 2017, a year which saw the author move house four times in three different countries, start two new jobs, give birth to a beautiful baby girl, have no maternity leave, prepare courses and teaching materials for a new appointment, and try to work out the taxation and medical insurance systems in three different countries.

I would like to give a final word of thanks to the Palgrave Macmillan editors, Emily Russell and Carmel Kennedy, who were supportive throughout the publication of this book, and to Béla Nagy, the mapmaker, who did such a great job of drawing the maps.

CONTENTS

LIST OF FIGURES

LIST OF TABLES

CHAPTER 1

A Peasant Uprising on the Edge of a Triple Frontier

Until 1878 three empires, the Ottoman, Habsburg and Tsarist, chafed at the borders between the Carpathians, the Black Sea and the Danube. Thirty years after the Treaty of Berlin of 1878 the Ottoman side of this triple frontier had morphed into several independent and quasi-independent Balkan states, each of them striving to modernize and to emulate Western European ways. Romania, which had come into being in 1859 through the union of the Danubian Principalities Wallachia and Moldavia, formerly under Ottoman suzerainty, was the biggest, most peaceful and, by all accounts and purposes, the most stable and flourishing of the fledgling states thus formed. The other states born from the European fringes of the Ottoman empire were convulsed by social and political violence: the Macedonian question raged between independent Greece and autonomous Bulgaria, Serbia waxed increasingly bellicose and went as 'the land of assassinations, abdications, pronunciamientos, and coups d'état';[1] Bulgaria resented the territorial stipulations of the Berlin Treaty and came to blows with Serbia in a short-lived war in 1885. By comparison, their neighbour north of the Danube came across, at its best, as a bastion of order and civilization in the quicksands of the Balkan Peninsula and, at its worst, in the words of British diplomat Sir Frank

---

[1] *The Times,* 12 June 1903, quoted in Dejan Djokic, 'Historical Notes: Brutal Murder in Serbia: 1903', http://www.independent.co.uk/arts-entertainment/historical-notes-brutal-murder-in-serbia-1903-1103132.html (Accessed on 2.01.2018).

© The Author(s) 2018   1
I. Marin, *Peasant Violence and Antisemitism in Early Twentieth-Century Eastern Europe,*
https://doi.org/10.1007/978-3-319-76069-8_1

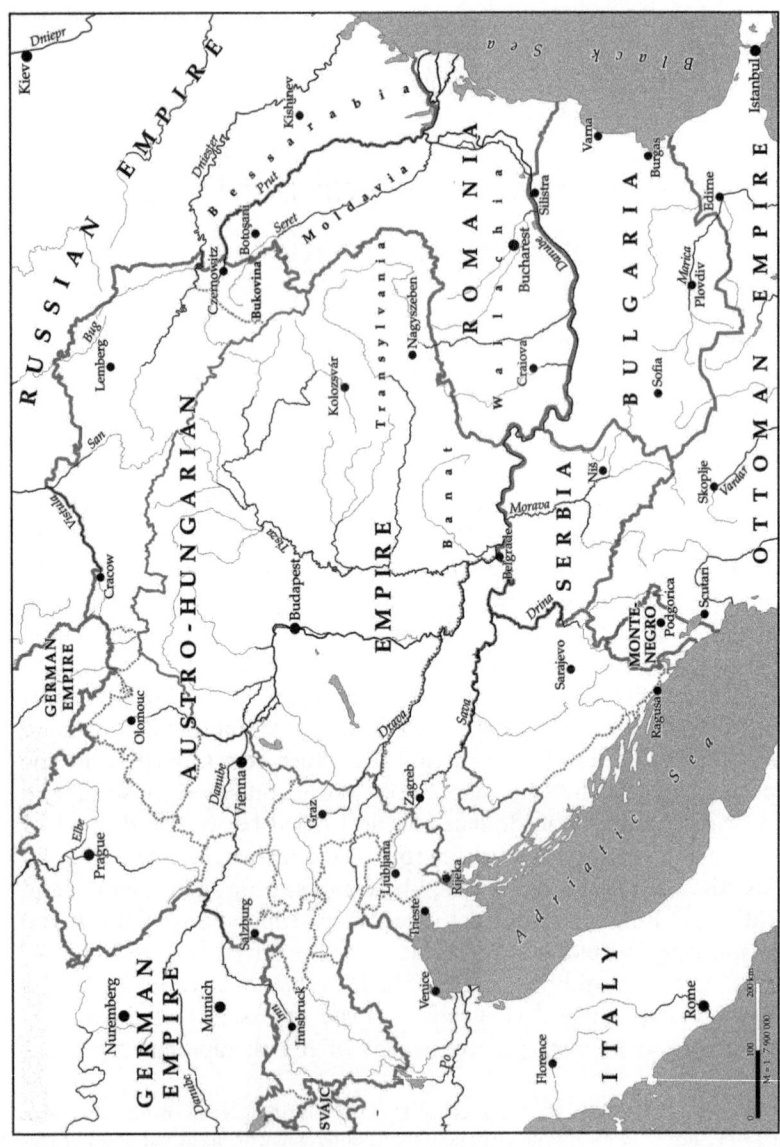

Fig. 1.1   Map of the triple frontier between Austria-Hungary, Tsarist Russia and Romania in 1907

Lascelles, as 'dull and uninteresting'.[2] Romania's Hohenzollern King Carol I proudly proclaimed in 1905, while Russia was in the grips of revolution and Hungary in throes of constitutional and political deadlock:

> Romania is the only country in which peace and order are reigning, while everywhere else around us menacing storm clouds are gathering and serious complications are in the offing. Europe should be grateful to me for governing this country with foresight and wisdom and keeping political passions in check.[3]

Romania was a young state, a quarter of a century old: in 1866 Carol I of Hohenzollern came to the throne of the recently united Principalities of Moldavia and Wallachia; in 1878 the country gained its independence from the Ottoman Empire, having taken part in the Russo–Turkish war of 1877–1878 and made a difference to the outcome of the hostilities. By 1906, the year of the royal jubilee celebrating 40 years of Hohenzollern rule over the country, there was much to be celebrated as the state had been virtually built from scratch. Apart from the usual eulogies, which were customary upon such occasions, there was good reason to be proud of the country's achievements. The peasantry had been emancipated in 1864 and received land in several batches of land redistribution. More money than the young state could afford had been invested in railways, which by the beginning of the twentieth century extended to an impressive 3,500 kilometres.[4] Industrial development (oil rigs, paper and sugar factories), heavily subsidized by the state and cocooned by protectionist tariffs, seemed to be taking off: thus before 1914 'Romania's gross industrial output per capita was over twice those of Serbia and Bulgaria and probably Greece.'[5] But perhaps the greatest statistical achievement of the new state was in the realm of agriculture, Romania being primarily an agrarian state, with a population made up of peasants in proportion of 82%

---

[2] Patrick J. Bourne, 'Sir Frank Lascelles: a diplomat of the Victorian empire, 1841–1920', unpublished PhD thesis, University of Leeds, 2010, p. 112.

[3] Sorin Cristescu (Ed.), *Scrisorile Regelui Carol I din arhiva de la Sigmaringen 1878–1905*, București, Paideia, 2010, p. 523.

[4] http://www.zeno.org/Roell-1912/A/Rumänische+Eisenbahnen (Accessed on 19 May 2016); Bogdan Murgescu, *România și Europa. Acumularea decalajelor economice (1500–2010)*, Polirom, București, 2010, pp. 144–145.

[5] John R. Lampe, 'Varieties of Unsuccessful Industrialization: The Balkan States Before 1914', *The Journal of Economic History*, Vol. 35, No. 1, (Mar., 1975), p. 60.

and land tenure dominated by great landowners. Despite the fact that agriculture was conducted traditionally, without recourse to modern farming techniques, and also despite the agricultural crisis of the 1870s, the end of the nineteenth, beginning of the twentieth century saw a huge increase in Romanian grain production and export, so much so that 'by 1910 Romanian wheat export value had climbed past that of the U.S. to fourth place in the world.'[6] Grain represented up to 80% of Romanian exports until the First World War.[7]

The acquisition of independent statehood gave a boost to a feverish adoption of institutions and practices from the West, which were imported wholesale and uneasily grafted onto autochthonous mores and practices: Western, so-called 'Frankish' fashion flooded in and eventually replaced the Oriental style of dress; the Constitution of 1866, which was patterned on the Belgian constitution, was retained and added to; two universities came into being in Bucharest and in Iași; the army was built from scratch and a military academy followed shortly in an attempt to make up for the lack of qualified personnel; museums, academies and a literary canon were enthusiastically created from scratch. The capital city Bucharest underwent an architectural facelift, with French-style boulevards and buildings that had the locals praise the place as the 'little Paris', one of the many in the region.

As these imports could not be entirely and effectively absorbed by Romanian society at the time, this led to the formation, at its best, of cultural and political hybrids and, at its worst, of empty forms or forms without content, as a prominent Conservative Romanian politician, Titu Maiorescu, put it. This was also the case in the political sphere, where constitutionalism and parliamentarianism, being grafted onto a patriarchal, pre-capitalist society, created a mere façade of liberal practices and concealed clientelism behind a veneer of constitutionalism. The lynchpin in the political architecture of the state was King Carol I, who appointed the Prime Minister, under whose government parliamentary elections were called and usually won by the party thus forming the government. Two parties dominated the political scene and succeeded to power: the Conservatives, representing the interests of great landowners, and the

---

[6] John R. Lampe, 'Varieties of Unsuccessful Industrialization: The Balkan States Before 1914', *The Journal of Economic History*, Vol. 35, No. 1, (Mar., 1975), p. 63.

[7] Murgescu, *România și Europa*, p. 123.

Liberals, who brought together small landowners and the emerging professional classes (bankers, merchants). Voting was restricted to the wealthy few and peasants had no political say at all.[8]

All in all, by the beginning of the twentieth century the Romanian Kingdom seemed to be going full steam ahead on the path of, albeit imperfect, modernization. A lot had been achieved, a lot more was yet to be done.

In spring 1907 a devastating peasant uprising engulfed the fledgling kingdom, shook it up from its very foundations and made a mockery of its strenuous, decade-long efforts at projecting the image of a civilized modern state. The uprising was (and still is to date) the most violent and destructive episode in Romanian history ever to occur in peacetime. Not even the 1989 revolution killed as many and destroyed as much: by the Romanian government's estimate at the time, which is generally thought to be a major understatement, the casualties were around 2,000 dead; by the bleakest of estimates, the death toll was 11,000. Destruction of property ran in the millions of Franks. Although at its peak the uprising only lasted a couple of weeks, it encompassed the whole country, threatened to destabilize the state and saw extremes of violence perpetrated on the part of both the rebellious peasants and the authorities. The troubles broke out in the north of the country, close to the Russian border, and were initially dismissed as nothing more than Jew bashing, they then rattled southwards with surprising celerity and savage, diehard violence.

The uprising started out as a conflict between peasants and the local leaseholder in the village of Flămânzi, county Botoşani, northeastern Romania. In pre-1914 Romania land tenure was dominated by the great property, the big landowners cultivating their land extensively and, increasingly towards the end of the century, by means of subletting their estates to leaseholders (*arendaşi*), who sought to maximize their profits at the expense of the peasants. Quite a few, though by no means all, of the leaseholders were 'foreigners' (Jews, Greeks, Armenians), who traditionally were in charge of trade and industry and increasingly came to be associated with the negative aspects of inceptive capitalism. The conflict was allowed to escalate through a combination of tardiness, empathy with the

---

[8] Keith Hitchins, *A Concise History of Romania*, Cambridge and New York, CUP, 2014, pp. 127–132.

plight of the peasants and antisemitism on the part of the local and regional authorities.[9]

The uprising started on estates leased out to Jewish entrepreneurs. News of the uprising in Botoşani trickled down from one village to the next and electrified the entire Romanian countryside like a shockwave. The intensity and violence of rebellion was not the same everywhere, but the rapid spread and the unprecedented synchronization of events caught the authorities off guard and by the end of the day nothing short of all-out military repression served to redress the situation. Peasants moved from verbal protest and threats to devastation of property and arson, driving out the local leaseholders, driving out 'foreigners', stealing what could be stolen and destroying everything else, in several cases, savagely murdering administrators and estate employees with whom they had an axe to grind.

By mid-March the whole country was in uproar, the entire army had been mobilized and the reserves were called up. In the south of the country armed peasants gathered in paramilitary formations and struck back against the army. In the early stages of the uprising there were more cases of defection and insubordination among new peasant recruits than the army commanders cared to admit to. The change of government in mid-March brought to power ministers who were determined to put an end to the conflagration by all means and at all costs. Heavy artillery was used, savage beatings and executions without trial were common, and reprisals were ordered against the villages that refused to turn in their ringleaders. The maximum figure of 11,000 dead that has been circulated in historical literature is not beyond doubt and contestation. There are no reliable statistics (official or otherwise) that can serve as an indicator of the extent of human loss. Fragmentary data is available for some of the most affected counties. On the basis of that and also bearing in mind that many deaths went unreported one can infer a figure that comes close to the 11,000 circulated at the time.

Admittedly, peasant disturbances were no rare occurrence in the region and even the mighty Tsarist Empire had barely recovered from its revolutionary turmoil of 1905–1907. Unlike Russia, Romania was not a great power and could ill afford to host such an implosion of social order. As the

[9] *Marea răscoală a ţăranilor din 1907*, Bucureşti, Editura Republicii Socialiste Românâ, 1967, 68–69; G.D. Creangă, *Grundbesitzverteilung und Bauernfrage in Rumänien*, Erster Teil, Leipzig 1907, 150–155; Karl Scheerer, *Die Rumänische Bauernaufstände vom Frühjahr 1907*, Mainz 1971, 32, 33, 43.

uprising extended and took on an increasingly anarchic character, the German-language Hungarian daily *Pester Lloyd* came to doubt whether Romania could avoid dissolution as a state. The prospect of this along with the causes of the upheaval were, according to the newspaper, of the utmost importance to the European powers that took a direct interest in the region. In words that the events of 1914 rendered prophetic, the newspaper wondered if the fate of the European order might not one day come to depend on one of these Balkan state's internal problems.

> Should law and order fail completely and should the inconceivable occur, that is, that the capital is threatened or even besieged, then that would be the end of the Romanian Kingdom. For there is no salvation for a state that is incapable of suppressing anarchy by its own forces. The European powers, and in particular those with a direct interest in the Orient, cannot remain indifferent to the course of events in this unfortunate country or to their causes. The Balkan question is once again brought to international attention by these events and in a form that the wisdom of diplomacy had not even imagined. They saw true danger in the Balkan states' expansionist endeavours and their outwardly directed unrest. It has now become evident that the domestic conditions of these half-Asiatic countries – and it would be good if they were only half Asiatic – hold out greater danger and even more fierce unrest and developments. Are law and order well established in Serbia and Bulgaria? Is there any guarantee that they won't follow the Romanian example? It is possible that the Romanian unrest could develop into a matter of European concern?[10]

If Romania collapsed, as the above worst-case scenario feared, what implications would that have on the bordering countries, Austria-Hungary and Tsarist Russia?

The triple frontier demarcated borderlands that were fairly similar in kind, if not in name. Romania bordered on Tsarist Bessarabia in the east, on Austrian Bukovina in the extreme north and on Hungarian Transylvania and the Banat in the west. These were provinces with complex historical heritage and trajectories, sharing a motley of ethnicities and religions, as well as a majority of Romanian population, and with comparatively low economic development: there were Romanians, Ukrainians, Russians, Hungarians, Austrians, Germans, Jews, Roma, Bulgarians and other ethnicities on all sides of the border in varying

---

[10] *Pester Lloyd*, 27 March, 1907, p. 2.

proportions. This was a region dominated by latifundia with recently emancipated peasantry and increasingly plagued by antisemitism. Low literacy rates, low level of taxes paid and investments made, poor infrastructure and rudimentary land cultivation singled out these border-lands among the poorest in the two empires. Romania's underdevelopment was not, therefore, much different from that of the neighbouring imperial borderlands. As the Austrian author Karl Frazos pointed out, the whole region evinced a striking superimposition of West and East, cutting-edge, superficial modernity and deep-core medieval backwardness,[11] all of this turgidly and painfully transitioning to a capitalist, market-dominated system, which created uneasy hybrids and at times combined the worst of the old and new systems together.

If this borderland region shared the same problems and characteristics, why was it that only Romania caught fire in 1907 whereas the neighbour-ing imperial provinces (Transylvania, the Banat, Bukovina and Bessarabia) remained relatively peaceful? Why did the conflagration not cross the fron-tiers? What were the factors that increased the social combustibility of a province or, as the case may be, rendered it fireproof?

Information in the form of rumour, news, preconceived ideas, wishful thinking and downright invention formed the lifeblood of the 1907 social upheaval and was of such a nature as to galvanize whole communities, hundreds of miles apart, into synchronous action. How did this informa-tion ripple through the social strata of Romania and how did it seep through the borders? How did news of the Romanian peasant uprising ripple across the triple frontier, what was its potential for contamination and what did the authorities in the neighbouring states make of it? What reactions and spectres did it trigger? This book sets out to map the helter-skelter of fears and opinions, real or imaginary, self-reflection, finger point-ing, *Schadenfreude*, that the 1907 peasant uprising in Romania conjured up and fed on. In so doing, it seeks to account for the varying degrees of combustibility within the provinces that formed the triple frontier and to pinpoint those factors that made the difference between isolated flares of social discontent and major conflagration; it will, in other words, account for the conductibility and combustibility of the three systems across the triple frontier using the coursing of news and rumour about the uprising through the body social and body politic of the frontier territories very

---

[11] Karl Emil Franzos, *Aus Halb-Asien. Culturbilder aus Galizien, der Bukowina, Südrußland und Rumänien*, Erster Band, Leipzig, Verlag von Duncker&Humblot, 1876, pp. iv–v.

much like a dye test[12] is used in medicine to reveal the working of internal organs.

In the present book I have opted for a narrative structure of concentric circles starting with the spread of the uprising in Romania, the background to it, and moving on to its reverberations across the triple frontier among the local and regional authorities, in the press of different colours and affiliations, and in the diplomatic exchanges of the time.

Chapter 2 'Rumour and Violence: the Making of an Uprising' follows the spread of the uprising in Romania and provides an account of how, within a matter of weeks, a localized incident snowballed into a country-wide rebellion threatening to remove all state authority and making a mockery of military action. It explores the ways in which peasants from distant villages got wind of the uprising elsewhere, how news circulated and what happened to this information in the process. Popular rationales for joining the uprising, newspaper reading strategies and dissemination as well the role of popular mythologies are brought to bear on the speedy spread of violence careering from one village to the next.

Chapter 3 'Jews, Strangers and Foreigners' explores the second set of rumour mills, this time the ones that shaped the responses of the Romanian authorities to the crisis and as such it is an exploration of Romanian offi-cials' obsession with foreigners. Representatives of both the Conservative and Liberal governments, instead of confronting the actual economic, social and cultural causes of the uprising, preferred to 'export' the blame and pin it onto the handy construct of 'the foreigner'. The chapter offers an analysis of the scapegoated Jewish community, of official fears regard-ing potential Russian and Bulgarian threats as well as the peasants' animos-ity against 'foreigners'. The misguided official responses to the agrarian crisis were instrumental in allowing the peasants' simmering discontent to get out of hand.

Chapter 4 'The Peasant Question' opens up the discussion of the deep causes of the uprising, analysing from a cross-border perspective the status of the main actors of the 1907 uprising, the peasants and their economic predicament, in contrast to their peers across the triple frontier in Austria-Hungary and Tsarist Bessarabia. The transnational comparison between land tenure and the position of the peasantry in Romania and in the

---

[12] A dye test presupposes the injection of a contrast substance into a patient's bloodstream so the working of internal organs such as the heart or kidneys can be more clearly monitored and abnormalities more easily detected.

neighbouring imperial provinces aims to identify those factors pertaining to the legal framework and social practice that set Romania apart from its neighbours and led to different outcomes.

Chapter 5 'Eyes of the State' picks up where the previous chapter left off and proposes a study of the administrative and policing system in Romania at the time of the uprising. This, I am arguing, is vital to understanding why the uprising reached such a scale and spread out in such a short time. By comparing this to the administrative systems across the border in Austria-Hungary and Tsarist Bessarabia, the chapter inaugurates the second part of the book, which traces the reverberations of the uprising across the triple frontier at the level of administration, public opinion and diplomacy.

Chapter 6 'Paper Worlds' presents press reactions to the uprising on the Austro-Hungarian and Russian sides of the border in an attempt to capture of the multiplicity of interpretations and knee-jerk reactions that pervaded the public space and which, in many cases, said more about the fears, concerns and preconceptions of public opinion in the neighbouring countries than about the uprising proper.

Having mapped the reactions of the local and regional administration and of the press in the previous two chapters, I close my study with an analysis of the highest circle of news propagation: diplomatic reactions. Thus Chapter 7 'The Diplomacy of the Uprising' charts the coursing of information through the diplomatic structures of Austria-Hungary and Tsarist Russia, relying on correspondence between the consulates in Romania and the imperial metropolitan centres. The main concerns of the diplomats, their risk assessment advice and appraisal of the contamination potential of the uprising, as well as the measures suggested and taken, form the core of this final chapter.

BIBLIOGRAPHY

Patrick J. Bourne, 'Sir Frank Lascelles: A diplomat of the Victorian empire, 1841–1920', unpublished PhD thesis, University of Leeds, 2010

G.D. Creangă, *Grundbesitzverteilung und Bauernfrage in Rumänien*, Erster Teil, Leipzig, 1907

Sorin Cristescu (Ed.), *Scrisorile Regelui Carol I din arhiva de la Sigmaringen 1878–1905*, Paideia, București, 2010

Karl Emil Franzos, *Aus Halb-Asien. Culturbilder aus Galizien, der Bukowina, Südrußland und Rumänien*, Erster Band, Verlag von Duncker&Humblot, Leipzig, 1876

Keith Hitchins, *A Concise History of Romania*, CUP, Cambridge and New York, 2014

John R. Lampe, 'Varieties of Unsuccessful Industrialization: The Balkan States Before 1914', *The Journal of Economic History*, Vol. 35, No. 1, (Mar., 1975)

Marea răscoală a țăranilor din 1907, București, Editura Republicii Socialiste România, 1967

Bogdan Murgescu, *România și Europa. Acumularea decalajelor economice (1500–2010)*, Polirom, București, 2010

Karl Scheerer, *Die Rumänische Bauernaufstände vom Frühjahr 1907*, Mainz, 1971

CHAPTER 2

Rumour and Violence: The Making of an Uprising

On 8 February 1907 the peasants of Flămânzi, a commune in Botoșani County, northern Romania, rebelled against the local estate authorities. They were inhabitants on one of the great latifundia that dominated land tenure in Romania. The landowner, Prince D.M. Sturdza, just like many of his peers in Romania at the time, had been lending his estates to mon-eyed leaseholders (*arendași*), who in turn made a profit by subletting land to the local peasants at usurious rates. In Moldavia the land rental market was monopolized by two Jewish families, the Fischers and the Justers, who competed with one another and thus pushed land rent up every ten years or so: whoever promised to extract the higher rent from the peasants secured the leasehold for another decade. Peasant protest was directed against oppressive work and land-rental contracts, and against a recently introduced tax, the five lei tax, which was meant to provide assistance in years of crop failure.[1] The previous year, 1906, had brought one of the best crops in decades and lots of empty promises for better contractual terms for the peasants from the two leaseholders outbidding one another for the renewal of the estate leasehold. Spring 1907 added frustrated expectations to older grievances. Within a month peasants across the whole country, north and south, were in open rebellion. The Conservative

---

[1] P.G. Eidelberg, *The Great Rumanian Peasant Revolt of 1907: Origins of a Modern Jacquerie*, Leiden, Brill, 1974, pp. 190–191, 200.

© The Author(s) 2018
I. Marin, *Peasant Violence and Antisemitism in Early Twentieth-Century Eastern Europe*,
https://doi.org/10.1007/978-3-319-76069-8_2

13

government headed by Gheorghe Grigore Cantacuzino, also known as the Nabob, was replaced on 12 March 1907 with a new, Liberal government, led by the very owner of the Moldavian estate on which the first acts of peasant violence took place.[2] It took another month and heavy artillery to put down the uprising, the last spasms of which had more the appearance of guerrilla warfare than of a traditional peasant uprising. How did the country go up in flames within the timespan of a month? What were the factors that virtually turned it into a giant conductor for rebellious electricity? How did news spread out and galvanize distant communities into synchronic action in a country with poor infrastructure and in which the overwhelming majority of the population were illiterate? Was the uprising a matter of contamination of previously peaceful communities by news of rebellion elsewhere or was it a matter of seizing a unique opportunity to strike while the iron was hot and settle ongoing disputes and grievances? These are the questions that the present chapter seeks to answer by concentrating on the role of rumour and news circulation in driving forward the uprising, the channels and media of information propagation and the way in which this flow of hearsay rippled through the population. Of particular interest here are the peasant mythologies that fuelled the uprising, which are frequently noted in historical bibliography but usually dismissed as figments of popular imagination and indicative of little more than peasant superstitious backwardness. Taking my cue from rumour theory, in this chapter I unpack the function of these mythologies and show how their primary role was one of legitimation, control and mobilization. In so doing, I seek to go beyond the simplistic value judgments that characterize contemporary 1907 coverage of the uprising as well as the present-day historiography on the topic. By taking rumours seriously, I am trying to restore agency to the peasants and show how their seemingly fantastic readings of the situation were anything but idle concoctions or signs of miscomprehension.

PROPAGATION OF THE UPRISING

How did things get out of hand so quickly? How did peasants at one end of the country get wind of what was happening at the opposite end of the country given that technological channels were so scarce at that

---

[2] Scheerer, *Die Rumänische Bauernaufstände*, p. 55.

time, the rate of illiteracy was high and also given the fact that the uprising started at that time of the year when the roads had not yet thawed out? Unlike Lefebvre's *Grande Peur*, which rattled the French countryside in July 1789, the 1907 peasant uprising in Romania peaked in March when most of the country was still covered in snow or barely thawing out.[3]

As the Figures 2.1, 2.2, 2.3, and 2.4 show, there was simmering discontent reported all over the country as early as January 1907, if not earlier. The last decades of the nineteenth century and the first years of the twentieth century were punctuated by peasant outbursts dotted around the country, with a dress-rehearsal major uprising in 1888, which was strikingly similar to the 1907 one.[4] Thus the impression one gets is not one of impending spread and contamination of the conflict from one region to another, but rather of ignition of a powder keg ready to blow up and of a synchronization of already existing flares. As we shall see further on in this chapter, the time factor and the need to act immediately were prominent in peasant rumour that fuelled the uprising.

There were a number of in-built features of Romanian society at the time that increased the conductibility of the system to social unrest, very much like water renders otherwise non-conductive substances conductive to electricity. One such systemic feature were the economic practices that the majority of the peasant population was embedded in at the time. The very lifestyle of the peasants lent itself to a propagation of the uprising. As Eugene Weber put it in reference to nineteenth-century France, peasants because of their way of life were quite mobile and got about quite a bit: cattle markets, fairs, inter-village marriages/relations, peasants working outside the village in railway workshops and sawmills; or answering the call of the state (army service, law suits).

Even more conducive to peasant assemblies and to disturbances was the system of land rental contracts between peasants and the local landowner or leaseholder. These contracts were due to be renewed annually, so every year in early spring great numbers of peasants would go out in sizeable groups to see the local leaseholder or landlord, each side being

---

[3] I am thankful to Professor Leen Van Molle for pointing out this difference to me and for her useful questions and comments.

[4] N. Adăniloaie, *Răscoala țăranilor din 1888*, Editura Academiei Republicii Socialiste România, București, 1988, p. 138.

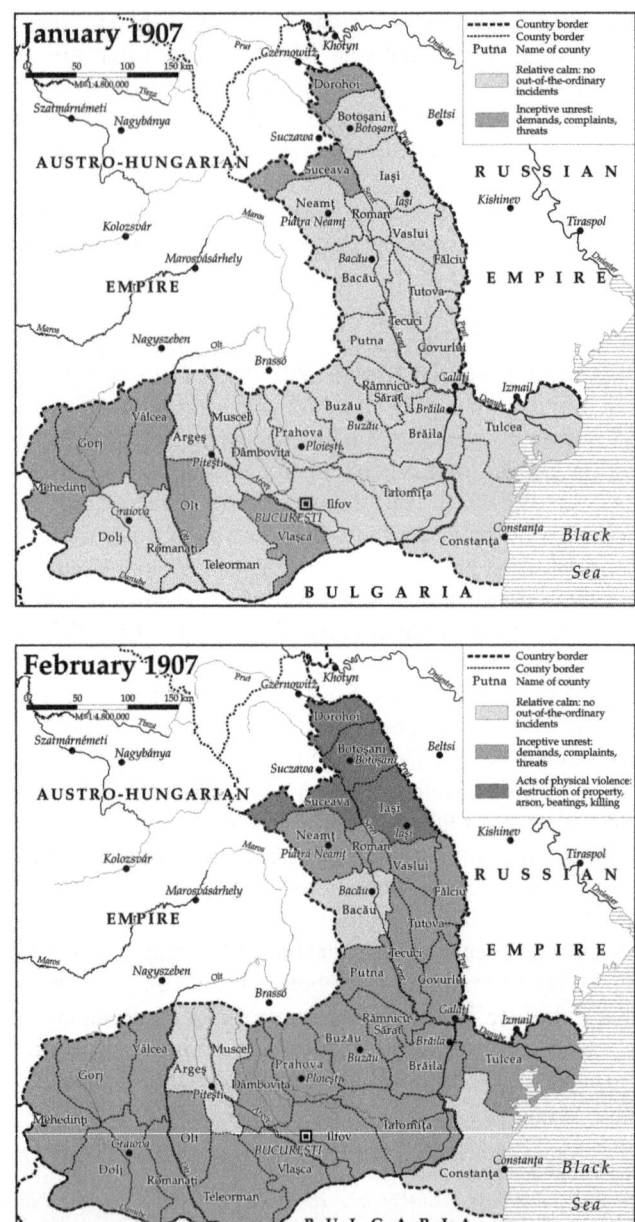

Figs. 2.1–2.4   Maps showing the propagation of the peasant uprising in Romania from January until April 1907

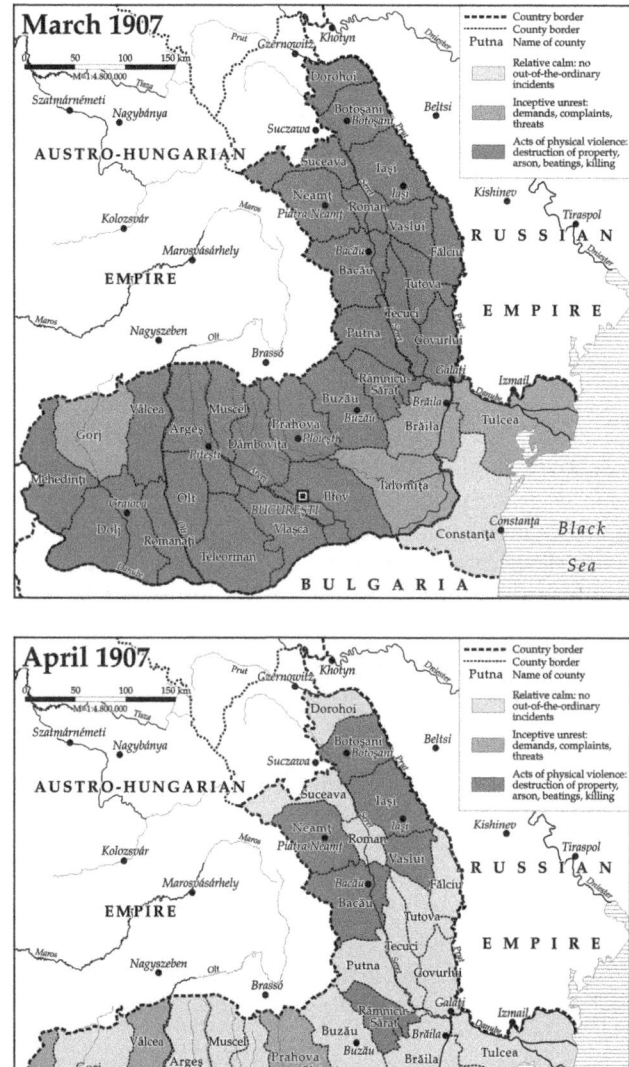

Figs. 2.1–2.4   (Continued)

intent on negotiating a more favourable contract for themselves. These occasions were highly charged and likely to degenerate into conflict, but they were also a commonplace practice, whose inbuilt antagonism usually left the authorities unconcerned. A priest from Tecuci County in Moldavia showed the difficulty in assessing the peasants' intentions and purposes until it was too late, given that these agricultural 'pilgrimages' took place every year: 'Everything seemed calm and legal, all the more so as everybody knows that here every year people go in groups to the landowners and the leaseholders to strike deals for fields to plough and pastureland.'[5] So the fact that a lot of peasants got together was nothing out of the ordinary at that time of year and certainly no telling sign of impending uprising.

Another systemic source of propagation was administrative in character and had to do with the way in which property was owned and rented out. Thus a leaseholder could sublease land to peasants from several adjoining villages and even counties, thus land interests and issues ended up straddling local administrative divisions, which rendered communication and spread of news easier as well as facilitated peer comparison and peer pressure.[6] A memorandum by a local teacher from the village of Tupilați, County Roman, described how peasants in his village were instigated by peasants from another village who rented land from the same leaseholder and had successfully browbeaten him into granting them more favourable terms, then bragged about it to the local peasants, whom they egged on to do the same.[7] The leasehold monopoly in Moldavia further contributed to contamination once trouble started on one of the estates held by the same leaseholder. Given the power of these land entrepreneurs, an uprising on one of their estates was bound to have an echo. Thus, as Eidelberg points out,

the fact that the initial revolt occurred on a very large property, part of a vast network of leased estates under the same family management, assured the initial revolt of maximum publicity. The Flămânzi peasants' demands

---

[5] Andrei Oțetea, Ion Popescu-Puțuri (Eds.), *Documente privind marea răscoală a țăranilor din 1907* (henceforth quoted as *Documente*), București, Editura Academiei Republicii Socialiste România, 1977, Vol. 2, p. 681: priest's letter to the *Proiereu* of Tecuci dated 7 October 1907.

[6] *Documente*, vol. 3, p. 268.

[7] *Documente*, vol. 2, p. 489.

(that land be leased to them at twenty-five lei a *falce* = 1.43 hectares) were subsequently to be repeated throughout the district of Botoșani on many other estates neither owned by Sturdza nor leased by Fischer.[8]

News of the uprising percolated to the peasants through a combination of old and new ways of communication: it was relayed by word-of-mouth, by letters home from conscripts; it was picked up while travelling and meeting people or conveyed through official announcements by the mayor or the village priest; in some cases, it was extracted from intercepted telegraph/telephone conversations.

The layout and nature of the roads channelled and conditioned the direction of the news flow. Thus, in Moldavia the main thoroughfare ran north to south, with no paved roads running east to west. Such paved roads, Eidelberg notes, were 'vital for winter transport' and their absence accounts for the 'spread of the revolt: north and south from Flămânzi, but not east or west. It remained centralized in the Cristești-Cotnari chain of communes until the end of February, without spreading to the rest of Botoșani or linking up with the similar Dorohoi uprisings to the north.'[9] Conversely, the impracticality of the roads during wintry conditions made difficult the progress of troops sent out by the central authorities to suppress the uprising.

SOCIAL INTERSTICES

How permeable was the village world and how much access did peasants have to the outer world? Which were the places where peasants got together and exchanged ideas? The rural world evinced a number of interstitial spaces,[10] where exchange of information took place intensively as a matter of course, such as the village pubs, cattle markets and regional fairs. Inceptive state modernization and centralization created new infrastructure and opportunities for peasants to leave their village and liaise with urban life.

---

[8] Eidelberg, *The Great Rumanian Peasant Revolt*, pp. 200–201.

[9] Eidelberg, *The Great Rumanian Peasant Revolt*, p. 201.

[10] See also Schenda's concept of 'Soziotop', or social places, such as inns, taverns and pubs, which fostered and shaped communication: Rudolf Schenda, *Von Mund zu Ohr. Bausteine zu einer Kulturgeschichte volkstümlichen Erzählens in Europa*, Vandenhoek & Ruprecht, Göttingen, 1993, p. 90.

Pubs

Local pubs were the most circulated of village communal places, where locals and travellers alike got together, some attracted by alcohol, others by the company, others still by the need for news. Just like cafes in towns and cities, village pubs served as forums of news and ideas, where newspapers were read out loud and strangers stopped by to rest and share novelties from outside. They were places of social interaction, information transmission and (from the point of view of the authorities) contamination. Unlike cafes, pubs also added the prospect of inebriation to the explosive mix of ideas, which made easier the transition from word to action. Given this high-traffic function of pubs, during the uprising the Minister of the Interior ordered county prefects to close down pubs and inns and cancel weekly cattle markets and fairs in both villages and towns.[11] A March 1907 informative note to the Giurgiu police related how a Transylvanian waiter, who had settled in Bucharest, went to a pub and told the peasants there about the uprising in Moldavia urging them to do the same if they wanted a better life.[12] An 18 March police chief's report to the Vâlcea prefect listed the measures taken to prevent the spread of the uprising, one of them being to close down the pubs in the villages along the national road, where people from other communes were passing by.[13]

Railways

Journeys either by land or by water, which temporarily cooped up people in small spaces, created opportunities for communication, pooling and exchanging stories and news, blowing off steam or just while-away-the-time escapism.[14] In particular trains and railways were vital infrastructure for news and people circulation: they took people from here to there, brought news and newspapers into towns and villages, brought in troops to quell the uprising, took reservists away to put down fellow peasant risings elsewhere. But maybe their most important function in the economy of the uprising was that of socialization. Trains brought (and still do bring) together people from far-flung regions, people who would otherwise

[11] *Documente*, Vol. 3, p. 504.
[12] *Documente*, Vol. 3, p. 506.
[13] *Documente*, Vol. 4, p. 265.
[14] Schenda, *Von Mund zu Ohr*, pp. 75–76.

never have seen or talked to one another, favoured exchange of experience and personal stories, showed that the plight of one peasant or village was not singular, brought news of what was happening in other parts of the country and how the peasants dealt with their problems there.

The social segregation of train classes ensured that peasants found themselves huddled up in a third-class carriage with a lot of other peasants. Many peasant encounters on trains might well have unfolded as Liviu Rebreanu described it in *Răscoala*, a 1932 novel about the 1907 peasant uprising:

> It was warm in the carriage, and there were quite a few passengers, mostly peasants, some from Ialomiţa, others from Muscel, Teleorman, or even farther. Tongues loosened in the warmth. But the seven from Amara, sitting huddled together in a corner and smouldering with rage, only spoke a word from time to time. Lupu Chiriţoiu grumbled that they had spent a terrible lot of money in vain. Luca admitted he was right, and swallowed dryly. However, gradually, as if coming to themselves, they began to talk their experiences over, and weigh them up. Every one of them felt he must add something, or at least sigh. If it had not been like it was, things might have turned out differently. Other passengers began to join in their lament, some out of interest, some because they had already heard about such things, or had suffered similar experiences themselves.[15]

As we shall see in the following chapters, the social-forum function of train journeys was recognized and eventually capitalized on by the Romanian authorities, who in the wake of the devastating uprising organized a special secret police unit that listened in on train conversations and collected information on the mood of the peasantry. The conversations they reported on were not dissimilar to the fictionalized one above.

Tribunals were yet another type of social interstice where exchanges between same-class people but also, more importantly, cross-class encounters took place. As a local village inspector wrote to the Ilfov Prefect on 28 February 1907, awareness-raising brochures were being distributed to peasants in the hallways of the Bucharest tribunal.[16] The Gorj Prefect notified the Minster of the Interior that, in order to prevent peasant overcrowding, he had disposed the discontinuation of tribunal proceedings across the

---

[15] Liviu Rebreanu, *The Uprising*, Trans. P. Crandjean and S. Hartauer, Peter Owen Ltd., London, 1965, pp. 168–169.

[16] *Documente*, vol. 3, 309.

county.[17] The Olt Prefect moved to a similar measure, requesting permission from the Minister of Justice that 'court cases should be suspended for a few days at the county tribunal and court house in Slatina [...], this way preventing the peasants from going into the town and keeping them away from information regarding unrest elsewhere in the country'.[18]

Military recruitment was, paradoxically, another systemic practice that favoured news dissemination as well as contributed to social unrest. The great, unprecedented movement of troops was in itself a tell-tale sign of turmoil elsewhere, for all the authorities' efforts to suppress news circulation. Official efforts to put down the uprising by calling up all reservists from among the peasant population more often than not backfired and fuelled the unrest. In some places the drafted peasants went to the nearest town in big groups and ended up joining the uprising.[19] In other places, reservists showed up without any papers so the authorities were at a loss who had called them up and whether to believe them.[20] As a consequence, requests were sent to the Prime Minister to put a stop to the general conscription of reservists as 'it overcrowded the towns and disrupted public services'.[21] Botched-up conscriptions, which left hosts of young peasants stranded in towns or on trains poured gas onto the fire: the conscripts got together, got drunk and started devastating. Moreover, any letters or otherwise conveyed news coming from these recruits were bound to make an impact on the native village as, traditionally, soldiers and recruits were a link between rural communities and the outer world and additionally possessed the authoritativeness that comes with experience and literacy. Thus in a letter sent to a peasant by his nephew who had been drafted into the army, the latter urged his uncle: 'here everyone has revolted and they called in the prefect, who called the landowner and gave them signed papers saying that they'll give them the whole of the estate [...] if we don't rebel now, then we won't get anything, everybody in all the other counties have revolted, mayor, prefect and all, they came out boldly, they are not sitting on their hands!'[22]

---

[17] *Documente*, vol. 4, p. 297.
[18] *Documente*, vol. 4, p. 307.
[19] *Documente*, vol. 2, pp. 301, 307.
[20] *Documente*, vol. 3, p. 239.
[21] *Documente*, vol.2, p. 299.
[22] Schenda, *Von Mund zu Ohr*, p. 71; *Documente*, vol. 2, pp. 462, 414; vol. 3, pp. 340, 362, 558.

Information Purveyors

If the peasants did not go out into the world, the world inevitably came to them. This happened via newspapers and rural-urban intermediaries such as peddlers and newspaper subscription collectors. News was the lifeblood of the uprising.

Peddlers

Long after the uprising had been put down, prefects recommended tighter control over peddlers, salt and gas sellers roaming from village to village and spreading rumours:

> they go from one commune to the other and bring with them wild rumours: that such and such a village has rebelled, that such and such an *arendaş* has been killed, that the peasants should act now; there was even a story that everybody should bring in their crops because in the autumn the students will be coming and will set fire to everything including the flour mills.[23]

Just how far such peddlers could get during their commercial travels is made clear in Austrian writer Leo Katz's autobiographical novel *Brennende Dörfer* (Burning Villages), offering a view of the Romanian uprising from the Austrian side of the border. In this novel, the figure of Mendel Flicker stands out prominently: a Jewish peddler who shuttled across the border between Bukovina and Moldavia and covered hundreds of kilometres in his weekly circuit through the villages:

> Flicker was not the real surname of Mendel Flicker. He was a furrier. To this day I have never known his real name. All through the week, from Sunday morning till Friday evening, be it summer or winter, he walked through the villages and mended the peasants' furs and boots. His area of activity stretched over the Sereth district and deep into Romania, all the way to Dorohoi and Botischani. There was hardly a peasant who did not know him. He lived with the peasants, helped them with their work, ate out of the same bowl as them and returned home on Saturday in the late afternoon, without money but with a sack full of food. [...] I loved Mendel dearly. He was to me the embodiment of the big wide world out there. He was always on the

---

[23] *Documente*, vol. 3, p. 538.

move, always met new people, travelled long distances, and walked the hundred kilometres from Sereth to Botischani.[24]

Mendel Flicker was one of the Mercure-like characters populating the village world who plied their trade while at the same time functioning as messengers and story tellers.[25]

Cultural Circles and Popular Banks

Literate peasants could disseminate ideas from newspapers and brochures at the village forums created by cultural circles and popular banks. These were more often than not well-off peasants. A report drawn up by local authorities in Turnu Măgurele pointed to such practices among their villagers: one of the suspected peasants, who was also the president of the Popular Bank, was thus said to have discussed issues regarding peasant oppression at the hands of foreigners and *arendaşi*.[26]

Newspapers

The most conspicuous carriers of news and also the most suspected by the authorities were newspapers. In every village there was bound to be a handful of well-off peasants who subscribed to newspapers. These more often than not were read out loud in the pub or in other village forums. Illiteracy was no impediment to news acquisition; on the contrary, it made for participatory public reading.

What did the authorities think of newspapers? Given that the leitmotif of official response to the uprising was that the peasants must have been instigated from outside, the local as well as central authorities viewed newspapers as instrumental in exciting the population. Some voices were more balanced in their assessment of the impact of the printed word. Thus, a Dorohoi judge pointed out that they were not able to identify the ringleaders, but thought that the uprising was the result of mutual instigation and the general background of lack of proper administration and justice. Newspapers and external news may have indirectly affected the peasants by 'opening their eyes to their rights and their actual

[24] Leo Katz, *Brennende Dörfer*, Verlag für Gesellschaftskritik, Wien, 1993, pp. 131–132.

[25] Schenda, *Von Mund zu Ohr*, p. 66.

[26] *Documente*, vol. 3, p. 382.

predicament'.[27] By contrast, the Putna prefect wrote to the Conservative Prime Minister Cantacuzino on 8 March 1907 that 'newspapers hugely contribute to the spread of the uprising, printing rumours and fanciful, exaggerated provocative news. The peasants read the newspapers voraciously and imitate.'[28]

Control and suppression of newspaper distribution were thus assiduously recommended across the country by prefects and mayors as well as dictated by the Ministry of the Interior. On 7 March, the Tecuci prefect requested the Minister of the Interior to authorize stopping the distribution of newspapers to the countryside as 'sensationalist news excite the rural population and the spirits are already agitated in counties Vaslui, Tutova and Putna.'[29] In a telegram dated 9 March 1907, the Dâmbovița prefect asked the Minister of the Interior to give orders to stop newspaper vendors travelling on the railway line Bucharest—Titu—Pucioasa as 'very many peasants read daily about the peasant unrest in northern Moldavia.' The prefect had forbidden the sale of newspapers at the stations in his county but he insisted that newspaper sellers should not be allowed to travel in the first place.[30] A Craiova prefect's instructions distributed to the local gendarmerie on 9/22 March 1907 included the close supervision of train stations to 'prevent suspicious individuals – disguised or not – from distributing manifestos, newspapers and brochures'.[31] Responding to such notifications, by mid-March the new Minister of the Interior C. Nicolaescu sent out a circular telegram to all prefects regarding local newspapers, which 'should be directed not to print news which are likely to trigger panic or unrest [...] Newspapers from other counties should be withheld if publishing such news'.[32]

Where found, newspapers were confiscated and the owners as well as distributors were often among the prime suspects of the local authorities. On 15 March, the mayor of Păușești Măglași notified the Vâlcea prefect that they confiscated an issue of *Gazeta țăranilor* from one of the inhabitants. A report dated 21 April from a village inspector to the Vâlcea prefect pinpointed a subscription collector ('*încasator*') for *Vorbe bune*, a newspaper from Balș, as the main disseminator of 'anarchical

[27] *Documente*, vol. 2, p. 280.
[28] *Documente*, vol. 2, p. 701.
[29] *Documente*, vol. 2, p. 637.
[30] *Documente*, vol. 3, p. 556.
[31] *Documente*, vol. 4, p. 43.
[32] *Documente*, vol. 3, p. 73.

ideas' among the local peasants. Subscription collectors seem to have been pet suspects as they were found to bring with them other printed materials in addition to newspapers. On 12 March 1907, the Prefect of Teleorman communicated to one of the ministers that brochures had been brought into villages by the subscription collector for the newspaper *Gazeta Țăranilor*.[33] A 30 March report by a village inspector throws light on the network and circulation of printed matter: A copy of the brochure *Către săteni* was confiscated from a railway worker, who in turn had it from another villager, whose house was then searched, where the authorities found another copy of the brochure and three copies of *Gazeta țăranilor*.[34]

Metabolization of News

For all the authorities' fears and precaution the actual influence of newspapers on the spread of the uprising seems to have been mixed. There were places where peasants had revolted and yet had had no contact with newspapers. News of the uprising elsewhere seeped in through different channels. On 23 March, a peasant by the name of Avram Văsii testified to how news of an uprising elsewhere trickled down to his village by hearsay, from one person to another:

> No one brought in any books that talked about land and I didn't hear any-
> one read any newspapers. I know the village secretary and the mayor read
> them but they didn't tell us anything. A few days before the uprising I heard
> people saying that there's an uprising in Moldavia [...] I didn't hear any talk
> of land or contracts. I don't know who brought the news about the uprising
> in Moldavia. I saw no stranger coming into the village and talking about the
> uprising.[35]

A 28 March peasant deposition from Râmnicu Sărat, similar to the previous one, tells how one of the villagers went around calling people to make a contract with the landlord because "the students" ordered it. If it had not been for this, they would never have heard about the uprising elsewhere. No one read out any newspapers to them. He did not hear of

---

[33] *Documente*, vol. 3, p. 381.
[34] *Documente*, vol. 4, pp. 256, 291, 449.
[35] *Documente*, vol. 3, p. 95.

anyone bringing a book from Bucharest about land. No strangers came into the village.[36]

In other places newspaper reading did make an important difference, in particular through its public, participatory quality. As a Tecuci prefect explained to the Minister of the Interior on 14 May, the uprising had spread not because of instigation by students or any other agents, rather 'the uprising took place under the influence of newspapers and news circulating from village to village'.[37] An assessment of the uprising by a judge in Ploieşti, dated 2 June 1907, dwells on the role of newspapers in the spread of the unrest: the course of the uprising was reported on by newspapers and spread out by word of mouth, much exaggerated. The peasants returning home from the towns where they had been for business, told everybody at home about the extent of the troubles, brought newspapers with them and related what they had heard in town.[38]

In the newspaper reading process the most important elements were the reader and the setting. The setting was, as shown by the mayor of Tunari-Dimieni, of Ilfov County, more often than not the village pub. In his 10 March letter to the Ilfov prefect, the mayor detailed the measures he took to contain the spread of brochures from Bucharest:

> 1) all inhabitants who go to Bucharest – where most of these brochures come from – will upon their return be confidentially sounded if they received such printed matter and if they did we will confiscate it; 2) policemen have been posted at the entrance to the village and they have been directed to signal the entrance of any stranger, peasant or townsman; 3) Given that the great majority of the inhabitants are illiterate and that, if they were to receive such brochures they would undoubtedly go to the pub, where they would have either the pub keeper or other people read it to them and in this way other people will learn the content, especially in the evening when the inhabitants come back home – I disposed that pubs should close at 7pm and pub keepers have been instructed to alert us whenever a stranger or a local came into their pub carrying such manifestos.[39]

If it was not a pub and the village literates, then other public places and literate people lent themselves equally well to the deciphering of

---

[36] *Documente*, vol. 3, pp. 104–105.
[37] *Documente*, vol.2, p. 669.
[38] *Documente*, vol.3, p. 277.
[39] *Documente*, vol.3, p. 323.

newspapers. In his witness deposition of 13 April 1907, Pandele Condeiescu, the commander of a Danube ship, recounted his conversation with Zimnicea peasants who went to Bucharest to insist that no railway be built between Zimnicea and the Danube, as that impinged on their carting business. 'As they saw me reading out of a newspaper, they asked me what the latest news from Moldavia was, how the uprising was going, and said that there was bound to be an uprising here as well because people could no longer put up with the poverty and lack of land.'[40]

Central in the purveyance of news was the actual reader, a village Hermes, who mediated, filtered and explained the information to his audience. As testified by the local authorities and by official statements by peasants themselves, reading was interpreting. Just as it was being deciphered, the information was processed for explanatory purposes. It was made relevant to the situation of the audience, to their concerns. Thus, a peasant interrogatory from Turnu Măgurele dated 3 April 1907 shows the imaginative quality of newspaper reading, as one of the peasants read out of a newspaper that 'orders have been given to drive all foreigners out of the country, that is, the Greeks and Jews'.[41] During an interrogatory dated 31 March in Râmnicu Sărat the landless peasant Radu I. Băjenaru told the judge he had heard Ştefan Negulescu reading out newspapers and saying the peasants had started killing elsewhere and no one was stopping them, because there was no army and urged the others to do the same, or they won't get any land.[42]

During the uprising tendentious reading notoriously turned an innocuous political tract into a general call to uprising. The brochure, which was entitled *To the Villagers* (Către Săteni) and had been issued by the organizers of a peasant congress in autumn 1906, had circulated ever since especially in southern Romania. It bore as a motto an excerpt from a speech given by Queen Elisabeth of Romania in August 1906 and subsequently printed on postcards and widely circulated: 'Rise up, my good people, live up to your duty and you will be amazed of your own power.'[43] In the

---

[40] *Documente*, vol.3, pp. 414–415.

[41] *Documente*, vol. 3, p. 396.

[42] *Documente*, vol. 3, p, 108.

[43] Elisabeth, Queen of Romania, Sinaia, 1 August 1906, quoted in *Documente*, vol. 3, p. 499; Alexandru A. Mareş, 'Procesul "Omului de la 1907". Date privitoare la biografia lui

interpretation of village readers this motto became a rallying call and an order from the Queen to the peasants to rise up and show the world their might.

The brochure itself called for peasant organization and concerted action, but also emphatically advised against violent means and urged to moderation and legality. Regional authorities spelt out the difference between the actual content of the brochure and the glossing of the actual text by sundry ad-hoc readers. General Prosecutor Leonescu of Iași county assessed the impact of the brochure in these terms: 'There is no instigation to an uprising in the text of the brochures by Kogălniceanu, which we have confiscated from the peasants, unless those who read them out loud gave them a completely different interpretation.'[44] In early February 1907 the Dorohoi Prefect, V. Miclescu, on the other hand, was convinced that unrest in the commune Hudeștii Mari on 31 December 1906 had been provoked by schoolteachers, who 'tendentiously interpreted a brochure, which had been distributed to the inhabitants'.[45] The same prefect showed how the peasants rejected authorities' objections that the peasants were engaging in illegal action claiming that they were urged to do so by the motto of the brochure.[46] At the other end of the country, this time in Ilfov county, near Bucharest, the same complaint was voiced by a local village inspector in his report to the Ilfov prefect: 'Mr Prefect, we have ordered that, until further notice from you, all such brochures should not be allowed to circulate through the villages as the villagers claim they were sent by Her Majesty the Queen herself as the title of the brochure suggests.'[47] As a peasant from a village near Bucharest stated in his deposition in the court case against V.M. Kogălniceanu, he together with two other fellow villagers went to Bucharest to see V. Kogălniceanu and give him 'a petition for land, pasture and woodland, as the booklet said' [...] 'Judging by his booklet, we thought Kogălniceanu represented the authorities because those among

Vasile M. Kogălniceanu', *Revista Arhivelor*, 2008, p. 191: http://www.arhivelenationale. ro/images/custom/image/serban/RA%201%202008/15_mares,_alexandru.pdf (Accessed on 2 April 2017).

[44] *Documente*, vol.2, p. 216.
[45] *Documente*, vol.2, p. 228.
[46] *Documente*, vol.2, p. 230.
[47] *Documente*, vol.3, p. 302.

us who could read said that the the name of the Queen herself was signed in the book.'[48]

The pro-domo-sua interpretation of the brochure was a common way of assimilating news from outside. Judge Vesper Erbiceanu from Iași wrote in his report to the General Prosecutor that 'the peasantry, because of their lack of education and mental discipline, evince an inclination for misinterpreting facts, distorting them and viewing them through a seditious prism. I could thus ascertain that in some villages the telegram put on display by the administration in the first days of March whereby the decision of the government was being communicated to vote a law against "*arendași* trusts" was interpreted by the peasants as – to use their words – "a state order to drive the Jewish *arendași* out of the village" and that is how the unrest started.'[49]

Such misreading of official discourse was not unique to the peasants of Romania nor was it confined to episodes of rebellion. As Willard Sunderland pointed out in the case of Russian colonists on the Eastern Frontier, officialese and technical jargon were reduced to concepts more amenable to the peasant mind:

> There was also the 'language problem.' Most peasant-based information on colonization and the frontier was relayed in oral form and was couched in words and inflections that made ready sense to peasant listeners. By contrast, information from outside the village world often came to the peasants in written form and could be easily misunderstood or misused. Words like 'subsidy' (posobie) and 'irrigation' (irrigatsiia) sounded strange to peasants and tended to be garbled. The term 'colonization' (kolonizatsiia) even created confusion. As one official noted in 1891, a party of about eight hundred settlers once appeared in the Central Asian town of Kazalinsk requesting permission to settle near a place that they called nizatsiia. In Russian, they wanted to settle 'near nizatsiia' (i.e. okolo nizatsii). The settlers had thus taken a process and turned it into a geographical location.[50]

[48] 'după cărțulia lui am crezut că Kogălniceanu este om al stăpânirii, fiindcă cei știutori de carte spuneau că este iscălită și regina pe cărțulie' – Alexandru A. Mareș, 'Procesul "Omului de la 1907". Date privitoare la biografia lui Vasile M. Kogălniceanu', *Revista Arhivelor*, 2008, p. 196: http://www.arhivelenationale.ro/images/custom/image/serban/RA%20 1%202008/15_mares,_alexandru.pdf (Accessed on 2 April 2017).

[49] *Documente*, vol.2, p. 353.

[50] Willard Sunderland, 'Peasant Pioneering: Russian Peasant Settlers Describe Colonization and the Eastern Frontier, 1880s–1910s', *Journal of Social History*, Vol. 34, No. 4, Summer, 2001, p. 897.

Tim Buchen also cites a case of glaring misreading of the printed word in Austrian Galicia in 1898, when the inhabitants of the small town of Kalwarya took a commercial leaflet for a ink stain removal product to mean an official order to attack the Jews based on the fact that in Polish the word for an ink stain was the same as that for a Jew (*żyda*).[51]

Contributing to the alteration of official communications was also the collective, participatory nature of information dissemination, whereby obscure meanings were either glossed over or attributed a new meaning, which was more relevant to the environment and concerns of the audience. The same logic of replacing an unfamiliar word by a more familiar one lies at the root of meaning alterations that go by the name of folk etymology in semantics. A village audience was never a passive receptacle of news; it actively processed and instrumentalized it.[52]

Rumour Mills

Just like early-twentieth-century pogroms in Tsarist Russia[53] or antisemitic agitation in Austrian Galicia,[54] the Romanian peasant uprising of 1907 saw an exacerbation of rumour mongering and fed on an extraordinary combination of partially accurate information, folk mythology, wishful thinking and wild leaps of popular imagination. Information was seldom conveyed accurately (apart from the basic fact of a rebellion in this or that village) and huge variation and inventiveness occurred when explaining on whose authority the uprising had started. Why should peasants rebel? Because orders from above have come to do so; because the King is dead, and the Queen ruled so in a letter;[55] because there are orders from the Russians that the peasants should kill all landowners;[56] because the 'seven emperors' have ordered it; because 'the students' have ordered it. These were variations on a more general template of authority

---

[51] Tim Buchen, *Antisemitismus in Galizien: Agitation, Gewalt und Politik gegen Juden in der Habsburgermonarchie um 1900*, Metropol Verlag, Berlin, 2012, pp. 175–176.

[52] Schenda, *Von Mund zu Ohr*, pp. 201, 213, 215.

[53] Klaus Richter, 'Kišinev or Linkuva? Rumors and threats against Jews in Lithuania in 1903' in *Revista Română de Studii Baltice și Nordice*, 2011, Issue 3 (1), pp. 117–130.

[54] Tim Buchen, *Antisemitismus in Galizien*, pp. 169–196.

[55] *Documente*, Vol. 3, p. 426.

[56] *Documente*, vol.2, p. 690.

invoked by peasants throughout the region: the Tsar, the Habsburg *Kaiser*, the not-so-dead Prince Rudolf. In Austrian Galicia, for instance, figures of authority ranged from the monarch, down to local MPs in the Viennese parliament, and even the occasional 'fine gentleman riding a bicycle'.[57]

In the case of the 1907 Romanian peasant uprising, the myth of the Tsar was not new (similar rumours circulated during a previous peasant uprising in the south in 1888) and was not completely without foundation in reality. There had been Russian troops quartered in Romania (before 1859, in the Principalities of Moldavia and Wallachia) during the Crimean War and more recently during the Russo-Turkish war of 1877–1878, which in itself created the impression of Tsarist power over and involvement in the region. In 1877 the entry of the Russian troops into Romania took place without prior permission from the Romanian authorities. Grand Duke Nicholas even took the liberty of disseminating a proclamation from the Russian Tsar to the local population and only notified the Romanian authorities post-factum. Writing to Prince Carol, he justified the de-facto military invasion by pressing strategic reasons and added that 'as I gave the order to my troops to cross over the frontier of your Highness's state, I made sure I provided them with a proclamation to the inhabitants, to warn them we were entering as friends and that the entrance of our troops on Romanian territory was effected by virtue of an agreement between our two governments'.[58] In 1890 the Russian ambassador gave the Orthodox church in Iaşi an icon of victorious St George as a gift from the Tsar in acknowledgment of Romania's participation in the 1877–1878 war on the Russian side.[59] Additionally icon peddlers were among the most prolific rumour-mongerers. Through tangible military presence but also through religious association with the world of Orthodoxy, which did have a major bearing on peasants' lives, Russia and the mythologized figure of the Tsar was an important cognitive reference point for the Romanian peasants.

---

[57] Tim Buchen, *Antisemitismus in Galizien*, p. 175.

[58] ANR (Arhivele Naţionale Istorice Centrale), Fond Casa regală, Personale Carol I, Corespondenţă familie, Nr. act V J 90, anul 1877, Letter from Grand Duke Nicholas to Prince Carol, pp. 1–2.

[59] National Archives, London, FO 104/83, May 7, 1890 – Many thanks to Dr. Patrick J. Bourne for generously putting at my disposal his PhD thesis 'Sir Frank Lascelles: a diplomat of the Victorian empire, 1841–1920', defended at University of Leeds in 2010, and his research notes.

'The Students Are Coming!'

Students' omnipresence in revolutionary movements was a constant process of political protest and upheaval in the latter half of the nineteenth and beginning of the twentieth century in Central and Eastern Europe. More often than not, revolutionary networks were based on student networks. Student input and solidarity represented a new and informed challenge to the system, and showed the spread of higher education to be anything but a reliable source of civil servants for the state or a pliant tool of control of the intelligentsia. Education turned out to be a Pandora's Box, which could equally well create efficient state officials and high-minded terrorists. As Susan Morrissey has shown in the case of imperial Russia, students were a compelling and conspicuous presence in the emerging public sphere of the Tsarist Empire, from the Narodniki movement aiming to awaken the common people to their political function, to protests, demonstrations, strikes and nationwide networks.[60] At the turn of the twentieth century, Russia had nine universities and during the 1905–1907 upheavals 'the student movement played a critical role in the revolutionary process'.[61]

That students should figure prominently in peasant movements is, however, something that does not usually crop up in historical literature and is something of a Narodnik dream come true. If in the 1860s and 1870s the Narodniki failed in their going-to-the-people initiative, a quarter of a century later the spectre of revolutionary students haunted peasant imagination during the upheavals that shook up the countryside between 1905 and 1907 in Russia and in 1907 in Romania. The relationship between the Narodniki movement and the 'student obsession' evinced by the peasant movements of early-twentieth century is a tempting one to postulate but not an easy one to demonstrate. The most probable explanation is that, rather than it being a question of memories of student visits lingering on in the minds of the peasants across more than a generation, peasant fascination with students is more likely to have been the combined result of traditional reverence for learned people as well as the gradual percolation into the village world of news of urban unrest and the conflation effected in official discourse between students and revolutionaries.

---

[60] Susan Morrissey, *Heralds of Revolution: Russian Students and the Mythologies of Radicalism*, OUP, Oxford & NY, 1998, pp. 4, 9.

[61] Morrissey, *Heralds of Revolution*, p. 115.

Closer to the 1907 events in Romania was the social turmoil that shook up Russia between 1905 and 1907. As Maureen Perrie has shown, post-factum regional reports pointed out that in 1905 in certain parts of Russia 'the peasants themselves came to use the word "student" to refer to anyone, including peasants, with radical or oppositional views.' Such a report explained that 'the term "student" [was] losing its academic character and [was] becoming a political category. Of the inhabitants of a whole number of villages it [was] said that they "[had] gone and turned into students".'[62]

In the 1860s Romania acquired two universities, one in Iași and one in Bucharest. By the turn of the century, the first generations of students were already actively involved in public life and in rowdy street protests. For years before the 1907 peasant uprising, student demonstrations had become a commonplace in the life of the big cities and in the press: they engaged in antisemitic demonstrations, cultural nationalistic protests and 'occupy' movements (see for instance students preventing the delivery of a French-language lecture on Romanian poetry at the Atheneum and the occupation of the National Theatre in protest against the inclusion of French-language plays), and solidarity protests (such as the successful pressure put by the students on the government to fire the manager of the National Theatre in Bucharest for manhandling student protesters or, in 1907 during the uprising, the demonstrations that pressured the authorities into releasing the students they had arrested for agitation in Iași).[63] Such was the prominence and the success of student protests that, as the German consul in Bucharest remarked, 'small wonder that they feel called upon to comment and take a stance on any and all public questions and use noisy demonstrations to intimidate the government into submission!'[64] Student enthusiasm and activism lent themselves equally boisterously to worthy causes, as for instance their support for improving the lot of the

[62] V. G. Tan, Novoe krest'yanstvo (The New Peasantry) (Moscow, 1905), p. 115, quoted in Maureen Perrie, 'Russian Peasant Movement of 1905–1907: Its Social Composition and Revolutionary Significance', *Past and Present*, 1972(57), pp. 123–155; p. 135.

[63] PAAA (Politisches Archiv des Auswärtiges Amts), Berlin, R 9652, Rumänien Allgemeine Angelegenheiten 1906–1907, Report no. 83, 27 March 1906, pp. 4–12; Report no. 88, Bucharest, 31 March 1906, pp. 1–4; Report no. 89, 2 April 1906, pp. 1–2; Report no. 102, 19 April 1906, pp. 1–4; Report no. 38, Bucharest, 14 March 1907, pp. 1–3; Scheerer, *Die Rumänische Bauernaufstände*, pp. 98–104.

[64] PAAA, Berlin, R 9652, Rumänien Allgemeine Angelegenheiten 1906–1907, Report no. 40, Bucharest, 20 March 1907, p. 5.

peasantry, or misguided ones, such as their frequent outbursts against Jews and foreigners. This mixture of good and bad high-mindedness was, in the eyes of the same German consul, proof of their immaturity.[65]

Within the mythology that fuelled the momentum of the 1907 peasant uprising in Romania and lent legitimacy to peasant protest and violence, the students upstaged by far all other real or imagined sources of higher authority. For the peasants they represented a sort of *Deus ex machina*: they were the only ones who would intercede for them with the government and the monarch; as more often than not the local authorities were corrupt and oppressive, peasants clung to the image of these young outsiders, who (so they thought) would help them obtain land and justice. They were variously portrayed as saviours or avengers: they were the only ones who genuinely wanted to help them, who were not likely to side with the cliquish local authorities and who strove to improve peasants' lot.

This perception was not entirely fanciful. Students from Iaşi University in northern Moldavia did write petitions on behalf of the peasants and some of them visited villages and talked to the peasants as part of an economic enquiry they conducted.[66] They sent telegrams to the Prime Minister asking for intercession and student assemblies publicly expressed their support for the peasant cause.[67] Extant correspondence from the close networks of Romanian and Bessarabian students who studied at Iaşi University and see-sawed between Romania and Tsarist Bessarabia also testifies to this quixotic involvement. Thus a letter from Mihail Vântul, a student in Iaşi, to Sergiu Cujba, a Bessarabian poet and socialist student, described the adventures of a group of Iaşi students in their attempt to provide moral support to the rebellious peasants:

> The three of us and Polihron, having heard of the uprisings, went to the countryside to see how the uprising was taking place and to protest against the vandalism of the army or of the administration. We ended up in the midst of the military camp and were arrested. After two prosecutors failed to find a reason to keep us under arrest, the administrative inspector Bogdan thought fit to play the Russian governor and arrested us anyway, illegally, and sent us to Bucharest. We never arrived there as we were sent to Galaţi

---

[65] PAAA, Berlin, R 9652, Rumänien Allgemeine Angelegenheiten 1906–1907, Report no. 40, Bucharest, 20 March 1907, p. 6.

[66] *Documente*, Vol.2, pp. 128, 175–176.

[67] *Documente*, vol. 2, pp. 310, 355.

instead. As we protested they returned us to Iaşi, where the tribunal let us free, including Polihron. The students went on strike and behaved very well, and should be praised for it. Please try as hard as you can and, if you can't do it yourself, ask Cazacu to forward to a newspaper, maybe to *Adevărul*, these letters from two students, who wanted to talk at an assembly about the agrarian question and Chuza[68] wouldn't give them the floor and called them crazy. The newspapers in Iaşi wouldn't publish either of them. So even if they are published late, please do your best to get them into print so we can offer them [the peasants] moral support.[69]

Further grist to the students-are-coming rumour mill was provided by a local attempt to sort out land relations by resorting to student expertise. In Dorohoi County, one of the landowners agreed to rent his land directly to the peasants and intended to call in students to conduct an economic study on the situation of his peasants.[70]

By mid-March 1907 a full-blown cult of the students had come into being among the peasants. A medical student from Iaşi had occasion to witness this as he travelled to his place of recruitment (Dumbrăveni, Botoşani County). At Paşcani railway station, groups of peasants who had also been called up for military recruitment found out he was a student and immediately surrounded him 'in a compact mass' and deluged him with questions and petitions:

> Some were asking what was being done for them in Bucharest, when they would be given land, others complained about the high price of land, pasture and timber; others, about the cheapness of labour [...] On the train I showed my surprise at the cult they had for the students, so one of them said to me: 'If we go to the mayor, he curses us, Mr Vice-Prefect beats us, Mr Prefect won't even listen to us, and Mr Minister has stacks of our petitions filed away, and we heard that only the students are on our side (*ţin cu noi*), that they'll come to us and teach us what to do in order to get land, because we don't know anything'.[71]

---

[68] A. C. Cuza (1857–1947) was a Professor of Political Economy at University of Iaşi and a Conservative MP, who espoused nationalist and antisemitic views. After the First World War he founded the League for Christian National Defense (Liga Apărării Naţional Creştine), one of the prominent antisemitic parties of interwar Romania.

[69] ANR, Fond Pelivan 1449, Dosar 119, Vol XLVI Scrisori vechi 1900-, pp. 54–56.

[70] *Documente*, Vol.2, p. 240.

[71] *Documente*, Vol. 2, pp. 384–387.

The farther away a village was from the university town of Iași and its rural neighbourhood, where actual students had been active, the more disconnected from reality the rumours about students were or, rather, the more they created a reality of their own. In Vaslui County rumours circulated of students devastating properties.[72] Farther south in Râmnicu Sărat County, villagers called on the people to make contracts with the landlord because 'the students have ordered it'.[73] In Teleorman County on the Danube, students were rumoured to be coming and threatening to set fire to the houses of those who opposed the uprising.[74] The same rumours made the round of the neighbouring county of Romanați, where in one village the inhabitants were so convinced that such orders actually existed that they forced the mayor to show them the order saying they should put fire to the landlord's properties.[75] Incidentally, similar suspicious behaviour had been displayed by the French population during the 1789 Revolution, when townsmen accused local authorities of hiding news from their deputies.[76] In the other Danubian county of Vlașca, the student mythology snowballed even further, testifying to the identification of the peasants with the postulated student revolutionary ethos:

In many communes there took part in the uprising mayors, garrison chiefs, priests, teachers, unlike the bad elements, who were condemned for various offenses and who in exchange for some advantages they thought they could obtain would assume the role of ringleaders under the name of *Students, that is to say, the destroyers of the landowners and the liberators of the peasantry.* They claimed to have been delegated by seven emperors and by Her Majesty the Queen. In other communes *the Students* were thought to be only the representatives of the HM the Queen and claimed to have received orders from her to the effect that, between 11 and 15 March, they should go to Bucharest so that HM the Queen can distribute to them land wrested from the hands of the usurping landowners.[77]

The same conflation of peasant rebels and students is borne out by testimonies from other counties (see for instance a deposition from Vâlcea

---

[72] *Documente*, Vol.2, p. 579.
[73] *Documente*, Vol.3, p. 104.
[74] *Documente*, vol. 3, p. 424.
[75] *Documente*, vol.4, pp. 138, 139.
[76] Georges Lefebvre, *The Great Fear of 1789: Rural Panic in Revolutionary France*, Transl. Joan White, NLB, London, 1973, p. 71.
[77] *Documente*, vol. 3, p. 528.

County, according to which rebellious peasant leaders called themselves students[78]), but also by the bemused authorities and by the peasants themselves.

Additional proof that the myth of the students went beyond a joke is that the authorities themselves from the highest to the lowest levels strove to provide an explanation as to who those students actually were. In April 1907 Prime Minister Ion I.C. Brătianu urged county prefects to throw light on the matter: 'From the interrogatories of some who were arrested as instigators we could ascertain that the rebellious population gave the name of students to certain individuals or even to fellow peasants. I urge you that, together with the local prosecutor, you should find out what made the peasants give the name of students to heads of devastating and arsonist bands, who were those who gave them this name and led the peasants to think the name of student is synonymous to that of ringleader or revolutionary.'[79] The Tutova prefect wrote to the Minister of the Interior on 13 May that 'what led the peasants to give the name of students to peasant ringleaders was the fact that those instigators, more often than not ex-convicts, were often strangers to the place and walked about dressed in German dress[80] (*îmbrăcați nemțește*), wearing peaked caps (*chipiu*) and holding a red flag, urging people to join the devastation.'[81] In Mehedinți County (Romania's western-most county at the time) the prefect wrote that 'the peasants don't know what the word "students" means – they use it as a synonym for ringleaders (*capi de răsculați*).'[82] The Romanați prefect wrote to the Minister of the Interior that the students were, for some, supernatural beings, for others learned men who came from the town to save the peasants from the boyars.[83]

That these official explanations and renditions of peasant perception were pretty accurate is borne out by subsequent testimonies of surviving peasants who took part in the uprising and reminisced about it after the Second World War. Quite a few of these testimonies, especially where the peasants came from the southern counties, mention the students: 'Students giving out typed leaflets inciting to ask for land'; 'students were

[78] *Documente*, vol. 4, p. 274.

[79] *Documente*, vol. 3, p. 430.

[80] 'German dress' meant they were wore townspeople's outfits as opposed to peasant clothes.

[81] *Documente*, vol. 2, p. 633.

[82] *Documente*, vol. 4, p. 230.

[83] *Documente*, vol. 4, p. 165.

coming with the revolution'; 'students from Iaşi were coming with the revolution'; or 'students were coming from Moldavia'; 'learned people from Moldavia, people who had schooling'; and 'the coming of the students was talked about as something certain.'[84] Although these testimonies were submitted 50 years after the uprising and targeted at a Communist audience, they nevertheless corroborate insights about peasant behaviour as communicated by 1907 official correspondence. These survivors' testimonies are evidence to the same identification process that becomes apparent in 1907 depositions and interrogatories. They show how rumours created a reality of their own, how the students mutated from actual physical persons, to disembodied rumours, mythological figures, then how the peasants themselves started competing with this image ('they say the students are coming with the revolution? why should they come? we can make our own revolution, no need for the students to come.'[85]) and ended up identifying themselves with it ('We are students! we want land! we want to quell the boyars to give us land!'[86]).

What's in a Rumour?

Regarding the proliferation of these peasant mythologies and their meaning in the economy of the 1907 peasant uprising, rumour theory provides explanatory tools on at least two levels: (1) it explains the frenzied propagation of rumours in terms of a specific typology of rumour and (2) it explains away the impression of a disconnect from reality that many of the rumours during the peasant uprising evinced.

By drawing on the rumour typology introduced by Allport and Postman (home-stretch rumours, fear rumours and wish rumours), one concludes that the 1907 peasant uprising was predominantly fuelled by the first category, that of home-stretch rumours, which proliferate 'when the public is expecting a momentous event to occur' and replicate all the more 'the nearer the realization of a hope seems to be'.[87] In the case of the peasant uprising, the great momentous event hoped for, yearned after, obsessed about, was land redistribution. The peasants

---

[84] *Amintiri despre răscoala din 1907*, henceforth *Amintiri*, Editura de Stat pentru Literatură Politică, Bucureşti, 1957, pp. 69, 134, 155, 159, 195, 212, 216, 238.

[85] *Amintiri*, p. 256.

[86] *Amintiri*, p. 44.

[87] Gordon Allport and Leo Postman, *The Psychology of Rumour*, New York, Russell&Russell, 1947, pp. 47, 63.

wanted land at all costs, or as the next best thing, favourable lease contracts for land. Rumours that peasants elsewhere got better land deals for their troubles spread like wildfire and engendered the firm conviction that unless you rebel you won't get any land. This was accompanied by a frenzied sense of urgency, of a window of opportunity that will never again open up: unless you act now, unless you join the uprising now, all efforts will have been in vain. This was not an instance of self-delusion, but rather a clear sign that the peasants were able to learn from previous experience: isolated flares of peasant unrest punctuated the period 1880–1907 with a major uprising in 1888, which shared all of the characteristics of 1907 but was quickly put down because of lack of synchronization between north and south.

Rumour has been variously defined as 'unverified and instrumentally relevant information statements in circulation that arise in contexts of ambiguity, danger or potential threat, and that function to help people make sense and manage risk'; rumours amount to 'making collective sense of an ambiguous situation' in contexts where there is 'a perceived threat or people feel an acute need for security', so their basic function is that of controlling a threatening situation.[88] Depending on their genetic context, rumours can engender fears or alleviate them,[89] but in all situations they are a form of collectively making sense of the world out there and, even more importantly, they have an instrumental value (they serve a purpose that is personally relevant to the rumour purveyor). In the case of the 1907 peasant uprising the major point of interest was impending land redistribution and seizing an opportunity that was not likely to arise again.

Another vital element in the process of rumour mongering as highlighted by rumour theory is that of ambiguity and lack of reliable standards of evidence. Dysfunctional channels of communication further increase the production of rumours.[90] From this point of view, the rural world of 1907 Romania presented itself as a hotbed of rumour: the impossibility of checking rumours' veracity given that central authority and its dictates had always been mediated, always at a remove (news had to be

---

[88] Nicholas DiFonzo & Prashant Bordia, 'Rumor, Gossip and Urban Legends', *Diogenes*, February 2007, vol. 54 no. 1, 19–35 – pp. 19–21.

[89] Cass Sunstein, *On Rumors: How Falsehoods Spread, Why We Believe Them, What Can Be Done*, Farrar, Strauss and Giroux, 2009, p. 6.

[90] Bordia et al., 'Uncertainty during Organizational Change: Is it all about Control?', *European Journal of Work and Organizational Psychology*, 2004, 13 (3), 345–365; p. 346.

read out to the others by the literate members of the community; it percolated through several filters before it reached ordinary peasants).
Distrust of village and regional authorities ran high and the chain of communication between villages and higher authorities was disjointed at best,
if not altogether non-existent. The peasants' way of learning about developments elsewhere was primarily through hearsay (what in rumour theory
is called 'informational cascades'[91]), while the authorities relied on corrupt
subordinates or on the newspapers for their knowledge of what was happening on the ground.

As regards the theoretical proposition that rumours are about making
sense of and managing threat, I would actually qualify this and point out
that it may not always be a case of coping with threat but rather of crisis
management: crises presuppose a systemic upheaval that can bode ill or
well for the community. In the case of the 1907 peasant uprising, it was
not so much impending peril (at least not for the peasants) as impending
opportunity that drove the rumour mills. So I would slightly qualify this
definition of rumour as a threat-control strategy and present rumour as a
form of community revelation (and the implicit preparation for it or acting
on it): an impending irruption of something good or something bad into
your life.

Mythologizing the Better to Get a Grip on Reality

The above-mentioned rumours afford a view of the Romanian countryside in the early years of the twentieth century: their seemingly 'fanciful'
nature is as relevant and as revealing of the village world at the time and
its relation to towns and local and central authorities as any hard metrics
to be had from archival material and official sources. It is not so much
the content of these rumours that is important as their performative
value: the effect they have on people and what actions they engender.
To use J.L. Austin's phrase, they are an instance of 'doing things with
words'.

There is a stark contrast between the patronizing view of the peasantry
held by the authorities (civil servants, clergy) and the unprecedented
organization and initiative of the peasants. For all their backwardness they
were very adept at seizing upon modern tools and strategies as well as

---

[91] Cass Sunstein, *On Rumors*, pp. 8, 21: informational cascades 'occur because each of us
tends to rely on what other people think and do'.

effectively using knowledge acquired in the army such as guerrilla warfare, cutting communication lines, intercepting correspondence/telegrams. Many peasants may have misunderstood rumours/news, but that is not the point. The point is how they used this information to serve their own purposes. For all the misreading of information—unwitting or purposeful—what comes out of the plethora of official correspondence is the peasants' ability to instrumentalize rumour and misinformation, to turn it around so it served their purposes. This uprising mythology could be dismissed as an instance of hazy/oversimplistic grasp of the structures of authority in the state, of misguided expectations and a disconnect from reality. But such a patronizing perspective holds little explanatory value and fails to account for the amount of social energy that went into these mythologies, or their wide spread, or even the fact that the authorities themselves took them seriously. A much more satisfactory explanation would be that this mythological framework functioned as a very effective strategy of mobilization, getting everybody to act NOW, moving people to action. As Tim Buchen put it in his book on antisemitism in Galicia, 'rumours were the self-empowerment of a community, who reinforced their own values and their own world view by means of us-and-them narratives.'[92]

This was vital in a context where only unity of purpose and concerted collective action could achieve the desired goal. The student mythology and other similar instances of folk rumour-mongering meant seizing a piece of information and turning it into a rallying call. These peasant mythologies evince a strong performative function of language in action: by making things up, the peasants postulated a source of authority and then acted on it: the order may have been fictitious, but the effects of the actions deriving from it were as real as could be. This ties in with rumour theory, which stresses the function of rumour as a form of informational coping and control. In this case rumour became a collective way of seizing a rare opportunity to be heard and to have their complaints redressed; it was a way of exerting control.[93] This psychological

---

[92] Tim Buchen, *Antisemitismus in Galizien*, p. 174.

[93] Control as defined by Greenberger and Strasser is 'a psychological construct reflecting an individual's beliefs in his or her ability to effect a change, in a desired direction, on the environment.' Bordia et al., 'Uncertainty during Organizational Change: Is it all about Control?', *European Journal of Work and Organizational Psychology*, 2004, 13 (3), 345–365 – p. 349.

category maps onto the notion of agency in sociology and political science. Through wild rumours the peasants of 1907 were in fact exercising agency, were seizing on an ambiguous situation and steering it to their own benefit.

BIBLIOGRAPHY

N. Adăniloaie, *Răscoala țăranilor din 1888*, Editura Academiei Republicii Socialiste România, București, 1988

Gordon Allport and Leo Postman, *The Psychology of Rumour*, Russell&Russell, New York, 1947

Amintiri despre răscoala din 1907, Editura de Stat pentru Literatură Politică, București, 1957

Prashant Bordia et al., 'Uncertainty during Organizational Change: Is It All About Control?', *European Journal of Work and Organizational Psychology*, Vol. 13, No. 3, 2004, 345–365

Patrick J. Bourne, 'Sir Frank Lascelles: a diplomat of the Victorian empire, 1841–1920', Unpublished PhD Thesis, University of Leeds, 2010

Tim Buchen, *Antisemitismus in Galizien: Agitation, Gewalt und Politik gegen Juden in der Habsburgermonarchie um 1900*, Metropol Verlag, Berlin, 2012

Nicholas DiFonzo and Prashant Bordia, 'Rumor, Gossip and Urban Legends', *Diogenes*, Vol. 54, No. 1 (Feb., 2007), 19–35

P.G. Eidelberg, *The Great Rumanian Peasant Revolt of 1907: Origins of a Modern Jacquerie*, Brill, Leiden, 1974

Leo Katz, *Brennende Dörfer*, Verlag für Gesellschaftskritik, Wien, 1993

Georges Lefebvre, *The Great Fear of 1789: Rural Panic in Revolutionary France*, Trans. Joan White, NLB, London, 1973

Alexandru A. Mareș, 'Procesul "Omului de la 1907". Date privitoare la biografia lui Vasile M. Kogălniceanu', *Revista Arhivelor*, 2008: http://www. arhivelenationale.ro/images/custom/image/serban/RA%201%202008/15_ mares,_alexandru.pdf (Accessed on 2 April 2017)

Susan Morrissey, *Heralds of Revolution: Russian Students and the Mythologies of Radicalism*, OUP, Oxford and NY, 1998

Andrei Oțetea, and Ion Popescu-Puțuri (Eds.), *Documente privind marea răscoală a țăranilor din 1907*, Editura Academiei Republicii Socialiste România, București, 1977

Maureen Perrie, 'Russian Peasant Movement of 1905–1907: Its Social Composition and Revolutionary Significance', *Past and Present*, No. 57, 1972

Liviu Rebreanu, *The Uprising*, Trans. P. Crandjean and S. Hartauer, Peter Owen Ltd., London, 1965

Klaus Richter, 'Kišinev or Linkuva? Rumors and threats against Jews in Lithuania in 1903' in *Revista Română de Studii Baltice și Nordice*, 2011, Issue 3 (1)

Karl Scheerer, *Die Rumänische Bauernaufstände vom Frühjahr 1907*, Mainz, 1971

Rudolf Schenda, *Von Mund zu Ohr. Bausteine zu einer Kulturgeschichte volkstümlichen Erzählens in Europa*, Vandenhoek & Ruprecht, Göttingen, 1993

Willard Sunderland, 'Peasant Pioneering: Russian Peasant Settlers Describe Colonization and the Eastern Frontier, 1880s–1910s', *Journal of Social History*, Vol. 34, No. 4, Summer, 2001

Cass Sunstein, *On Rumors: How Falsehoods Spread, Why We Believe Them, What Can Be Done*, Farrar, Strauss and Giroux, 2009

CHAPTER 3

Jews, Strangers and Foreigners

There were two sets of rumour mills that fuelled the 1907 peasant uprising. As seen in the previous chapter, instrumental in the rapid spread of the peasant rebellion were the village rumour mills, which, for all their fantastic notions and sometimes wide-off-the-mark understanding of the sources of power, were nevertheless empowering and pragmatic in their overall effect of general mobilization. Parallel to the village rumour mills, and at times echoing them and bouncing information off of them, was a second set of rumour mills, the official ones. These were fundamentally disempowering and self-destructive, testifying to the elites' disconnect from reality and the worlds-apart perception of strangers and foreigners held by the authorities as opposed to ordinary peasants. The rumours that haunted the ruling class were the compounded consequence of knee-jerk reaction shaped by historical precedent, incapacity to rule properly and assume responsibility for it, and scapegoating.

FOREIGNERS: CAN'T LIVE WITH THEM, CAN'T LIVE WITHOUT THEM

Borderland polities, which were historically caught up in a 'shatterzone of empires', survived by dint of an astute game of alliances and playing one power off another.[1] These survival strategies and the constant meddling of

---

[1] Alfred Rieber, *The Struggle for the Eurasian Borderlands: From the Rise of Early Modern Empires to the End of the First World War*, Cambridge and New York: Cambridge University

© The Author(s) 2018
I. Marin, *Peasant Violence and Antisemitism in Early Twentieth-Century Eastern Europe*,
https://doi.org/10.1007/978-3-319-76069-8_3

45

great powers into their affairs enhanced the sense that all things foreign were deleterious as well as rendered reliance on things foreign unavoidable. Moreover, fledgling nationalism, such as practiced in the young states that emerged from the fringes of the Ottoman Empire, suffered from an inferiority complex and was thus virulently xenophobic. It was not hate for hate's sake, it was hate for the sake of self-preservation and self-affirmation. It was not a question of 'we don't like foreigners', it was a question of 'the foreigners are stifling us, they won't let us live and prosper'.

The beginnings of the Romanian state were marked by rapid modernization, institutional construction and consolidation, massive imports (cultural, administrative, legal), and fast and lopsided development, which yanked forward a small part of Romanian society at the cost of the relentless impoverishment of the peasant population, which formed an overwhelming 82% of the total population. Just like in Tsarist Russia, modernization was effected not for the benefit of the peasantry, but at their expense.[2] As Keith Hitchins has pointed out, the population of Romania at the end of the nineteenth century and the beginning of the twentieth century, was from an ethnic and confessional point of view, 'remarkably homogenous': in 1899, 92.1% of the population was Romanian and 91.5% were Orthodox. Jews were 'the only significant minority in Romania during the period'.[3]

Massive investment into state infrastructure (building and manning institutions from scratch: railways, army, bureaucracy, banks etc.) presupposed equally massive reliance on foreign capital and also required skills for negotiating favourable (as opposed to colonial) terms with the foreign investors. Thus, 80% of joint-stock industrial capital came from outside the country, 92% of investment in the petroleum industry was foreign as was 46% to 94% of stock in the timber, metallurgical, paper and sugar industries. Added to this foreign input were the entrepreneurial and commercial skills, which were mostly Jewish, German or Austrian.[4] The

Press, 2014, p. 318; Omer Bartov and Eric D. Weitz, *Shatterzone of Empires: Coexistence and Violence in the German, Habsburg, Russian, and Ottoman Borderlands*, Indiana University Press, 2013.

[2] A. Gerschenkron, 'Russia: Patterns and Problems of Economic Development 1861–1958', *Economic Backwardness in Historical Perspective. A Book of Essays*, Frederick A. Praeger Publishers, New York, Washington, London, 1962, pp. 125–126, 131.

[3] Keith Hitchins, *Rumania 1866–1947*, Clarendon Press, Oxford, 1994, p. 164.

[4] John R. Lampe, 'Varieties of Unsuccessful Industrialization: The Balkan States Before 1914', *The Journal of Economic History*, Vol. 35, No. 1, (Mar., 1975), pp. 68, 69, 78, 79.

railways were built with foreign capital secured at disadvantageous rates and employing almost exclusively imported raw materials and skilled labour, triggering none of the beneficial backward and forward linkage effects (to use Albert Hirschman's terms) that industrialization fostered in Western Europe.[5] It was this overwhelming and inescapable financial dependence on foreign capital and the self-contradictions of fledgling, immature statesmanship, rather than the actual ethnic structure of the population, that stoked up official xenophobia.

As we shall see in the next chapter, agriculture was the main branch of Romanian economy that 'accounted for two-thirds of the gross national product and supplied over three-quarters of the country's exports'. Agricultural production increased but not because of the increased productivity of the land (through the use of fertilizers or machinery) but because of the expansion of cultivation surfaces and merciless exploitation of the peasant.[6] Land tenure was dominated by latifundia, absentee landlords and the land-lease system (*arendași*). This was conducive to high rents, land speculation and capitalist monopolies that left the peasantry at the mercy of capitalist sharks, and kept it in a check-mate situation by legislation that precluded genuine economic emancipation.

In 1907, just like during previous episodes of internal crisis such as the 1888 peasant uprising in southern Romania, the preoccupation of the Romanian government with foreigners and foreign involvement became most acute. This was in addition to the usual political recriminations that targeted the opposition. Double-barrelled blame assignation to the opposition and foreign agitators had also cropped up in 1888, when the Liberal government pinned the blame for the uprising on the opposition and the Russian emissaries: they put the peasants up to it; the plan had been long in the making but it backfired as the uprising started too late, after the Brătianu government fell.[7] A carbon copy of this same justificatory trope was to resurface in 1907 among both the Conservatives and the Liberals, this time with the slight variation that the uprising had started too early, rather than too late.[8] King Carol himself espoused this view of the causes

[5] Murgescu, *România și Europa. Acumularea decalajelor economice (1500–2010)*, pp. 144–145.

[6] Hitchins, *Rumania 1866–1947*, pp. 167, 169.

[7] PAAA, Berlin, R 9637 Allgemeine Angelegenheiten Rumäniens, March–April 1888, Report no. 52, 10 April 1888, p. 3.

[8] PAAA, Berlin, R 9653, Rumänien Allgemeine Angelegenheiten April–December 1907, Report no. 59, 7 April 1907, pp. 4–5.

of the 1888 peasant uprising, which he described in his personal correspondence as 'a consequence of antagonistic passions and of Russian
influence'.[9] He put down peasant troubles in Romania to 'pan-Slavists and
nihilists', who infiltrated among the peasants under various guises, and to
bad crops: 'In spring [1889] we could have another peasant uprising,
which affects us more than a workers' strike affects Belgium, because here
an uprising immediately impinges on state revenues and great landowners'
income. Let us hope Parliament will vote laws in the peasants' favour
through which deleterious propaganda [Socialist, nihilist and pan-Slavist]
could be at least in part counteracted.'[10] A few years later, in 1905, the
King described Romania as a safe zone amidst conflicted neighbours
(Russia and Hungary) and considered that the only harm could come
from contamination with the political and social troubles across the
frontier:

> For years now the peasants have been endeavouring to get land and they
> want to divide the great estates among themselves. Every year thousands of
> peasants become owners of land through the sale of plots, but there are over
> 100,000 who at the moment have to make do without anything and are
> instigated by the Socialists.[11]

The uprising of 1907 was haunted by rumours of strangers and foreigners roaming the countryside, who were viewed as either engenderers or
catalysts of the rural troubles and kept the authorities guessing as to their
identity, agenda and whereabouts. To the very end, representatives of the
Conservatives claimed that the uprising was a cunning conspiracy. For
example, Take Ionescu stated in an interview for *Frankfurter Zeitung* that:

> without a unitary organization there would not have been such a sudden
> and unitary uprising. One cannot yet establish the goal of this plot. It may
> be more of a general anarchist purpose or it may be a devious foreign plot –
> the means of agitation at least are most certainly of foreign origin. [...] I
> have on me a whole file with proof of anarchy. Everything points to the
> existence of a plot based in Bucharest. I think the movement started too
> early and was not completely organized; they would otherwise have started

[9] Sorin Cristescu (Ed.), *Carol I. Corespondența personală (1878–1912)*, București, Triton, 2005, pp. 237–238.

[10] Cristescu (Ed.), *Carol I. Corespondența personală*, pp. 243–244.

[11] Cristescu (Ed.), *Carol I. Corespondența personală*, p. 435.

with the destruction of the railways. They probably planned a great uprising during harvest time, which would have destroyed the entire crop.[12]

The former head of the Conservative government, Cantacuzino, explained the uprising in similar conspiratorial terms to *Neues Wiener Abendblatt*:

> A defining feature of this uprising is the fact that, just like the uprisings that the Carbonari instigated in Italy, it was planned under the utmost secrecy and excellently organized. [...] There is among peasants undoubtedly much discontent. But they seem to have been instigated to rise up by foreign influences. The events in Russia, especially in neighbouring Bessarabia, where the situation of the peasantry is similar to ours, were as contagious as an epidemic. Arrests were made where it was seen that there were foreign emissaries who went from village to village under the most varied disguises and disseminated a great number of instigating pamphlets and brochures. In the last few days even, several people have been arrested, some of them disguised as priests, others as women, who, although could speak no Romanian, instigated the rural population by distributing pamphlets.[13]

Among the Liberals, too, there were voices that took seriously the hypothesis of a plot/foreign conspiracy. As pointed out in the previous chapter, the student rumours, which circulated profusely among peasants, were given much attention by Brătianu, the new Minister of the Interior. The uprising was punctuated by rumours of strangers and foreigners stoking up peasant discontent: Russian agents, students, peddlers disseminating political messages and so forth. Extant testimonies from peasants and local authorities as well as diplomatic reports seldom or never bear out these alleged infiltrations. Mayors' reports and peasant depositions denied the existence of any agitators, be they Potemkinists, Russian revolutionaries, socialists or any other type of instigating foreigners.[14]

The authorities' dogged belief in external involvement was symptomatic of a particular way of relating to and explaining social unrest, which was fundamentally extra-punitive. This is not something new and to a certain extent is shared by all governments. Extra-punitive crisis management, when kept in check, can buttress the dwindling legitimacy of a

---

[12] *Documente*, Vol. V, p. 345.
[13] *Documente*, Vol. V, p. 349.
[14] *Documente*, vol. 2, pp. 205, 215.

regime by deflecting blame and as such it is a very common political strategy. When it ceases to be a mere political strategy and defence mechanism, and comes to pervade all political thought and shape official reactions and attempted remedies, it has the opposite effect: of blinding the government to the real problem and as such leading to a snowballing of the crisis. This is what happened in Romania in spring 1907.

The enduring reaction of the Romanian authorities to the peasant crisis was twofold: (1) the culprits for the peasant situation were the Jewish leaseholders and (2) the uprising was the product of external agitation: the peasants must have been put up to it and would never have rebelled otherwise. This was in keeping with both the rampant antisemitism of the establishment and the patriarchal and patronizing view of peasants as children, under age, incapable of mature action, and as such easily swayed. It also reflected the widespread notion, which was equally shared by authorities across the border, that social unrest was very much like a disease, catching, contaminating, coming from outside, never from inside.

THE STATUS OF JEWS IN ROMANIA

Blaming the uprising on Jewish exploitation rang true because there were a considerable number of Jews among the notoriously exploitative leaseholders and also because for decades antisemitic discourse had been lavishly used in Romanian politics and public debates. But how many Jews were there in Romania at the time and what was their status within the young Romanian state?

The status of Jews in the Romanian Kingdom was emblematic of the structural duality of the Romanian state: on the one hand, denying citizen rights to ordinary Jewish population (on account of their allegedly posing a threat to autochthonous economic development) and thus placing them in a limbo legal category, neither here nor there (this was not very different from the situation of the Dobrogea population, who, although nominally enjoying Romanian citizenship, were in practice in as much of a political and social limbo as the Jewish population)[15]; and, on the other hand, the reality of elites and state institutions favouring big, foreign and autochthonous, capital for land rental purposes against the needs and demands of local peasants. As Andrew Janos put it,

---

[15] Enache Tuşa, *Imaginar politic and identități colective în Dobrogea*, Editura Institutului de Științe Politice și Relații Internaționale, București, 2011, p. 170.

For the Liberal bureaucracy, however, the problem, was more complex. As nationalists, they could not but lament the rise of an alien entrepreneurial class in their midst, but as economic rationalists and a class dependent on public revenue, they could not but welcome the contributions made by Jewish talent and capital to the modernization of the economy. The conflict was well reflected by the waverings of Romanian liberals between total rejection and emancipation in the twenty-five years between 1839 and 1864. Their dilemma was in part resolved by the formula that found its way into the Constitution of 1866 (in force until 1923). On the one hand, this document provided legal protection to Jewish capital and urban property. On the other, it denied Jews the rights of citizenship, and hence access to bureaucratic positions, ownership of rural property, and the exercise of political rights. By this formula Jews could participate in developing the modern, urban economy without posing a threat of competition to landowners, bureaucrats, and professional politicians.[16]

In Romania by the end of the nineteenth century the status of the Jewish population was inextricably bound up with the issue of state independence and international recognition; it was also part of the process of squaring new-fangled concepts such as citizenship with the inchoate social realities on the ground and, not least, defining the Romanian nation in legal terms. The Romanian Principalities changed hands several times across the nineteenth century: under exclusive Ottoman suzerainty until 1830 (Treaty of Adrianople), under Russian control until the Crimean War, under joint Great Power and Ottoman control until 1858, and finally independent following the Russian-Turkish war of 1877–1878. The legal status of the Jews fluctuated with each change of hands. Under Ottoman (Phanariot) rule, legal stipulations were comparatively inclusive (with some exceptions especially regarding the right to own land in the countryside). The paradox of Jewish legal status in the Principalities (later the Romanian state) was that, while the state was weak, legal categories were relatively tolerant and inclusive; as the state coalesced into being and acquired modern, liberal institutions (its first constitution), legal categories became more restrictive and exclusive (discriminating), bearing out the truism that liberalism could be bound up with great illiberalism.

---

[16] Andrew Janos, 'Modernization and Decay in Historical Perspective: The Case of Romania' in Kenneth Jowitt (Ed.), *Social Change in Romania 1860–1940*, Berkeley, California, 1978, p. 92.

The first proto-constitutional laws that the Romanian Principalities ever had were imposed under Russian occupation (*Les reglements organiques*) in 1830–1831. Their stipulations granted progressive political structures and rights that were unthinkable in Tsar Nicholas I's autocratic Empire, but they also inherited the state-driven antisemitism of their powerful neighbour. For the first time native Jews were categorized as 'foreigners' (*străini*) and explicitly referred to in the very text of the law as a deleterious influence on the country.[17] The dissolution of the Russian protectorate resulted in a temporary removal of explicit antisemitic legislation. By the stipulations of the 1856 Paris Conference, all citizens of the Principalities should enjoy political and religious freedom, but the issue of civic and political rights was left to the local Moldovian and Wallachian governments to decide. Under Prince Cuza (1859–1866) a partial emancipation was effected, which was however reversed a few years later, after his deposition, by the introduction of the first Romanian Constitution in 1866. Article 7 of the latter unequivocally enunciated: 'Romanian citizenship can only be acquired, maintained and lost in accordance with the rules stipulated by the civil laws. Only foreigners of Christian faith can acquire the quality of being Romanian.'[18] This was followed by a spate of expulsions on the grounds of vagabondage and by state-condoned violence against Jewish communities.[19]

In Romania the question of the emancipation of the Jews did not develop as an internal debate born of domestic necessity, but was, from the very beginning of the state, an external imposition and an element of international pressure (see for instance the Strousberg Affair, whereby Germany conditioned their recognition on Romania buying off the railway network at an exorbitant price[20]). The Berlin Treaty of 1878 imposed on Romania (just as it did on Serbia and Bulgaria) the obligation of treating all their subjects as equal before the law and in their civic and political rights. Article 44 stipulated that 'in Romania the difference in religious beliefs and confession cannot be held against anyone as a ground for exclusion from civil and political rights, taking up public office, posts, awards, or plying various trades and professions.'[21] In exchange for signing

[17] Carol Iancu, *Evreii din România (1866–1919). De la Excludere la Emancipare*, Trans. C. Litman, Editura Hasefer, Bucharest, 1996, pp. 46–47.

[18] Iancu, *Evreii din România (1866–1919)*, pp. 58–65; p. 72.

[19] Iancu, *Evreii din România (1866–1919)*, p. 94.

[20] Iancu, *Evreii din România (1866–1919)*, p. 202.

[21] Iancu, *Evreii din România (1866–1919)*, p. 182.

the Treaty, Romania acquired full state independence. The 'Jewish' clause was endlessly negotiated with, and led to, fierce internal political debates. As pointed out in a memorandum of 1879 (which was part of an intensive diplomatic campaign conducted by the Romanian government to sidestep the emancipatory impositions of the Berlin Treaty),[22] the young Romanian state had the largest Jewish population by comparison to its total population in all of Europe.[23] According to the 1899 census, the Jews represented 4.5% of Romania's total population (10.5% of the Moldavian population and 1.8% of the Wallachian population).[24] The Romanian authorities accepted the citizenship stipulations imposed by the Treaty of Berlin in principle but objected to their immediate and wholesale application as deleterious to national interests. Among the reasons invoked for such a position were: the example of other European countries, which opted for a gradual integration of their Jewish population; the counter-example of Jewish emancipation in French Algeria, which, as was argued, was done at the expense of the Arab population, causing social unrest; and the commonly shared prejudice of Romanian and French statesmen, who looked upon the Jewish community as a caste impossible to assimilate and opposed to assimilation. As Romania adopted France as its role model, both from an institutional and from a social mores point of view, it followed almost as a matter of course that it should take its cue from the same country regarding the native Jewish population. Romanians defended their own autochthonous anti-Jewish prejudice by borrowing arguments from the French:

> Algerian Jews have been posing as a dominant race ever since they were emancipated and they look to exploit the Arabs, whose lands and property they seize callously. And far from growing close to those to whom they owe such great advantages, they remained confined, just like in the past, to the narrow limits of their caste. They do not join in the efforts of the nation; on the contrary, they seek to shun the responsibilities imposed on them by the title of citizen, without ever neglecting, however, to claim the advantages deriving from it. This is the testimony of all those who know Algeria and which can be confirmed by an old soldier and distinguished statesman such

---

[22] Iancu, *Evreii din România (1866–1919)*, p. 184.

[23] HHStA (Haus-, Hof- und Staatsarchiv, Vienna), PA Rumaenien 1880, Karton 50, Judenfrage, Memoire sur la revision de l'Article 7 de la Constitution Roumaine, Paris 1879, pp. 12–13. Cf. Carol Iancu, *Evreii din România*, pp. 161–162.

[24] Iancu, *Evreii din România (1866–1919)*, p. 162.

as General Chanzy, who was governor of this French dependency for six years and who is now French diplomatic agent in St Petersburg.

In this respect we can invoke yet another incontestable authority, that of Mr Thiers, who as Prime Minister and chief of the Executive, presented in August 1871, through Mr Lambrecht, Minister of the Interior, a law project which aimed to abrogate the 1870 emancipation decree. His exposition of reasons behind this law project is remarkable; it seems to have been written for the Jews of Romania. Speaking of the Jews of Algeria, the drafter of the exposition mentions: 'They preserved their traditional ways and institutions, which have allowed them survive through the ages without assimilating... They do not consider themselves to be part of the political community. They remain to a certain extent strangers to this community. They can never be expected to cast votes dictated by political considerations or by an apprecia-tion of municipal interests. They are and will continue to be a foreign body, endowed with its separate existence [...] The Jews [...] have only with great reluctance rendered military service; their temperament and mores are so absolutely opposed to a useful incorporation into our army; they are inca-pable of military service.'[25]

Romanian reluctance to emancipate the native Jewish population resulted in endless debates in Parliament and legal artifice aimed at observ-ing the letter, but not the spirit, of the Berlin Treaty stipulations in this respect. As pointed out by Count Hoyos, the Austro-Hungarian diplo-matic agent in Bucharest, the changes made to the Constitution were meant to 'remove the word "non-Christian" from the legal text without, however, settling the Jewish Question one way or another, or only giving the impression that this has been settled.'[26] And, as usual, this was not about the Jews or foreigners per se, but rather the Jewish Question was a function of political factionalism.[27]

Attitudes to Jews were not only shaped by economic and political inter-ests, but also by the wider international configuration in which Romania was embedded at the time, in particular by the tug-of-war between external influences and models (the French and the German), which translated into yet another layer of political factionalism. Supporters of the French influ-

---

[25] HHStA, PA Rumaenien 1880, Karton 50, *Judenfrage*, Memoire sur la revision de l'Article 7 de la Constitution Roumaine, Paris 1879, pp. 14–15.

[26] HHStA, PA Rumaenien 1878–1879, Karton 49, p. 13/verso (report no. 18 from Count Ladislaus von Hoyos to Count Andrassy, 21 January 1879).

[27] HHStA, PA Rumaenien 1878–1879, Karton 49, pp. 72/verso, 73/recto (report no. 53 from Count Hoyos to Count Andrássy, 3 March 1879).

ence and more importantly promoters of national self-reliance (*prin noi înşine*) such as the Liberal Brătianus couched their antisemitism in terms of anti-Germanism. Dimitrie Brătianu in particular was keen to remove all foreign influence from Romania in all domains. He lumped together Jews and Germans as a harmful invasion onto the Romanian economic scene:

> The Germans and the Jews have already imperceptibly occupied a good part of our towns and, when they take full possession of these, they will move on to the countryside. I speak not only of the Moldavian towns but also of Bucharest, in whose busiest streets one can hardly hear a word of Romanian spoken. [...] We are losing our towns, our trade and industry are being wrenched away from us, and soon the turn will come for our land to be taken away from us, and with that we will be stripped of our language, religion and our Romanian soul. – Just like the Jews, the Germans too have no fatherland. Like migrating birds, they fly around and leave behind, light-heartedly, their native towns. The German leaves his home and hearth, his friends and relatives without problems, packs his nationality in his backpack, – for, just like the Jew, the German remains a German irrespective of whether he wins or loses – and goes, without so much as a thought of return, to America, Australia, or wherever he thinks he can earn a *Kreuzer*, and buy a pint of beer and a pound of meat. These Germans are all the more dangerous as, given their advanced culture, the ease with which they work, and their utter lack of national and patriotic feelings, they have no compunction in squeezing out those who received them as friends. More than this: the German is by nature pliant, obsequious, and patient, he deprecates himself (*er verkleinert sich*), offers you his services, asks you to take him in your house out of pity, and when you answer his request, he silently works away until he has impoverished you and thrown you out of your own house.[28]

Dimitrie Brătianu's views seem to have been part of a wider trend against German-ness, which as expressed at a Romanian journalists' congress, 'is overtly threatening the Danubian Principalities. The press will energetically fight any direct or indirect attempt to colonize the country with Germans; it will oppose with equal energy the systematic invasion of Jews, this true vanguard of German-ness'.[29]

[28] H. B. Oppenheim, *Die Judenverfolgungen in Rumaenien*, Berlin, Verlag von Georg Stilke, 1872, pp. 6 - Holocaust Museum – digitized material: Die Jüdische Gemeinde zu Breslau Sygn. 105/244.

[29] H. B. Oppenheim, *Die Judenverfolgungen in Rumaenien*, Berlin, Verlag von Georg Stilke, 1872, pp. 7 – *Holocaust Museum* – digitized material: Die Jüdische Gemeinde zu Breslau Sygn. 105/244.

By opting for case-by-case 'naturalization' as opposed to a general, unconditional emancipation of the native Jews, three legal categories came into being: foreign Jews (under the protection of other states), native Jews (who were Romanian subjects, but not citizens) and citizens (Jews enjoying full civic and political rights).[30] The middle category was thus a political limbo in which the majority of the Jewish population in Romania was stranded. As Constantin Dobrogeanu-Gherea pointed out in a 1913 interview given to *România Muncitoare*, 'a witty foreigner who knew Romania well once told him jokingly, "I don't understand why Romania is agonizing so much over the Jewish Question since there are no Jews in Romania. [...] For a man to exist in a modern state, to genuinely be, they must be the citizen of one country or another."'[31]

Post-1879 Romanian legislation consolidated and made more explicit the non-belonging of Jews to the Romanian state resulting in a series of oxymoronic laws that made Jews liable to state obligations but excluded them from state careers and benefits. Thus, militarily, the Jewish population as 'foreigners under no other state protection' had to do military service but were precluded from making a career in the army. In the words of General Manu, 'all Jews are Romanians as far as military service is concerned, once that comes to an end they become foreigners once again.'[32] While access to free education was sanctified by the 1866 constitution, subsequent laws confined this right to Romanian citizens only.[33] An 1881 law on 'foreigners' facilitated the expulsion of any inhabitants who were deemed 'dangerous to state security'.[34] In 1884 another law, this time against peddling, deprived many Jews of their livelihood and was misapplied so bribe money could be extorted from better-off Jews.[35] In 1887 the law of rural communes prevented 'foreigners' from settling in the countryside and, following the recategorization of several towns as rural communes, led to the expulsion of the local Jewish population.[36]

[30] HHStA, PA Rumaenien 1880, Karton 50, Judenfrage, Memoire sur la revision de l'Article 7 de la Constitution Roumaine, Paris 1879, p. 19.

[31] Constantin Dobrogeanu-Gherea, *Opere Complete*, Vol. 5, Editura Politică, București, 1978, Vol. 5, p. 168.

[32] Iancu, *Evreii din România (1866–1919)*, p. 218.

[33] Iancu, *Evreii din România (1866–1919)*, pp. 220–222.

[34] Iancu, *Evreii din România (1866–1919)*, p. 230.

[35] Iancu, *Evreii din România (1866–1919)*, pp. 227–228.

[36] Iancu, *Evreii din România (1866–1919)*, p. 233.

The Economics Behind Antisemitism

There had been Jews in the Romanian Principalities for hundreds of years. Some migrated from Spain and settled mainly in the south (Sephardi for the most part), others came from the Tsarist Empire and Polish territories and settled mainly in the north-east (Ashkenazi in their great majority). Religious prejudice existed throughout this time. Just like everywhere else in Europe, in the nineteenth century anti-Judaism (religious antagonism) gradually mutated into antisemitism (racially and economically motivated animosity). In the Romanian context it was less the racial arguments that predominated as the economic ones. From the latter half of the nineteenth century, Jews were accused of monopolizing Romanian trade and industry, of being unfair competition to the fledgling Romanian middle class, of being the plague of the countryside. The Conservative Petru Carp rejected these economic prejudices with the famous words:

> Do you want to win the battle against the Jews? Work as hard as they do, be as thrifty and moderate as they are, and you will have nothing more to fear. I said this before and I am repeating it today: the solution to the Jewish question lies in labour competition.[37]

As Carol Iancu has pointed out, no in-depth study of the social structure of the Romanian-Jewish population and its economic role is available to date, but there are mid-nineteenth-century statistics for Moldavia showing the clear predominance of Jews in the trade and among skilled and highly skilled craftsmen. An indefinite number of Jews were pub keepers and village moneylenders, and a handful were involved in large-scale trade, banking and industrial enterprises.[38]

In the context of the 1907 peasant uprising, the Jews were associated with the exploitative land rental system, namely with the *arendaşi*, or leaseholders. Great estates took up almost half the cultivable surface in Romania and were in the majority rented out to big capitalists. In Moldavia, where the uprising started, the estates were monopolized by capitalists of Jewish faith. They amassed so much land and were able to dictate prices and wages to such an extent that part of Moldavia came to be referred to as Fischerland (the land dominated by the Fischer brothers).

[37] Iancu, *Evreii din România (1866–1919)*, pp. 140–141.
[38] Iancu, *Evreii din România (1866–1919)*, p. 160: in 1853 of all the craftsmen and apprentices in Moldavia 16,037 were Jews and 8268 Romanians.

As will become apparent in the next chapter, countrywide, the leasehold-ers were not exclusively Jewish, but rather a medley of nationalities and confessions. Some were Romanian citizens, others were Austro-Hungarian or Tsarist subjects.[39] In southern Romania, in Wallachia, the leaseholders were mostly Greek, Armenian as well as Romanian.

Raubwirtschaft *or Plunder Economy*

As shown by the head of the statistical institute G.D. Creangă, the extrac-tive leasehold system was not an unfortunate cancerous overgrowth of a fledgling economy, it was a system wholeheartedly embraced by Romanian landowners and Romanian state institutions alike. The majority of great landowners preferred to make a profit at all costs, which they chose to spend abroad rather than reinvest and develop their estates. They were reluctant to invest in draft cattle because, as part of the onerous agricul-tural contracts they imposed on the peasants, they could conveniently use the peasants' cattle.[40] As the German Consul in Bucharest remarked, 'even the greatest of landowners, like Prime Minister Cantancuzino with his 3 Million Franks income, cultivate their land without capital, without live stock and almost without any other implements (*bewirtschafteten ihr Land ohne Kapital, ohne lebendes und fast ohne todtes Inventar*).'[41] More enter-prising landlords did invest in agricultural machinery, but they did not use it for intensive agriculture, based on more rational exploitation of the land, but rather as an aid for their more and more extensive agriculture and exploitation of the peasant (see Table 3.1).[42]

To minimize effort and maximize profit, the landlords, many of whom had a political career in the capital, resorted to the extractive land-lease system. Their estates were rented out to the highest bidder for periods ranging between three and ten years. The leaseholders had even less of an incentive to invest and develop the estates or show ethical consideration

[39] *Documente*, Vol. 2, p. 596.

[40] Dimitrie Ionescu, *Agrarverfassung Rumäniens. Ihre Geschichte und Ihre Reform*, Leipzig, Verlag von Duncker & Humblot, 1909, p. 59.

[41] PAAA, Berlin, R 9652, Rumänien Allgemeine Angelegenheiten 1906–1907, Report no. 47, Bukarest, 25 March 1907, pp. 4–5.

[42] G.D. Scraba, *Starea socială a săteanului. După ancheta privitoare anului 1905, îndeplinită cu ocaziunea expoziţiunii generale romăne din 1906 de către secţiunea de economie socială*, Institutul de arte grafice Carol Göbl, Bucureşti, 1907, pp. 78–79; Ionescu, *Agrarverfassung Rumäniens*, pp. 52, 59, 64, 67–68.

Table 3.1   Number of cattle in 1900 Romania

Category of owner	Number of cattle
Great landowners and leaseholders	6,207
Small land-owning farmers	650,062
Landless workhands and sharecroppers	61,429

Source: Ionescu, *Agrarverfassung Rumäniens*, p. 59

for the local peasants as they were in possession of the estates for a short period of time and sought to make the most of it. The type of extensive agriculture they practised was not, strictly speaking, capitalist in character given that the leaseholders' investment was confined to the first rent, the rest of the money being extracted out of the peasants by subleasing.[43]This exploitative system was appositely described by contemporaries as *Raubwirtschaft*, or plunder economy. The term gained currency at the time especially in reference to colonial exploitation of the resources of a territory without making any improvements or without any attempt at sustainability. A variation of it, *Raubbau*, had been used before in the sense of rudimentary land cultivation to depletion, without using any fertilizers or crop rotation. For the most part, Romanian peasants engaged in such basic agriculture.[44] The peasants' *Raubbau* reflected their landlords' *Raubwirtschaft*.

Not all the Jewish leaseholders who became infamous in 1907 for their exploitative practices were Romanian citizens. In other words, the carefully crafted Romanian legislation, which was meant to exclude the Jewish population from citizenship rights on the grounds of unfair competition and alleged economic danger, was utterly useless in preventing this type of colonization of the country by foreign capital. The great landowners *chose* to use foreign capital and rent out their estates to Jewish and other leaseholders because they wanted to make more profit:

> The president of the Appeal Court (*Cassationshof*) Pherekyde,[45] whose wife is one of the mainstays of dancing, singing and comedy charities for the poor

[43] Ionescu, *Agrarverfassung Rumäniens*, p. 64.

[44] PAAA, Berlin, R 9637 Allgemeine Angelegenheiten Rumäniens, Report no. 62, 22 April 1888, p. 5.

[45] Charles Pherekyde was one of the great landowners in Wallachia, where the worst of the uprising took place. See also R. W. Seton-Watson, *A History of the Roumanians*, CUP, 1934, p. 387.

peasants, has leased out his estate, which he had leased out to the peasants last year for 120 thousand Franks, to the Fischer brothers for 200 thousand Franks. He must therefore share with his Jewish leaseholder Fischer the blame for the discontent of his peasants.[46]

A few respectable landowners such as Kalinderu, the administrator of the Crown Domains, were acknowledged by the German consul as exceptions to the rule.

Mr Kalinderu, for instance, teaches his peasants how to cultivate vegetables and gives them seed and guidance. Those who take good care of their vegetable gardens get prizes (*Belohnungen*) in the form of fruit trees and the like. But in this area much remains to be done and it is precisely the richest of landowners, as for instance Prime Minister Cantacuzino, whose possessions are twice as extensive as all the Crown Domains put together, who continue to exploit the peasants (*treiben noch immer das Bauernlegen*) and are opposed to any legal improvement.[47]

By providing agricultural education and guidance, argued Kiderlen, Kalinderu had shown that the plight of the peasantry could be improved without more demands for land. 'This, however, took decades of hard work. That is why no one else follows his example.'[48]

Amidst the legislative flurry brought about by the shock of the uprising, the German diplomatic representative in Romania pointed out the uselessness of yet more legislation: 'they'll vote more thickly-paragraphed and beautifully-worded laws, but that won't be much help to the peasant because most of them will remain a dead letter (*auf dem Papier bleiben*). [...] There would be a way out and it would come at less material cost to the great landowners: if only the boyars and others like them decided to administer their own estates directly and send their sons away to learn agriculture.' The disappointing reality was that the great landowners were not used to 'work', which was a word applied only to the poor.[49]

---

[46] PAAA, Berlin, R 9652, Rumänien Allgemeine Angelegenheiten 1906–1907, Report no. 44, Bucharest, 23 March 1907, pp. 7–8.

[47] PAAA, Berlin, R 9652, Rumänien Allgemeine Angelegenheiten 1906–1907, Report no. 186, Sinaia, 2 October 1906, pp. 14–15.

[48] PAAA, Berlin, R 9653, Rumänien Allgemeine Angelegenheiten April–December 1907, Report no. 51, Bucharest, 28 March 1907, pp. 6–7.

[49] PAAA, Berlin, R 9653, Rumänien Allgemeine Angelegenheiten April–December 1907, Report no. 147, Bucharest, 3 December 1907, pp. 5–6.

The aversion to hard work of the landed elites and their lack of interest in their own estates and the welfare of the peasant population was made worse by the chronic politicization of the bureaucracy and public services and the lack of a skilled middle class and professionals specialized in agriculture and administration. Universities churned out students in law and philosophy rather than furnishing them with sorely needed skills in administration, economy and agriculture. Students did show a fitful interest in the peasants' plight. That is how the viral rumours about students coming with the revolution started to circulate among peasants in the first place. A handful of students from the University of Iaşi proposed making inquiries into the peasant condition. But these never resulted into anything serious and, according to the German consul Kiderlen, student protests were volatile and politically coloured. They evinced a combination of 'demands for solving the peasant question and antisemitism'.[50]

Accusing the Romanian political parties of opportunistic chauvinism, Kiderlen noted that the attacks against foreigners were bound to subside again when the government would attempt to cover the great expenses incurred in 1906, which were unlikely to be covered from domestic capital or loans. 'The majority of Romanian landowners work with very little capital and the annual excess they squander away in Paris and other pleasant places. Romania will therefore soon be back knocking on Berlin bankers' doors and, when the knocking will take a while to be answered, the chauvinism boosted by this year's good crop will rapidly disappear.'[51]

Romanian legislative logorrhoea, which masked the fecklessness of the politicians (see Take Ionescu's more than three-month absence from Romania while he was Minister of Finance in 1906 or his brushing off concerns about Romania repaying her debts; neglect and *Schlamperei*—leaving grain out all exposed to the elements, or the excedent of 45 million Franks after two years of good crops[52]), created a climate of heavily legislated lawlessness. Kiderlen once again captured this antinomy to perfection:

[50] PAAA, Berlin, R 9652, Rumänien Allgemeine Angelegenheiten 1906–1907, Report from Bucharest, 20 March 1907, p. 5 recto and verso.

[51] PAAA, Berlin, R 9677, Die Finanzen Rumäniens 1905–1908, Report no. 13, 9 Januarz 1906, p. 3.

[52] PAAA, Berlin, R 9677, Die Finanzen Rumäniens 1905–1908, Report no. 13, 9 Januarz 1906, p. 2; Report no. 189, Sinaia 4 October 1906, p. 2; Newspaper cutting *Finanz Chronik*, 8 September 1906.

There are plenty of good laws in this country, but they are applied only to the weak or to the opposition. For the government and their cronies, they do not exist. I will never forget the exclamation (*Stoßseufzer*) of a German citizen, who rented big estates here and became a wealthy man: 'I would love to go back to Germany, but I couldn't possibly live again in a country where I too would have to obey the law.'[53]

This reality of heavily legislated lawlessness endured well into the twentieth century. As late as 1937 a journalist from *Adevărul* was making a similar point: 'The greatest and most fruitful revolution which could be accomplished in Romania would be simply to apply the existing laws.'[54]

This was the great paradox of Romania at the beginning of the twentieth century: it had laws galore against domestic 'foreigners', that is the Jews (see the 1881 law on foreigners, the 1884 law against peddling, the 1887 law of rural communes, in addition to the already existing exclusion from citizenship rights enshrined by the Constitution), it publicly denounced Jewish and foreign influence as the root of all evils, while in practice the great majority of its landowners as well as state institutions leased out their estates to predatory capitalists (many of them foreigners but also Romanians), who created strangle-hold monopolies, as part of an unregulated capitalist bonanza. In perfect colonialist style, foreign capitalists came to Romania, rented properties and exploited the local population in a way they would never have been able to do in their native countries. They were allowed to do so by the Romanian political elites because these were unwilling/incapable of administering their own estates while happily sharing in the ever-growing profits extracted by the leaseholders at the expense of the ever more impoverished peasantry.

The even more egregious side of this cohabitation between elites and foreign capital was the perfect impunity of some of the actual exploiters. As the great leaseholders were, in a considerable proportion, foreigners, they had the double of advantage of not coming under the incidence of Romanian laws and, in case of trouble, of appealing for help and intercession to their diplomatic representatives. Austro-Hungarian and German diplomatic correspondence are rife with requests for help received from their citizens based in Romania and also show the constant pressure these

---

[53] PAAA, Berlin, R 9653, Rumänien Allgemeine Angelegenheiten April–December 1907, Report no. 51, Bucharest, 28 March 1907, p. 5.

[54] Joseph Rothschild, *East Central Europe between the Two World Wars*, University of Washington Press, Seattle and London, 1998, p. 322.

diplomats exerted on the Romanian authorities during the uprising for protection of their citizens' life, limb and wealth, as well as asking for damages. Those leaseholders who did come under the incidence of Romanian laws were, in their turn, protected by the politicking landowners whose estates they managed.[55]

As a consequence, the wrath of the peasantry was vented on ordinary, local Jews living in market towns, who had the misfortune to be Romanian subjects but not citizens, and who were as such outside the protective loop of any state. Violence was visited not on the big culprits, but on ordinary Jews, who had nothing to do with the system and enjoyed no protection from a 'home country'. When things deteriorated, the big leaseholders had the means to get out in time and could always reach out for consular protection. Small-town Jewish merchants, who were not involved in land dealings but were all the same the target of peasant wrath, were completely without protection. A contemporary article in the socialist newspaper *Adevărul* captured this injustice:

> Where has antisemitism brought us? The small man is battered, while the culprits are allowed to get away. The Romanian Jew is equally in need of help as the poor Romanian peasant. If we genuinely want to help, then both of them (Jew and peasant) must benefit from it. By nurturing antisemitism, we only harm both.[56]

This complex relationship between antisemitism as a red herring and peasant discontent bears striking resemblance to the land question in Poland after the First World War. As shown by Joel Cang, in Poland 'nearly one third of the total arable land in the country [was] in the hands of the gentry' and well into the interwar period 'three million Polish farmers [were] forced to maintain themselves and their families on less than two hectares of land'. This was down to the great power wielded by the big Polish landowners:

> not even Mr. Witos, the peasant leader, and three times prime-minister of Poland, dared touch their land and divide it among the peasants. Even Marshal Pilsudski dared not tackle land reform and he rather made up with the nobles. But the peasant still needs the land. He will never be lifted from his nineteenth century level until he is given more land. Instead of being

---

[55] Ionescu, *Agrarverfassung*, p. 56.
[56] Excerpt from *Adevărul* quoted in *Pester Lloyd*, 23 March 1907, p. 3.

given land the peasant is advised to "go to the town" and oust the Jews. It is thus their desire to retain their vast holdings which determines the antisemitic policy of the conservatives in Poland.[57]

RUSSIAN RED HERRING OR ONCE BITTEN TWICE SHY

The second great obsession of Romanian statesmen was that of foreign intrigue and contamination. Here Russian influence took pride of place. Since the acquisition of state independence in 1878 and the stipulations of the Treaty of Berlin that concluded the Russo-Turkish war of 1877–1878, Romanian public opinion had been haunted by the spectre of a malevolent Russian influence and interference in Romanian internal affairs. Such suspicions were not surprising in a country that had historically experienced frequent occupation by foreign armies, the most recent being the Austrian occupation of the Principalities in 1852 and, even more of a smarting memory, the march of the Tsarist army across Romania without asking for permission in 1877 at the beginning of the Russo–Turkish war. The forced retrocession by Romania of southern Bessarabia to the Tsarist Empire as part of the Berlin Treaty stipulations created more bad blood and resentment in Romania. Even the Russians recognized this, as shown by the Russian Finance Minister Sergei Witte's admission in private conversation to the German consul in St Petersburg in 1898:

> We behaved disloyally to Romania. After promising not to take one yard of Romanian territory, we kept for ourselves a good chunk and in exchange gave Romania the marshland of Dobrogea taken from the Turks. This hurt and antagonized the Romanians and justly so. Today this antagonism has been overcome and we are on the best of terms.[58]

In 1905, following the diplomatic malaise over the retrocession of the Potemkin warship and crew, the Russians showed up in the Romanian port of Constanța with five battleships and torpedo boats without notifying the Romanian authorities, although they did issue an apology subsequently claiming it was an oversight.[59]

---

[57] Joel Cang, 'The Opposition Parties in Poland and Their Attitude towards the Jews and the Jewish Problem', *Jewish Social Studies*, Vol. 1, No. 2 (Apr., 1939), pp. 247–248. Many thanks are due to Dr. Sarah Cramsey for suggesting this reference to me.

[58] PAAA, Berlin, R 9730: Rumänien Acta betreffend die Verhältnisse in der Dobrudscha, Report from St Petersburg, 29 July 1898.

[59] Sorin Cristescu (Ed.), *Carol I. Corespondența personală*, p. 431.

The Liberals, headed by Brătianu and Sturdza, were staunch believers in a Russian conspiracy and claimed to have solid proof of Russian machinations. The political crisis of 1888 and the violent peasant uprising in the spring of the same year whipped up a frenzy of accusations of Russian foul play and agitation. King Carol himself believed in Russian interference as he attributed the 1888 peasant uprising to a 'nihilist movement acting in Russia's interest'.[60] P.P. Carp, the doyen of the Conservatives, believed in agitation by Slavic agents propagandizing among the peasants.[61]

Fear of Russian political machinations was not without substance or precedent. There were good reasons to distrust Russian intentions. In 1889 King Carol confessed to Kiderlen, the German consul in Bucharest, that he had the Russian consul Khitrowo followed, 'not by the government police but by His own agents'. One of the deciphered telegrams Khitrowo received from St Petersburg read: '*On est furieux du discour Carp. Cependant ne montrez pas les griffes. Épargnez aucune peine pour maintenir Catargi au pouvoir.*'[62] Khitrowo was indeed an arch-intrigant and did attempt to destabilize Romanian politics by turning one party against another and fostering in-fighting, but it remains a matter of debate how successful he actually was. According to the British diplomat Sir Arthur Henry Hardinge, Khitrowo's scheming was 'very barren in Roumania' and 'there was nothing Russia could do "in the way of getting a real Russian party" in Romania, and could only play one party off against another in the hope that Romania would collapse "from her own anarchy" at a moment of national emergency.'[63]

As with most fears, Romanian fear of the Russians started from something all too real. It was, however, boosted out of all proportion and snowballed into Russo-phobia, to the extent that all bad things were imagined to come from Russia and, conversely, all bad things happening to Russia were by default good news for Romania. Such was for instance the pervasive rejoicing among Romanian officials at the Russian troubles in the hope that Romania might get Bessarabia if the Tsarist Empire disin-

[60] Cristescu (Ed.), *Carol I. Corespondenţa personală*, p. 237.

[61] PAAA, Berlin, R 9637: Allgemeine Angelegenheiten Rumäniens March–April 1888, Report no. 60, 20 April 1888, p. 5.

[62] PAAA, Berlin, R 9821 Beziehungen Rumäniens zu Russland 1889–1919, Report no. 100, Bucharest, 4 May 1889.

[63] Patrick J. Bourne, 'Sir Frank Lascelles: a diplomat of the Victorian empire, 1841–1920', unpublished PhD thesis, University of Leeds, 2010, p. 126: quote from A. Hardinge to White, 13 May 1890, FO 364/1.

tegrated. The German General Consul even had a conversation with a former Romanian Minister of Foreign Affairs, who suggested to him that, in case of Russian disintegration, Germany should take Russian Poland and Romania should take Bessarabia.[64]

Russian contamination and/or machinations were easy to invoke in 1907: the uprising had started (or so it seemed to contemporaries) on the Russian border; this was the very border which, for the previous couple of years at least, had been oozing with Bessarabian, Odessa and Kishinev refugees as well as with fleeing revolutionaries, and which had been keeping Romanian ministers busy racking their brains how to stave off this Russian emanation[65]; throughout the uprising copious rumours coursed from local to central authorities that instigators of Russian nationality incited the peasants to ask for more land; according to peasant rumour, the order to kill landowners came from the Russians; in Covurlui County one of the dead was held to be a Russian deserter making propaganda; just like during the 1888 peasant uprising in southern Romania, fanciful rumours circulated about the Russian Tsar ordering the redistribution of land.[66]

However, the firm conviction of Conservative Prime Minister Cantacuzino that the Russians were to blame for the peasant uprising was not so much an instance of reading all of these signs and being deluded by them, but rather a blatant example of 'none so blind as those who won't see'. Thus, prior to the outbreak of the uprising, several prefects from Northern Moldavia came to Bucharest, asking for advice from the government and voicing fears that there would be serious peasant troubles at the beginning of the year. Rather than taking this information on board and looking into the causes of discontent, Cantacuzino insisted on 'blaming it all on Russian contamination and considered that tighter border supervision was the solution to the problem'.[67] Cantacuzino was one of the many landowners who were convinced of the inherently docile nature of the

[64] PAAA, Berlin, R 9818 Beziehungen Rumäniens zu Rußland 1906–1914, Report no. 167, Sinaia 11 July 1906, p. 5; Report no. 191, Sinaia, 4 October 1906, p. 2. See also R 9652: Rumänien Allgemeine Angelegenheiten 1906–1907, Report no. 5, Bucharest, 2 January 1906, p. 8.

[65] PAAA, Berlin, R 9652: Rumänien Allgemeine Angelegenheiten 1906–1907, Report no. 5, Bucharest, 2 January 1906, pp. 1, 5, 6.

[66] *Documente*, vol. 2, pp. 186, 690, 745.

[67] PAAA, Berlin, R 9652: Rumänien Allgemeine Angelegenheiten 1906–1907, Report no. 19, Bucharest, 21 February 1907, p. 3.

Romanian peasant and, as such, completely impervious to any other explanation of peasant unrest except for Russian revolutionary contamination.

N.V. Leonescu, the General Prosecutor of the Court of Appeal in Iaşi, was called in by Prime Minister Cantacuzino on 9 February 1907 and addressed as follows:

> Mr Prosecutor, I called you in for reasons of state. According to the reports I have from the prefects in upper Moldavia, there are going to be widespread peasant uprisings in spring provoked by secret agents and in particular caused by the bad behaviour of Jewish leaseholders towards the peasants. Please take the necessary measures so that your subalterns suppress all such attempts and inform me immediately.[68]

This, however, was not the main reason why the Prosecutor had been summoned:

> There is however something much more serious than this. [...] All the prefects within the jurisdiction of your court of appeal complained about you being too harsh on the local gendarmes, that you sue them for the smallest of complaints against them, and they end up wasting their time and being absent from work. You will understand, Mr Prosecutor General, that such a situation is untenable. We need order and cannot tolerate this. You must understand the gravity of this.[69]

The Prosecutor confirmed that there would indeed be uprisings in the spring but 'not caused by agents crawling all over the countryside but by the very people who man the administrative apparatus', through their abuses and inhumane treatment of the peasants. He also offered to prove this to the prime minister with documents. 'The Prime Minister told me it was not necessary, that he did not want me to send him any reports, but just to write to him and keep him informed. "I cannot tolerate this, I won't stand for such a state of affairs."'[70]

It was not only the Conservative government that had Russo-phobic knee-jerk reactions. Among the first measures of precaution taken by the new Liberal government was the arrest of former Potemkin sailors who

[68] N.V. Leonescu, *Anul 1907. Răscoala ţăranilor*, Atelierele grafice "Lumina Moldovei", Iaşi, 1924, pp. 31–32.

[69] Leonescu, *Anul 1907*, pp. 32.

[70] Leonescu, *Anul 1907*, pp. 32.

were working in Romania at railways, factories and oilrigs. Since July 1905 around 100 Potemkin sailors had been allowed to settle in Romania after the famous rebellion: the Romanian authorities, very much to the frustration of the Tsarist government, confiscated the ship and accepted that the crew turned themselves in as deserters. The ship was eventually returned to the Russians, but the crew was not handed over as at that time there was no extradition treaty in place between Romania and Tsarist Russia. In March 1907, as the uprising was spreading apace, 77 former sailors from the Potemkin were arrested in Buzău and Prahova counties.[71] Three Potemkin workers at the Railway Workshops in Iași were kept under surveillance, but gave no occasion for suspicion.[72] These Potemkinists were 'fairly harmless people', observed the German consul Kiderlen in his 7 April report to the German Minister of Foreign Affairs, 'their ringleaders have long left the country and many of [the remaining Potemkinists] are married to Romanian women and try to scrape a living. These people, who don't speak Romanian very well, and who are notorious for not leaving their work places, are supposed to have suddenly stirred up the peasantry in the whole of Romania! Their employers, among them being in the first place German oil companies, have intervened in their defence.'[73]

Long after the uprising was suppressed, the hunt for Potemkin sailors on Romanian territory continued. A lot of time and energy was put in by the Romanian government into keeping tabs on Potemkinists' whereabouts in Romania. A decree of 23 May 1907 made it mandatory for former Potemkin sailors to choose a place to settle and not to leave without official permission. As the former sailors did not always stay put and moved across the country in search of employment, this occasioned numerous searches by the local authorities and a flurry of correspondence between them and the central authorities about individual Potemkinists, alleged Potemkinists and fake Potemkinists who could not be accounted for. The incentive to pass oneself for a Potemkinist came from fact that Potemkinists were allowed to stay in the country without passports.[74] Tables with surveillance information were printed out centrally and distributed to all county and village authorities with the purpose of tabulat-

---

[71] *Documente*, vol. 3, pp. 141, 251.

[72] *Documente*, vol. 2, p. 356.

[73] PAAA, Berlin, R 9653, Rumänien Allgemeine Angelegenheiten April–December 1907, Report no. 59, 7 April 1907, pp. 2–3.

[74] ANR, Arhiva CC al PCR, Fond 59/6066, pp. 66–67.

ing information on the elusive foreigners.[75] A Ministry of the Interior circular to all county prefects of March 1908 alerted to the danger posed by foreign defectors and Potemkinists 'who settle in border counties and maintain relations with like-minded people across the border' and urged the prefects to feed back information on the number of foreigners in their county.[76] This alert comes across as an official inconsistency in that subsequent correspondence between the Ministry and county prefects shows that the Romanian authorities had no problem taking in defectors from all the armies of the neighbouring countries (Russians, Bulgarians, Turks, Serbs and Austro-Hungarians) as long as they were not wanted for murder in their home country and that they were not revolutionaries.[77]

The Romanian authorities' attitude to foreigners was in keeping with the fairly common susceptibility of governments in the region to anarchists and revolutionary contamination. Up until 1907 the Romanian secret police concentrated its attention exclusively on anarchists and spies; the peasants slipped under the radar, which comes in striking contrast to the avalanche of secret police reports and notes following 1907 (with the caveat that, given the state of the archives, this might yet turn out to be an optical illusion). While useful as qualified workers, Potemkinists were treated like a political pest, with Romanian authorities wanting to get rid of them and being only too happy to accede to their request for emigration to America, while the neighbouring governments showed apprehension at the prospect of Potemkinists journeying through their country. The Austro-Hungarian Foreign Minister Aehrenthal reacted to news that the Romanians were considering letting the Potemkinists emigrate with a panicky 'don't send them over our border!'[78]

Next on the list of suspects were the Lipovans, old Russian believers who had found refuge in north-eastern Moldavia, Bukovina and Dobrogea after the seventeenth-century Orthodox schism in Russia. They cropped up in official correspondence as participants in the unrest in Botoşani and Iaşi and were rumoured to want to burn down Târgul Frumos. In Tulcea on the Danube they were rumoured to rebel; they spoke out against being

[75] ANR, Arhiva CC al PCR, Fond 50/6065, Dosar Prefectura Judeţului Vâlcea. Anul 1907. Corespondenţa relativă la Potemchiniştii din Rusia, pp. 3–5.

[76] ANR, Arhiva CC al PCR, Fond 59/6066, p. 17.

[77] ANR, Arhiva CC al PCR, Fond 50/6067, pp. 51, 55, 66, 70, 81; Fond 59/6066, pp. 129–154.

[78] MOL (Magyar Országos Levéltár), K 26 Miniszterelnök, Letter from Aehrenthal to Hungarian Prime Minister Wekerle, 9 April 1907.

drafted and motivated their refusal in religious terms: they would not go out and shoot Christians (which came as a variation on the theme of conscription refusal—some Romanian peasants refused to go out and shoot their relatives; Lipovans refused to shoot fellow Christians).[79] In addition to religious reasons, there must have been also an element of antagonism to authority implicit in the Lipovans' attitude, Lipovans traditionally opposing repressive authority. It appears from extant documents that the unrest reported in Tulcea County was mostly to do with the botched-up mobilization: hosts of young men called to arms, some refusing, others lolling around in groups, getting drunk and riotous.[80]

FEAR OF BULGARIANS

Bulgarian peasants in southern Romania figure among the most rebellious population during the 1907 uprising: in Băilești, one of the villages that were shelled by the army, 500 Bulgarians reportedly intended to put fire to Prince Ştirbey's palace. Army intervention exacerbated the conflict as the rebels put up barricades and violent clashes ensued with scores of dead and over 100 wounded.[81]

It was not, however, these Bulgarian peasants that government officials feared but rather the would-be malignant intentions of the Bulgarian state: both Liberals and Conservatives, as pointed out by Kiderlen, the German Consul, claimed that 'the peasants had been stirred up by the Bulgarians, who had an interest in destabilizing Romania so it could not take part in any future Balkan events' (um Rumänien bei den späteren Vorgänge im Balkan Lahm zu legen).[82] A high ministerial official said to the German Consul: 'If the Bulgarians were to come now, we are completely defenceless because of the currently raging civil war!'[83] In the newly acquired Dobrogea, the Romanian authorities introduced measures against the local Bulgarian population and thereby forced them to look to the Bulgarian state. 'An honest and effective administration would be a

---

[79] *Documente*, vol. 2, pp. 118, 336–347; vol. 3, pp. 582–585.

[80] *Documente*, vol. 3, p. 582.

[81] *Documente*, vol. 4, p. 58, 66, 500.

[82] PAAA, Berlin, R 9653, Rumänien Allgemeine Angelegenheiten April–December 1907, Report no. 59, 7 April 1907, p. 1.

[83] PAAA, Berlin, R 9652 Rumänien Allgemeine Angelegenheiten 1906–1907, Report no. 40, Bucharest, 20 March 1907, pp. 13–14.

better bulwark against any Bulgarian claims that might arise', concluded Kiderlen.[84]

Proof that the uprising had nothing to do with the number of non-Romanian population but rather with economic and administrative structures is the fact that of all the regions of Romania, Dobrogea, which was integrated into the new state with a special status and had a totally different social make-up, remained peaceful and untouched by the raging anger and destruction. Here peace and quiet reigned for the most part, the most trouble-free being Constanța County, from where the prefect had nothing to report to Bucharest: no unrest, no agitation, no students, no uprising-related arrests, just some local discontent but nothing out of the ordinary. The worst that could be reported back from Constanța County was an abortive attempt by a Romanian publican to incite Muslim inhabitants to claim land. This was dismissed as a misunderstanding: the accused claimed that the discussion was misunderstood by the Muslims, whose Romanian was very poor.[85]

PEASANTS' XENOPHOBIA

Ernest Renan once quipped that nationalism presupposed a shared mistaken view of the past and a common hatred of their neighbours. Romanian peasants were decidedly not in the nationalist loop by this definition and this is best shown by their divergent view of foreigners and their different brand of xenophobia. In the case of the Romanian peasantry, the animosity against foreigners and strangers had a different rationale.

A recurrent slogan in many of the rural devastations of spring 1907 was 'Drive out all foreigners!' Wherever rebellious peasants managed to get into towns, they devastated shops (some of them belonging to Jews in Moldavia, and to Greeks, Bulgarians and Macedo-Romanians in Wallachia). But proof that peasants once riotous were indiscriminate is that deployed troops were given instructions to protect Romanian businesses. More often than not, foreigners were targeted not for being foreigners but for acting as servants or coercive tools for the great landowners and leaseholders. In Argeș County, Turkish servants had been hired by the landowners to intimidate the peasants. Elsewhere, there were grievances against Turks

---

[84] PAAA, Berlin, R 9730: Rumänien Acta betreffend die Verhältnisse in der Dobrudscha, Report no. 39, Bucharest, 18 March 1907, p. 16.

[85] *Documente*, vol. 3, p. 576.

and Bulgarians who had been hired by the landowner and these, as a peasant deposition went, 'shot at their children and raped their women'.[86] In
the eyes of the peasants, strangers/foreigners were associated with oppressive landlordism or, alternatively, they represented the face of spoliating
capitalism. As Olga Crisp once put it in the case of Polish Galicia, the
peasant's first brush with the money economy was more often than not
through the Jew.

To this must be added the unquantifiable influence of newspaper and
official discourse: whenever news trickled down to village level via newspapers, it more often than not took the form of xenophobic discourse (orders
have come to drive out all foreigners, the students have ordered us to drive
out all foreigners.)[87] Official blame assignation was predominantly antisemitic and xenophobic and provided a frame of reference for the peasants
when it came to formulating discontent.

The more tangible cause of peasant xenophobia was, however, work-
related. Migrant workers, whether foreigners or peasants from other
Romanian counties, who were contracted by landlords and leaseholders as
temporary work hands, were a means of blackmail and removed all possibility of negotiation over fairer wages and land prices. Under these circumstances, the peasant withholding his labour would only have
repercussions on himself and he would stand to lose more than the leaseholder in case of a standoff.[88] An official inquiry into the condition of the
Romanian peasant, which was occasioned by the Royal Jubilee Exhibition
of 1906 and based on 4,858 questionnaires sent to village mayors and village school principals, highlighted this as one of the causes of the low
remuneration of peasant work:

> One of the reasons why the peasant's work is so badly paid is also the ability
> of the landowners and leaseholders to bring in outside workers (*muncitori
> străini*). In 1905 their number was 57,908, out of whom 30,383 [were] in
> Moldavia, 20,626 in Muntenia, 3,835 in Oltenia and 3,064 in Dobrogea. In
> Ialomița, which is the county that brings in most workers for fieldwork, the
> cause is the great expanse of cultivated land. Not the same can be said of the
> counties in northern Moldavia, where the villagers in Dorohoi County, for
> example, go to other counties for work, being replaced by workers from

[86] *Documente*, vol. 3, pp. 394, 396, 468, 469, 470; Vol. 2, p. 132; Vol. 4, pp. 193, 380, 407, 408.
[87] *Documente*, vol. 3, p. 396.
[88] *Documente*, vol. 3, p. 222.

Bukovina. The same happens, to a lesser extent, in the counties of Mehedinţi and Vâlcea, from where every summer hundreds of villagers migrate to the plains and especially to the counties of Brăila, Ialomiţa and Constanţa, their place being taken by foreign workers.[89]

As the excerpts from these survey questionnaires show, the term 'străin', which in Romanian covers anything from foreigner, to stranger, outsider or simply an unknown person, was more often than not used in the sense of internal migrants from neighbouring communes, or neighbouring counties, or from across the country. It was seldom that it was used to mean foreigner, in either a national or religious way. 'Străin' was anyone from outside the narrow circle of the village commune.

SHOOTING ONESELF IN THE FOOT

The fact that in spring 1907 the Romanian authorities saw foreigners everywhere and blamed the uprising on them is evidence of the poor grasp that the fledgling state had on its own territory and population, but also, more importantly still, it shows that this very blindness lay at the root of the problem. The shifting of the blame onto others precluded any meaningful self-critical engagement with the problem of land ownership and peasant condition. Thus the problem grew as economic conditions worsened. As Dobrogeanu-Gherea put it:

> Our government were perfectly right to look for instigators after every peasant uprising; only they were not looking in the right place. There are indeed instigators or rather one big and powerful instigator, with a countrywide organization, with branches and agents in every village and every peasant hut. This is a much more powerful instigator than those that the government were looking for. It is the state itself with its whole modern-bourgeois organization and its democratic institutions that conducts these instigations.[90]

The Romanian authorities were in a state of almost schizoid denial: on the one hand, as Constantin Stere put it, they waxed lyrical about Article

[89] Scraba, *Starea socială a săteanului*, p. 190.
[90] Constantin Dobrogeanu–Gherea, *Neoiobăgia. Studiu economico-sociologic al problemei noastre agrare*, Editura Librăriei Socec et comp, 1910, p. 149.

7 of the 1866 constitution that effectively kept autochthonous Jews away from Romanian citizenship (the invoked reason behind this being a protectionist one); on the other hand, the great majority of Romanian statesmen, who were also great landowners, did not have the least compunction to lease their estates to great capitalists, be they 'baptized or circumcised', as the phrase circulated in the foreign press during the uprising; instead of renting their land out to the peasants, latifundia owners preferred to make a higher profit out of what was essentially real-estate speculation and not for one moment showed interest in the fate of the co-national peasants or what the subrental system did to them. The same antisemitism that was so hypocritically legislated also blinded the local authorities to the implications of the first signs of uprising in spring 1907. As unrest started on Jewish-administered estates in northern Moldavia, the first reactions were 'serves them right', rather than recognizing that the peasants were not interested in what religion the leaseholders belonged to, but rather were out to get all those who exploited them and stood between them and the much coveted land.

It is not clear to what extent the conspiracy theories Romanian statesmen indulged in (about Russian contamination or meddling, Bulgarian destabilizing agents, anarchist or opposition conspiracy) were the result of sheer self-delusion or were part of an attempt to save face with the international public opinion. By the beginning of April 1907 the Liberal government was looking for the 'Big Organization', as intimated by both Sturdza and Brătianu to the German consul Kiderlen, and claimed to already have a few leads to it: 'To my question as to where the leads led to, both of them had to admit that unfortunately they did not know it yet.' Kiderlen doubted any foreign intervention or the existence of such an organization given the lack of coordination between rebellious flares across the country, the failure to disrupt key infrastructure such as railways or bridges and the absence of any attempt to occupy the capital. He did, however, venture a prophecy that if the Liberals continued to 'blame everything bad on foreigners in an attempt to shore up the country's tattered prestige, they were in for much more unpleasant surprises than the present, relatively short-lived uprising'.[91]

---

[91] PAAA, Berlin, R 9653, Rumänien Allgemeine Angelegenheiten April–December 1907, Report no. 59, 7 April 1907, pp. 3–6, 12.

BIBLIOGRAPHY

Omer Bartov and Eric D. Weitz, *Shatterzone of Empires: Coexistence and Violence in the German, Habsburg, Russian, and Ottoman Borderlands*, Indiana University Press, 2013

Joel Cang, 'The Opposition Parties in Poland and Their Attitude Towards the Jews and the Jewish Problem', *Jewish Social Studies*, Vol. 1, No. 2 (Apr., 1939)

Sorin Cristescu (Ed.), *Carol I. Corespondența personală (1878–1912)*, București, Triton, 2005

Constantin Dobrogeanu–Gherea, *Neoiobăgia, Studiu economico-sociologic al problemei noastre agrare*, Editura Librăriei Socec et comp, 1910

Constantin Dobrogeanu-Gherea, Opere Complete, Vol. 5, Editura Politică, București, 1978

A. Gerschenkron, 'Russia: Patterns and Problems of Economic Development 1861–1958'in Frederick A. (Ed.), *Economic Backwardness in Historical Perspective. A Book of Essays*, Praeger Publishers, New York, Washington, London, 1962

Keith Hitchins, *Rumania 1866–1947*, Clarendon Press, Oxford, 1994

Carol Iancu, *Evreii din România (1866–1919). De la Excludere la Emancipare*, Trans. C. Litman, Editura Hasefer, Bucharest, 1996

Dimitrie Ionescu, *Agrarverfassung Rumäniens. Ihre Geschichte und Ihre Reform*, Leipzig, Verlag von Duncker & Humblot, 1909

Andrew Janos, 'Modernization and Decay in Historical Perspective: The Case of Romania' in Kenneth Jowitt (Ed.), *Social Change in Romania 1860–1940*, Berkeley, CA, 1978

John R. Lampe, 'Varieties of Unsuccessful Industrialization: The Balkan States Before 1914', *The Journal of Economic History*, Vol. 35, No. 1 (Mar., 1975)

N.V. Leonescu, *Anul 1907. Răscoala țăranilor*, Atelierele grafice "Lumina Moldovei", Iași, 1924

Bogdan Murgescu, *România și Europa. Acumularea decalajelor economice (1500–2010)*, Polirom, București, 2010

H. B. Oppenheim, *Die Judenverfolgungen in Rumaenien*, Verlag von Georg Stilke, Berlin, 1872

Alfred Rieber, *The Struggle for the Eurasian Borderlands: From the Rise of Early Modern Empires to the End of the First World War*, Cambridge University Press, Cambridge and New York, 2014

Joseph Rothschild, *East Central Europe between the Two World Wars*, University of Washington Press, Seattle and London, 1998

G.D. Scraba, *Starea socială a săteanului. După ancheta privitoare anului 1905, îndeplinită cu ocaziunea expozițiunii generale române din 1906 de către secţiunea de economie socială*, Institutul de arte grafice Carol Göbl, Bucureşti, 1907

R. W. Seton-Watson, *A History of the Roumanians*, CUP, 1934

Enache Tuşa, *Imaginar politic and identităţi colective în Dobrogea*, Editura Institutului de Ştiinţe Politice şi Relaţii Internaţionale, Bucureşti, 2011

CHAPTER 4

The Peasant Question

The 1907 peasant uprising in Romania destroyed lives and property with a fury born of long-pent-up tensions and irreconcilable social antagonisms. It spread and encompassed the whole country in a matter of weeks. The rebellious wave did not, however, cross the frontier into Tsarist Bessarabia, the eastern borderland of an empire that had barely recovered from major social turmoil, nor did it ripple through into Austria-Hungary's borderlands, Bukovina and Transylvania respectively, two of the most underdeveloped regions of the Habsburg empire. This chapter explores the deeper differences in law and practice that defined the condition of the peasantry around the triple frontier and resulted in a different, more explosive degree of social combustibility on the Romanian side of the border. If there was rural poverty all around the triple frontier, why was it that only Romania's peasantry waxed rebellious and not their peers across the border?

Similar Borderlands?

Along the triple border between Austria-Hungary, Tsarist Russia and Romania lay some of the least developed regions of the two empires and the frontier counties of the similarly underdeveloped fledgling Kingdom of Romania. In all the provinces involved (Transylvania, Bukovina, Bessarabia, Moldavia and Wallachia), a combination of dwarf and small

© The Author(s) 2018
I. Marin, *Peasant Violence and Antisemitism in Early Twentieth-Century Eastern Europe*,
https://doi.org/10.1007/978-3-319-76069-8_4

property and latifundia existed; with some regional exceptions, agricultural technique was rudimentary, there was little if any mechanization, and illiteracy was high; the ability to tap into the new opportunities of loans and mortgages was correspondingly low and sometimes misguided. Therefore the bulk of the peasantry around the triple border was, from the point of view of land distribution and land usage, fairly similar in their respective conditions.

The counties buttressing the triple border on the Transylvanian side were in the great majority among the poorest and most underdeveloped regions of Habsburg Hungary. Only in the Ruthene and Croat inhabited territories were some of the indices of development (level of taxes paid, ability to take out loans and insurance, literacy rates, railway density) lower than in these border regions.[1] The region was predominantly divided into small properties (between 5 and 100 hold - 1 hold = 0.5 hectare) and was outside the big rental loop: the renting system was practised on a considerable scale in particular in central and western Hungary, where the great property predominated.[2]

In Tsarist Bessarabia, with the notable exception of the well-off colonists in the south, agriculture retained its traditional character until after the First World War. An American report for the Hoover Commission of 1919 highlighted the underdevelopment of land cultivation in Bessarabia while remarking on the black-earth quality of the soil:

> the working of the land is very primitive and out of date in comparison with the western countries. Agricultural machines are known only to a few rich landowners, but the greater part of the machines were destroyed by the bolsheviks. The same is the case with fertilizers, while the soil is rich and it produces without any fertlizer, its producing capacity could be greatly increased by chemicals, but so far only large landowners took advantage of this, the great majority, if using any fertilizer at all, they are using manure. Much improvement is seen in this respect, however, in the Cetatea Alba and Izmail Districts.[3]

---

[1] Nagy Mariann, *A magyar mezőgazdaság regionális szerkezete a 20. század elején*, Gondolat Kiadó, Budapest, 2003, pp. 227–233.

[2] Nagy, *A magyar mezőgazdaság regionális szerkezete a 20. század elején*, pp. 443–444.

[3] Cpt John Kaba, *Politico-Economic Review of Bessarabia*, June 30, 1919 (US army, member of the Hoover commission for Romania), p. 15.

Similarly, wine growing, which would in later years turn the province into the Soviet 'wine cellar', was at the turn of the century traditionally pursued, as the peasants, who formed the 'majority of vine growers, [were] not yet acquainted with the methods of modern technique, and work[ing] their land as their ancestors did before them'.[4]

Low agricultural efficiency reflected the low rates of literacy. According to 1907 Hungarian statistics, the rate of literacy varied between 20% and 74% in Transylvania and the Banat (Romanian counties had lower rates of literacy, between 20% and 46%).[5] Compared to Romania, these 'backward' regions of Hungary seemed to be slightly better off. In Romania as a whole less than a quarter of the total population (17.33% by the 1899 census) was literate.[6] In Bessarabia, literacy rates were even more abysmal compared to either of the two neighbouring states: 'only 156 out of 1000 were able to read and write' in 1909,[7] that is, less than 16% of the total population. This of course varied form one ethnic group to another: the German and Jewish population were the most literate in the province, which was a consequence of religious injunction but also, in the case of the German population, of colonization privilege: after the loss of autonomy in 1828, Bessarabia embarked on a path of Russification, which forbade tuition in Romanian. By contrast, German colonists were allowed to retain their German-language schools.[8]

EXPLOSIVE ROMANIA

Of all of the above variations on peasant poverty and underdevelopment along the triple frontier, it was the Romanian case that turned out to be the most explosive. What made poverty unbearable to the point of general rebellion was, as we shall see in what follows, neo-serfdom, that is, the perpetuation of serfdom in a new guise, and the conversion of Romanian agriculture into a colonial-style plunder economy, or *Raubwirtschaft*.

---

[4] Ion G. Pelivan, *The Economic State of Bessarabia*, Paris, Imprimerie des Arts et Sports, Paris, 1920, p. 13.

[5] *Magyar Statisztikai Évkönyv*, Új folyam 1907, Budapest, Az Atheneum irodalmi és nyomdai részvénytársulat könyvnyomdája, 1909, p. 306.

[6] G.D. Creangă, *Grundbesitzverteilung und Bauernfrage in Rumänien*, Erster Teil, Leipzig, Verlag von Duncker und Humbolt, 1907, p. 165.

[7] Ion G. Pelivan, *The Movement and Increase of Population in Bessarabia from 1812 to 1918*, Paris, Imprimerie des arts et des sports, 1920, p. 17.

[8] Em. de Martonne, *What I have seen in Bessarabia*, Paris, 1919, p. 22.

Romania nominally emancipated its peasantry in 1864, that is, 14 years later than the Habsburg Monarchy (1848) and three years later than Russia (1861). In 1864 the Romanian peasants were declared legally free of *corvées* and other manorial dues, and the land they used became rightfully theirs, albeit only up to two-thirds of the landlord's possessions. 'The new holdings could not be sold or alienated for thirty years'[9] and the burden of redemption payment fell on the peasants. The pattern of land tenure continued to be dominated by latifundia with the additional development, towards the end of the nineteenth century, of absentee landlordism and the *arendaşi*, or leaseholder system.

The 1864 emancipation act was one of a series of such pieces of legislation that, while pointing forwards, actually looked backwards. Such were the 1830 and 1831 Organic Statutes, which were passed under Russian occupation and which, while decreeing rights of ownership over the land, bereft the peasantry of their customary use of communal land and forests.[10] Similarly, the 1864 act freed the peasant from manorial dues but distributed so little land that the peasants were forced to go back to working for the landowners. Two subsequent laws of agricultural contracts purported to clarify agrarian relations but in effect only entrenched the exploitative system all the more by virtually legislating peasant forced labour.

The 1864 Act of emancipation was a result of political infighting rather than genuine wish for reform and careful planning; the law was passed *against* the will of the local potentates, the boyars, by Prince Alexander Ioan Cuza, who within two years was deposed and replaced with a German prince. Prince Cuza's reformist legislation remained in place after his deposition but the boyars made sure that nothing changed. The old hold of the great landowners over their peasants was kept intact through administrative subterfuge and subsequent legislation: the initial agrarian law of 1864 and two subsequent laws of agricultural contracts ensured that (1) the peasants never had sufficient land for subsistence and (2) they would *have to* enter into sharecropping contracts with the big landowners. This legal framework set the scene for chronic land hunger, which was compounded by several other factors: the initial land distribution, which fell

---

[9] Hugh Seton-Watson, *Eastern Europe between the Wars 1918–1941*, Harper Torchbooks, 1967, p. 202.

[10] Radu Rosetti, *Pentru ce s-au răsculat ţăranii*, Atelierele grafice Socec, Bucureşti, 1907, pp. 48–49.

short of actual peasant needs; the 'pulverization' tendency implicit in the traditional peasant practice of subdividing land for inheritance purposes; rural overpopulation ('from 1859 to 1899 the Romanian population grew by 54%'[11]) as well as rudimentary cultivation techniques.

As a consequence of this legislative framework, for the great majority of Romanian peasants emancipation did not result in increased independence and prosperity, nor did it result in a gradual modernization of agriculture. It had a polar-opposite effect: it led to exploitation, poverty and a new, more insidious form of serfdom, which the *Narodnik* émigré Constantin Dobrogeanu-Gherea called neo-serfdom. This presupposed the replacement of the old, legal ties with new, economic ones, forcing peasants into disadvantageous labour relations with the big landowners while being nominally free and, some of them, endowed with a scrap of land.

The division of land showed the clear domination of the great property and latifundia, which were concentrated in the hands of few thousand owners. Thus, according to G.D. Creangă, the director of the Statistical Institute[12]:

- Properties of up to 10 ha formed 40.29% of total arable land and were stretched thin among almost 90% of the population:

  25.74% – up to 5 ha
  14.55% – between 5 and 10 ha

- Those of 50–100 ha – 8.89%
- Properties of 100–500 ha – 10.43%
- Great property of over 500 ha – 38.29%

The crux of the matter was, however, that for 39% of the landowning population who owned up to three hectares of land, it was impossible to cover basic needs by working their land and they were 'unconditionally dependent on great landowners and *arendaşi* (leaseholders)' for additional work.[13] 'Basic needs' meant the maize and wheat necessary to make bread for sheer subsistence and did not include any other type of food, clothing, heating and lighting fuel nor land and church taxes, or loan interests, which according to Creangă's calculations redoubled the house-

---

[11] Charles and Barbara Jelavich, *The Establishment of the Balkan National States, 1804–1920*, University of Washington Press, Seattle and London, 2000, p. 120.

[12] Creangă, *Grundbesitzverteilung*, p. 89.

[13] Creangă, *Grundbesitzverteilung*, pp. 107–108.

hold expenditure in the case of a landless family and trebled it in the case of a poor peasant family with little land.[14]

There were also smallholders who could barely cover subsistence needs but were vulnerable to any weather vagaries or economic fluctuations. Those who owned between three hectares and five hectares, accounting for around 30% of the total population, could barely make ends meet even if they were thrifty, and had no possibility of improving their condition. It cannot have been a coincidence that the worst of the 1907 uprising took place in counties where the great majority of the peasant population owned between three hectares and five hectares of land: Ialomiţa (63%), Teleorman (60%) and Vlaşca (57%).[15] The peasants owning between five hectares and ten hectares were comparatively better off, independent of great landowners and *arendaşi*, and especially those owning between seven hectares and ten hectares, obtaining a land yield of up to four times in excess of their basic subsistence needs.[16] The borderline owners of five hectares to seven hectares formed 10% of the population and the truly independent ones, with seven hectares to ten hectares, represented only a small part of the peasant population, 4.24% by Creangă's estimate. By contrast the great property (over 100 hectares) occupied 69% of all cultivable land and was in the hands of 4,171 landowners. As Creangă concluded, 'the ratio of land to landowners was worse even than in Russia, where 23.8% of the landowners possessed 79.9% of the total land surface; in Romania, 39% of landowners possessed 48.68% of the total surface of cultivable land.'[17]

As many peasants were forced into disadvantageous sharecropping contracts with the big landowners and their leaseholders, another exploitative feature of the system came into play. Romania had no land cadaster or any clear legislation that would regulate land delimitation. Consequently double standards in measuring land were endemic when agricultural contracts were drawn up. As part of an agricultural contract, peasants rented land from the landowner or leaseholder more often than not in exchange for working some of the landowner's land. As a rule, the acre of land that the peasant received for his own subsistence was one-quarter smaller than

[14] Creangă, *Grundbesitzverteilung*, pp. 103–106.
[15] Creangă, *Grundbesitzverteilung*, p. 116.
[16] Creangă, *Grundbesitzverteilung*, pp. 107–109.
[17] Creangă, Grundbesitzverteilung, p. 162:

the acre of land he was contractually bound to work for the landowner.[18] The lack of a cadaster and the lack of demarcation for peasant property (whether it be communal land or pastureland) led to rife intra-community litigation, endless trials and local animosity.[19] Although they invoked the high costs involved in conducting a comprehensive land survey, the boyars were actually opposed to this, as it would mean giving up their hold on the peasantry. Uncertainty of land possession and relations and the lack of proper delimitation of landed property led to numerous trials, which were usually won by the powerful boyar or their leaseholders. Moreover, pastureland, which was concentrated in the hands of the big landowners, functioned as a means of coercion to get the peasant to agree to the terms of the boyar.[20]

Endemic Poverty

The great majority of the peasants in Romania lived at or below subsistence level. Bad years with poor crops wrought havoc in the countryside and led to famine. A testimony of just how precarious the situation was even for the few better-off peasants once disaster struck comes from the historian and politician Radu Rosetti (1853–1926):

> The peasants, especially those with little land, which was of poor quality and far away from their homesteads, or without roads (to their land) and without watering places, had to rent land from the landowners and *arendași*. Most peasants were in need of money: for taxes, which started to grow considerably, for the redemption payment and for other needs arisen from the new circumstances.[21]

As money was a rare commodity at the time, they had to commit to working for the landowners. These land rental contracts (*învoieli*) were renewed every year and struck at usurious rates making life miserable even for the most provident and hard-working peasants:

---

[18] Ionescu, *Agrarverfassung Rumäniens*, p. 65.

[19] Scraba, *Starea socială a săteanului*, pp. 48–49.

[20] PAAA, Berlin, R 9652, Rumänien Allgemeine Angelegenheiten 1906–1907, Report no. 186, Sinaia 2 October 1906, pp. 2–3.

[21] Constantin Dobrogeanu-Gherea, *Neoiobăgia. Studiu economico-sociologic al problemei noastre agrare*, Editura Librăriei Socec et comp, 1910, p. 55.

I know peasants (I can give names), who are not lazy drunkards, but indus-
trious and thrifty workers, who employ workhands (*cu ajutor în casă*), and
who worked hard for 15 years to pay off the debt incurred in the winter of
1866–67, when they had to buy maize to feed their family. It was not until
the summer of 1881 that they managed to rid themselves of the debt.[22]

Those peasants who signed land-rental contracts (about half of the total
number of family heads) were forced to accept onerous conditions: they
worked for a pittance, many times pledging their work in advance for a
fraction of its actual worth in exchange for money to pay taxes or food to
survive the hungry gap in the winter; these contracts came with such a
heavy workload and so exploitative terms that the peasants not only were
not able to make ends meet but they remained perpetually in debt.[23] A
leaseholder MP once remarked in Parliament: 'I don't know how it happened. I lent money to the peasants in the winter, they worked all the year
round and at the end of the year, they were still in debt, often more so
than at the beginning.'[24] This was not only due to contractual terms but,
more often than not, to ploys and stratagems on the part of the land-
owner/leaseholder, who would in practice impose on the peasants even
more exploitative terms than the actual contract stipulated: under the pretext of non-fulfilment of contractual obligations, the leaseholder/landlord
could prevent the peasants from harvesting their own crops until he
deemed they fulfilled any outstanding dues or alternatively the lease-
holder/landlord could put off indefinitely the contractual division of the
crop (*dijma la tarla*). The result was the burdening of the peasants with
even more work, securing their indebtedness for the following year, which
was to be paid off in labour, and the inevitable going to waste of their part
of the crop, which they could not lift off the field; as late as December of
the harvest year or March of the following year peasant crops could be
seen rotting away in the fields.[25]

[22] Rosetti, *Pentru ce s-au răsculat țăranii*, p. 450 – cited in Dobrogeanu-Gherea,
Neoiobăgia, p. 56.

[23] *Marea răscoală a țăranilor din 1907*, București, Editura Republicii Socialiste România,
1967, pp. 111–112; G.D. Scraba, *Starea socială a săteanului. După ancheta privitoare anului 1905, îndeplinită cu ocaziunea expozițiunii generale române din 1906 de către secțiunea de
economie socială*, Institutul de arte grafice Carol Göbl, București, 1907, pp. 85, 102, 108;
Dimitrie Ionescu, *Agrarverfassung Rumäniens. Ihre Geschichte und Ihre Reform*, Leipzig,
Verlag von Duncker & Humblot, 1909, p. 47.

[24] Ionescu, *Agrarverfassung*, p. 51.

[25] *Marea răscoală a țăranilor din 1907*, pp. 83–85.

Such was the degradation of the condition of the peasantry that death at the hands of the army seemed the least of evils. Moldavian Prosecutor Leonescu described such an encounter with famine-stricken peasants in Vaslui County in autumn 1904 when he was called in together with army troops to conduct an inquest into an uprising against the local leaseholder. One desperate peasant came up to him and said:

> Mr General Prosecutor, I see you have lots of troops with you. I pray you, do a Christian deed and order them to shoot me. I have eight children at home and maize only for four days. Rather than see them starve to death under my very eyes, better die first.[26]

Poor peasants were left at the mercy of the state, which, in famine years, distributed meagre relief in the form of maize and sowing seed. King Carol I himself was painfully aware of the ravages of famine in his country and the huge costs incurred by the state to keep it at bay. His correspondence shows constant concern for the harvest throughout the years and also his brooding over the economic nadir of his reign in 1905. Thus in January 1905 he reflected:

> I look back with pain to the past year, which has inflicted so many wounds on us. For my country it has been the worst year of my long reign. We now suffer greatly the consequences of the bad harvest; two-thirds of the population must be fed by the state, otherwise people would be starving. Huge shippings of maize from South America are being distributed to the peasants.[27]

By February of the same year, things had not improved:

> We're looking forward to springtime because the cattle are out of fodder and sheep are dying by the hundreds. The state has to buy in large quantities of maize for the peasants and for sowing.[28]

His stock-taking of the situation in April 1907 revealed that 'the government has spent 35 million [Franks] to buy in maize from America and

---

[26] N.V. Leonescu, *Anul 1907. Răscoala țăranilor*, Atelierele grafice "Lumina Moldovei", Iași, 1924, p. 15.

[27] Sorin Cristescu (Ed.), *Carol I. Corespondența personală (1878–1912)*, București, Triton, 2005, p. 426.

[28] Cristescu (Ed.), *Carol I. Corespondența personală*, p. 429.

fodder to at least in part cover the great needs [of the peasants]. If we get a good crop we will be able to cover half of these huge expenses.'[29]

As D.A. Sturdza, leader of the Liberal Party, showed during a Romanian Academy session, 'if you look at financial reports regarding the public budget or at the registers of state or county debt, you will see that every two or three years the state or individual counties buy in maize to distribute to famine-stricken peasants. And I'm talking here only of the maize necessary for bare subsistence, clothing is an entirely different matter.'[30] This, as the German Consul in Bucharest pointed out, was both insufficient and counterproductive:

> No one does anything against the exploitation of these people by foreign and native, Jewish and Christian leaseholders and usurers. If in one year the misery becomes too great, the government distributes maize and seeds; but even this takes place badly (*in ganz verkehrter Weise*); they accustom the peasants to relying on this distribution and thereby increase their fecklessness and lack of provision (*Mangel an Voraussicht und Vorsorge*). This distribution is of course very discretionary (*nach Gunst und Ungunst verfahren*), the material is often wasted and, according to the custom of the land, stolen.[31]

As the German Consul reiterated in a later report: 'By distribution of state land and, in bad years, of food and seed out of political calculation (*aus parteipolitischen Gründen*), they have only achieved to increase the peasant hunger for more, without genuinely helping them, and have reinforced them in their conviction that the state must provide for them.'[32]

While unfairly judgmental of the peasants and their would-be 'fecklessness' (although this was understandable, as he did not know the ins and outs of agricultural contracts), the Consul did make a vital point about the condition of the Romanian peasantry at the time. The Romanian peasants could best be described as 'beggars of the State'. On the one hand, they were both in law and in practice on the losing side: some had a scrap of land, but not enough to make a living on and could not do much with it

---

[29] Cristescu (Ed.), *Carol I. Corespondența personală*, p. 429.

[30] Constantin Stere, *Publicistică*, Editura Universul, Chișinău, 2006, p. 146.

[31] PAAA, Berlin, R 9652, Rumänien Allgemeine Angelegenheiten 1906–1907, Report no. 27, Bucharest 3 March 1907, pp. 4–5.

[32] PAAA, Berlin, R 9652, Rumänien Allgemeine Angelegenheiten 1906–1907, Report no. 47, Bucharest 25 March 1907, p. 9.

(sell or mortgage); land delimitation was ill-defined so they were endlessly cheated by the local potentates; they were at the mercy of corrupt local authorities and greedy leaseholders; as we shall see further on, they were illiterate and completely devoid of agricultural knowhow. On the other hand, the state gave them bits of land from time to time (usually after episodes of peasant unrest) and gave alimony (the above-mentioned food and seed) in hungry years. In this context, it is little wonder that the Romanian peasant should come across as land hungry and lacking in entrepreneurial spirit.

G.D. Creangă viewed the Romanian land redistribution as a badly managed process of internal colonization, which in itself was in keeping with foreign diplomatic descriptions of Romanian agriculture as *Raubwirtschaft*, or plunder economy, a phrase that at the time was applied to extractive colonial rule:

> The state distributed plots of less than 10 ha [...] and no longer cared about the fate of the peasants thus endowed with land. On the contrary, its slogan since 1864 until now seems to have been: 'I gave you a plot of land. Now grow wealthy and multiply yourselves' and the consequence of this indifference was that, in default of any advice, any help and any agricultural knowledge, the peasants did no different than the German medieval peasants who threw the seed on the ground and shouted 'Now grow by yourself'. Moreover, the state-directed land sales were led in many cases by financial reasons in that the state demanded an unusually high price for the land bought by the peasants.[33]

Added to this were the neglect, arbitrariness and vagaries of the as yet inchoate and highly politicized administrative apparatus.[34]

The Bane of Leaseholding

By far the most oppressive feature of the land tenure system in Romania was the widespread practice of great landowners leasing out their estates to capitalist lessees, or *arendaşi*, rather than to their own peasants. Big leaseholders were preferred to the peasants because they offered higher rents and were deemed more reliable in their payments. Estates were rented out at auction to the highest bidder. The successful leaseholders

[33] Creangă, *Grundbesitzverteilung*, p. 82.
[34] Creangă, *Grundbesitzverteilung*, pp. 83–84.

were able to pay increasingly higher rent not because of a more rational exploitation of land but because they shifted all costs onto the peasants. Between 1865 and 1907 land rent increased up to ten times while peasant work remuneration decreased.[35] The peasants, who were, in their great majority, in dire need of land for sheer subsistence, subrented land from the leaseholder, who forced them to work more for less pay.

The law, as subrental contracts showed, was all on the leaseholder's side. Contracts were lopsided and stipulated in great detail the rights of the landowner/leaseholder and the work obligations of the peasants, with great attention to the timings of the leaseholder's agricultural works, but offering no protection to peasants and showing no consideration for the timings of their fieldwork or for their livelihood in general. They also commonly included clauses that ran completely against the law or which completely enslaved peasant labour: see, for instance, stipulations to the effect that contracted peasants were not free to work on another estate, or forcing the peasant to continue working the landlord's land (for pay) even when they had paid off their debts to them, or contracts that automatically included all the people living in the same house.[36]

Big leaseholders were not proper farmers or agricultural specialists. They were land speculators, extractors on behalf of the great landowners and of state institutions. Their practices could not easily be associated with fully fledged capitalism as their actual investment in the rented estates was minimal, being confined to the initial rent payment, which they then recuperated two- or threefold from the local peasants. Their business style was along the lines of inceptive capitalism, that is, land usury.[37] As a contemporary rural newspaper pointed out, 'the leaseholder brings no financial capital to the exploitation of the estate and even less scientific capital. If someone were to write a history of leaseholders they would find that more often than not the leaseholder brought nothing else to the estate than a stack of registers, a good beating stick and a huge dose of cunningness.'[38]

Leaseholders tended to accumulate large estates and create monopolies, which were instrumental in forcing the peasants to exploitative

[35] Rosetti, *Pentru ce s-au răsculat țăranii*, pp. 672–687; Scraba, *Starea socială a săteanului*, p. 67.

[36] Scraba, *Starea socială a săteanului*, pp. 162–163, 167–168, 176, 186–187.

[37] Scraba, *Starea socială a săteanului*, pp. 64, 67–68; *Marea răscoală a țăranilor din 1907*, p. 67; Ionescu, *Agrarverfassung*, p. 64.

[38] *Marea răscoală a țăranilor din 1907*, p. 68.

contractual terms. This system, as vividly described by Constantin Stere, was practised just as oppressively by Jewish and Gentile entrepreneurs alike, with the blessing of the great landowners:

> In these counties (Botoşani, Dorohoi and Suceava) we find in all its glory the *Fischer-esque* system, which was first used by the *Fischer* brothers (so they deserve to give their name to it), then found adherents among all faiths and nationalities, genuine *Fischeroids*, irrespective whether they are or not subjects of foreign powers or true-blue descendants of Trajan. The system is brilliant in its simplicity: by concentrating huge latifundia by means of rental (*arendare*) into the hands of a powerful association you force the peasant into complete submission: bereft of land and in need of pasture, the peasant is forced to accept the law of the latifundia potentate. As a peasant put it at the Congress of Popular Banks: wherever you go, you still run up against him. A vivid illustration of the 'free competition' glorified in political economy textbooks. The success of the system was ensured by the happy combination of 'foreign capital' (autochthonous capital would not suffice for such a vast operation), on the one hand, and the villainous uselessness (*nemernicia*) of our boyars, who, being incapable of administering their own estates, found a way to reconcile their lyrical support for Article 7 of the Constitution [*the article of the 1866 Constitution debarring non-Christians from becoming Romanian citizens*] with the peasant's land hunger by passing those estates into the hands of 'foreign capital'.[39]

G.D. Creangă pointed out that this system was not an anomaly or a foreign blight, which the fledgling state was struggling with and sought to contain, but rather it was a state-promoted, state-condoned, state-directed development. The state itself and not just individual landowners resorted to the exploitative system of *arendaşi* and drew profit from the monopolies and the high rents extorted by the lessees from the peasants:

> The trust [of the Fischer brothers] rented land not just from private persons but also from the State, whose duty should have been that of furthering the welfare of the peasant and preventing, *not* supporting, the build-up of monopolies; [they rented land also] from the Department of Schools (*Schulkasse*), whose duty is the spreading of education among peasants; from the Saint Spiridon charity, whose goal is the preservation of peasant health, and not making peasants' life even more difficult. How can one reproach

---

[39] Constantin Stere, 'Fischerland', p. 366.

private individuals with supporting and promoting this system when the State itself and its authorities set such an example?[40]

This extractive, exploitative system, which Dobrogeanu-Gherea called *neo-serfdom*, ₁made it impossible for Romanian peasants to make a self-sufficient living, while at the same time being silent on, and thus permitting, huge accumulations of land in the hands of capitalist entrepreneurs without scruples.

The condition of the peasantry had been precarious for years before the 1907 uprising. In 1888, the year in which a violent but localized peasant uprising broke out in southern Romania, the German consul in Bucharest was describing peasant–landlord relations as follows:

> Between peasant and great landowner there is hardly any human relationship (*kaum irgend eine menschliche Beziehung*). The latter lives in Bucharest, the biggest city in Romania, or abroad, and squanders, without any concern for the peasants' wellbeing, the income of his estate, which comes up to at least 7% of the value of the estate due to the exploitation of the peasant workforce.[41]

These huge profits made by the great landowners through the mediation of leaseholders were not reinvested into the estates with a view to raising their productivity by intensive technology-driven cultivation, but rather were spent abroad thus creating a haemorrhage of domestic capital.

The peasants, for their own part, were in their overwhelming majority illiterate and had no knowledge of agricultural techniques and, even if they had had, they lacked the necessary capital to invest in technology and machinery. They used no fertilizers and cultivated the land as their forefathers had done hundreds of years before. The same diplomatic sources referred to this as '*Raubbau*', cultivation to exhaustion. The great landowners' *Raubwirtschaft* went hand in hand with their peasants' *Raubbau*.

The consequences were not just poor crops and endemic poverty but also poor nutrition and widespread diseases among the peasantry. As contemporary bacteriologist Victor Babeş showed in his work 'The Illnesses of the Romanian Peasant' (*Boalele ţăranului român*):

[40] Creangă, *Grundbesitzverteilung*, p. 151.
[41] PAAA, Berlin, R 9637 Allgemeine Angelegenheiten Rumänien, Report no. 62, 22 April 1888, pp. 8–9.

the peasant's small plot of land, which he cultivates with low-quality seed and much too late, which is left unweeded, sown with one type of grain only and unfertilized, does not yield enough nutrients to the peasant and this condition will only get worse [...] the Romanian peasant suffers and dies not only of infectious diseases, which can be cured, but also of another type of diseases, squalor diseases, which are in direct connection to the state's neglect of the peasant's economic status.[42]

At the medical congress organized in Bucharest in 1906 Dr. Gheorghe Marinescu shocked his audience with statistics revealing the inroads made by pellagra into peasant society. The disease was caused by poor nutrition based exclusively on maize. According to him, 'the number of people suffering from the disease, which in Italy was almost disappearing, grew five times in Romania in the last ten years' and the measures taken so far against it were 'downright laughable'.[43] In a broad survey of Romanian doctors' reports on the state of the peasantry, Constantin Bărbulescu remarks on the comparatively positive image of the peasantry conveyed in 1860s medical reports as opposed to the unremittingly bleak image depicted by doctors' reports at the end of the nineteenth and beginning of the twentieth century. In 1877–1878 medical reports described peasants in almost exclusively negative terms.[44]

The sorry state of the Romanian peasantry was, as pointed out by Constantin Stere, best illustrated by the plunging figures of domestic consumption for maize, which was the staple food for the majority of the population. Table 4.1 shows the difference between domestic production and export.[45]

So by 1903 the average Romanian peasant had at their disposal 146 kilograms of maize per head per year whereas the bare minimum for subsistence was, according to Creangă, between 350 and 400 kilograms (in Germany the minimum quantity was deemed to be 450 kg).[46] This was

[42] Victor Babeș, 'Fragmente din lucrarea *Boalele țăranului român* (1906)' in Ioan Scurtu and Sorin Teodorescu (Eds.), *1907 în viziunea contemporanilor*, Editura Semne, București, 2007, pp. 177–119.

[43] PAAA, Berlin, R 9652, Rumänien Allgemeine Angelegenheiten 1906–1907, Report no. 192, Sinaia 6 October 1906, pp. 1–2.

[44] Constantin Bărbulescu, *România medicilor. Medici, țărani și igienă rurală în România de la 1860 la 1910*, Humanitas, București, 2015, pp. 31, 221.

[45] Stere, 'Foametea constantă și chestia agrară', *Publicistică*, p. 145.

[46] Creangă, *Grundbesitzverteilung*, p. 102.

Table 4.1 Differences in domestic production, consumption and export of maize in turn-of-the-century Romania

Years	Production (in freight carriages)	Export (in freight carriages)	Domestic Consumption (in freight carriages)	Population	Consumption per head (in kg)
1876	125,000	**26,000**	99,000	4,300,000	**230**
1886–1890	157,000	60,000	97,000	5,000,000	194
1891–1895	158,000	72,000	86,000	5,500,000	156
1896–1900	160,000	70,000	90,000	6,000,000	150
1901–1903	192,000	**102,000**	90,000	6,300,000	**146**

in the context in which production increased marginally, exports increased almost five times and the total population increased by half.

The same Stere who provided the Table 4.1 also painfully remembered the remarks of a Bulgarian professor of Political Economy and Rector of the University of Sofia: 'I am surprised that after three years of rich crops and only after one year of bad crop (and only partially so as there was a good crop of wheat and plums even if the maize crop was poor), the Romanian government has to provide sustenance for the entire population and for the livestock. In Bulgaria this would be impossible even after three consecutive years of bad crops.'[47]

Romanian agriculture represented a great paradox in the region in that it managed to combine great outward success with great domestic failure. As John Lampe observed:

By 1910 Romanian wheat export value had climbed past that of the U.S. to fourth place in the world. Even when the expansion of cultivated land slowed down after 1895, this grain-led increase was not prompted by rising productivity, in the manner described for pre-1914 Hungary by Scott Eddie. It was instead the result of a sharp, probably cyclical increase in world grain prices and subsequent pressure on the peasantry to turn over a larger marketable surplus to the boyar estates. Calculations by Marvin Jackson reveal that the annual rise in real crop output per capita after 1900 was literally nil.[48]

[47] Stere, 'Cauzele mișcărilor agrare', *Publicistică*, p. 147.
[48] John R. Lampe, 'Varieties of Unsuccessful Industrialization: The Balkan States before 1914', *The Journal of Economic History*, Vol. 35, No. 1, (Mar., 1975), p. 63.

So soaring grain exports occurred despite the retention of antiquated methods of cultivation and not owing to modernization and increased productivity but to other means: extending cultivation surfaces, so much so that they cannibalized vital pastureland and common land, and trapping and exploiting peasant labour.

As Bogdan Murgescu has pointed out, there were discussions and proposals for increasing agricultural productivity especially during the crisis of 1875–1878 and these included proposals to 'limit emphasis on wheat and maize production and cultivate instead other crops which were deemed more lucrative (barley, rye, millet, rapeseed) and revitalize cattle breeding for export'. These pragmatic proposals were, however, trumped by nationalistic concerns over state independence and the agonizing debate about granting Jewish population rights and citizenship.[49]

Romania not only did not diversify its crops and remained for the most part mono- and bicultural but they continued their relentless exports throughout the agricultural crisis despite the dumping prices of American grain. Its neighbours, by contrast, sought to steer clear of the worst of the crisis. In the Hungarian half of the Austro-Hungarian Monarchy the proportion of population employed in agriculture dropped from 80% to 64% between 1870 and 1910, while agricultural products formed only 58% of Hungarian exports, many of them being processed foods.[50] Most importantly, as grain prices plummeted, Hungary switched to animal husbandry, which had become 'the most important branch of Hungarian agriculture by the late 1880s.'[51] Fellow Balkan states such as Serbia and Bulgaria also differed from Romania in terms of proportion of grain exports: thus, in 1897, whereas Romania exported 46% of its total harvest, Serbia exported only 12.5% and Bulgaria 27%.[52]

An essential aspect of Romanian agricultural output and its impressive growth was that it was predicated on a fundamentally unsustainable system. It was a system of land cultivation to exhaustion and work force exploitation, with no regeneration loop in place and ultimately no

---

[49] Murgescu, *România şi Europa*, p. 136.

[50] Katherine Verdery, *Transylvanian Villagers. Three Centuries of Political, Economic, and Ethnic Change*, University of California Press, Berkeley, Los Angeles, London, 1983, p. 199.

[51] Verdery, *Transylvanian Villagers*, p. 197.

[52] John R. Lampe & Marvin R. Jackson, *Balkan Economic History, 1550–1950. From Imperial Borderlands to Developing Nations*, Indiana University Press, Bloomington, 1982, p. 173.

possibility of genuine, long-term progress. Bogdan Murgescu has made this point clearly and wondered if the sacrifice of the peasantry on the altar of national economy and state consolidation was effective in the first place (by the First World War Romania was far from having caught up with Western economies) and, secondly, was it worth it, given that this growth was unsustainable?[53] John Lampe put it even more decidedly:

> The weakness of the mainly agricultural foundations of the pre-1914 Romanian economy augured badly for the future. The nearly virgin lands of a century before had now filled up with a peasant population tied to ever-smaller plots (there was no primogeniture) and to traditional methods even on the large estates. Any prolonged downturn in world grain prices would have spelled disaster for agriculture and capital accumulation. Any attempt to extract a larger exportable surplus or to increase productivity within the existing system of land tenure ran the risk of a peasant revolt still more widespread than the uprising of 1907. In addition, this peasant population was untrained for other work and by this time largely immobile.[54]

AUSTRIA-HUNGARY

Across the border in the provinces of the Habsburg Monarchy the peasantry had been emancipated in 1848 amidst revolutionary turmoil, which posed an existential crisis to the system and brought home to all the warring parties the need for reform. The peasants came out on the winning side as their allegiance became a trump card for Vienna and Budapest. Ignoring the peasants and their wishes could have disastrous consequences: in the 1830s and 1840s there were violent uprisings that stressed the need for emancipation (such as the Slovak uprising in northern Hungary in the 1830s or the 1846 Galician massacre). By 1848 emancipating the peasants had become an impending necessity. The emancipation from serfdom decreed by the Hungarian revolutionary government in 1848 was not cancelled during the neo-absolutist era by the restored imperial authorities; no redemption dues were levelled on the peasants and no legal tricks precluded the latter from making full use of their land ownership.

By 1900 in the Hungarian half of the Monarchy, to which the two eastern borderland provinces Transylvania and the Banat of Temesvár

---

[53] Murgescu, *România și Europa*, pp. 147–148.

[54] Lampe, 'Varieties of Unsuccessful Industrialization: The Balkan States Before 1914', *The Journal of Economic History*, pp. 83–84.

Table 4.2 The distribution of landed property in Hungary in 1910 (1 hold = 0.5 hectare)

Size of property	Total number of landed properties (%)	Land surface (%)
Dwarf (0–5 hold)	52.3	6
Small (5–100 hold)	46.82	49
Intermediate (100–1000 hold)	0.74	14
Large	0.14	31

belonged, 68.6% of the total population were employed in agriculture. By 1910 the proportion had dropped to 64%. According to the 1895 statistics there were 2,795,885 landed properties (farms) distributed as shown in Table 4.2.[55]

Within the vital category of small properties (5–100 hold), properties of 5–10 hold represented 9% of all property land, those of 10–20 hold 14%, those of 20–50 hold formed 16% of the land, and those of 50–100 hold 6.55% of the total land.[56] This meant that half the landed properties were small and they took up half of the agricultural land; the other half were dwarf properties (and landless peasants), but they only cultivated 6% of the arable land; while the large and intermediate properties represented barely 1% of the properties and yet occupied 20% of the land. In the Transylvanian borderland 45% owned 5.3 hectares of land per family in the post-emancipation period.[57]

Emancipation in Hungary did not automatically equal prosperity or even equal chances of achieving it: of the 1,538,096 serfs that were freed 'only 46.6% became owners of various tracts of land (only 36.8% owned plots large enough to produce for the market) and 57.4% were emancipated without any land whatsoever (7.1% were emancipated without owning a house to live in)'.[58] This created a numerous rural proletariat and a

[55] R. Vargha, *Hungary*, Budapest, 1906 – cited in Doreen Warriner (Ed.), *Contrasts in Emerging Societies. Readings in the Social and Economic History of South-Eastern Europe in the Nineteenth Century*, Indiana University Press, Bloomington, 1965, p. 111; Verdery, *Transylvanian Villagers*, p. 199.

[56] Dr. Beck Lajos, *A magyar földbirtok megoszlása. Agrár-statisztikai tanulmány*, Budapest, Pallas Irodalmi és nyomdai Résvénytársaság, 1918, pp. 36, 39, 40:

[57] Verdery, *Transylvanian Villagers*, p. 219.

[58] Joseph Held (Ed.), *The Modernization of Agriculture: Rural Transformation in Hungary, 1848–1975*, Columbia University Press, Boulder, Colo., 1980, p. 135.

social problem, which resulted in outbursts of rural unrest throughout the 1890s and early teens of the twentieth century.[59]

Emancipation did create the premises of modernization and within two generations progress was made in Hungarian agriculture, but the distribution of accumulated wealth saw huge variations from east to west. As Held points out,

> Changes occurred at the most rapid rate in western Hungary, while the eastern areas were showing a slow, sluggish progress. On the other hand, half a century of capitalist development left the north-eastern and eastern regions practically untouched. The latter regions continued to use production methods characteristic of the feudal age, although there was some progress in the adoption of power tools such as the steel plough and mechanical threshers. The differences in developmental levels thus not only continued to exist, but in some instances they were even aggravated.[60]

Thus the percentage of two-or-three-field system usage was by 1908: 41.4% in Transylvania and 19.6% in the Banat. Peasants' reluctance to give up this age-old system as well as problematic new legislation (*mezőori törvény*) and off-putting red tape contributed to the retention of ineffective cultivation techniques.[61]

For all the uneven development of Hungarian agriculture and the partial continuation of practices and social relations typical of the ancient regime, there was one major advantage that Habsburg Hungary had over countries like Romania. Its imperial setting meant that it benefited from a steady internal market for its agricultural produce and also had access to credit within the empire, which proved to be a life-saving boon during the agricultural crisis in the 1870s. Drawing on the work of Hungarian historians such as Berend and Ránki, and Hanák and Katus, Katherine Verdery has stressed the need to reconsider

> The orthodoxy that Hungary's connection with the empire was crippling, and impeded industrial development by prolonging an agrarian economy and depressing the accumulation of capital. [...] far from being an impediment, Hungary's inclusion in the empire after 1848 accelerated Hungarian industry, relative both to the empire's western half and to other East

[59] M. Lampland, 'Corvee, Maps and Contracts: Agricultural Policy and the Rise of the Modern State in Hungary during the Nineteenth Century', *Irish Journal of Anthropology*, 3, 1998.
[60] Held, *Modernization of Agriculture*, p. 98.
[61] Held, ibid., p. 101.

European economies. [...] It is crucial to observe that because of the influx of Austro-Bohemian funds into Hungarian industry and the favourable prices for Hungary's protected agricultural goods, both resulting from the imperial connection, Hungary's industrial development did not require forced transfers of value from agriculture through low agricultural prices. While not all cultivators benefited from the good agricultural incomes possible in these years – Transylvanians were among those who benefited less – to the extent that taxation drove peasants into marketing commodities, at least these were not grossly undervalued. Hungary's access to imperial capital made even its agricultural taxation comparatively light, until outside funds retreated between 1896 and 1906. Thus, despite the political oppression of non-Magyars within the new Hungarian state, the economic situation of non-Magyar peasants in Transylvania was better than it would be after Transylvania passed (1918) from Hungary into a Romanian state that did not enjoy the advantages of Hungary's access to a more developed imperial economic system.[62]

Verdery has vitally pointed out that industrialization in Hungary was not done at the expense of the rural world, so that there were 'no forced transfers of value from agriculture through low agricultural prices'.[63] This is also borne out by the most recent scholarship on Hungarian agriculture before 1914, with Mariann Nagy stressing the great importance of the common market within Austria-Hungary in buffering the shock of foreign market competition and vagaries.[64]

Hungarian Borderlands

In the provinces flanking the triple border, Transylvania and the Banat, five of the eight frontier counties (Krassó-Szörény, Hunyad, Szeben, Fogaras and Beszterce-Naszod) were inhabited by a majority of Romanian population (70%),[65] two (Csík and Három Szék) had Hungarian (Székely) majority and one (Brassó) had mixed population in equal pro-

---

[62] Verdery, *Transylvanian Villagers*, pp. 199–200.

[63] Verdery, *Transylvanian Villagers*, p. 200.

[64] Mariann Nagy, 'Interaction between institutional change and market forces in Hungary in the second half of the 19th century', conference paper given at the Rural Studies Conference: http://www.ruralhistory2013.org/papers/3.7.3._Nagy.pdf (accessed on 23 June 2016)

[65] Nagy, *A magyar mezőgazdaság regionális szerkezete a 20. század elején*, p. 227.

portion (Saxons, Hungarians and Romanians each formed a third of the population).

In the 'Romanian' counties, according to the 1895 census, peasant properties between 5 and 20 hold (equivalent of 2.5 hectares to 10 hectares) predominated, those above five hectares ensuring self-sufficiency. As a consequence there was a comparatively high proportion of self-sufficient properties and also of supporting family members (*segítő családtagok*), whilst the resort to wage labour was infrequent in the region. Wheat and maize were staples of peasant production: they accounted for 70% of cultivated land in the Romanian-inhabited regions of Transylvania. As a contemporary Hungarian description mentioned, 'maize forms the main diet [of the Romanian peasant] and is cultivated in great quantities. His bread consists mostly of polenta; wheat or rye flour bread can only be seen on the table of well-off people'.[66]

The Székely-inhabited counties of Csík and Három Szék were embedded in the mountainous frontier where the Eastern Carpathians changed direction westwards. These were counties with low population density and a high proportion of forest, which took up almost half of the territory. Meadows represented 15% and arable land a mere fifth of the total surface, 20% of which was left fallow as land cultivation still followed the traditional two-field system. The two counties show how, with high odds against it (comparatively low rates of literacy, traditional land tilling techniques, rudimentary cattle growing), moderate prosperity was attainable if a number of conditions obtained. State help was available in these two counties: important sums of money were invested for improving the local livestock, farms using manure were encouraged, agricultural schools were placed at peasants' disposal. In addition to this, the pattern of land tenure was also favourable: plots of less than 100 hold (50 hectares) formed 80% of all properties; the Székely region had one of the highest proportions of self-sufficient households, whilst those who could not make ends meet hired out their labour as day workers; the land rental system, which reached cancerous proportions across the border in Romania, was infrequent here. Most importantly perhaps, for all the region's comparative poverty, there existed initiative (state-led and private) regarding improvement and modernization of production techniques: trips were organized by the local authorities to the Saxon counties where groups of Székely small farmers learnt about the latest developments in cattle breeding and vegetable growing.[67]

---

[66] Nagy, *A magyar mezőgazdaság regionális szerkezete a 20. század elején*, pp. 227, 270–273.
[67] Nagy, *A magyar mezőgazdaság regionális szerkezete a 20. század elején*, pp. 262–266.

The Saxons, living side by side with Hungarians and Romanians in equal proportion, served as role models of agricultural prowess. The region they inhabited was not favourable for agriculture, consisting of mountains and poor soil. This they remedied through extensive use of fertilizers (the manure farm (*trágyátelep*) was a Saxon peasant's pride and joy and the first place newly weds visited before making their way to the marital house), vocational education and apprentice farms (*tangazdaságok*) as well as investment in mechanization. Usage of agricultural machinery not only placed them at the forefront of the peasantry in the region but also put them in a position of competition with the more advanced Western counties of Hungary. Thriving Saxon dairy cooperatives made full use of the growing demand for such produce from neighbouring towns, whilst— similar to the Romanian and Székely counties—land was predominantly divided into properties between 5 and 20 hold (2.5–10 hectares), which were for the most part self-sufficient with low levels of wage labour.[68] The Saxon story of agricultural success must be connected to the high rates of literacy among their population, who ranked among the most literate in eastern Hungary (60% in Brassó county), but also to the historical privilege as colonized population fostered by the Hungarian Kingdom.

Austrian Bukovina

Belonging to the Austrian half of the Monarchy, Bukovina was the Empire's easternmost province, which bordered on northern Romania, the very part of the country where the 1907 uprising started. Bukovina, which was hived off to the Austrian half of the Monarchy after 1867, partook in full peasant emancipation with all its consequences, positive and negative. Habsburg emancipation led to the setting up of peasant associations, banks and loan institutions,[69] but also in many cases full, unlimited ownership opened the door to the proletarianization of peasants and large-scale emigration. Bukovina evinced common traits to the rest of the Empire, to which it added a few of its own derived from its geographical make-up.

The province was situated at the eastern extremity of the Empire, bordering on Romania and Tsarist Russia, and had been acquired in 1775,

[68] Nagy, *A magyar mezőgazdaság regionális szerkezete a 20. század elején*, pp. 266–270.

[69] Alois Brusatti (ed.), *Die Habsburgermonarchie 1848–1918*, Band I: Die Wirtschaftliche Entwicklung, Verlag der Österreichischen Akademie der Wissenschaften, Vienna, 1973, pp. 456–457.

being a splinter of the historical Principality of Moldavia. Of the entire territory of this province (1,044,164 hectares), more than half was taken up with forest, arable land being concentrated in the north-east, between the Prut and Dnister Rivers and along internal river valleys. As such, forestry was the main source of income in Bukovina and not agriculture.[70] The distribution of land according to 1907 statistics shows a clear predominance of dwarf property[71]:

from 0–50 Ar [1 Ar = 100 m^2]	....	38.37%
from 50 Ar to 1 ha		20.37%
from 1 ha to 5 ha		31.29%
over 5 ha		8.69%

Bukovinian peasants had at their disposal associations and loan opportunities. Numerous *Landwirtschaftliche Vereine u. Genossenschaften* were set up, some without ethnic affiliation, many specifically targeted at one of the several ethnic groups that made up the population of the province. Thus, side by side with *deutsche landwirtschaftliche Kasinos*, there were also 'Reuniunea agricultorilor' and several *rumänische landwirtschaftliche Kasinos*.[72] As regards credit institutions, there were 149 Ruthene *Spar-und Darlehenskassenvereine*, 156 Romanian ones and 71 German *Spar-und Darlehenskassenvereine*.[73] This corresponded to the ethnic breakdown of the population: out of a total of 511,964 inhabitants, 219,000 were Romanians, 186,000 were Ruthenes and 32,000 were German, to whom were added 47,772 Jews (further ethnic groups included Hungarians, Armenians, Lipovans and Poles).[74]

---

[70] P.S. Aurelianu, *Economie Natiunala. Bucovina. Descriere economica insocita de ua charta*, Bucuresci, Tipografia Laboratorilor Romani, 1876, pp. 30, 31, 44–46; Creangă, *Grundbesitzverteilung*, p. 179: 'according to the agricultural statistics of 1897: 288184 cultivable land; 131,758 meadows; 8121 gardens; 451,230 forests; 164,899 uncultivable land; – out of a total surface of 1,044,192 ha.'

[71] Michael Lytwynowytsch, *Die bäuerlichen Besitz- und Schuldverhältnisse im Wiznitzer Gerichtsberzirke*, Czernowitz, 1911, p. 17.

[72] *Statistisches Jahrbuch des Herzogtums Bukowina für das Jahr 1908*, II. Jahrgang, Zusammengestellt und veröffentlicht vom statistischen Landesamte des Herzogtums Bukowina, Czernowitz, 1911, pp. 116–117

[73] *Statistisches Jahrbuch des Herzogtums Bukowina für das Jahr 1908*, II. Jahrgang, pp. 402–413.

[74] *Heimatkunde der Bucovina*, Czernowitz, Verlag von H. Pardini, 1872, pp. 48–49.

The presence of loan institutions did not, however, automatically mean cheap and easy access to credit for the peasant dwarf holders, as pointed out by a 1903 report by the Bukovinian provincial government (*K. K. Landesregierung*) to the Austrian Ministry of the Interior:

> The only large credit institution in the province, the Czernowitz Land Credit Society, does not manage to cover peasant demand. Their loans are, moreover, too expensive due to costly formalities. The society only issues big loans so that the peasants are wrongly induced (*verleitet*) to take out more money than they need, which they then cannot profitably invest in their property. The Raiffeisen banks, whose beneficial influence is acknowledged, have just come into being and do not have at their disposal all the necessary means.[75]

Just as in the case of Hungarian agriculture, the transition from a feudal type of economy to capitalist market relations was anything but easy or smooth. Population increase and the tradition of dividing land among heirs led to chronic land atomization. As Michael Lytwynowytsch, an imperial judge in Bukovina, observed in 1911, within a quarter of a century, since the mid-1880s, the average surface of a peasant property as well as its net yield had all but halved.[76] The peasants continued to use the time-honoured three-field system of agriculture, which meant that the yield was poor. A peasant property of 5 hectares was barely enough to feed the owner's family and, as the average property was more often than not much smaller than five hectares, the peasants had to make ends meet by means of wage labour.[77] The same complaint that had been voiced in Hungary about peasants' spirit of enterprise, or rather the lack thereof, comes from Bukovina as well. Lytwynowytsch remarked on the peasants' 'complete lack of enterprise initiative (*der vollständige Mangel der Unternehmungslust*)', which was reflected in the way peasants used the available system of loans and mortgages: 'only a fifth of all mortgage loans were used for productive purposes', the rest being resorted to for paying off debts.[78]

---

[75] ANR, Fondul Guvernământul Bucovinei, Mapa 75/II, p. 2.

[76] Lytwynowytsch, *Die bäuerlichen Besitz- und Schuldverhältnisse im Wiznitzer Gerichtsberzirke*, p. 19.

[77] Lytwynowytsch, *Die bäuerlichen Besitz- und Schuldverhältnisse im Wiznitzer Gerichtsberzirke*, p. 18.

[78] Lytwynowytsch, *Die bäuerlichen Besitz- und Schuldverhältnisse im Wiznitzer Gerichtsberzirke*, p. 10.

The life of the average Bukovinian peasant at the turn of the twentieth century was by no means full of the joys of spring. Official Bukovinian reports in the early teens of the twentieth century identified the deterioration of peasant property and agriculture and, even more worryingly, the waves of emigration depleting the local peasant population. The main causes for this were endemic indebtedness and consequent loss of land, land fragmentation, lack of local industry, drunkenness, and the difficulty of obtaining cheap and easy credit. Officials thus worried about the prospect of a 'mass pauperization of the rural population'.[79]

The initial terms of peasant emancipation did not always lead to a smooth, clear-cut division of landed property and decade-long litigation was quite a common occurrence: there were litigations between former landowners and peasant communities, litigations within and among peasant communities, or between the peasants and the commission that administered land distribution (*die Bukowinaer k.k. Grundlasten-Ablösungs-Landes-Commission*). While verdicts were not always in favour of the peasant communities, the justice apparatus did function and, in some cases, petitions were placed before the Emperor's eyes and received imperial approval.[80] What comes out of official documents for Austrian Bukovina is a concern for the plight of the provincial peasantry and attempts to provide solutions to ameliorate it: proposals submitted for debate in Parliament, inter-ministerial discussions, official conferences and various initiatives (such as the setting up of district farmers' associations and an agricultural council).[81]

TSARIST BESSARABIA

Across the Tsarist border in Bessarabia two great land reforms swept over the bulk of the peasants. The great peasant emancipation edict of 1861 brought about little change for the better and equally little impact had the radical agrarian reform implemented by the Romanian authorities when

[79] ANR, Fondul Guvernământul Bucovinei, Mapa 75/II, Report from the Austrian Ministry of Justice to the Austrian Ministry of the Interior, 2 May 1903, pp. 117–119.

[80] ANR, Fondul Guvernământul Bucovinei, Mapa 134/5, pp. 25–57: documents regarding the complaint lodged by the Gogolina peasant community on account of their being deprived of communal grazing land.

[81] ANR, Fondul Guvernământul Bucovinei, Mapa 75/II, 1901 report from the Provincial Government of Bukovina (K. K. Landesregierung für die Bukowina) to the Ministry of Agriculture, pp. 1–2.

the Tsarist Empire collapsed and the province changed hands after the First World War. This was not because conditions could not be improved or there were in-built obstacles to peasant emancipation but, quite the contrary, because, for historical reasons, the condition of the peasantry in this Tsarist borderland had been comparatively better than that of the rest of the Empire and incomparably better than that of the peasantry in the Principality of Moldavia (later on to become part of Romania), from which they was severed in 1812.

As Ion G. Pelivan, a representative in the Bessarabian Assembly (*Sfatul Țării*), observed in 1920, 'the great act of liberation of February the 19th, 1861 did not have for Bessarabia, with her free peasantry, the same importance as for the central provinces of Russia. This act only changed the position of a small number of gypsies, who were farm-hands in the employ of Bessarabian boyars and put an end to Russian refugees who came from the centre of the Empire and were wandering in Bessarabia, in their great fear of slavery which reigned at that period in their region.'[82] A similar note was struck at roughly the same time (1920) by the Sorbonne professor Emile Martonne, who remarked how little impact the post-First World War Romanian land reform seemed to have had on the peasants of Bessarabia: 'very few of them have understood the series of events that followed the Russian revolution. Even the agrarian reform does not seem to interest them equally. There are villages of "*răzeși*", or peasants who have been landowners for many generations.'[83]

How was it possible that a province (or the splinter of a province) would fare better than the original country following annexation by an empire notoriously known for the poor condition of its peasantry, whose class name was almost synonymous with serfdom? There were several contributing factors to this paradoxical outcome: time, context and dynamics of social/political empowerment and disempowerment within the Tsarist Empire. When Bessarabia was annexed in 1812, the mood was high in the Tsarist Empire fostered by Russian victory and massive reverse in the Napoleonic wars as well as the liberal policies of Tsar Alexander I. The combination of wartime necessity and the Tsar's open-minded attitude to government led to the decision that the newly acquired borderlands (Congress Poland, Finland, Bessarabia) should be rendered stable and

---

[82] Ion G. Pelivan, *Bessarabia under the Russian rule*, Paris, Imprimerie J. Charpentier, 1920, p. 41.

[83] de Martonne, *What I have seen in Bessarabia*, p. 28.

loyal by means of autonomy, preservation of ancient rights and privileges, and various exemptions.

Bessarabia thus benefited from this favourable context on all levels, social, political, religious and cultural. Following annexation, the province was declared autonomous and local authorities were co-opted into the imperial government. One of the Romanian boyars Scarlat Sturza was appointed governor of the province, another Romanian 'Gabriel Bannlescu Bodoni was made metropolitan of the diocese of Kishinev and Hotin',[84] all rights and privileges of the local boyars were recognized, to which were added the privileges of Russian nobility, which was gradually introduced into the new borderland.[85] Ordinary population were kept happy by means of exemption from taxes (for three years initially, then extended by another two) and from military service (which was eventually introduced in 1874). The peasantry, who were free before annexation, retained this legal status and their ancient property, where this was the case. According to Pelivan, 'in comparison with all the other provinces where the spirit of centralisation and red tape routine dominated in the most dreadful manner, where the words "Liberty of the Peasantry" were considered as a crime against all fundamental laws, the situation in Bessarabia was bearable.'[86]

Legally speaking most peasant population in Tsarist Bessarabia were free (with the exception of a few thousand enserfed Roma on church and private estates) and were divided into three main categories:

(1) ordinary peasants, who had no land of their own, but worked the boyars' land in exchange for tithe and labour dues;
(2) the 'Mazils', who, according to Pelivan, 'were the descendants of the ancient boyars' who had been 'dismissed from their functions' and 'inherited property from their ancestors, which, notwithstanding its having been parcelled out into thousands of plots, assured them material as well as moral independence. The Mazils retained their old-time privileges and their own organisation (they had their Captain) and the Russians confirmed this to them by the law of 1818 as well as by the law of March 10th 1847.'[87]

---

[84] Pelivan, *Bessarabia under the Russian rule*, pp. 6–7.

[85] Dinu Postarencu, 'Introducerea instituției nobiliare în Basarabia' in Maria Danilov (Coord.), *Nobilimea basarabeană în epoca reformelor din imperiul rus*, Academia de Științe a Moldovei, Chișinău, 2013, p. 64; Cristina Gherasim, 'Confruntări din cadrul adunării nobilimii basarabene în anii 40–50 ai secolului al 19-lea', ibid., p. 77.

[86] Pelivan, *Bessarabia under the Russian rule*, pp. 6–13.

[87] Pelivan, *Bessarabia under the Russian rule*, p. 47.

(3) the '*răzeși*' or landed free peasants, who historically possessed land granted to them by Moldavian princes for loyal military service. 'The *răzeși*-tenure,' as Pelivan explains, 'is an old kind of land holding by which every *răzeș* is the hereditary proprietor of his plot of land, but de facto only, because by right he is only co-proprietor in the old judicial unity. The *răzeși* like the *Mazils*, owning land given to their ancestors by the princes of Moldavia in return for having served in the regiments which defended the Eastern frontier of the country, had never been obliged, like the peasants, to farm the land of the boyars. They had therefore never done any menial or servile work.'[88]

As landed peasants or (in the case of the *Mazils*) descendants of small boyars and possessors of privilege, these last two peasant categories were well known for their feistiness and strong opposition to any attempts to curtail their historical rights.[89] Not unlike the Szeklers in Transylvania and the *Schwaben* in southern Hungary, historical enfranchisement translated into a strong sense of community assertiveness and frequent use of legal channels to obtain redress and satisfaction. The *răzeși*, in particular, were in constant conflict with their boyar neighbours and the most legally minded of all Bessarabian peasants:

> one cannot imagine a '*răzeș*' who has not just been summoned to appear before the Justice of the peace or some higher court or who is not the proud owner of a pile of documents dating back to the time of Stephen the Great, which he insists on showing to Mr. Lawyer or His Worship the Judge. It is on this account that no social class knows the agrarian laws better and more thoroughly than the '*Răzeși*'. It is also for the same reason that the knowledge of law and justice is more developed among the *Răzeși* than anywhere else.[90]

To these were added a smaller number of colonists, who successfully fulfilled the role of a middle-sized propertied peasantry. Given the sparse population when the province was acquired in 1812 (through war refugees and relocation of population in some cases such as the Tartars in the Bugeac) several waves of colonization brought German and Bulgarian

---

[88] Pelivan, *Bessarabia under the Russian rule*, p. 49.
[89] Pelivan, *Bessarabia under the Russian rule*, pp. 46, 49.
[90] Pelivan, *Bessarabia under the Russian rule*, pp. 49–50.

population in the southern parts of Bessarabia. Just like colonists elsewhere in the region these enjoyed extensive privileges (tax exemption and exemption from military service) and received plenty of land (60 desiatin - 1 desiatin = 1.09 hectares) as well as state protection. By the beginning of the twentieth century it was these colonists that represented the middle stratum of the local peasantry, well above subsistence level, literate and well-off enough to take advantage of technological advancements in the field of agricultural machinery. On visiting one of the German colonies in southern Bessarabia in 1920, Emile Martonne described the German colonists as 'an aristocracy of hard-headed landholders' and went away with a 'vivid impression of prosperity', wealth as well as order and method, at the same time stressing the source of this prosperity: one must remember 'they were singled out for favours: almost all of them own between 30 and 50 hectares',[91] that is, up to ten times more land than needed for bare subsistence.

As part of the same drive to colonization, several Jewish agricultural colonies were set up in northern Bessarabia disproving ingrained prejudice against the Jews as a community unsuited to field work.[92] These colonies survived the onslaught of the anti-Jewish May laws and endured through a combination of agricultural activities and traditional Jewish trade and crafts.[93]

By 1909 cultivable land in Bessarabia was split between peasant tenure (48.6%), the great property (mainly native boyars, whose land and privileges were not affected by the change of borders in 1812, but also non-natives, who received grants of land for services done to the Tsar), who held 43.2% of the arable land, and state, church and other institutions (8.2%).[94]

Whilst the historical emancipation edict of 1861 made little difference to the bulk of the Bessarabian peasantry, a subsequent law given in 1869 granted full land ownership to the peasants for the land they cultivated. According to land quality the peasants received between 8 and 13 desiatin (1 desiatin = 1.09 hectares), which was much more generous than elsewhere in the Empire and incomparably more than that which peasants received in neighbouring Romania. Whilst within a couple of generations,

[91] de Martonne, *What I have seen in Bessarabia*, p. 21.

[92] Mariana Hausleitner, *Deutsche und Juden in Bessarabien. 1814–1914. Zur Mindenheitenpolitik Russlands und Großrumäniens*, IKGS Verlag, München, 2005, pp. 29–62.

[93] *Recueil des Matériaux sur la situation économique des israélites de Russie*, vol. 1, Jewish Colonization Association, Paris, Alcan, 1906–1908, pp. 101–102.

[94] Pelivan, *The Economic State of Bessarabia*, p. 7.

this land inevitably became fragmented through inheritance subdivision, there were however checks in place that ensured that plots of land could not dwindle to under 2 hectares and the land remained within the peasant commune. By the late-nineteenth century individual peasants still had enough land so that they seldom went out and hired their labour for extra income.[95] Bessarabia, moreover, was one of the few Tsarist provinces that had a share of the meagre 8% of Tsarist Empire peasants who could comfortably live off their land.[96]

As the autonomy of the province was abolished in 1828, the 1869 law of land distribution was passed and implemented without the agreement of the Bessarabian great landowners.[97] Although by no means perfect in its implementation (redemption dues were a source of much abuse and injustice to the peasant on the ground), this law showcased how the peasants could gain from the tension between the Tsarist authorities and the provincial elites. The local nobility opposed it and petitioned the Tsar not to extend the reform to Bessarabia because, as they claimed, it did not apply to it as Bessarabian peasants were free and, secondly, because the great landowners would be ruined. Their petition was turned down by the imperial authorities.[98] The rationale for favouring the peasantry was to undercut the power of the local elites, which came in the context of the backlash created by the Polish rebellion in 1863–1864, following which 'pro-peasant' changes were introduced 'for political reasons' in the western provinces of the Empire. The most notable of these were the default terms of the system of land redemption dues: when peasants and landowners failed to agree on terms, these default terms came into effect. These were more favourable to the peasants in the western provinces, Bessarabia included.[99]

It was not the first time that Bessarabian landowners had been thwarted by imperial design. Imperial permission was asked to introduce serfdom (or some form of servile relations) in Bessarabia as well.[100] This was not

---

[95] Zamfir C. Arbore, *Basarabia în secolul XIX*, București, Institutul de arte grafice Carol Göbl, 1898, p. 419.

[96] Creangă, *Grundbesitzverteilung*, p. 165.

[97] Pelivan, *Bessarabia under the Russian rule*, p. 41.

[98] Arbore, *Basarabia*, pp. 131–132.

[99] Andrei Markevich and Ekaterina Zhuravskaya, 'Economic Effects of the Abolition of Serfdom: Evidence from the Russian Empire', Document de travail (Docweb) no. 1502, Centre pour la recherche economique et ses applications, http://www.cepremap.fr/depot/docweb/docweb1502.pdf (Accessed on 19.02.2016), p. 11.

[100] Arbore, *Bessarabia*, p. 131; cited in Pelivan, *Bessarabia under the Russian rule*, p. 40.

granted and a few years after annexation the imperial authorities took steps towards reassuring the peasant population that serfdom would not be introduced in Bessarabia, as rumour had it at the time, setting in motion a wave of emigration.[101]

During an 1890 visit to Izmail, southern Bessarabia, the British diplomat Frank Cavendish Lascelles laid stress on this regional triangle between provincial elites, imperial authorities and the local peasantry: Russian rule, he pointed out, was beneficial to the peasantry and workmen, if not to commerce; courts usually decided suits in favour of the peasantry; the same policy of keeping the lower classes happy at the expense of the elites was pursued in Bessarabia as it was in Poland, Finland and the Baltic states.[102]

Thus, although Bessarabia lost its autonomous status in 1828 and full-scale Russification of the entire administration ensued, the curbing of boyar power and influence over local administration and legislation helped preserve the freedom and relative prosperity of the Bessarabian peasantry in a way that did not happen in the sibling principality of Moldavia, where the situation of the autochthonous peasantry worsened as the century wore on. A Darwinian island-effect is noticeable in the agricultural evolution of this Tsarist province, which was severed from the Principality of Moldavia and took a different administrative and cultural course than its original state. Conditions worsened increasingly across the nineteenth century for the peasantry in the Romanian Principalities. In 1805 Moldavian peasants were officially classified into well-off, middling and poor (*fruntași*, *mijlocași* and *codași*), which corresponded to the number of draught cattle they possessed: 16 oxen, 12 and 4, respectively. 'Sixty years later,' pointed out Constantin Stere, 'for peasant emancipation and land distribution a new classification came into being; this time, a well-off peasant was one who had four oxen'.[103] The two fundamental pieces of legislation that shaped the fate of the Romanian peasantry for a century to come, whilst nominally clarifying relations (the 1831–1832 Organic Statutes) and liberating the peasantry (the 1864 law of peasant

---

[101] Victor Taki, '1812 and the Emergence of the Bessarabian Region: Province-Building under Russian Imperial Rule' in *Euxeinos* 15/16 (2014), p. 15; Andrei Cușco an Victor Taki, *Бессарабия в составе российской империи (1812–1917)*, pp. 166–167.

[102] National Archives, London, FO 104/83, June 7 1890. Many thanks to Dr. Patrick J. Bourne for generously putting at my disposal his PhD thesis 'Sir Frank Lascelles: a diplomat of the Victorian empire, 1841–1920', defended at University of Leeds in 2010, and his research notes.

[103] Stere, *Publicistică*, p. 147.

emancipation), in practice increased their dependence on the great land-owners and disempowered them. About the Organic Statute applied in the Principality of Moldavia in 1832 the French lawyer and future Finance Minister Élias Regnault (1801–1868) observed:

> the Organic Statute is not only a monument of robbery and oppression, it is also a powder-keg of civil war, which will one day result in fire and slaughter [...] the oppressed peasants, being unable to put up opposition, are seeking asylum abroad. Moldavian peasants are crossing over into Bukovina, Bessarabia and Dobrogea, those from beyond the Milcov river [*i.e. the Wallachian peasants*] are fleeing into Transylvania, Serbia and Bulgaria.[104]

Bessarabia 'missed out' on these developments and, paradoxically, the condition of its peasantry was all the better for being part of the Tsarist Empire, in which it figured as an atypical border region.

The comparatively better condition of Bessarabian peasantry is also reflected in the low levels of social combustibility. Although there was occasional peasant unrest in various quarters of the province (among the Mazils, or among the disgruntled inhabitants of particular villages) and troops were at times called in to restore order, these isolated flares of peasant discontent never escalated into full-blown, province-wide uprisings. Even in the troubled years of revolution 1905–1906, when major uprisings devastated the Black Earth regions of the Tsarist Empire, Bessarabia was among the provinces that incurred least damage and peasant destruction. A British diplomatic report quoting a memorandum of the Tsarist Ministry of the Interior published in *Odesski Listok* regarding 'losses caused by the agrarian disorders in 19 provinces of European Russia and Esthland' listed Bessarabia at the very bottom of the pile of sustained damages. While almost half of the included provinces incurred losses between 1 million and 9 million roubles, Bessarabia reported a mere 4,540 roubles' worth of losses.[105]

CROSS-BORDER COMPARISON

The social combustibility of the peasantry around the triple frontier between Romania, Austria-Hungary and Tsarist Russia was determined by several structural factors: (1) how land reform was implemented; (2) who

---

[104] Élias Regnault, *Istoria politică şi socială a Principatelor Dunărene*, p. 356 – cited in I. Nistor, *Românii şi rutenii în Bucovina*, Bucureşti, Librăriile Socec, 1915, p. 105.
[105] London National Archives, FO 371/120, Russia 1906, p. 286.

paid for the land and what could be done with it; (3) peasant access to pasture and forest; (4) how land leaseholds were regulated; (5) initiatives for improvement of agriculture; and (6) peasant agency and social safety valves such as the possibility of emigration.

How the Reform Was Implemented

In Austria-Hungary peasant emancipation occurred with the explicit aim of creating a self-sufficient, self-standing peasantry. In Romania emancipation was warped from the very beginning as, under the appearance of empowerment, it tied the peasant to land and former landowner. In Tsarist Bessarabia, owing to the tug-of-war between imperial authorities and provincial elites, land reform was introduced against the wishes of the great landowners and for the benefit of the peasantry. This initial design of the reforms translated into different geographies of land exploitation.

Land distribution occurred in Bessarabia as a consequence of an 1869 law that entitled to a plot of land peasants who lived and worked on state, church or private estates. The actual land division was the result of an agreement between landlord and peasants and in case of conflict the Regional Administration for Peasant Problems and local and regional justices of the peace arbitrated. The village community as well as the peasant had rights of ownership over the land.[106]

Romania was the most egregious case in terms of how the legal stipulations of land reform were put into practice on the ground. As the reform was made *by* the great landowners *for* the great landowners, and as there was no state institution that acted as a neutral arbiter in the tug-of-war between peasants and landlords, the distribution of land was effected to the detriment of peasants: the worst-quality land was given to them, land that had no direct access to water or scattered in remote places, measurements were made to the landowner's advantage, the local authorities, mayor, gendarme, estate administrator were all on the landowner's side. Contemporaries remarked again and again on the plight of the peasant as being at the mercy of local authorities and their landlord, more often than not cheated out of his rights, with no one to turn to for redress. It was the pervasive sense of being both wronged and forsaken, left to fend for

---

[106] Valeriu Scutelnic, 'Regulamentul despre relațiile agrare ale țăranilor regiunii Basarabia', *Revista de Istorie a Moldovei*, no.1, 2007, http://www.history.asm.md/index.php/ro/publicatii/reviste/398--revista-de-istorie-a-moldovei-nr-1-69-2007 (accessed 29.07.2015)

themselves, that contributed to the bitterness and fierceness of the 1907 peasant uprising, perhaps even more so than poverty itself.

In Hungary following 1848 and until the restructuring of the empire into a dual entity, Austria-Hungary, property rights fell in the purview of urbarial courts, which settled disputes and any issues regarding property rights. These courts were mostly resorted to by the great landowners rather than the peasants.[107] After the 1867 restructuring of the empire, Hungarian local and regional institutions took over responsibility for landed property disputes.

Who Paid for the Land and What Could Be Done with It

As regards redemption of land and manorial dues, the situation was once again more favourable to peasants in Austria-Hungary and Tsarist Bessarabia. Parteniu Cosma, President of the Romanian National Party and director of the *Albina* Bank in Hermannstadt (Sibiu), noted the contrast between Hungary and Romania:

> Here [in Hungary] the former landowners received compensation for the land they had to give up to peasants and for all the urbarial dues, but this they received from the state. This was paid for by increasing the land tax by 35%, the bulk of which was of course paid by the great landowners. In Romania, on the contrary, the peasant himself had to pay for the meagre land he received [...] In other words, emancipation was done without any sacrifice on the part of the former landowner and without any sacrifice from the state.[108]

This, however, applied only to urbarial serfs, the cost of whose emancipation was endorsed by the state. All other categories of Hungarian enserfed peasants had to pay redemption dues.[109]

Technically speaking, in Romania redemption dues were not for the land received but for the amount of corvée work that the landowner was deprived of following peasant emancipation. This, however, amounted to

---

[107] Zoltán Szász, 'The Social Stratification of the Peasantry', *History of Transylvania*, Volume III. From 1830 to 1919: http://mek.oszk.hu/03400/03407/html/383.html (Accessed 30.07.2015)

[108] Parteniu Cosma, *Răscoala țărănească în România*, Sibiu, Tiparul Tipografiei Arhidiecezane, 1907, p. 6.

[109] Verdery, *Transylvanian Villagers*, p. 219.

the value of the land or more and, given that the new labour relations were so skewed in favour of the great landowner, the Romanian peasant ended up paying redemption dues while never really ceasing to be a serf. In Bessarabia, the land was to be paid for by the peasants within 20 years. Even though this gave rise to tensions between peasants and landowners,[110] redemption dues will not have had the same backbreaking impact on the peasantry as they did in Romania, as the distributed land was in the Tsarist province almost twice as much as in Romania and more fertile.

The nature of land ownership differed around the triple frontier. In Hungary full ownership of the land meant that the peasant could dispose of his bit of land as he saw fit: he could mortgage it, sell it, he could use it as a basis for further investment. All of these the Romanian peasant could not do.[111] In his theory of neo-serfdom Dobrogeanu-Gherea, too, emphasized this major handicap crippling peasant development: 'the first essential condition of serfdom – being tied to the land – was achieved to a certain extent by the very law of emancipation of 1864, which decreed the inalienability of land.'[112] And indeed the law of 1864 stipulated that the peasant could not sell or take out a loan on his land for a period of 30 years. In 1884 the constitution was modified so the period of inalienability was extended by another 32 years.[113] This stipulation only went out of use in 1929.[114]

Dobrogeanu-Gherea made no bones about it: this was no unfortunate side-effect of emancipation, it was a deliberate strategy on the part of the ruling class:

> The covert but fairly obvious tendency of this first land distribution was to render impossible the independent life of the small property, to make it impossible for the peasants to live off their land and to make them economically dependent on the great landowners by having to work their land as well.[115]

That this was not just another conspiracy theory enunciated by a Marxist is proved by Partenie Cosma's testimony: in a 1876 conversation

---

[110] Arbore, *Basarabia*, pp. 137–138.
[111] Cosma, *Răscoala țărănească în România*, pp. 5, 19.
[112] Dobrogeanu-Gherea, *Neoiobăgia*, p. 64.
[113] http://www.legex.ro/Legea-0-1864-6.aspx (Accessed on 30.11.2017)
[114] Seton-Watson, *Eastern Europe between the Wars 1918–1941* p. 202.
[115] Dobrogeanu-Gherea, *Neoiobăgia*, pp. 50–51.

with Ion Brătianu, the latter admitted to him that the 'agrarian law was put together the way it was out of high reasons of state, for if they completely emancipated the peasant from his former lord, then the great landowners would not have been able to cultivate their land for lack of workhands as at that time the rural population of Romania was quite sparse and mechanization unknown'.[116] In 1900 a similar admission was made to Cosma by someone who would later become a prefect in Romania: 'in our country the interests of the great landowners do not allow for the emancipation of the peasantry.'[117] Officially the inalienability of peasant land was presented as 'a measure against the improvidence and stupidity of the peasant, who would otherwise become a proletarian'.[118] This attitude combined the interests of the great landowners with the reactionary view, not uncommon before and after emancipation, that 'the peasant is lazy, drunkard, and used to the whip, does not understand freedom and cannot make good use of it [...] In other words, the peasant is treated like a child and consequently must be kept under close supervision'.[119]

In Bessarabia the inalienability of newly acquired land was decreed by the 1869 law in the following terms:

> The land bestowed on the peasants retains the name of communal land (*pământ obștesc* – *mirskaia zemlia*) and peasants will pay redemption dues for it according to the law. This land will belong to the rural commune (*selskoe obshestvo*) and cannot become private property, neither in part nor in whole, and constitutes peasants' inalienable land, which serves to feed the rural class.[120]

The difference between Romania and Tsarist Bessarabia was that in the latter the distributed land was enough for peasants to make ends meet, whereas in the former, land was chronically insufficient. In Bessarabia a peasant could sell their land to another member of the rural commune, which in time led to peasant stratification, while the property of heirless couples remained in the hands of the rural commune.[121]

[116] Cosma, *Răscoala țărănească în România*, pp. 6–7.
[117] Cosma, *Răscoala țărănească în România*, pp. 9–10.
[118] Dobrogeanu-Gherea, *Neoiobăgia*, p. 64.
[119] Dobrogeanu-Gherea, *Neoiobăgia*, p. 63.
[120] Arbore, *Basarabia*, p. 135.
[121] Arbore, *Basarabia*, p. 136.

Access to Pasture, Forest, Water

As mentioned above, Parteniu Cosma, President of the Romanian National Party in Hungary and director of the *Albina* Bank in Hermannstadt, dwelt on the much better situation of the Hungarian peasant in contrast to the Romanian:

> Our peasant became absolute owner of the land he worked as a serf [...] In addition to this, he also acquired pasture and forestland from the previous landowner so that after emancipation he could work for himself only and he and his family could live off their property without falling back on the help of the former landowner and without being at his mercy. He can now prosper even, which can be seen in the considerable number of industrious peasants who have since made good fortunes and can even send their children to university at their own cost.

In Romania, by contrast, the peasant was given some land but *not*

> the possibility of cultivating it [...] for one cannot cultivate land without livestock and without a house and economic appurtenances (*zidiri economice*). You cannot build a house and live in it without wood for timber and fire. You cannot keep livestock without pastureland. These have remained in possession of the former landowner, who will continue to exploit the peasant as he likes.[122]

And indeed, according to Hungarian agricultural statistics dating from the year 1900, common forest and pastureland played a central role in Hungarian agriculture. Along the triple border: in Transylvania 52.34% of the total forest and 55.99% of the total pastureland were common, while in the Banat 17.75% of forest and 62.79% of pastures were for public use.[123]

In Romania pastureland remained in the hands of the great landowners and became a way of coercing the peasant into onerous contracts. The 'price of using pastureland has gone up to a level hitherto unknown in the history of rural economy', pointed out Constantin Stere. 'Pastureland usage for a big animal from St George's day until St Demeter's [*i.e. from April till October*] costs 20–40, even 60 lei, which is 3–4 times more than

---

[122] Cosma, *Răscoala țărănească în România*, pp. 4–6.

[123] *A Magyar Korona országainak Mezőgazdasági Statisztikája*, Negyed Rész, Budapest, Pesti Könyvnyomda-Részvénytársaság, 1900, pp. 30–35.

in the neighbouring countries!'[124] Moreover, peasants had poor access to their own land and to watering places, which also became a means for the great landowner to force them into exploitative deals.[125]

In Bessarabia the land reform law of 1869 stipulated that, although forest was not included in the redistribution,

> land covered by shrubs and bushes, meadows and pastures, which the peasants had been using according to old custom, remained in peasant possession. In the plains the land covered by reeds and thatch, from where the peasants got their fuel, remained the property of rural communes. [...] The land reform law also stipulated that watering places for cattle such as ponds, streams, ravines, fountains and springs, constituted communal property of the landowner together with the village community. In case the landowner wants to keep them for himself, then he will have to provide at his own cost other watering places for peasants' cattle and these places must be located as close to the village as those he kept for himself. Should these new watering places be farther out, then they must be separated out from pasture land and fields, making good roads across private property for villagers' cattle to pass.[126]

By 1919 in Bessarabia peasant fraternities owned about 10% of the forests.[127]

The Nature of Land Leaseholds

How Much Land? How Many Leaseholders?
According to G.D. Creangă, in Romania 56.88% of property over 50 hectares was leased out and the number of leaseholders who rented estates of over 50 hectares, was 3,332. Out of these, 2,417 (75.24%) were Romanian; 443 (30.13%) were foreign citizens; and 472 (14.16%) were Jews.[128] One assumes that the 'Jews' category does not refer to foreign nationals of Jewish faith, but to Romanian subjects of Jewish faith, who at the time were not Romanian citizens.

---

[124] Constantin Stere, *Publicistică*, p. 149.
[125] Dobrogeanu-Gherea, *Neoiobăgia*, p. 50.
[126] Arbore, *Basarabia*, p. 134.
[127] Kaba, *Politico-Economic Review of Bessarabia*, p. 21.
[128] Creangă, *Grundbesitzverteilung*, p. 137, pp. 144–145.

Table 4.3   The distribution of leaseholders across provinces in 1906 Romania

Provinces	Romanians	Foreigners	Jews	Total No.
Moldavia	556	106	440	1,102
Wallachia	1,304	249	25	1,578
Oltenia	387	75	7	469
Dobrogea	170	13	–	183

In terms of percentage of leased property, Creangă concluded that 63.34% of the total rented property went to Romanians, 17.79% to foreigners and 18.87% to Jews. The proportion of nationality to land size varied so that the proportion of Romanian leaseholders decreased from 83.19% for properties between 50 hectares and 100 hectares to 51.11% for properties over 5,000 hectares, which reflected the increase in the proportion of foreign leaseholders from 7.18% to 24.45% and of Jewish leaseholders from 9.63% to 24.44% for the same surface categories.[129]

The distribution of leaseholders across provinces, according to Creangă, is shown in Table 4.3.[130]

The Iași General Prosecutor N.V. Leonescu's chart for nine counties in northern and central Moldavia breaks down the landowners and leaseholders into two categories only, Romanians and foreigners, leaving one to guess as to which one the autochthonous Jewish population was included into (see Table 4.4):[131]

As Leonescu concluded, the number of landowners who cultivated their own estates was 243, and among the leaseholders 273 were Romanians and 385 were foreigners. Leonescu also bears out Creangă's assessment of the relationship between size of land rental and nationality:

> Romanian landowners and *arendași* cultivated small estates. The biggest and best estates were leased out to foreign *arendași*. Of the foreign leaseholders, one had 13 estates; three had 8 estates; one had 6 estates; three had 5 estates; six had 4 estates. Foreign *arendași* who had several estates encircled the landowners who cultivated their own estates and the Romanian *arendași*. By means of extensive cultivation they made unequal competition

[129] Creangă, *Grundbesitzverteilung*, p. 145.
[130] Creangă, *Grundbesitzverteilung*, p. 145.
[131] N.V. Leonescu, *Anul 1907. Răscoala țăranilor*, Atelierele grafice "Lumina Moldovei", Iași, 1924, pp. 17–18.

Table 4.4   Landowners and leaseholders in northern and central Moldavia

County	Estate Managers (Esploatatori de moşii)	Romanians (Owners and leaseholders)	Foreigners (arendaşi)
Bacău	121	90	31
		46 landowners who worked their own land **44** arendaşi	
Botoşani	118	56	62
		31 landowners who worked their own land **25** arendaşi	
Dorohoi	157	87	70
		49 landowners who worked their own land **38** arendaşi	
Fălciu	66	41	25
		13 landowners who worked their own land **28** arendaşi	
Roman	72	42	30
		20 landowners who worked their own land **22** arendaşi	
Suceava	70	38	32
		20 landowners who worked their own land **18** arendaşi	
Vaslui	102	68	34
		26 landowners who worked their own land **42** arendaşi	

(*continued*)

Table 4.4   (continued)

County	Estate Managers (Esploatatori de moșii)	Romanians (Owners and leaseholders)	Foreigners (arendași)
Iași	118	50	68
		17 landowners who worked their own land 33 arendași	
Neamț	77	44	33
		21 landowners who worked their own land 23 arendași	

to the landowners who cultivated their own estates and to the Romanian *arendași*: they coerced the former to stop cultivating their own estates and to lease them out; and forced the latter out of the leasehold business or into associating with a foreign *arendaș*.[132]

Leaseholders and Their Modus Operandi

While the above figures offer a necessary view of the distribution of land to leaseholders according to nationality and, in the case of Jews, religion, as well as showing how much land was rented out rather than farmed by the owners themselves, there is, however, a limit to their explanatory power. Creangă for instance goes into tremendous detail and provides chart upon chart of data and percentages, which betray the fervour of the statistician but are nothing more than trivia, which may satisfy a nationally minded reader, but by themselves provide little insight into the workings of the system or the cause of its oppressiveness. It is Creangă's merit that he furnishes detailed information on the leaseholdings of the Fischer brothers and of the Juster brothers, the masterminds behind the two infamous cartels that dominated land business in Moldavia. Detailed estate-by-estate information on their rented property across the country shows how big statesmen such as Cantacuzino and Sturdza were faithful customers as were institutions such as the Saint Spiridon Hospital Charity, the state itself and insurance companies such as Dacia-România, whose members were Romanian landowners and statesmen.[133]

[132] Leonescu, *Anul 1907*, pp. 19–20.
[133] Creangă, *Grundbesitzverteilung*, pp. 154–155.

The oppressive feature of the system resided not in the predominance of the leasehold or the percentage of foreigners or Romanian subjects of Jewish faith among the leaseholders but in the set of practices that defined the rental system and the legal framework it was embedded into. As contemporary authors pointed out, exploitative practices were common to all leaseholders, irrespective of their nationality or religion.

> The Fălciu commune borders on the Prut river and the estates Bogdănești, Berzeni, Golia, Ronzești, Gogești and Miclești. These estates were leased out to Mendel Melegzon. Hliza Zangol (estate) was rented to Iacob Filipescu, Bogdana (estate) was leased out to Vasile Constantinescu and Boziea estate was leased out in parts to Mendel Melegzon, Vasile Moțoi, Irimiea Bodeanu, Ghiță Duca and Gh. Filip. All these leaseholders, the Jew and the Romanians, were in cahoots with one another refusing to sub-lease any land for food and grazing to the Fălciu villagers so as to impoverish them. So that the two hundred inhabitants of Fălciu could not keep goats nor cows for their food and that of their children.
>
> [...] The district (*plasa*) of Munteni in Vaslui County consisted of three communes of *răzeși*, all three communes were leased out to the Greek arendaș Topale. He was the only arendaș and disposed of the fate of the peasants as it suited him.[134]

Notwithstanding the competition between foreign and autochthonous capital and the chicanery between landlords and leaseholders when it came to dealing with the peasants they all acted in the same way. As Prosecutor Leonescu pointed out:

> All were in agreement with one another as to how to treat the working peasant. The mayors legalized agricultural contracts without the peasants being present and without their consent. [...] there were legal cases that showed that some landowners and leaseholders forced their peasants to work on their estates for a second year, without having paid them for their work of the previous year. The gendarmes forced them to work on the order of the mayor and sometimes even without it.[135]

Creangă too reinforced this point showing that:

---

[134] Leonescu, *Anul 1907*, p. 18.
[135] Leonescu, *Anul 1907*, pp. 19–20.

[l]easeholds are numerous in those counties where the landed property belongs to a small number of people, who cannot themselves cultivate it, or where the number of peasants who don't have enough land is so high that they are forced to pay any rent in order to get more land. This critical situation (*Zwangslage*) is exploited by leaseholders and entrepreneurs, in that they persuade the landowners to lease out their land to them for higher rent; then they seek to extract this land rent twofold or threefold from the peasants, forcing them to ever more onerous agricultural contracts, which brings the leaseholders a profit of 100%–200%.[136]

State-run leaseholds were not part of an unregulated capitalist bonanza. The possibility of imposing terms on the lessees did exist and was occasionally made use of. There were official regulations conditioning the leasing of state-owned land. A general set of regulations was published in 1901 in *Monitorul oficial* and added to later on. 'The leaseholder must cultivate the land in such a way that he does not grow the same autumn crop in one place for two years in a row.' Or 'the leaseholder must allow the fourth part of arable land to rest every year'.[137] State-owned land was leased out at auctions organized by the government and the lease duration varied between four and ten years. The auction result papers show that the state could and did reject some bids, accepted counter-bids from higher bidders and in a few cases agreed to lease out the land to village communities. Some of the auction result entries stipulated special conditions under which the leasehold was to be had. These varied from the injunction that the leaseholder should leave space for a road on the edge of the rented plot of land, or buy at his own expense the necessary materials for the good functioning of the mill, or give land to the local priests, or allow the local peasants to use the pond as watering place for their cattle.[138] So in the case of state-owned land, there were two sets of conditions: the official regulations and the special conditions (which were estate-specific) appended to leasehold contracts at auction. The general conditions were aimed at preserving land quality through crop rotation but, for all their well-meaning import, they fell short of agricultural modernization: they preserved the status quo and did not in any way encourage or constrain the leaseholder to use fertilizers or new technologies in order to extract a higher profit from the land. The modality and morality of gains extraction from the

---

[136] Creangă, *Grundbesitzverteilung*, p. 139.
[137] ANR, Fond 451, MAD Arendări, Dosar 3307, pp. 5–6.
[138] ANR, Fond 451, MAD Arendări, Dosar 3306, p. 18, Dosar 3302, pp. 75, 123.

rented land fell outside the purview of these regulations. There is the occasional note in the margin of auction lists specifying that this or that leaseholder was stripped of the rented land for 'failure to pay' (*neplata de câştiguri*). There is no such note to the effect that a leaseholder was deprived of his land for onerous contracts imposed on the local peasants. Bidding and outbidding were encouraged with no stipulation in place that would prevent that a higher price offered should lead to a more severe exploitation of peasant work.

Leaseholding Across the Triple Frontier
The leaseholding system of land tenure was not specific to Romania. Rented properties and subletting of land represented common practice both around the triple frontier under discussion and across Europe as a whole. With the exception perhaps of Ireland, where leaseholds were con-ducive to exploitation and impoverishment of the rural population, Romania seems to be singular in the development of a leasehold system that was unfair to the bulk of the population and extractive in character. There were leaseholds as well as Jewish population in both Austria-Hungary and Tsarist Bessarabia and yet the combination of the two did not have the same result as it did in Romania. By considering how Jewish emancipation and the implementation of leaseholds occurred across the border we are providing two elements of comparison to Romania and thus placing its development into wider, cross-border perspective. In Austria-Hungary the Jewish population had been fully emancipated since 1867 and leaseholds were a common practice in agriculture. In Tsarist Bessarabia, on the contrary, antisemitic legislation was in place and the authorities looked upon it as too lenient; leaseholds were, similarly, an important fea-ture of the land-tenure system. On neither side of the border, however, did the leasehold acquire cancerous proportions.

Austria-Hungary was the least systemically antisemitic of the three states around the border and provides the starkest contrast to develop-ments in Romania. The two halves of the Monarchy had different ratio-nales for emancipating the Jews but the result was roughly the same. In Austria the Jews for the most part assimilated to German language and culture, and were without exaggeration the best representatives of the supranational state concept promoted by the Habsburg authorities. In Hungary, emancipation was effected at the same time, but here the Jews became staunch allies of the Hungarian national project.

Hungary provides perhaps the most meaningful term of comparison to the Jewish question in Romania. In addition to fundamental dissimilarities, there were also a number of similarities in the two states, which make for a revealing comparison between Hungarian and Romanian Jewish policies. Modern state building started at relatively the same time in both states (from the 1860s onwards); this was accompanied by virulent national projects, which led to aggressive policies of Magyarization in Hungary and rampant xenophobia in Romania; in both cases the nation was presented as under siege (linguistically the same metaphor of an island in a sea of Slavs applied, and was applied, to the two language groups, Hungarians and Romanians, the former speaking a Finno-Ugric language and the latter, a Romance language). The two states, however, reached completely different conclusions as to the best way to relate to their Jewish population. Two polar-opposite processes came into being: Hungarians actively embraced the Jews in their policies of Magyarization while Romanians across the border sought to exclude them by every possible means. On one side of the border (the Romanian), Jews were deemed to be an economic bane and a threat to the nation, while across the frontier they were viewed as great boosters to economic modernization and staunch allies of the Hungarian nation. This great disparity can be explained by looking at where the Jews featured within the two nation-building projects and how they fitted in, or failed to. Animosity to, or alternatively acceptance of, the Jews was also a function of the economic configuration and the extent to which the dominant nation in the respective states felt threatened or displaced by Jewish economic activities.

In Hungary ethnic Hungarians made up less than half of the population (the rest was a combination of Romanians, Serbs, Croats and Slovaks). By contrast Romania was ethnically homogenous and the only considerable non-Romanian group they had to come to terms with were the Jews. Hungarians represented the dominant nation in the state and, if anything, suffered from a complex of superiority (legal and economic). Romanians achieved state independence in 1878 and were masters of their own country but suffered from an inferiority complex, both in relation to the Western world and in relation to their Jewish population. The tendency in Hungary was to assimilate all nationalities and religions into one single political and, eventually, ethnic nation, the Hungarian. The Romanians felt no need to create Romanians out of other ethnic/religious groups since Romanians formed the great majority of the population. So basically the Hungarians had political and economic power, but were in a numeric minority in their state; the Romanians had the numbers, demographically speaking, and had just acquired political power, but economically they felt dependent on 'foreigners' such as Jews or Greeks/Armenians, who traditionally dominated the trade and incipient capitalist institutions such as the banking system. This is how it came about that Hungarian endeavours were targeted at making up the numbers, while Romanian policies aimed at nationalizing their economy and creating an ethnically Romanian middle class.

The two states thus practiced two types of aggression: exclusionary and inclusionary. It so happened that in Hungary the Jews fitted, like a glove, the Magyarizing national project of the Hungarian elites and so did not pose a threat to their economic power. Once emancipated, the Jews of Hungary enthusiastically assimilated and came to view themselves as Hungarians of Mosaic faith. Indeed, assimilation offered itself as the best solution for the progressive faction of Hungarian Jewry in their struggle for community modernization against the Orthodox Jews.[139] The inclusionary effect of Hungarian nation-building was a blessing for the Jewish community but was an act of aggression on the national aspirations and sensibilities of the non-Hungarian nationalities. Hungary gave its Jews what Romania and Russia would never have dreamt of giving theirs. Since the *Ausgleich*, Hungarian Jews enjoyed full emancipation and their religion was accepted among the other state religions and supported by means of state funding. The Hungarian state treated the Jews as full Hungarian citizens, greatly prized their contribution to the economy and promoted a 'sympathetic image of the hard-working, resourceful, useful, Magyarizing Jew'.[140]

Hungary was, by no means, a Jewish utopia: antisemitism did exist and emerged as a consequence of emancipation[141] but was kept in check by state legality. Most inclined towards antisemitism were those who stood to lose by the transition to a capitalist economy, the small landowners, who were on the wane at the end of the nineteenth and the beginning of the twentieth century.[142] The animosity of Hungarian small landowners towards the

[139] William O. McCagg, *A History of Habsburg Jews, 1670–1918*, Indiana University Press, Bloomington, 1989, p. 133.

[140] Raphael Patai, *The Jews of Hungary: History, Culture, Psychology*, Wayne State University Press, Detroit, 1996, p. 360.

[141] Raul Cârstocea, 'Uneasy Twins? The Entangled Histories of Jewish Emancipation and Antisemitism in Romania and Hungary, 1866–1913', *Slovo* 21(2), 2009, p. 71.

[142] Patai, *The Jews of Hungary*, pp. 367, 377.

Jews resulted in instances of social exclusion, not on a large scale, but rather symbolical: Jews were denied access to clubs and were excluded from certain social occasions. The Jews did not win many favours either among the political leaders of the non-Hungarian nationalities, who fought against the violent Magyarization policies and must have regarded Jewish assimilation to the Hungarian nation as a counterweight to their endeavours: 'by 1910 there were almost 1 million Jews in Hungary[143] – 75% of whom declared Hungarian as their mother tongue'.[144] Finally, state philosemitism was no guarantee of grassroots compliance as proved by the 1881 Tiszaeszlár blood libel trial and the subsequent anti-Jewish riots.[145] The fact that forensic evidence and a scientific approach were used in the trial and that the accused were eventually acquitted shows that whilst antisemitism was indeed present in Hungary it was effectively contained by existing laws and procedures.[146] By contrast, at roughly the same time, across the border in Romania, blood libel and anti-Jewish riots resulted in the imprisonment of Jews for defending themselves against their attackers.[147]

The Hungarian economy thrived as a consequence of Jewish emancipation. The Jews, as the most literate community in Hungary, figured prominently and efficiently in all domains that presupposed a high degree of literacy, skills and qualifications. 'By 1890 in most middle-class occupations the Jews were represented in proportions that far exceeded their proportion in the general population (5%).'[148] And even more interestingly from the point of view of this cross-border comparison, in Hungary by virtue of their full emancipation the Jews could and did own land and the extent of their involvement in agriculture was considerable: in the decades before the First World War, they owned 20% of the larger estates and rented more than half of them[149]; of the middle-sized estates they owned 19% and rented 62%.[150] This forms an interesting comparison with

[143] McCagg, *A History of Habsburg Jews*, p. 125: this exceeded the Jewish population in Galicia

[144] Patai, *The Jews of Hungary*, p. 431

[145] Patai, *The Jews of Hungary*, pp. 364, 365.

[146] http://www.yivoencyclopedia.org/article.aspx/Tiszaeszlar_Blood_Libel (accessed on 23.04.2014)

[147] Carol Iancu, *Evreii din România (1866–1919). De la Excludere la Emancipare*, Trans. C. Litman, Editura Hasefer, Bucharest, 1996, pp. 109–111.

[148] Patai, *The Jews of Hungary*, p. 433.

[149] Patai, *The Jews of Hungary*, p. 375.

[150] Patai, *The Jews of Hungary*, p. 438.

the similar predominance of Jewish lessees in eastern Romania (Moldavia) and their being reviled as exploiters of the peasantry.

Jews fared equally well in the Austrian half of the Monarchy, with the great difference that here emancipation was effected under the auspices of a supranational concept of state (*Staatsgedanken*) and the Jews did not so much assimilate to the German nation (or *Volksnation*) but rather to German-ness as a liberal-cosmopolitan cultural and political community (*Kulturnation*).[151] Just as in Hungary, Austrian Jews were looked upon as a religious community and not as a nationality (Yiddish, for instance, was not recognized as one of the *Landessprache*, nor was it taught in schools).[152] While in Hungary antisemitism was kept in check by state policies, in Austria it started making headway into mainstream political discourse from the 1870s onwards. State philosemitism in Hungary was due, as pointed out above, to the happy alliance between the Magyarization project of the Hungarian elites and Jewish willingness to embrace it, as well as to the monolithic political system whereby political power was exclusively concentrated in the hands of the Hungarian magnates. In Austria, no similar state-driven nationalist project took place and power was dispersed across a deeply factionalized political spectrum where antisemitism took off as a handy electoral strategy (the case of Georg Schönerer and, more famously, of the successful mayor of Vienna, Karl Lueger).[153]

The rise of a virulent type of antisemitism in Vienna and in *Reichsrat* politics did not hinder the flourishing of regional Jewish communities. This was the case of Bukovina, where the progressive (Maskilim) section of the Jewish community succeeded, with the help of Austrian administration, in modernizing and assimilating to the German culture emanating from Vienna.[154] The Jews in Bukovina were gradually emancipated between 1849 and 1860, with 1860 as the landmark for full acquisition of rights: the possibility of buying land.[155] Just as in Hungary, this full social recognition catalyzed assimilationist tendencies and fostered strong

---

[151] Martin Broszat, 'Von der Kulturnation zur Volksgruppe: Die nationale Stellung der Juden in der Bukowina im 19. und 20. Jahrhundert', *Historische Zeitschrift*, Bd. 200, H. 3 (Jun., 1965), p. 580.

[152] Broszat, 'Von der Kulturnation zur Volksgruppe: Die nationale Stellung der Juden in der Bukowina im 19. und 20. Jahrhundert', *Historische Zeitschrift*, pp. 580–1.

[153] McCagg, *A History of Habsburg Jews*, p. 164.

[154] McCagg, *A History of Habsburg Jews*, pp. 172–173.

[155] Broszat, 'Von der Kulturnation zur Volksgruppe: Die nationale Stellung der Juden in der Bukowina im 19. und 20. Jahrhundert', *Historische Zeitschrift*, p. 575.

loyalties to the Austrian state on the part of the Jewish community, who 'came to view Austrian state interests as their own'.[156] The success story of the Jewish community in Hungary was replicated in Austria. In Bukovina, where there was no dominant nation[157] nor a nationally assertive landed aristocracy as in neighbouring Galicia, within a few generations the Jews became, socially and economically, the most prominent local communities. They came to dominate the free professions and the trade, they virtually kick-started local industry and most of the German-language press in Bukovina was in their hands.[158] They made full use of their unrestricted citizenship rights and ventured into agriculture as well, the peculiarity of their involvement with this branch of economy being that they usually went for large estates, unlike the German peasants, who owned mainly smallholdings.[159]

Hungarian versus Romanian Leasehold Systems

In Hungary the *haszonbéres* or leaseholding system mainly affected the great property, which was concentrated in central and western Hungary, while leaseholding was rare in the eastern borderlands. According to the map of land tenure in Transylvania published in *Magyar Korona országainak Mezőgazdasági Statisztikája* for the year 1900, the land renting system (*haszonbéres/Pacht*) was minimal with a predominance of small property. Although great and middle property varied a lot throughout the region, they never went beyond one-third of the property. Transylvania is described in these statistics as dominated not by cultivable land (*Ackerland*) but by meadows, pastureland and especially woodland.[160]

In Hungary leaseholds dated back to the early-nineteenth century and started out as investments made by big merchants, who sold the produce of the rented estates. It therefore comes as no surprise that among these

---

[156] Broszat, 'Von der Kulturnation zur Volksgruppe: Die nationale Stellung der Juden in der Bukowina im 19. und 20. Jahrhundert', *Historische Zeitschrift*, p. 576.

[157] Broszat, 'Von der Kulturnation zur Volksgruppe: Die nationale Stellung der Juden in der Bukowina im 19. und 20. Jahrhundert', *Historische Zeitschrift*, p. 576.

[158] Broszat, 'Von der Kulturnation zur Volksgruppe: Die nationale Stellung der Juden in der Bukowina im 19. und 20. Jahrhundert', *Historische Zeitschrift*, p. 577.

[159] Broszat, 'Von der Kulturnation zur Volksgruppe: Die nationale Stellung der Juden in der Bukowina im 19. und 20. Jahrhundert', *Historische Zeitschrift*, p. 578.

[160] *A Magyar Korona országainak Mezőgazdasági Statisztikája*, Negyed Rész, Budapest, Pesti Könyvnyomda-Részvénytársaság, 1900, Annex 1 and ff.

great traders there were quite a few Jews, who capitalized on their knowledge of the market and salesmanship.[161]

The nature and extent of Hungarian leaseholds underwent vital changes after the emancipation of the peasantry and that of the Jewish population. Peasant emancipation made leaseholding a necessity for many, even big landowners, who had lost their serf workforce and were in ever-greater need of money.[162] By contrast, this was not the case in Romania, where the post-emancipation legislation had ensured that the peasant remained tied to the land. In Hungary, given the different nature of peasant emancipation (full emancipation as opposed to the Romanian *neo-serfdom*), leaseholds had a different function than in the neighbouring country, were effected on a smaller scale and under different legal conditions. It was uncommon for Hungarian landowners to lease out all their land. This is reflected in the comparatively low percentage of pure leaseholds (as opposed to mixed leaseholds), the average being around 25% of the land in 1895, while in 1911 36.8% of latifundia were rented out and 47% of their income came from this.[163] The usual procedure was for the landowner to lease out part of their land while retaining some for their own usage. Cases where whole estates were rented out were rare and occurred when the owner happened to be under-age or, if of age, engaged in a profession or if there were several owners who did not want to divide the land. Integral rental was more often than not a sign of social downfall as with members of the middle gentry, who were more likely to lease out their estates and live off the rent, squandering it, getting into debt and eventually losing their estates altogether.[164]

Just as in Romania, more often than not big capital was Jewish in origin, with 49.5% of the estates above 100 hold (50 hectares) and 75% of the estates above 1,000 hold (500 hectares) rented by Jews, with the highest numbers in the north-eastern parts of Hungary. After Jewish emancipation, 20% of the properties above 1,000 hold and 18% of those between

---

[161] Gyurgyák János, *A Zsidókérdés Magyarországon*, Osiris Kiadó, Budapest, 2001, pp. 85–86.

[162] Puskás Julianna, 'Zsidó haszonbérlők a magyarországi mezőgazdaság fejlődésének folyamatában: Az 1850-es évektől 1935-ig', *Századok*, 126. (1992) 1. p. 35–58; p. 37.

[163] Puskás Julianna, 'Zsidó haszonbérlők a magyarországi mezőgazdaság fejlődésének folyamatában: Az 1850-es évektől 1935-ig', *Századok*, 126. (1992) 1. p. 35–58; p. 39.

[164] Julianna Puskás, 'Die Kapitalistische Grosspachten in Ungarn' in Vilmos Sandor & Peter Hanak (Eds.), *Studien zur Geschichte der Oesterreichisch-ungarischen Monarchie*, Budapest, 1961, pp. 196–197, 204.

200 and 1,000 hold belonged to Jewish landowners. Even more importantly still, after Jewish emancipation leaseholds further consolidated and their duration increased (for instance, by the end of the 1930s some leaseholds had been in the same family for three generations), which had obvious consequences on the amount of improvement and modernization conducted on the estate.[165] Thus, while there was countrywide variation in technology and cultivation, leaseholds in Hungary do not seem to have had the bad fame that they had across the border in Romania. Julianna Puskás relied on 1895 Hungarian statistics to show that, countrywide, leaseholds were better equipped with machinery and used more modern tilling techniques.[166]

Animosity against Jewish landowners and leaseholders in Hungary was usually kept within bounds and targeted only those instances of Jews buying land from heavily indebted gentry. The worst that antisemitic writers of the time could say about land-owning or land-renting Jews was that 'they take over with real cupidity the good old Hungarian land' and 'begin as small leaseholders or owners and end up as great latifundia owners'. This in itself cannot begin to compare with the hatred accumulated against Jewish leaseholders in Romania at the same time.[167] As we shall see further on, non-Magyar nationalities such as the Saxons or the Romanians came in for similar animosity on the part of the Hungarian establishment for buying up Hungarian estates and distributing them among their co-nationals.[168]

Factors such as increased duration of leasehold, improvements and modernization as well as continued involvement of the original landowner with the exploitation of the rented land were non-existent in the Romanian case. In Romania the leasehold system took the form of asset stripping. Most lease contracts were for a period of three to five years, and never for more than 12 years. Hereditary leaseholds were rare. This in itself was a

---

[165] Puskás Julianna, 'Zsidó haszonbérlők a magyarországi mezőgazdaság fejlődésének folyamatában: Az 1850-es évektől 1935-ig', *Századok*, 126. (1992) 1. p. 35–58; pp. 38–40.

[166] Puskás Julianna, 'Zsidó haszonbérlők a magyarországi mezőgazdaság fejlődésének folyamatában: Az 1850-es évektől 1935-ig', *Századok*, 126. (1992) 1. p. 35–58; p. 41.

[167] Petrássevich Géza, *Zsidó földbirtokok éa bérlők Magyarországon*, quoted in Gyurgyák János, *A Zsidókérdés Magyarországon*, p. 86.

[168] Attila Gábor Hunyadi, *Cooperative Networks in Transylvania belonging to Hungary and Romania. Nation-Building and Modernization by Cooperatives in Transylvania as part of Hungary (1867–1918) and Romania (1918–1940)*, LAP Lambert Academic Publishing, Saarbrücken, 2016, pp. 34, 48.

disincentive to make any investment as the contract period was too short to see it pay off. More egregiously still, the actual leasehold contracts actively discouraged such initiatives by stipulating that all investments will remain part of the estate and the leaseholder will not be able to redeem them at the end of the contract. Thus, a rental contract from Tecuci County for one of the estates of D.A. Sturdza, the Liberal Prime Minister under whose government the 1907 uprising was suppressed, stipulated: 'Any new improvement or building which the leaseholders make will remain after the expiry of the contract on the estate without any reimbursement from the landowner.' Another lease contract, dated 1909, pointed out that 'The leaseholder is free to make any improvements and erect any buildings on the estate and all of it will remain for the use of the estate with no payment or reimbursement, even if the contract should, by any means, come to an end before its term.' Yet another, concluded in Botoşani County: 'Any building that might be built by the leaseholder for agricultural exploitation will belong to the estate from the first day with no reimbursement and will remain on the estate without destroying it. The exception to this are the machines of the fire mill, which the leaseholder is free to erect should he wish to do so.'[169]

The obstacles placed by the great landowners in Romania on investment into agriculture modernization as well as the relatively short duration of the contracts were instrumental in shaping Romanian land-tenure relations in this period and defining its exploitative character. In the words of Radu Rosetti, this resulted into a general tendency among leaseholders in both Moldavia and Wallachia to 'not so much exploit land intensively as to exploit the peasant completely. The first priority of landowners and leaseholders today is to figure out how much work they can extract out of the peasant without paying for it, only speculating the peasant's need for 1. pastureland; 2. land for food; 3. woodland'.[170]

The rapid succession of leaseholders and the auction-like system of securing a leasehold (the estate going to the highest bidder, with leaseholders outbidding one another) resulted in a spiralling increase of land rent for the peasants. Thus a 1907 inquiry into the level of land rent paid on 142 estates out of 210 concluded that between 1870 and 1906 land

---

[169] *Marea răscoală a ţăranilor din 1907*, p. 70.

[170] Rosetti, *Pentru ce s-au răsculat ţăranii*, p. 505 – quoted in *Marea răscoală a ţăranilor din 1907*, pp. 68–69.

rent had increased between 150% and 500%.[171] This was not accompanied by a commensurate increase in the level of work payment and by a change in the style of agriculture practiced. There was, moreover, no legislation that precluded such rampant exploitation.

Jewish Question and Leaseholds in Bessarabia

Bessarabia provides the third type of land administration in this cross-border comparison. It was different from the Hungarian case in essential ways (no Jewish emancipation, no modernization of agriculture) and fairly similar to the Romanian leasehold-dominated pattern of land tenure, without however producing the economic stranglehold that the leaseholds in Romania did. Bessarabia, as we shall see further on, had both leaseholds and Jewish leaseholders but these, although they had a bad name in the public sphere, did not have the disabling effect that similar land-rental practices had in Romania.

The Jews in Bessarabia lived in a society where even the application of antisemitic laws was considered to be too lax. In 1903 Kishinev, the capital city of Bessarabia, was the scene of one of the bloodiest pogroms to date in the Tsarist Empire. This violence propelled the Tsarist backwater to a sad notoriety and transformed the toponym Kishinev into a word of threat used against Jews as far as Lithuania.[172] Bessarabia had been gradually integrated into the Pale of Settlement, which came into being by governmental decree at the end of the eighteenth century following a Moscow merchants' petition 'to be shielded from Jewish competition' and included Ukraine, New Russia and the former territories of Poland. The three partitions of Poland in the eighteenth century had brought into the Tsarist Empire a large intake of Jewish population. The Tsarist authorities opted for the segregation of the Jews from the rest of the population, a policy that stemmed primarily from the Russian government's 'misgivings as [Jews were] likely to outperform Russians and drive them from business'.[173]

---

[171] *Creşterea arenzii pământului în bani şi în dijmă, a păşunatului şi a preţurilor muncilor agricole de la 1870–1906*, Bucureşti, 1907, p. IV – quoted in *Marea răscoală a ţăranilor din 1907*, p. 74.

[172] Klaus Richter, 'Kišinev or Linkuva? Rumors and threats against Jews In Lithuania in 1903', *Revista Română de Studii Baltice şi Nordice*, Vol. 3, Issue 1 (2011), p. 119

[173] Geoffrey Hosking, *Russia and the Russians from Earliest Times to 2001*, Penguin, London, 2002, pp. 258–259.

Up until 1835 Bessarabia enjoyed an autonomous status in the Tsarist Empire, which meant that the limitations of the Jewish Statute of 1804 did not apply to Bessarabian Jews. The second half of the nineteenth century saw the loss of Bessarabia's autonomy and, with this, the wholesale application of Tsarist Jewish legislation to the new province, which had become fully integrated into the fabric of the empire as a *gubernia*. Restrictions on residence in the border area were enforced and disrupted Jewish life all the more so as, with the cession of southern Bessarabia to Moldavia after the Crimean War, Kishinev itself came to form part of the border area. This resulted in expulsions. The return of the southern counties from Romania to Russian Bessarabia in 1878 did nothing to alter this situation as four years later the May Laws were enforced across the empire forbidding Jews to settle outside towns or to own or lease land outside towns, or to trade on Sundays/Christian holidays. Moreover, starting from 1835, the Jews in the Tsarist Empire were lumped together with nomadic and semi-nomadic peoples from Siberia and the Tsarist Asiatic territories under the name of *inorodtsev*, foreigners. This was a legal category that had come into being in 1822. Inclusion into this category was 'despite the fact that Jews were a sedentary people and inhabited a European, rather than Asian milieu'.[174]

The number of Jews in Bessarabia increased tenfold over less than a century as a consequence of the province being included in the Pale of Settlement: in 1812 there were 20,000 Jews in Bessarabia; by 1897, there were 228,620 representing 11.8% of the total population and predominantly making up the urban population of the province.[175] As Charles King has pointed out, in Bessarabia 'city life was dominated by Jews and Russians. There were over 50,000 Jews in Chisinau in 1897 (half the population) and almost all the city's factories were owned by Jews; [there were also] 16 separate Jewish schools'.[176] The Jewish population engaged mainly in commerce and liquor distilling (in villages they acted as money lenders and innkeepers) and were also busy craftsmen: Bessarabia being a richly wooded

---

[174] John W. Slocum, 'Who, and When, Were the Inorodtsy? The Evolution of the Category of "Aliens" in Imperial Russia', *Russian Review*, Vol. 57, No. 2 (Apr., 1998), pp. 173–190; p. 174.

[175] Eliyahu Feldman and Theodor Lavi, 'Bessarabia' in Michael Berenbaum and Fred Skolnik (Eds.), *Encyclopedia Judaica*, Vol. 3, 2nd Edition, Detroit, Macmillan Reference USA, 2007, p. 495.

[176] Charles King, *Moldovans: Romania, Russia and the Politics of Culture*, Hoover Institution Press, Stanford, CA, 1999, p. 23.

province the Jews specialized here in particular in the building, pottery and wood industries, but there were also quite a few bakers, butchers and tailors among the local Jewish population.[177]

Due to the vagaries of nineteenth-century Tsarist legislation regarding the Jews, several Jewish agricultural colonies were founded in northern and central Bessarabia in which lived around 11,000 Jews. These colonies had been set up between the 1830s and the 1850s and the land received by the colonists was less than that which the rest of the population received after the land reform: on average 3.71 desiatin. Subsequent restrictive legislation against the Jews did not affect the land held by these colonies. The Jewish colonists' tendency was not to accumulate land and engage in extensive agriculture, but rather to cultivate intensively, growing special crops such as tobacco, vineyards, fruit trees and vegetables. In their cultivation of cereals their methods of land tilling were as rudimentary as those of the Christian peasants around them. An important characteristic of the colonists was the fact that they did not engage in agriculture exclusively but also plied other trades such as carting, various crafts and or acting as grain sellers and middlemen. They also rented land from neighbouring villages and, if practicing money lending, received the usufruct of land as gage.[178]

> None of the Jewish estates seem to be especially noted for their methods of farming, nor, on the other hand, did I hear any complaints against the owners of such estates made by their peasant neighbours. Nothing in my time disturbed the peaceful, neighbourly relations between Jewish landowners and the working class.[179]

Despite the predominant agricultural backwardness of colonial agriculture, progressive agricultural experiments were conducted beginning with the end of the nineteenth century. This was the case of the model farms

---

[177] *Recueil de Matériaux sur la situation économique des israélites de Russie*, vol. 1, pp. 381–383.

[178] Andrei Oișteanu, *Imaginea evreului în cultura română. Studiu de imagologie in context est-central european*, 2nd Edition, Humanitas, București, 2004, p. 215.

Recueil de Matériaux sur la situation économique des israélites de Russie, vol. 1, pp. 51–53, 101–104, 109–110, 113–114; S.D. Urusov, *Memoirs of a Russian Governor*, Transl. by Herman Rosenthal, London&New York, Harper and Brothers Publishers, 1908, pp. 156–158.

[179] Urusov, *Memoirs of a Russian Governor*, p. 156.

and agricultural schools set up by the Jewish Colonization Association (I.C.A.) for the rural Jewish communities. One of these schools located in Soroka in north-eastern Bessarabia made a deep impression on the Tsarist governor at the beginning of the twentieth century:

> for the first time I took account of the fact that agricultural books were not only a pleasant distraction for readers gifted with imagination, but were a very real force. On the thirty desyatins of black freshly spaded earth there no weeds to be seen. On the large and small beds, which were separated from each other, stood, row on row, slender, vigorous apple and pear trees, straight as arrows, and of different ages and varieties – not a crooked one, not a diseased one, not one that was backward in growth could be seen; everything grew per order, and as if in a picture. [...] The model drying establishment for fruit and vegetables, and also the cannery, which I found in full operation, permitted me to observe the method of preserving the garden produce, and convinced me on the spot of the clean handling and excellent quality of everything.[180]

The governor thus enthusing about the proficiency of the Jewish agricultural school in Soroka was Prince Sergey Dimitrievich Urusov, Governor of Bessarabia between 1903 and 1904, who took up his post in the wake of the Kishinev pogrom and, in this capacity, was asked by the Russian central authorities to provide an analysis of the state of the Jewry in the province. In his 1907 memoirs, which are the most informed as well as sympathetic account of the condition of Jews in Bessarabia, Urusov depicted an atmosphere of all-pervasive antisemitism among the provincial authorities, which exacerbated the restrictions imposed on the Jews by the 1882 May laws and created the general impression that the Jews were outside the protection of the law and as such fair game for all sorts of abuse. So deep-seated was this attitude that the new governor concluded that the mere application of the laws and fair treatment of the Jewish community in Bessarabia was likely to incur one the accusation of philosemitism. This was the case of V.N. Goremykin, the Prosecuting Attorney of Bessarabia, who, as described by Urusov, 'was not, properly speaking, a judophile, but simply an intelligent and educated man, free from animosity and intolerance towards all non-Russian nationalities. But, as is well known, with us it is just these qualities which give one the name of a judophile. V.N. Goremykin did not escape the unpleasant effects of his impartial

---

[180] Urusov, *Memoirs of a Russian Governor*, p. 118.

and strictly lawful attitude towards the Jews'.[181] It was Goremykin who warned Urusov of 'the tactical blunder of showing an open philo-Semitism'.[182] Thus all measures taken with a view to staving off violence against the Jews had to be cloaked in the euphemistic guise of order keeping: 'I only endeavoured to impress upon the functionaries the necessity of fulfilling their official duty in maintaining public order and safety: "We do not guard the Jews, but the public order!" was the watchword I gave the Bessarabian police.'[183]

Much of the stoking up of spirits that led to the 1903 pogrom was effected by the local press, in particular the antisemitic newspaper *Bessarabets*, edited by the right-wing journalist Pavel Krushevan. Krushevan belonged to the demagogic Russian nationalists that blamed the Jews for all the ills in the land. He was tolerated by the local authorities, by the press censorship bureau and by the secret police. In the words of Senator Z, head of the bureau, 'Krushevan's tendencies and activity had a sound basis and from a government's point of view it was undesirable to suspend his publication.'[184]

How much truth was there behind the endemic accusations that Jews monopolized land lease in Bessarabia and that they exploited people? Knowing next to nothing about the province when he arrived as a governor, Urusov was willing to give the antisemites the benefit of the doubt: 'I was inclined to admit that, as a new-comer to Bessarabia, I had not yet been able to observe to the full extent the unsightly and injurious role of the Jewry.'[185] Personal experience and interactions with the Jewish community debunked one by one the prejudices and accusations against the Jews or at least showed them to be the consequence of a system of repression that forced people into illegal practices. The behaviour of the Bessarabian Jewry was shaped by the constrictive set of laws and formal and informal practices in which they were embedded. This amounted to a system of full duties with diminished or no rights, not unlike the one practiced across the border in Romania. The Jews had to bribe their way to obtain what the rest of the population enjoyed as natural rights whilst being expected to fulfil all the duties of an ordinary

[181] Urusov, *Memoirs of a Russian Governor*, p. 84.
[182] Urusov, *Memoirs of a Russian Governor*, p. 83.
[183] Urusov, *Memoirs of a Russian Governor*, p. 54.
[184] Urusov, *Memoirs of a Russian Governor*, p. 79.
[185] Urusov, *Memoirs of a Russian Governor*, p. 54.

citizen. The discriminatory legislation led to further, informal discrimination and abuse, which in turn fed into the vicious circle of corruption. Talking about Ustrugov, the former vice-governor of Bessarabia, and his elaborate system of oppression of the Jews, Prince Urusov noted how 'his inventions for the evasion of the law to the injury of the Jews were, at any rate, not less original than those invented by the Jews themselves for the evasion of the law in their own favour.'[186]

Governor Urusov showed how complaints that the Jewish inhabitants of the Pale of Settlement were congested into a small space were indeed justified, given that settlement was not permitted throughout the Pale but only in designated towns and cities. The result, pointed out Urusov, was an 'artificial overcrowding in towns', with the consequence of dire poverty, cut-throat economic competition and rising social tensions:

> The observer is struck by the number of Jewish signs in Bessarabian towns. The houses along second-rate and back streets are occupied in unbroken succession by stores, big and small, shops of watch-makers, shoe-makers, locksmiths, tinsmiths, tailors, carpenters and so on. All these workers are huddled together in nooks and lanes amid shocking poverty. [...] There are scores of watch-makers in small towns where the townsfolk, as a rule, have no watches. It is hard to understand where all these artisans, frequently making up seventy-five percent of the total population of a city or town, get their orders and patrons. Competition cuts down their earnings to the limit of bare subsistence on so minute a scale as to call in question that theory of wages. The struggle for mere bread breeds mutual hatred and informers, and compels many Jews to resort to the vilest methods to kill off competitors and, as much as possible, to reduce artificial overcrowding in the trades. [...] The result is that in such communities there is a wholesale exodus of the artisans and small merchants of other nationalities from their occupations, and along with this comes the usual complaint against the invasion of the Jews into all branches of industry and commerce, to the exclusion of everybody else. Anti-Jewish discontent grows in proportion to the increasing number of Jews, preparing this way the ground on which pogroms have of late so richly bloomed.[187]

Urusov could not detect any endemic exploitation of Christians by the Jews, but rather remarked on the latter's 'usual traits: knowledge of the market, clever use of credit, quick floating of capital in connection with

[186] Urusov, *Memoirs of a Russian Governor*, p. 33.
[187] Urusov, *Memoirs of a Russian Governor*, pp. 147–148.

small margin of profits'.[188] He also pointed out, following conversations with peasants and rural folk, that those who usually complained about such exploitation were not from among those who were said to be exploited: 'Indeed, the alleged sufferers do not, in most cases, understand those who plead for them, and before the invariably negative answer as to the weight of Jewish oppression can be drawn from the peasants, it has to be made plain to them in what this traditional oppression is supposed to consist.'[189]

The restrictions against Bessarabian Jews were by no means watertight. Interdictions to settle in rural areas, to buy or lease land, to reside in border areas were the subject of negotiation and bribery, the Jews constituting a valuable source of illegal income for the local administration and the meagrely paid police. Thus rather than contest in court the decision of the local police to expel them from the villages, Jewish tradesmen preferred to reach an informal agreement with the police.[190] In the frontier areas, it was cheaper for Jewish merchants to bribe the frontier police, who could arbitrarily decide they did not qualify for a free border pass, rather than apply for an expensive passport.[191]

Land Lease

The administration of great property in Bessarabia was not dissimilar to that of Romania in that great landowners preferred to rent out their estates to middlemen, who in turn sublet them to the local peasants. What follows is Urusov's description of the system:

> In Bessarabia an estate is a share of land stock yielding a large dividend and easily transferrable, a marketable commodity circulating among enterprising persons owing to the rapid upward movement in the price of land. [...] High yields of valuable cereals and proximity to harbour facilities and the frontier line have raised the lease rate of land in Bessarabia to a high level. Fertilizers were seldom used in my time. Farming with stock owned by the farmer was infrequent, except in the northern districts of the province. As a rule, the Bessarabian landowner kept for himself his vineyards and a patch of land; the rest he leased – most of it to a Jew, who subleased it in small lots

---

[188] Urusov, *Memoirs of a Russian Governor*, p. 162.
[189] Urusov, *Memoirs of a Russian Governor*, p. 163.
[190] Urusov, *Memoirs of a Russian Governor*, p. 34.
[191] Urusov, *Memoirs of a Russian Governor*, p. 30.

to peasants. The landowner himself, living in town or abroad, was little in touch with the peasants. Outward display of luxury, enjoyment of the blessings of urban life, the tendency to get much and spend still more – these were the conspicuous traits of the Bessarabian landowners that in Bessarabia robbed the land-ownership of noblemen of its hereditary character and its stability.[192]

Just as in Romania the land-lease system was detrimental to agricultural modernization and was viewed as a speculative business transaction:

> Our frequently changing chance tenant avoids investing his capital for making improvements on the land of another. He carries on his farming in a rapaciously wasteful manner, and at the expiration of his lease he returns the estate to its owner in an exceedingly ruined condition. Bessarabian landowners very often lease their land for long terms without incommoding the tenant by making his tenure conditioned on his cultivating the land with his own stock, on the use of fertilizers or, in general, on the adoption of any definite agricultural system. The Bessarabian tenant is therefore not so much a farmer as he is middleman and a responsible agent for subletting separate sections of the estate to the neighbours in need of land. His object is to get, during his lease term, a maximum amount of differential rent from his peasant sublessees. Such use of land on lease cannot deserve encouragement in any respect. The estates in such cases deteriorate, the relations with the neighbours become still worse and, therefore, most cases of agrarian friction usually centre around lands held on long-term leases by separate persons.[193]

Other contemporary authors such as Arbore remarked on the ploys used by leaseholders to secure cheap work hands for the summer by lending money to peasants over the winter when they were cash strapped and asking to be paid back in labour. The peasants would often fail to do the required work while trying to get on with their own fieldwork and this was the cause of additional conflict.[194] This, however, does not come across as a generalized feature of the leasehold system in Bessarabia and certainly did not lead to preposterous indebtedness such as pledging one's work five years in advance, which happened across the border in Romania.[195]

---

[192] Urusov, *Memoirs of a Russian Governor*, p. 66.
[193] Urusov, *Memoirs of a Russian Governor*, p. 157.
[194] Arbore, *Basarabia*, p. 419.
[195] Ionescu, *Agrarverfassung Rumäniens*, p. 51.

Slightly better administered in terms of use of income were the extensive landed properties that belonged to foreign monasteries. These came into being following historical land grants by Moldavian boyars and princes. As estimated by governor Urusov, these lands represented around 200,000 desiatins and their income was divided into five: two parts went to their foreign beneficiaries, two parts 'were laid aside to carry out the will of the testator in Bessarabia, where the estates were located, as a fund from which the institutions of the local zemstvo received subventions for building schools and hospitals; and the one remaining part covered the expenses of the central and local administrations'.[196]

Jewish Leaseholds

Jewish land lessees were an important feature of land tenure in Bessarabia, with great landowners preferring to rent their estates out to Jews irrespective of whether the former harboured antisemitic feelings or not. The rental process involved intricate strategies of breaking the law by hiring proxies and bogus tenants and bribing local authorities so as to circumvent the laws that said Jews could not buy or take land on lease nor could they reside in the countryside. It was usually rich and influential landowners who could afford the luxury of having a Jewish leaseholder and the illegality of the process rendered the whole business all the more lucrative for the big landowner as the Jewish lessee was thus at their mercy.[197] In addition to being regular and reliable payers, Jewish leaseholders also had the great quality of keeping a low profile and not antagonizing their neighbours. As Urusov pointed out,

> A Jewish tenant runs his farm business in such a way as to avoid any friction with neighbours, and affords no ground for litigation and disputes, endeavouring to settle every difficulty in a peaceful way without resort to the courts or the authorities. A Jew will not collect his debts by such methods as seizing the grain in the stacks, selling his neighbour's property, and the like. He bides his time, jogs the debtor's memory, chooses the right occasion, and gets his bill without the aid of the police or the sheriff. He does not mar the mutual relations of owner and neighbour, and creates no basis for disputes and hostility. On account of all this, I have for example never received or heard any complaints from the people of the province against Jewish

---

[196] Urusov, *Memoirs of a Russian Governor*, pp. 88–89.
[197] *Recueil de Matériaux sur la situation économique des israélites de Russie*, vol. 1, p. 222.

tenants, while we had some litigation in connection with difficulties in which either landowners themselves, or especially non-Jewish tenants, were principals. I think it entirely correct to say that Jewish landlease in Bessarabia is an evil in so far as it is land lease and not because it is Jewish. At any rate, this conclusion will not be questioned either by the landowners or by the peasants of Bessarabia.[198]

A similar point was made by Dobrogeanu-Gherea in the case of Jewish *arendași* in Romania:

[the Jewish *arendaș*, unlike his Romanian counterpart] is unable to turn to account his full power of exploitation because of his lack of political rights and because of his being a Jew. His position is inferior also in relation to those who are being exploited, for whom he is not a boyar, nor is he an upstart (*ciocoi*), but just a Jew; it is inferior also in relation to the administration, whose lower-level employees he is admittedly adept at placating, but whose high-level employees remain hostile to him. His position is also made difficult by the antisemitic current, which is so strong, by the hostile public opinion and by the press, which is antisemite in great proportion; but, most of all, it is the regime itself [that makes his position difficult] in that it, on the one hand, gives him all the advantages of neoserfdom, while on the other hand using his Jewishness to mount a diversion and turn him into a scapegoat for the regime's sins. For all these reasons, the Jewish *arendaș* finds it much more difficult to exploit *á outrance* and not because he does not wish it – of course he does – but because he is under too much supervision, so he can only push it so far but not as far as the Christian *arendaș* can (*nu poate să întindă prea mult coarda, căci la el se rupe mult mai curând decât la colegul creștin*). If he feeds rotten cheese to the peasants, a Jewish *arendaș* risks getting bad press about it from Liberal or Conservative newspapers; whereas the *arendaș* who is a voter for the first electoral college and an MP can give his peasants even worse cheese and he will never be denounced by the newspapers or will, instead, be praised for giving them splendid Dutch cheese, and this because the newspaper is Liberal or Conservative and the *arendaș* MP is either or both.[199]

All in all the Jews owned 3.9% of the total cultivable land in Bessarabia and took on lease another 5.7%, so that the total of land cultivated by Jews

[198] Urusov, *Memoirs of a Russian Governor*, p. 159.
[199] Dobrogeanu-Gherea, *Neoiobăgia*, p. 182.

was around 9.6%, which was less in proportion to their numbers (11.65% of the total population of the province).[200]

Local Initiatives

In Hungary there were local initiatives that improved the condition of the local peasantry and made a difference within a narrow circle of social and economic relations, but, with some exceptions, these never reverberated upwards to the centre or sideways to the neighbouring communities. Thus in multi-ethnic Transylvania (eastern Hungary) in the Székely[201] counties there existed initiative (state-led and private) as regards improvement and modernization of production techniques: state help was available with important sums of money invested for improving the local livestock, farms using manure were encouraged, agricultural schools were set up. Trips were organized by the local authorities to the Saxon[202] counties where groups of Székely small farmers learnt about the latest developments in cattle breeding and vegetable growing.[203] Both the Székely and the Saxons were historically colonized and privileged communities. The Saxons in particular were a success story in the region, with high rates of literacy and the necessary wealth and know-how to tap into the latest agricultural techniques and make full use of new trends in market demand (extensive use of fertilizers and emphasis on dairy and vegetable farming). The Romanian-inhabited counties of Transylvania had the lowest rates of literacy and correspondingly low levels of development (the old rotation system of land cultivation was retained here, use of fertilizers and modern technologies was not common, the cultivation staple remained maize crops).

This reinforces Held's view of the effects of land reform in Hungary: emancipation did create the premises of modernization and within two generations of the emancipation progress was made in Hungarian agriculture, but the distribution of accumulated wealth saw huge variations from east to west. As Held points out, 'changes occurred at the most rapid rate in western Hungary, while the eastern areas were showing a slow, sluggish

---

[200] *Recueil de Matériaux sur la situation économique des israélites de Russie*, vol. 1, p. 225.

[201] The Székely people were a colonized population speaking an old dialect of Hungarian, who were encouraged to settle within the Carpathian arc by medieval Hungarian kings and functioned as border guards.

[202] German-speaking population who settled in Transylvania as colonists in the medieval period.

[203] Nagy, *A magyar mezőgazdaság regionális szerkezete a 20. század elején*, pp. 262–266.

progress. On the other hand, half a century of capitalist development left the north-eastern and eastern regions practically untouched. The latter regions continued to use production methods characteristic of the feudal age, although there was some progress in the adoption of power tools such as the steel plough and mechanical threshers. The differences in developmental levels thus not only continued to exist, but in some instances they were even aggravated.'[204] Thus the percentage of two- or three-field system usage was, by 1908, 41.4% in Transylvania and 19.6% in the Banat.[205]

The one movement in Hungarian agriculture that spread to all ethnic groups was the cooperative movement. As Attila Hunyadi has shown, before the First World War 'there were approximately 800 national cooperatives organized mainly in their own national centres.'[206] Given the endemic suspicion between the Magyar elites and the non-Magyar political leaders, these cooperatives were organized along national lines and as independent networks, with the notable involvement of the Orthodox Church in the case of the Serbian population and of the Catholic Church in support of Slovak cooperatives.[207] More often than not, the resulting banks and credit cooperatives had an explicit political aim, as in the case of the Romanian Ardeleanca Bank, whose director stated that 'they had the duty to regain the Romanian small-owners (peasants) out of the sphere of influence of Hungarian and Saxon banks'.[208] As Hungarian franchise was limited at the time and based on property credentials, Romanian political leaders found in this cooperative system the most effective way of creating a peasant middle class that would qualify to vote and thus strengthen Romanian politics in Hungary.[209] Similarly, Saxon land-acquisition cooperatives bought up Hungarian estates and divided them among their co-nationals thus 'defending and increasing Saxon national property and creating social protection for the national community'.[210] The additional incentive for setting up cooperatives and banks was, as the Hungarian Minister of Commerce put it in a report to the Prime Minister, the fact

[204] Joseph Held (Ed.), *The Modernization of Agriculture: Rural Transformation in Hungary, 1848–1975*, Columbia University Press, Boulder, Colo., 1980, p. 98.

[205] Held, ibid., p. 101.

[206] Hunyadi, *Cooperative Networks*, p. 23.

[207] Hunyadi, *Cooperative Networks*, pp. 23–24.

[208] Hunyadi, *Cooperative Networks*, p. 26.

[209] Hunyadi, *Cooperative Networks*, p. 48.

[210] Hunyadi, *Cooperative Networks*, p. 34.

that, 'as commercial institutions, according to the principles of economic liberalism, they could avoid state control'.[211]

In Romania, there was no interest among the political elites for improving the plight of the peasantry as the former were already masters in their own country and needed no reinforcement of their electoral powerbase. On the contrary, a strong peasant class would have posed a threat to their vested interests as great landowners. There were, nevertheless, sporadic, isolated initiatives aimed at improving the peasants' standard of living and modernizing agriculture. The most successful and much touted project was conducted on the Romanian Crown Domains (a collection of large estates scattered across the country and belonging to the royal family). Their administrator, Ion Kalinderu, a progressive lawyer and philanthropist, introduced the latest agricultural technology (constantly visiting and taking notes from prosperous estates in Austria-Hungary), built model farms and strove to raise the quality of life of the rural population (better housing, education and medical facilities, popular banks).[212] Others such as the Moldavian landowner Calimachi were inclined to 'experiment' with leasing land directly to the peasants,[213] as opposed to the common practice of leasing one's estate to an *arendaș*, or estate lessee. These, however, constituted the exception rather than the rule and failed to set an example for the bulk of great landowners, who continued to rely on traditional peasant labour and tools rather than engage in intensive agriculture. As Andrew Janos put it, the Romanian *boyars* were

> an economically declining class whose members were searching desperately for alternatives to economic entrepreneurship. After 1848, these alternatives were found for, as the lesser boyars moved into the apparatus of state to become political rather than economic entrepreneurs, the great landowners embraced the institution of neo-serfdom in an overall arrangement that recognized a market in grain but not in land and labour.[214]

[211] Hunyadi, *Cooperative Networks*, pp. 50–51.

[212] Narcisa Maria Mitu, 'Aspecte din viața și activitatea lui Ion Kalinderu', pp. 252–256, in *Oltenia. Studii. Documente. Cercetări*, Seria IV, nr. 2, 2014, Arhivele Naționale Serviciul Județean Dolj, Editura Sitech, Craiova, 2014: http://www.arhivelenationale.ro/images/custom/file/Revista%20OLTENIA%20pentru%20editura.pdf (Accessed on 29.07.2015)

[213] Andrei Oțetea; Ion Popescu-Puțuri (eds), *Documente privind marea răscoală a țăranilor din 1907* (henceforth quoted as Documente), București, Editura Academiei Republicii Socialiste România, 1977-, Vol. 2, pp. 240–241.

[214] Andrew Janos, 'Modernization and Decay in Historical Perspective: The Case of Romania' in Kenneth Jowitt (Ed.), *Social Change in Romania 1860–1940*, Berkeley, California, 1978, p. 83.

The attitude of the land-owning elite in Bessarabia as regards land cultivation contrasted with that of their peers in Romania. The Zemstvo, or Bessarabian provincial assembly, who were in their great majority recruited from among the great landowners, showed interest in modernization and technology. Governor Urusov had words of praise for the activity of the Bessarabian provincial zemstvo, who for all their inclination to squander money on quixotic projects, evinced a 'general character of enlightenment and progress', while the district zemstvos were instrumental in 'developing the fruitful activity of the local public institutions'.[215] As early as the period 1872 to 1875 the district zemstvos started popularizing modern agricultural tools and machines, the Orhei zemstvo leading the way by setting up a tool warehouse stocked with German implements, which were sold to peasants for cash or on credit.[216]

As the memoirs of the American agricultural scientist Louis Guy Michael testify, the Bessarabian zemstvo were interested in the latest techniques in agriculture and were willing to invite specialists to teach them these new methods. The inclination of the Bessarabian zemstvo towards agricultural modernization can be explained by the situation in which the great landowners in Bessarabia found themselves after the land reform of 1869: unlike Romanian landowners, Bessarabian landowners could not rely on the forced labour of the local peasantry as the latter had received enough land to render them independent of the great landowners. So the only way in which they could make up for the dearth of work hands and continue to draw profit from their estates was to bring in foreign workers (which they did) and to invest in technology that would increase production and intensify cultivation. When it came to sharing this with the local peasants, most of the landowners were strongly opposed. As L.G. Michael put it, 'it was a distinct shock to me that many of the landed gentry were openly opposed to the peasants in "their village" being taught how to grow more corn on their own little plots, claiming that this would make it more difficult to get them to work on the fields of the estates'.[217]

Across the border in Transylvania, the Banat and Bukovina, the peasants also gained in an indirect way from the general political friction between ethnic groups. One of the consequences of this national struggle

[215] Urusov, *Memoirs of a Russian Governor*, p. 71.

[216] Arbore, *Basarabia*, pp. 422–423.

[217] Louis Guy Michael, *More Corn for Bessarabia. Russian Experience 1910–1917*, Michigan State University Press, 1983, p. 35.

in both Austria and Hungary was the creation of a network of national banks.[218] In the Tsarist Empire land reforms were accompanied by the setting up of a rural bank (*Banque Paysanne*), which the Romanian authorities were tempted to introduce in Romania as well but eventually discarded as too 'socialist', too revolutionary.[219]

Peasant Agency Between Political Representation, Protest and Emigration

The three states under review had limited or no franchise (with the exception of the Austrian half of the Austro-Hungarian Monarchy, where universal male franchise was introduced in 1906) until after the First World War. As such, although the peasantry was invoked in political discourse, they did not wield much political power.

In Romania, where the political system was based on the succession to power of two main parties—Conservatives and Liberals, who held polar opposite views on the peasant question, peasant interest was demagogically invoked in order to consolidate or, as the case may be, to create political capital. The Liberals challenged the status-quo of a latifundia-dominated economy and encouraged the formation of a middle stratum of well-off peasantry and the development of autochthonous industry. For all their reformist energy, they were however completely unrealistic in their expectations and their policies: in a country where the overwhelming majority of the population belonged to the peasant class, which in its great majority were barely above subsistence level; where the peasant 'middle class' was so slim as to be something of a mythical beast; where domestic industry was so anaemic as to hardly function as an occupational alternative for proletarianized peasants; where moreover legal stipulations were still in place to prevent the ordinary peasant from selling or mortgaging his land—one cannot seriously have expected that the legislation and setting up of peasant banks and cooperatives, exclusively aimed at the mythical well-off middle peasant, would actually work. This, compounded with political instability and lack of continuity (Liberals and Conservatives came to power in rapid

---

[218] Anders Blomqvist, *Economic Nationalizing in the Ethnic Borderlands of Hungary and Romania. Inclusion, Exclusion and Annihilation in Szatmár/Satu-mare 1867–1944*, Stockholm Studies in History 101, Doctoral thesis in History at Stockholm University, Sweden, 2014, p. 114.

[219] HHStA, Wien, Karton 39, PA, XVIII, Bericht no. 44 B, Sinaia, am 6. September 1907, from Schönburg to Aehrenthal, p. 325 (recto/verso).

succession cancelling each other's policies) as well as an inability to tackle the pressing problems of the majority of the peasantry, led to the explosive situation that blew up in spring 1907.

In Hungary the peasantry was represented from 1890 onwards by the Social Democratic Party. As the great majority of the population in Hungary was employed in agriculture, the socialists had to widen their political scope to include the rural proletariat and poor peasants. They thus formulated programmes demanding the '12-hour working day, later to be reduced to 8 hours, the abolition of unpaid labour, payments in cash, equal wages for men and women and the end of child labour under the age of 14'. More radical demands included 'distribution of land and common ownership'.[220] The socialist movement resulted in a wave of rural strikes, which peaked in summer 1897. The outcome was the very opposite of the one intended: the Hungarian state closed ranks and rendered its policing system all the more efficient.

How much of a say did the peasantry have in government legislation? In none of the three countries did the peasantry have direct influence on legislative or policy processes. There were however indirect or illegal ways of pushing for reform. These too differed according to context.

In Austrian Bukovina, amidst general official concern for the pauperization of the peasantry, there were attempts on the part of both the authorities as well as some of the local landed elites to protect peasant interest and represent it in parliament. We find for instance for the year 1897 a complaint from a Polish landowner that Baron Nikolaus Mustatza, Austrian MP of Romanian nationality, 'had taken upon himself, as usual when it came to opposing Polish landowners, to represent the interests of the Romanian peasant community', who were in litigation with the said Polish landowner over pastureland.[221] In 1900/1901, another Bukovinian landowner and MP, Dr. Lupu, was proposing at a conference convened to discuss the problem of peasant mass emigration that the illiterate peasants' ability to take out mortgages (*Wechselfähigkeit*) should be curtailed and legal contracts should be notarized in an attempt to prevent peasants from mortgaging their land and losing it.[222]

---

[220] Warriner, *Contrasts in Emerging Societies,* pp. 108–109.

[221] ANR, Fondul Guvernământul Bucovinei, Ministerul de Interne, Mapa 134/5, German translation of Polish letter from Laura z Ortynski Kuliczkowski, dated 12.10.1897.

[222] ANR, Fondul Guvernământul Bucovinei, Ministerul de Interne, Mapa 75/II, 1902 report from the Bukovinian government to the Ministry of Justice, pp. 1–2.

In Hungary not only did peasant movements fail to force through favourable legislation, but the unrest and rural agitation they fostered had the contrary effect: even more restrictive legislation was passed, which made protests illegal. An 1898 law, which came to be nicknamed the Slave Law, laid down very strict working conditions for agricultural labourers and stipulated that 'strikes, meetings and even complaints were forbidden, on penalty of severe fines or imprisonment'.[223]Despite this law, rural unrest and strikes persisted and became an annual feature of the Hungarian agricultural calendar. The most powerful form of protest, however, was what has been called 'the emigration revolution'—massive rural emigration was the most influential form of expressing discontent in Hungary. As government official correspondence shows, this was a major cause for concern with Hungarian authorities. From Transylvania only 'between 1901 and 1914 nearly 210,000 persons departed – in all 10% of Transylvania's population of 2.5 million'.[224]

In Romania the peasants had even less direct agency over processes of land reform. The widespread system of land rental by great capitalist entrepreneurs (many of them foreigners, but by no means all of them) in combination with a dysfunctional and corrupt administration posed insurmountable obstacles to the feedback loop between the countryside and the state. With no safety valves in place (emigration was *not* an option given the costs involved, lack of know-how and infrastructure, and the crucial legal interdiction on selling land within 30+ years of acquisition), social tensions eventually came to a head in spring 1907, when the devastating peasant uprising shook up the state and threatened its very existence. It was only after the shock therapy of 1907 that some improvements were made and some of the most egregious exploitative elements of the system of land tenure were removed. Full land distribution and the dismantlement of the great latifundia only came after the First World War in 1921.

In the Bessarabian borderland of the Tsarist Empire there was, as pointed out above, room for manoeuvre for the peasantry as they benefitted from the antagonism between provincial elites and imperial authorities. It was not in the interest of the Tsarist authorities to grant too much power to the local elites, who tried to get as much out of their peasants as possible; at the same time a relatively happy local peasantry meant a stable secure borderland, which constituted a priority with central imperial

---

[223]Warriner, *Contrasts in Emerging Societies,* p. 109.
[224]Verdery, *Transylvanian Villagers,* p. 221.

authorities. Progressive land fragmentation eventually affected the Bessarabian peasantry just as it did their peers across the triple frontier. The legal stipulations regarding the limits of subdivision ensured that the plots of land per head of family did not shrink below two hectares. Well-off rural inhabitants such as the *răzeși* and *mazili* also acted towards preventing land fragmentation by changing inheritance practices (e.g. the introduction of the *minorat*, that is, the practice whereby land was inherited by the youngest male offspring of a given family) and emigration (internal, within Bessarabia, or elsewhere in the Tsarist Empire: in the neighbouring provinces but also as far as Yekaterinodar and the Caucasus).[225]

Emigration

One of the great differences between the agricultural systems around the triple frontier lay in the possibility of emigration. In both Tsarist Bessarabia and Austria-Hungary emigration, with its infrastructure of agents, travel companies and active recruitment campaigns, was a common practice. As Gur Alroey pointed out in the case of Jewish emigration from Bessarabia, the existence of a considerable number of ICA information bureaus in the Pale of Settlement was a vital factor in their decision to emigrate.[226] Among the Romanian peasantry in Bessarabia the above-mentioned practice of *minorat* (bestowing the land onto the youngest son) made the remaining siblings available for emigration. Across the border in Hungary emigration took on such proportions among the peasantry that the government came to fear a virtual demographic haemorrhage from the countryside and, although having initially allowed emigration, it changed its view by the beginning of the twentieth century and actively sought to put a stop to it.[227] The Austrian half of the Habsburg Empire had the right to emigration enshrined in its constitution and as such put up no barriers against it.[228] In Romania, by contrast, the government kept tabs on the comings

---

[225] Arbore, *Basarabia*, pp. 135–136.

[226] Gur Alroey, *Bread to Eat and Clothes to Wear: Letters from Jewish Migrants in the Early 20th Century*, Wayne State University Press, Detroit, 2011, pp. 28, 39.

[227] Katalin Stráner, 'Emigration Agents and the Agency of the Urban Press: Approaches to Transatlantic Migration in Hungary, 1880s–1914', *Journal of Migration History* 2 (2016), 352–374, pp. 355, 357.

[228] Gregor M. Kowalski, 'Constitutional Liberty in the Area of Emigration in Austria. Activities of Emigration Agencies in Lodomeria and Galicia', in Kaziemierz Baran (Ed.),

and goings of emigration agents from the neighbouring countries, whom it treated as a pest, debarring them from entering the country or intercepting their letters.[229] Romania did have lively internal migration, but international migration was negligible and in stark contrast to the emigration numbers from neighbouring countries such as Austria-Hungary. The great majority of émigrés from Romania were Jews.[230]

*   *   *

This cross-border comparison of peasant condition around the triple frontier between Romania, Austria-Hungary and Tsarist Russia has sought to foreground the structural differences of land reform in the three countries. These differences can be brought to bear on an explanation as to why Romania experienced the social implosion of 1907 and its neighbours did not. A general survey of the main indicators of prosperity and development shows that the borderlands around the triple frontier were fairly similar in terms of literacy rates, patterns of land tenure and level of agricultural know-how. All around the frontier there were illiterate peasants who engaged in subsistence agriculture, cultivated their lands as their forefathers had done hundreds of years before, had little incentive to improve their ways and were likely to be on the losing side in the new money economy. However, the broader context, the social and in particular administrative structures, in which this type of agricultural 'poverty' was embedded made a world of difference. In none of the three borderlands did emancipation in itself automatically lead to prosperity and modernization, but it does appear from the analysis in this chapter that, while there were winners and losers of the transition from the manorial system to capitalist agriculture, in some of the border provinces the peasants were not systemically doomed to poverty and there were ways of getting by or, if all else failed, there was at least the possibility of emigration. The legal framework as well as the gulf between the theory and practice of land reform spelt the difference between genuine emancipation, though no agricultural utopia (in Austria-Hungary and Tsarist Bessarabia) and

Constitutional Developments of the Habsburg Empire in the Last Decades before its Fall, Jagiellonian University Press, 2014, p. 61.

[229] ANR, Arhiva CC al PCR, Fond 59/6066, pp. 5, 7, 35, 88.

[230] Ulf Brunnbauer, *Globalizing Southeastern Europe: Emigrants, America, and the State since the Late Nineteenth Century*, Lexington Books, Lanham, 2016, pp. 47–48; Scraba, *Starea socială săteanului*, p. 190.

neo-serfdom (Romania). By 1907 the average peasant was better off living in either the Austro-Hungarian borderlands or in Tsarist Bessarabia than in Romania. This was painfully recognized by Romanian authors of the time, the most poignant indictment coming from historian Radu Rosetti:

> We conclude therefore that, out of all the countries where Romanians lived, it was in independent Romania, the very country where Romanians should have lived at most ease and enjoyed a decent life, that the bulk of the population, who formed the strength of the nation, were worst mistreated, most disenfranchised and stripped of their ancient rights over the land which they had soaked with their blood and sweat.[231]

BIBLIOGRAPHY

Gur Alroey, *Bread to Eat and Clothes to Wear: Letters from Jewish Migrants in the Early 20th Century*, Wayne State University Press, Detroit, 2011

Zamfir C. Arbore, *Basarabia în secolul XIX*, Institutul de arte grafice Carol Göbl, Bucureşti, 1898

Victor Babeş, 'Fragmente din lucrarea *Boalele ţăranului român* (1906)' in Ioan Scurtu and Sorin Teodorescu (Eds.), *1907 în viziunea contemporanilor*, Editura Semne, Bucureşti, 2007

Constantin Bărbulescu, *România medicilor. Medici, ţărani şi igienă rurală în România de la 1860 la 1910*, Humanitas, Bucureşti, 2015

Lajos Beck, *A magyar földbirtok megoszlása. Agrár-statisztikai tanulmány*, Pallas Irodalmi és nyomdai Résvénytársaság, Budapest, 1918

Anders Blomqvist, *Economic Nationalizing in the Ethnic Borderlands of Hungary and Romania. Inclusion, Exclusion and Annihilation in Szatmár/Satu-mare 1867–1944*, Stockholm Studies in History 101, Doctoral thesis in History at Stockholm University, Sweden, 2014

Martin Broszat, 'Von der Kulturnation zur Volksgruppe: Die nationale Stellung der Juden in der Bukowina im 19. und 20. Jahrhundert', *Historische Zeitschrift*, Bd. 200, H. 3 (Jun., 1965)

Ulf Brunnbauer, *Globalizing Southeastern Europe: Emigrants, America, and the State Since the Late Nineteenth Century*, Lexington Books, Lanham, 2016

Alois Brusatti (Ed.), *Die Habsburgermonarchie 1848–1918*, Band I: Die Wirtschaftliche Entwicklung, Verlag der Österreichischen Akademie der Wissenschaften, Vienna, 1973

---

[231] Rosetti, *Pentru ce s-au răsculat ţăranii?* quoted in Stere, *Publicistică*, p. 278.

Raul Cârstocea, 'Uneasy Twins? The Entangled Histories of Jewish Emancipation and Antisemitism in Romania and Hungary, 1866–1913', *Slovo*, Vol. 21, No. 2, 2009

Parteniu Cosma, *Răscoala țărănească în România*, Tiparul Tipografiei Arhidiecezane, Sibiu, 1907

G.D. Creangă, *Grundbesitzverteilung und Bauernfrage in Rumänien*, Erster Teil, Verlag von Duncker und Humbolt, Leipzig, 1907

Sorin Cristescu (Ed.), *Carol I. Corespondența personală (1878–1912)*, Triton, București, 2005

Maria Danilov (Coord.), *Nobilimea basarabeană în epoca reformelor din imperiul rus*, Academia de Științe a Moldovei, Chișinău, 2013

Constantin Dobrogeanu–Gherea, *Neoiobăgia. Studiu economico-sociologic al problemei noastre agrare*, Editura Librăriei Socec et comp, București, 1910

Eliyahu Feldman and Theodor Lavi, 'Bessarabia' in Michael Berenbaum and Fred Skolnik (Eds.), *Encyclopedia Judaica*, Vol. 3, 2nd Edition, Macmillan Reference USA, Detroit, 2007

János Gyurgyák, *A Zsidókérdés Magyarországon*, Osiris Kiadó, Budapest, 2001

Mariana Hausleitner, *Deutsche und Juden in Bessarabien. 1814–1914. Zur Mindenheitenpolitik Russlands und Großrumäniens*, IKGS Verlag, München, 2005

Heimatskunde der Bucovina, Verlag von H. Pardini, Czernowitz, 1872

Joseph Held (Ed.), *The Modernization of Agriculture: Rural Transformation in Hungary, 1848–1975*, Columbia University Press, Boulder, CO, 1980

Geoffrey Hosking, *Russia and the Russians from Earliest Times to 2001*, Penguin, London, 2002

Attila Gábor Hunyadi, *Cooperative Networks in Transylvania Belonging to Hungary and Romania. Nation-Building and Modernization by Cooperatives in Transylvania as Part of Hungary (1867–1918) and Romania (1918–1940)*, LAP Lambert Academic Publishing, Saarbrücken, 2016

Carol Iancu, *Evreii din România (1866–1919). De la Excludere la Emancipare*, Trans. C. Litman, Editura Hasefer, Bucharest, 1996

Dimitrie Ionescu, *Agrarverfassung Rumäniens. Ihre Geschichte und Ihre Reform*, Verlag von Duncker & Humblot, Leipzig, 1909

Andrew Janos, 'Modernization and Decay in Historical Perspective: The Case of Romania' in Kenneth Jowitt (Ed.), *Social Change in Romania 1860–1940*, Berkeley, California, 1978

Charles Jelavich and Barbara Jelavich, *The Establishment of the Balkan National States, 1804–1920*, University of Washington Press, Seattle and London, 2000

John Kaba, *Politico-Economic Review of Bessarabia*, June 30, 1919

Charles King, *Moldovans: Romania, Russia and the Politics of Culture*, Hoover Institution Press, Stanford, CA, 1999

Gregor M. Kowalski, 'Constitutional Liberty in the Area of Emigration in Austria. Activities of Emigration Agencies in Lodomeria and Galicia', in Kaziemierz Baran (Ed.), *Constitutional Developments of the Habsburg Empire in the Last Decades Before Its Fall*, Jagiellonian University Press, 2014

N.V. Leonescu, *Anul 1907. Răscoala țăranilor*, Atelierele grafice "Lumina Moldovei", Iași, 1924

A Magyar Korona országainak Mezőgazdasági Statisztikája, Negyed Rész, Pesti Könyvnyomda-Részvénytársaság, Budapest, 1900

Magyar Statisztikai Évkönyv, Új folyam 1907, Az Atheneum irodalmi és nyomdai részvénytársulat könyvnyomdája, Budapest, 1909

Marea răscoală a țăranilor din 1907, Editura Republicii Socialiste România, București, 1967

Andrei Markevich and Ekaterina Zhuravskaya, 'Economic Effects of the Abolition of Serfdom: Evidence from the Russian Empire', Document de travail (Docweb) no. 1502, Centre pour la recherche economique et ses applications: http://www.cepremap.fr/depot/docweb/docweb1502.pdf (Accessed on 19.02.2016)

Em. de Martonne, *What I Have Seen in Bessarabia*, Paris, 1919

William O. McCagg, *A History of Habsburg Jews, 1670–1918*, Indiana University Press, Bloomington, 1989

Louis Guy Michael, *More Corn for Bessarabia. Russian Experience 1910–1917*, Michigan State University Press, 1983

Narcisa Maria Mitu, 'Aspecte din viața și activitatea lui Ion Kalinderu', pp. 252–256, in *Oltenia. Studii. Documente. Cercetări*, Seria IV, nr. 2, Arhivele Naționale Serviciul Județean Dolj, Editura Sitech, Craiova, 2014: http://www.arhivele-nationale.ro/images/custom/file/Revista%20OLTENIA%20pentru%20editura.pdf (Accessed on 29.07.2015)

Mariann Nagy, *A magyar mezőgazdaság regionális szerkezete a 20. század elején*, Gondolat Kiadó, Budapest, 2003

Mariann Nagy, 'Interaction Between Institutional Change and Market Forces in Hungary in the Second Half of the 19th Century', Conference Paper Given at the Rural Studies Conference: http://www.ruralhistory2013.org/papers/3.7.3._Nagy.pdf (Accessed on 23 June 2016)

I. Nistor, *Românii și rutenii în Bucovina*, Librăriile Socec, București, 1915

Andrei Oișteanu, *Imaginea evreului în cultura română. Studiu de imagologie in context est-central european*, 2nd Edition, Humanitas, București, 2004

Andrei Oțetea and Ion Popescu-Puțuri (Eds.), *Documente privind marea răscoală a țăranilor din 1907*, Editura Academiei Republicii Socialiste România, București, 1977

Raphael Patai, *The Jews of Hungary: History, Culture, Psychology*, Wayne State University Press, Detroit, 1996

Ion G. Pelivan, *Bessarabia Under the Russian Rule*, Imprimerie J. Charpentier, Paris, 1920

Ion G. Pelivan, *The Economic State of Bessarabia*, Imprimerie des Arts et Sports, Paris, 1920

Ion G. Pelivan, *The Movement and Increase of Population in Bessarabia from 1812 to 1918*, Imprimerie des arts et des sports, Paris, 1920

Julianna Puskás, 'Die Kapitalistische Grosspachten in Ungarn' in Vilmos Sandor and Peter Hanak (Eds.), *Studien zur Geschichte der Oesterreichisch-ungarischen Monarchie*, Budapest, 1961

Julianna Puskás, 'Zsidó haszonbérlők a magyarországi mezőgazdaság fejlődésének folyamatában: Az 1850-es évektől 1935-ig', *Századok*, Vol. 126, (1992), 1

Recueil des Matériaux sur la situation économique des israélites de Russie, Vol. 1, Jewish Colonization Association, Alcan, Paris, 1906–1908

Klaus Richter, 'Kišinev or Linkuva? Rumors and Threats Against Jews in Lithuania in 1903', *Revista Română de Studii Baltice și Nordice*, Vol. 3, No. 1, 2011

Radu Rosetti, *Pentru ce s-au răsculat țăranii*, Atelierele grafice Socec, București, 1907

G.D. Scraba, *Starea socială a săteanului. După ancheta privitoare anului 1905, îndeplinită cu ocaziunea expozițiunii generale române din 1906 de către secțiunea de economie socială*, Institutul de arte grafice Carol Göbl, București, 1907

Valeriu Scutelnic, 'Regulamentul despre relațiile agrare ale țăranilor regiunii Basarabia', *Revista de Istorie a Moldovei*, No.1: 2007, http://www.history.asm. md/index.php/ro/publicatii/reviste/398--revista-de-istorie-a-moldovei-nr-1-69-2007 (Accessed 29.07.2015)

Hugh Seton-Watson, *Eastern Europe Between the Wars 1918–1941*, Harper Torchbooks, 1967

John W. Slocum, 'Who, and When, Were the Inorodtsy? The Evolution of the Category of "Aliens" in Imperial Russia', *Russian Review*, Vol. 57, No. 2 (Apr., 1998)

Statistisches Jahrbuch des Herzogtums Bukowina für das Jahr 1908, II. Jahrgang, Zusammengestellt und veröffentlicht vom statistischen Landesamte des Herzogtums Bukowina, Czernowitz, 1911

Constantin Stere, *Publicistică*, Editura Universul, Chișinău, 2006

Katalin Stráner, 'Emigration Agents and the Agency of the Urban Press: Approaches to Transatlantic Migration in Hungary, 1880s–1914', *Journal of Migration History*, Vol. 2, 2016, 352–374

Zoltán Szász, 'The Social Stratification of the Peasantry', *History of Transylvania*, Volume III. From 1830 to 1919: http://mek.oszk.hu/03400/03407/html/383.html (Accessed 30.07.2015)

S.D. Urusov, *Memoirs of a Russian Governor*, Trans. Herman Rosenthal, Harper and Brothers Publishers, London and New York, 1908

Katherine Verdery, *Transylvanian Villagers. Three Centuries of Political, Economic, and Ethnic Change*, University of California Press, Berkeley, Los Angeles and London, 1983

Doreen Warriner (Ed.), *Contrasts in Emerging Societies. Readings in the Social and Economic History of South-Eastern Europe in the Nineteenth Century*, Indiana University Press, Bloomington, 1965

CHAPTER 5

Eyes of the State

ROMANIA

The high combustibility of a social system does not depend only on oppressive poverty, exploitative relations, long unaddressed grievances and the lack of safety valves; it is also a function of the policing capabilities of the state, whether this means infrastructure, personnel, professional ethos or efficiency of crisis management strategies. A major social explosion occurs when a state becomes dysfunctional, when a regime has come to the end of its resources and loses its grip on reality and on its own population; or, alternatively, when a regime is so young that it has yet to acquire a grip. In 1907 Romania the poor grip of the state over its population was a consequence of fledgling statehood. Like all states that broke off from the Balkan fringes of the Ottoman empire, Romania was a young state, which, internally, was still finding its feet and, in terms of foreign policy, was eager to prove itself worthy of its freshly acquired state independence. The greatest challenge for Balkan fledgling states was to be taken seriously by the Great Powers and to pursue their own national interests rather than become mere pawns of neighbouring empires. Domestic problems were therefore addressed in earnest only when they started to affect the country's international image.

By 1907 Romania had been a unified state for less than 50 years and an independent one for 30 years. Basic laws and institutions had to be built from scratch, more often than not on a foreign model and, most importantly, this had to be done rapidly and artificially. Several spurts of

© The Author(s) 2018
I. Marin, *Peasant Violence and Antisemitism in Early Twentieth-Century Eastern Europe*,
https://doi.org/10.1007/978-3-319-76069-8_5

institutional development occurred throughout the nineteenth century. Vital changes were initiated through the Organic Statutes introduced to the Danubian Principalities under Russian occupation in the early 1830s. Following unification in 1859 a new wave of reforms swept over the country under Prince Cuza (secularization of church lands, mass education, land reform); finally, the most intensive legislative and institutional overhaul accompanied the rule of Prince Carol I of Hohenzollern (from 1881 King of Romania): Belgian-style constitution (1866), the first universities, consolidated army, gendarmerie law, several additions to the original law of land reform, all done with the enthusiasm of the neophyte as part of what Dobrogeanu-Gherea called a 'mania for legislation'.[1] The wholesale import of laws, institutions and mores was not without its critics, the most outspoken of them being the Conservative Titu Maiorescu, who denounced them as 'forms without content' (*forme fără fond*). Later on, in the early twentieth century this great foundational effort was vindicated by literary critic Eugen Lovinescu, who argued that simulation of foreign models was instrumental in stimulating an autochthonous content.

Given the fledgling nature of the Romanian state, how much did the state authorities know about what was going on in their own country? What did the state 'feelers' tell the central authorities about turn-of-the-century Romania? If one judges by the reports of the *Siguranţă*, or secret police, the place was crawling with anarchists, socialists, and foreign agents throughout the first decade of the twentieth century. This was not surprising given that the Macedonian question had been raging for more than a decade south of the Danube; political assassination at the hand of anarchists was at the order of the day; and by 1905 the best part of the Tsarist Empire was in revolution. Revolution and revolutionaries were very topical, but for several decades another kind of revolution had been in the making in their own backyard and the Romanian authorities were oblivious to it. Peasants crop up on the agenda of the secret police only after 1907. There had been periodical flurries of peasant violence and unrest throughout the 1880s, 1890s and early years of the twentieth century and yet the secret police did not consider the peasantry a potential threat to state security.[2]

---

[1] Henry L. Roberts, *Rumania. Political Problems of an Agrarian State*, New Haven, Yale University Press, 1951, p. 20.

[2] Alin Spânu, *Istoria serviciilor de informaţii/contrainformaţii româneşti în perioada 1919–1945*, Iaşi, Demiurg, 2010.

Infrastructure of a Fledgling State

Romanian statesmen kept a hold on their country through prefects and the police. This control was mainly aimed at securing electoral advantage, with the party in power deciding the fate of elections.[3] And therein lay one of the greatest problems of the fledgling Romanian state: vital civil services such as the administration and the police were hopelessly politicized. Civil servants were not chosen on the basis of their skills and qualifications but were party appointees. Repeated criticism of this problem comes across in the German General Consul's correspondence, who viewed it as a particularly harmful phenomenon and as an important factor in the escalation of the uprising:

> The greatest lack of the system is that of a qualified and professional civil service (*geschulten und pflichtbewußten Beamtenstandes*). The civil servants are here chosen according to party interest and they are mere agents of Mr Cantacuzino. Thus they have little concern for important economic interests; instead they are keen on whether the conservative club in their county leans towards Mr Take Ionescu or if the Liberal club has new members. The Liberals are no better. A classic example is that the current Liberal government have asked the local president of the Liberal club to take over the Prefecture until a new Liberal prefect is appointed! I have repeatedly talked with Romanian politicians about the possibility of creating a permanent class of civil servants, who would be qualified for the job and familiar with their duties. They always replied that, if it had not been for the constant Damoclean sword of instant dismissal without a pension hanging above their heads, people would not do absolutely anything.[4]

'The most important task of the future ruler', reiterated Kiderlen in a later report, 'is, in my humble opinion, the creation of a professional and politically independent class of civil servants, who would only be subordinated to the King, would be trusty supporters of the Crown, and do their duty irrespective of what government was in power'.[5]

[3] Charles and Barbara Jelavich, *The Establishment of the Balkan National States, 1804–1920*, University of Washington Press, Seattle and London, 2000, pp. 179–180.
[4] PAAA, Berlin, R 9653, Rumänien Allgemeine Angelegenheiten April–December 1907, Report no. 53, Bucharest, 28 March 1907, pp. 7–9.
[5] PAAA, Berlin, R 9653, Rumänien Allgemeine Angelegenheiten April–December 1907, Report no. 61, 8 April 1907, p. 6.

An insider's view of the system, equally damning in its criticism of the corruption and politicization of the local administration, comes from N.V. Leonescu, Prosecutor General at the Court of Appeal in Iași. He described administration personnel in 1907 Moldavia as follows:

> with a few exceptions, [they were] bad, neglectful, abusive, unskilled and unqualified for the post in hand. While the assistant to a judge had to have an academic title, a prefect could be any electoral agent who was devoted to the government. This was enough. The prefect, with the support of the government, sought to subordinate justice to the administration. People felt that; people knew that. The county administration was at the discretion of the prefect. In the great majority, the prefects were inebriated with the power they held, unaccountable and devoid of any special qualifications that were required to be a good administrator as well as lacking in common sense; they were of the opinion that administering a county was all about inflicting violence and fear; they tolerated illegalities for they themselves were guilty of them through the measures they took. They encouraged beating, which they thought necessary in order to rule effectively. I will not go into the letters and personal requests I received from several prefects asking that their gendarmes be allowed to beat people.[6]

Leonescu explained how corrupt and based on illegalities the administrative hierarchy was. The mayors, who were subservient to subprefects and easily swayed by the great landowners, were little gods in the villages: 'The mayor was administrator, he presided over agricultural contracts, made inquiries, acted as a local judge, put into practice his own sentences.'[7] Tax collectors were no better: 'they collected taxes twice, did the most outrageous things in order to collect them, in breach of the law which forbade the confiscation of certain household items. They stripped the peasants in the middle of the village, took objects out of their houses, bed linen, their cauldron so they could not boil their polenta anymore. All this was done with the support of the rural gendarme, who was yet another plague for the peasants'.[8] Village authorities and rural gendarmes lent a hand to the great landowner or his leaseholder by forcing the peasants to

[6] N.V. Leonescu, *Anul 1907. Răscoala țăranilor*, Atelierele grafice "Lumina Moldovei", Iași, 1924, p. 22.

[7] Leonescu, *Anul 1907*, pp. 12–13.

[8] Leonescu, *Anul 1907*, p. 13.

work his land, with 'no regard for age, sex or state of health'. It often happened that peasants who had not been hired and were under no contractual obligation were also forced to work the landowner's land.[9] Such treatment of the peasants at the hands of the local authorities bears out the point made by Charles Tilly that 'a good deal of violent behaviour occurs under the cover of law'.[10]

Apart from political control of the country's institutions, how much of a grasp did Romanian authorities actually have on the country as a whole? How much of a hold did they have over the bulk of the population, who were peasants and outside the electoral loop? As we shall see in this chapter, the answer is: not very much. This comes out of both contemporary critiques of the land-tenure system and the post-traumatic stock-taking of police capabilities in the wake of the 1907 peasant uprising. Official short-sightedness was caused primarily by a lack of personnel and proper infrastructure (physical and administrative), but was compounded by a number of other factors: antisemitism, misinformation and gross high-level mismanagement.

Romania, a country whose population was formed in its overwhelming majority of peasants (82% in 1912)[11] and whose main national product and export was grain, functioned without a land cadaster well into the twentieth century. Romania in 1907 not only lacked that, but also suffered from a disjointed administrative system, which made use of statistics and engaged in land assessment for fiscal purposes, but did not do so in a unified, centralized way. The 1907 work by G.D. Creangă on land distribution in Romania (which was commissioned by the Liberal government) starts by drawing attention to this major drawback:

> In the forty-three years [which have passed since the peasant emancipation of 1864] there has been no official study of the distribution of land property. As a consequence we don't have information on how much land the peasants own, that is, those peasants, whose one and only demand has always been 'We don't have any land, we need land'. We know equally little about the medium-sized property, which some legislators wanted to extend in

---

. [9] Leonescu, *Anul 1907*, p. 13.
[10] Charles Tilly, *Politics of Collective Action*, CUP, Cambridge, 2003, p. 19.
[11] Keith Hitchins, *A Concise History of Romania*, Cambridge and New York, CUP, 2014, p. 132.

order to create a middle class between the great landowners and peasants, which would be necessary for the normal development of agriculture. Even the surface of the great property has not been ascertained [...] The information available on land ownership is not methodically collected and attempts have often been made to prove that peasant property was more extensive than the great property.[12]

A similar study of the peasant question in Romania by Jormescu and Popa-Burcă drew attention to the same shortcoming of sporadic, incomplete information on land ownership. The number of various-size properties was roughly known but there was little data on the actual number of owners, which in the case of peasant property constituted vital information given that multiple ownership of a plot of land was a common occurrence.[13] One inevitably wonders how the authorities could ever have weighed the demands of the peasants without a rigorous, centralized system of land division and administration, and relying on such scattered, fragmentary input. As Creangă pointed out, a lot of the agrarian debates in Parliament took place in the absence of basic information or, worse, by basing assumptions and conclusions on erroneous information.[14]

Kiderlen, the German Consul, offered a cynical explanation for this glaring administrative gap. The high cost invoked by Romanian politicians to justify rejecting the project of a land cadastre was just a pretext. In reality, what was lacking was not money but political will to conduct a comprehensive land survey as it upset too many vested interests:

> The great landowners do not actually want to clarify land relations so they can manipulate the boundaries of peasant land to suit their needs. In particular the lawyers' clique is against the issuance of definite land documents (*gesicherte Grundakten*) as they would stand to lose a good part of their income by the decrease in property rights litigation.[15]

---

[12] G.D. Creangă, *Grundbesitzverteilung und Bauernfrage in Rumänien*, Erster Teil, Leipzig, Verlag von Duncker und Humbolt, 1907, pp. 24–25.

[13] C. Jormescu and I. Popa-Burcă, *Harta agronomică a României*, Bucureşti, Inst. de arte grafice "Carol Göbl", 1907, p. 33.

[14] Creangă, *Grundbesitzverteilung*, pp. 24–25.

[15] PAAA, Berlin, R 9652 Rumänien Allgemeine Angelegenheiten 1906–1907, Report no. 186, Sinaia, 2 October 1906, pp. 2–3.

Poor Policing

In Romania the setting up of an urban gendarmerie went back to the 1850s, when the previous territorial militias were legislated into a separate institution. Just as in the case of the Hungarian gendarmerie, to be presented later on in this chapter, the Romanian gendarmerie was initially subordinated to both the Ministry of the Interior and the War Ministry and, following the metamorphoses undergone in the armed forces in Romania between 1864 and 1868, shifted to the purvey of the War Ministry, and was subsequently anchored within the structures of the Ministry of the Interior. The rural gendarmerie only came into being in 1893 (after the major peasant uprising of 1888) and stipulated the introduction of order-keeping structures that would replace the older and less-effective rural militia in the Romanian countryside. All communes were to be manned by rural gendarmes, who were subordinated to the local mayors and operated under the higher supervision of county prefects.[16] This was the well-meaning letter of the law. Actual implementation left much to be desired and this showed in spring 1907. At the request of the Liberal Minister of the Interior Brătianu, the regional authorities took stock of the number of village gendarmes before and after the uprising. Out of the extant data for 21 out of the 32 counties that formed Romania at the time, one can ascertain that more than one-quarter of this sample had no rural gendarmes whatsoever in 1907, around one-third had gendarmes only in one or two communes, and only three counties (Constanţa, with 348 gendarmes across 42 communes, Tulcea with 81 gendarmes for 26 communes and Romanaţi with 179 gendarmes for 24 communes) had more sizeable contingents of rural gendarmerie.[17]

A Moldavian prefect's report of July 1907 addressed to the Minister of the Interior further reinforced this assessment:

> There is no such thing as a rural police. The local authorities could not care less. Anyone can walk undisturbed through villages and communes. Whenever I visited a village without announcing my visit, the mayor did not even know I had been there. There are few gendarmes around and they have

---

[16] *Jandarmeria română: 161 de ani de istorie în slujba legii, ordinii şi siguranţei publice*, Editura Ministerului Administraţiei şi Internelor, http://www.editura.mai.gov.ro/documente/biblioteca/2011/JANDARMERIA.pdf (Accessed on 25 August 2015).

[17] ANR, Fond Brătianu, Dosar 377, pp. 1–48.

no notion how to do their duty. As they have no horses, they waste a lot of time walking long distances. When they come back after their patrolling, they are completely exhausted and fall asleep in their clothes.[18]

The gendarmerie that was in place at the time was, according to contemporary testimony, corrupt and subservient to the local potentates. A searing indictment of the institution came almost two decades after the uprising from the man who was a nemesis of corrupt gendarmes at the turn of the century, Prosecutor General N.V. Leonescu, the head of the Iaşi Court of Appeal.

> The rural gendarmerie was an important institution of great significance in the state. It depended on three ministries, war, interior and justice. The gendarmes were badly recruited and badly led. In their capacity as police officers, they disobeyed the prosecutors. They followed the orders of the local administration, who were in favour of the landowners and against the peasants, the latter being looked upon as worse than foreigners in their own country. There were gendarmes going around the villages not to maintain order or discover crimes, but to force peasants to work the landowner's fields. They beat the peasants, arrested them without a reason, violated their domicile, perpetrated all kinds of abuse, and for all of these reasons I sued them.[19]

It became increasingly difficult to prosecute gendarmerie abuses as obstacles were put in place by the very Minister of Justice. Thus a 1903 circular order made it compulsory for the county commander of the gendarmerie company to be present during any inquest against a rural gendarme, which meant that if the commander chose not show up, the inquiry could not take place.[20]

Antisemitism

The 1907 peasant uprising started in Botoşani County as a conflict between peasants and the local leaseholder. The leaseholder was Jewish (and a foreigner); the peasants were Christian and Romanian. In the context of the

---

[18] Andrei Oţetea; Ion Popescu-Puţuri (eds), *Documente privind marea răscoală a ţăranilor din 1907* (henceforth quoted as *Documente*), Bucureşti, Editura Academiei Republicii Socialiste România, 1977, Vol.2, p. 588.

[19] Leonescu, *Anul 1907*, pp. 32–33.

[20] Leonescu, *Anul 1907*, pp. 50–51.

official antisemitism that dominated Romanian political culture at the time, this circumstance blinded the authorities to the major danger posed by the brewing conflict. The Jewish question acted as a smoke screen, which prevented the local authorities from perceiving the magnitude of the social and economic problem they had on their hands. Some of the local authorities thus fostered a false sense of security and reassurance by, on the one hand, recognizing that the peasants were indeed justified in their claims and outrage and, on the other hand, dismissing this as the Jews' fault (in other words, if it were not for the Jews and their exploitation, Romania would have been a happy country of prosperous peasants). Thus Văsescu, the Prefect of Botoşani, concluded in his 18 February report to the Minister of Justice:

> This is what we have ascertained and noticed everywhere: that the inhabitants, although in great numbers, did not take advantage of this to make threats or impose their will, they only took the opportunity to make known their complaints and to ask for justice and what they were entitled to. We did not detect anywhere any external influence (*influenţă străină*) or incitement from priests or school teachers, as the Jews claim. The Jews are the only culprits, for through their cupidity and their brutal behaviour they have exasperated the peasants.[21]

No mention that one of the first victims of peasant discontent was a Romanian estate administrator by the name of Constantinescu.[22] No mention either that those who chose to rent their estates to Jewish leaseholders and refused to rent them directly to the peasants were the great landowners, who were both partners in crime and moral culprits. G. Livaditti, the Prosecutor in Botoşani, informed the General Prosecutor in Iaşi that the state of anarchy one of the Jewish leaseholders was complaining about was non-existent: 'the state of anarchy Mr Juster is saying exists in the commune of Rădeni is a figment of his imagination, probably caused by the fact that the *arendaş* is aware of the inhabitants' animosity (*spiritele cam agitate*) against him.'[23] This instance of playing down Jewish leaseholders' complaints comes out as all the more self-defeating as in the same report

[21] *Documente*, Vol. 2, p. 73.
[22] *Documente*, Vol. 2, p. 66.
[23] *Documente*, Vol. 2, p. 77.

the prefect indicated that he was aware of the ominous potential of these conflicts:

> From all these we can observe that the inhabitants of the communes Flămânzi, Frumuşica, Rădeni and Deleni, although apparently quiet, are in a curious mood (*într-o stare de spirite curioasă*) and from one day to another we can expect more serious disturbances if the *arendaşi* of these estates will not agree to rent land to the peasants at the price they promised.[24]

As P.G. Eidelberg points out, this was not the only instance of the misreading of the situation that the regional authorities showed at the time. In the early stages of the uprising, when the peasants 'were still in a mood to negotiate', Prefect Văsescu presented their demands as 'relatively moderate' to the Justice Minister: he was of the opinion that peasants wanted only lower rents and not a radical change in the system of payment from labour to cash.[25]

The antisemitic self-delusion regarding the true causes of the uprising permeated all state echelons as proved by the correspondence between Gheorghe Rosetti-Solescu, the Romanian Ministry Plenipotentiary and Special Envoy in St Petersburg and Dimitrie A. Sturdza, the head of the new Liberal government that took over from the Conservatives mid-uprising. In a letter dated 17 March 1907, the diplomat reassures Sturdza:

> Thank you for the telegraphic information that you were so kind to send to the Legation. I had already indicated to the powers that be (*les facteurs dirigeants*) how much the Jewish press has tendentiously been exaggerating the situation, and I can assure you that here they have full confidence in the new government, whose composition is excellent for fruitful work. I am particularly glad to see the foreign affairs in your hands. At Solesci, where I do not have a Jewish leaseholder nor do I have the least trouble with the peasants, who have got rich since I became in charge of the estate, I have – thank God! – escaped without much damage, at least as far as I know. The good local elements appear to have even defended the property against gangs that came from elsewhere. In the meantime, with the complicity of a few village rascals, the wine cellar has been broken into, there have been wine orgies and seditious upheavals, with preposterous demands and worrisome threats!

---

[24] *Documente*, Vol. 2, p. 77.

[25] P.G. Eidelberg, *The Great Rumanian Peasant Revolt of 1907: Origins of a Modern Jacquerie*, Leiden, Brill, 1974, pp. 219–220.

My administrator fled to Iași; his brother hid in the forest; the mayor played dead! I am hoping there have not been other ravages, but so far I do not know anything for certain as I cannot obtain reliable information and this uncertainty worries me much.[26]

The official state of self-delusion and the underlying *Schadenfreude* were best captured by Liviu Rebreanu in his 1932 realist novel *Răscoala* (*The Uprising*), where the following dialogue takes place between two journalists in Bucharest:

'See this horseshoe, my boy?' he went on like a tutor, running his index finger along the convolutions of the frontier. 'You see it? Remember what I said about ten days ago when we discussed the peasant disturbances? Well, was I right, eh? See, they started up here in the corner, towards Bukovina, with the Jews, and it went on and on, with "Down with the Jews" and "Down with the side-whiskers". Do you remember that you, too, thought that the whole matter only concerned a few Jewish side-whiskers? And now, look, it has come down to Teleorman there! See? And the flames are gradually spreading; I assure you that in three or four days they will have reached Severin, that is, the length of the whole horseshoe. Now the gentlemen who shouted "Down with the Jews!" are in deep trouble, now they feel it on their own skins for the peasant isn't discriminating between Jew or Christian, now that he's risen to get justice. And just where there are no Jews, the disturbances are most serious. In Moldavia, it seems, there was no murder and no bloodshed, but in these parts [i.e. Wallachia] numbers of landlords and lease-holders have been slaughtered by the rebellious peasants.'[27]

High-Level Mismanagement

Not only some of the regional authorities, but also, more vitally still, the central authorities failed to grasp the magnitude of the social danger brewing away in the countryside. Several years after the uprising, Take Ionescu

---

[26] Rudolf Dinu, Adrian-Bogdan Ceobanu (Eds.), *Gheorghe Rosetti-Solescu. Corespondență diplomatică personală și oficială (1895–1911). Petersburg*, Editura Unversității Alexandru Ioan Cuza, Iași, 2016, pp. 289–290.

[27] Liviu Rebreanu, *The Uprising*, Trans. P. Crandjean and S. Hartauer, Peter Owen Ltd., London, 1965, pp. 241–242.

remembered in a speech given in parliament the prophetic warning he had received in early 1907 from the Jewish writer Ronetti Roman[28]:

> 'What is going on around Hârlău is much more serious than you are led to think. You sent in Mr Sfetescu, the Secretary General of the Interior Ministry, [...] and he is sending you reassuring reports. In reality the situation is this: if you do not take energetic measures today, [...] in two weeks' time you will be using canons.' This was the first time I had heard the word 'canon' used in reference to domestic repression. Subsequent events proved him right: in three, rather than two, weeks' time, canons were being used.[29]

The new Liberal Prime Minister Dimitrie Sturdza corroborated this image of high-level neglect in a confidential discussion with the Austro-Hungarian ambassador in Bucharest:

> Mr Sturdza told me in confidence that, upon taking up his post, he had found stackfuls of unopened reports and notifications from the countryside (*aus der Provinz*) on the table of the previous Prime Minister and Minister of the Interior, Mr. G. G. Cantacuzino.[30]

An informant from Romania described a similar situation to Sir Edward Grey, the British Foreign Minister: 'I am convinced that the Prime Minister, who was also Minister of the Interior, had been receiving worrying news for a long time [before the uprising] which warned him of the danger, but they were all discarded; I have information that at the War Ministry more than a hundred similar notifications were received, but they were not even read.'[31]

The Iași Liberal Prefect told the German vice-consul that there had been noted dangerous peasant movements one month before the uprising. Kiderlen, the German General Consul in Bucharest, also testified to the 'abysmal weakness and fecklessness' (*die bodenlose Schwäche und*

---

[28] Ronetti Roman was the pseudonym of Aron Blumenfeld (1853–1908), a Jewish writer who settled in northern Moldavia.

[29] Ioan Șerbănescu (Ed.), *Evreii din România in secolul XX. 1900–1920. Fast și Nefast într-un răstimp istoric. Documente și mărturii*, Vol. I, Editura Hasefer, București, 2003, p. 217.

[30] MOL, K 26 Miniszterelnök, Prinz Schönburg an Freih. von Aehrenthal, No. 15 A, Bukarest, 3 April 1907, p. 114.

[31] Ion Popescu-Puțuri et al., *Documente privind marea răscoală a țăranilor din 1907*, vol. V, Editura Academiei Republicii Socialiste România, București, 1987, p. 356: 22 March/4 April 1907, Bucharest, Report to Sir Edward Grey, MP.

Kopflosigkeit) of the government, pointing out that 'for weeks, for months even, individual prefects had been warning about the movement'.[32] The reaction of the Conservative Prime Minister Cantacuzino was, as shown in Chapter 3, to blame it all on Russian influence and reinforce the border, rather than look into the domestic causes of the discontent.

The situation was not helped by the fact that King Carol was in poor health at the time and had been ailing for several years. Just like the main Romanian politicians, the King himself was of the opinion that peasant uprisings were caused by foreign contamination/instigation in conjunction with bad crops. So the monarch was himself ill-placed to foresee the 1907 peasant troubles. In June 1906 he wrote: 'I am worried about the agrarian troubles [in Russia], which have reverberated up to our frontiers, because here in Romania as well the peasants are constantly asking for land. Fortunately we have had such a good crop [this year] that there is peace and contentment all over the country.'[33]

Shock Therapy Effect

Throughout the summer of 1907 and for years afterwards, a stream of reports poured into the Ministry of the Interior regarding '*starea de spirit*', the mood of the peasants. Following the uprising the authorities sent undercover agents into the villages and started making use of trains as platforms for spying on the population. The state was growing eyes and ears. The new Rural Gendarmerie Law of 1908 increased the manpower as well as decreed as one of the institution's fundamental tasks 'the active and permanent surveillance of the countryside and preventive operations'.[34] Telegrams from county prefects to Interior Minister Brătianu testified to the considerable difference this new law made when compared to the rural gendarmerie manpower of 1907.[35] Not all county gendarmerie effectives were increased (some of them depleted after 1907, others remained unchanged), but on the whole a distinctive improvement is noticeable.

---

[32] PAAA, Berlin, R 9653, Rumänien Allgemeine Angelegenheiten April–December 1907, Report no. 53, Bucharest, 28 March 1907, p. 6; Report from Iaşi, 9 April 1907, pp. 5–6.

[33] Sorin Cristescu (Ed.), *Carol I. Corespondenţa personală (1878–1912)*, Bucureşti, Triton, 2005, p. 442.

[34] Inspectoratul de Jandarmi Cluj, *Jandarmeria rurală: istoric şi fapte*, http://www.jandarmeriaardeleana.ro/Doc%20diverse/Jandarmeria%20rurala.PDF (Accessed on 25 August 2015).

[35] ANR, Fond Brătianu, Dosar 377, pp. 1–48.

Three months after the uprising, in July 1907, a Moldavian prefect provided the Minister of the Interior with a detailed report on the system of local surveillance he had put in place so as to get a more accurate picture of the mood sways of the peasant population and of their problems: 'In order to be well informed about the peasants' first reactions[36] [to problems] (*pentru a fi bine informat de gândul cel întâiu al țăranilor*), I sent in a secret agent who walks through the county collecting information and holding counsel with them. I was thus able to find out about many ills. I acted immediately with a view to calming some people down or imparting justice to others'. The agent thus infiltrated was, by the prefect's admission, nothing but a clever gendarme who obtained his information by passing for a student. Through him the prefect found out that 'for the coming autumn, in some villages the peasants are in cahoots and planning to refuse to pay for land as they had agreed; they will instead ask that the price of the *falce* be 30 Lei, as they had heard was the price elsewhere.' More worryingly still, 'reservists and part-time soldiers (*soldații cu schimbul*) are egging each other on that, if they should be called up for military duty, they should no longer obey their superiors' orders.'[37]

Orphans of the State

Official reports such as the following one testify to the great chasm between peasants and local authorities: 'The greatest of ills is the lack of affinity and closeness between the peasants and those who are called upon to impart administration and enlightenment. State employees are usually in a hurry, they apply the law without tact, without taking the necessary measures, without giving any explanations and often with brutality. This is why the peasants only see enmity and ill will coming from the authorities.'[38]

A striking and acute aspect of interactions between the village and the state also becomes apparent in post-uprising police reports: the post-emancipation breakdown of paternalism defining relations between peasants and landlord, its replacement with 'cold' capitalist relations, which, in the absence of a welfare state or an effective administrative system of complaint-and-redress, left the peasants stranded in a limbo: the old

---

[36] The idea behind this was that of nipping in the bud any problems that might otherwise escalate into an uprising: targeting the problem early and solving it before it snowballed.

[37] *Documente*, Vol.2, p. 588.

[38] *Documente*, Vol.2, p. 587.

connections and sources of support were severed and new ones could not be forged because of the corrupt administration and self-seeking absentee landlords.

Any expression of interest and concern from the outside was received by peasants with great surprise. The myth of the students took off and snowballed the way it did precisely because of this perception on the part of the peasants that no one else cared about them, no one else would listen to their grievances. The German Consul in Iași reported in April 1907 on the Iași Prefect's experience of mediating between landowners, peasants and leaseholders: he was deluged with petitions and grievances.[39] As the Vaslui prefect noted, 'in many places the peasants are amazed that the prefect comes to their village, goes into their houses, talks to them, asks them about their problems and their relations with the boyar. After an hour or two of talking, they take courage, ask questions, ask for explanations and the discussion almost always ends with the following words: "Mr Prefect, it is good like this, but how should we know when nobody teaches us? Whoever let us in on anything?"'[40]

The Chief of the Special Security Brigade in Cerna-Vodă described the transition from the land-owner to the leasehold system, the resulting intromission of strangers into the village and the withdrawal of support and benefits hitherto traditionally granted by the lord of the manor to the peasants. He talked about the Erbiceni estate, one of the properties of the Cantacuzino family in Moldavia, where his father had worked as an administrator and where the author of the report had spent his childhood. He stated that the previous owner Lascar Pașcani Cantacuzin

> cultivated his estate himself. [...] I spent my childhood in that village, there among the peasants I attended primary school. I know from my personal experience that at that time the school and the church, as well as their personnel, were supported with money and materials by the landowner, who had sums of money set aside in the estate budget for this very purpose. There was a medicine store at the manor house, which provided the peasants with cures for their ailments. The peasants were helped with food and even money when in dire straits. For every single birth, christening, wedding and funeral, as well as for the big religious holidays, the estate personnel had to honour the pageant at the manor house or themselves go to the peasants'

---

[39] PAAA, Berlin, R 9653, Rumänien Allgemeine Angelegenheiten April–December 1907, Report from Iași, 9 April 1907, p. 6.
[40] *Documente*, Vol.2, pp. 587–588.

houses, or attend the village festivities (the *hora*), building connections, in word and deed, between landowner, administrator and personnel, and between peasants and the school and the church.[41]

In a police report triggered by an article in the press that there was impending danger of an uprising in the village of Popricani, the author strikes a similar note in his analysis of peasant-leaseholder relations:

> The *arendaş* of the Popricani estate is Mr Nuhăm Solomonovici, who lives in Botoşani and very rarely comes to the estate. As far as I know, he was only twice at the estate this summer. Instead he sent to the estate his son Mozes, an 18-year-old youth, who not only doesn't know anything about estate business, but he is also cold to the inhabitants and sometimes refuses to talk to them. We know this from the estate administrator and the village mayor.[42]

By contrast, the newspaper article that had occasioned the official investigation quoted one of the local peasants, who complained about the new *arendaş* in the following terms: 'We've had other *arendaşi* before [...] we had Dr. Ilie Stroici, who would talk even to the children, and lent an ear to our problems and hardships and gave us fatherly advice. The new lease holder is skinning us alive (*jupueşte de pe noi şapte piei*) and won't so much as talk to us.'[43]

These testimonies reflect a widespread nostalgia in the wake of peasant emancipation, which was not only confined to Romania. We find similar attitudes of looking back with fondness on the good old days of serfdom in Hungary as well. Such were the problems posed by emancipation that serfdom came to be viewed in retrospect as the lesser of two evils. The unprecedented rural upheaval that emancipation triggered took its toll on the population and, just like any other major transition, it was fraught with the dangers of the newly acquired freedom and divided the population into winners and losers, to such an extent that many came to look back nostalgically onto the safety net of serfdom. For good or bad, servile relations created a patriarchal system, which admittedly stifled initiative but at least did not let one die. Just like the *zadruga* and the *mir*, it was an archaic, unprogressive system, but a survival one too.

---

[41] ANR, Fond Direcţia Generală a Poliţiei, Dosar 2/1909, folio 5 (recto and verso).

[42] ANR, Fond Direcţia Generală a Poliţiei, Dosar 2/1909, folio 14 (recto).

[43] ANR, Fond Direcţia Generală a Poliţiei, Dosar 2/1909, Newspaper cutting from *Fulgerul*, No. 43, 24 August 1909, 'Primejdie de răscoale', folio 8 (recto).

In 1936 Gyula Illyés reminisced about the days of serfdom as a 'happy age' and meditated that, for all its boons, 'freedom had dangerous side-effects': competition, mechanization and the pressure of the wider world brought prosperity to some, while it ground others into poverty.[44] This lost symbiosis was reflected on in fiction as well where the peasants were portrayed as orphaned of great landowner protection and at the mercy of unscrupulous members of the emerging middle classes. In the passage below an old Transylvanian peasant who got into trouble with a money-lender turns for help to the young landowner, whom he naively expects to afford as much protection as the old landowner:

> Juon, who was now well over sixty had known well Balint's maternal grand-father, the elder Count Tamas, and for many years had managed all the communal property of the village, always going to Denestornya for advice as Count Abady, to whom they had formerly owed allegiance as serfs, still took a fatherly interest in everyone who lived and worked on his properties. Besides, he was also the county court judge. Old Juon Maftye therefore proposed that should now go to the young *mariasza*, ask his help and tell him of their complaints, for there was no doubt that, just like his grandfa-ther before him, he was a mighty man, who would put all to rights.[45]

After emancipation, the young count could no longer help them as the old count did. Patriarchal protection no longer had legal grounds so the peasants had to fend for themselves.

The Feedback Loop

What did the police find out once they sent agents under cover to sound the rural population? One peasant told them that his fellow villagers were trying to get the landowner to sell them land at a lower price and, as he would not, they had decided to get together and write a petition to higher authorities.[46] Other peasants complained that the local administra-tor would not lease out enough land and pasture and they had been

[44] Gyula Illyés, *Puszták népe*, Budapest 1936, pp. 55–57 – cited in Doreen Warriner (Ed.), *Contrasts in Emerging Societies. Readings in the Social and Economic History of South-Eastern Europe in the Nineteenth Century*, Indiana University Press, Bloomington, 1965, pp. 106–107.

[45] Miklós Bánffy, *Transylvanian Trilogy*, vol. 1: 'They Were Counted', Translated by Patrick Thursfield and Kathy Bánffy-Jelen, Arcadia Books, London, 1999, pp. 500–501.

[46] ANR, Fond Direcţia Generală a Poliţiei, Dosar 2/1909, folio 2 (recto).

threatened that he would hire workers from Bukovina.[47] On a train journey, an undercover agent learnt about the hardships of local peasants, who
because of that year's bad crop were forced to sell their cattle for very little
money and thus pay off their debts.[48] Another train took peasants from
Roman to Podu Iloaiei, where a cattle market was being held and where
they hoped to take advantage of the dirt-cheap prices for cattle, whom
poorer peasants could not afford to feed over the winter.[49] On another
train more discontent was vented, this time against an oppressive administrator on one of the Cantacuzino estates: he was ruthless, maltreated the
peasants, leased them the worst land at exorbitant prices; the peasants
were thus minded to submit a petition to the 'Ministry' to have one of the
state-owned estates sold off to them, 'otherwise they'll starve to death
together with their wives and children'.[50] Peasants coming back from work
on the train complained that 'they were living like dogs as their village had
no priest' so over the holidays they were determined to get together and
make a complaint to the Ministry and the Metropolitan.[51]

Police surveillance and reports continued for years after the uprising.
By 1910 the railway brigade of the Police and State Security department
was still busy reporting peasant complaints: there were clashes between
peasants and the local *arendaş* in a village in Iasi county;[52] in another village, the *arendaş* refused to lease land to the peasants and the local mayor
demanded ten Lei as a fee for village guards; in another place the *arendaş*
demanded payment in labour rather than in money (which set back the
peasants' own work) and the notary charged peasants for everything;[53] the
local administration in another village (mayor, notary, priest and gendarme) all demanded discretionary informal payments from the villagers;[54]
one of the big Jewish *arendaşi* Froim Fischer played the system and placed
his own henchmen (among them, a Romanian lawyer from Iaşi) in charge
of several estates, thus avoiding the new legal stipulations that forbade the
leasing of more than one estate per person.[55]

---

[47] ANR, Fond Direcţia Generală a Poliţiei, Dosar 2/1909, folio 7 (recto).
[48] ANR, Fond Direcţia Generală a Poliţiei, Dosar 2/1909, folio 15 (recto).
[49] ANR, Fond Direcţia Generală a Poliţiei, Dosar 2/1909, folio 18 (recto).
[50] ANR, Fond Direcţia Generală a Poliţiei, Dosar 2/1909, folio 16 (recto and verso).
[51] ANR, Fond Direcţia Generală a Poliţiei, Dosar 2/1909, folio 27 (recto).
[52] ANR, Fond Direcţia Generală a Poliţiei, Dosar 2/1909, folio 32 (recto).
[53] ANR, Fond Direcţia Generală a Poliţiei, Dosar 2/1909, folio 34 (recto and verso).
[54] ANR, Fond Direcţia Generală a Poliţiei, Dosar 2/1909, folio 35 (recto).
[55] ANR, Fond Direcţia Generală a Poliţiei, Dosar 2/1909, folio 36 (recto).

By 1911 the number and subject matter of complaints had not altered: the surveillance notes talk about the same tug-of-war between peasants and *arendaş*, the same usurious rates and unfavourable terms practiced by the *arendaşi*.[56] In 1912 reports start to echo the prospect of war (the possibility of Romania taking part in the Balkan wars). News of this trickled down to the peasants. As one inhabitant of the village of Zărbeşti, Vaslui county, was overheard to have said to another on the train: 'Mr Carp[57] has leased out his estate because he knows there's a war coming and he made sure he had enough money coming in.' To which, the other peasant interlocutor (from Slobozia Voineştilor, Iaşi county) replied: 'it would be good if there were war because there would be fewer people and more land. For they in their village have only the land around the house of 2 or 3 *prăjini* and Mrs Negruţi, the estate owner, won't give them any more land to work and because they are so destitute they are going to plough the estate land by force. Better be shot dead than live in poverty; in their village the people were making a petition to his Majesty the King to give them land.'[58]

In 1913, the year of the second Balkan war, in which Romania took part, the police and county authorities were deluged with complaints from peasant reservists who had fought in the Bulgarian campaign. Their commanders had promised them tax exemption for the year when they were away and they returned home from the war only to find their land had been neglected and their families had not been given the help the authorities promised they would provide:

the mobilized peasants came back home and instead of seeing the improvements their families were supposed to have benefited from, as their commanders had told them on the battlefield, in some communes they found their families in dire poverty fleeced of whatever little wealth they had by the rapaciousness of some of the mayors, notaries and gendarmes. These failed to provide support with working the fields, which were left fallow, and requisitioned their cattle, whilst taking bribes from others, whose cattle were not taken, and appropriated themselves of the relief funds and food which were meant for the families of those taken to the front.[59]

---

[56] ANR, Fond Direcţia Generală a Poliţiei, Dosar 2/1909, folio 49 (recto).
[57] P.P. Carp (1837–1919), one of the prominent Romanian conservative politicians and great landowner.
[58] ANR, Fond Direcţia Generală a Poliţiei, Dosar 2/1909, folio 65 (recto and verso).
[59] ANR, Fond Direcţia Generală a Poliţiei, Dosar 2/1909, folio 84 (recto).

Amidst this injustice they were additionally expected to work the land of the *arendaş* as the rental contract required, irrespective whether their own crops went to waste. In a petition addressed to the Iaşi prefect, the formerly mobilized peasants asked for a commonsensical and totally humane exemption, at the same time harking back to 1907, the mere mention of which seems to have retained its power of persuasion: 'While we were serving under the flag, our commanders told us we would be exempted from labour dues – and what with winter drawing near and this being the time to do our own field work to provide food for the winter – we are respectfully asking Mr Prefect to exempt us from labour dues (*prestaţia*) as were all those who were concentrated in the spring of 1907 to put down the uprising.'[60] According to newspaper coverage, the authorities, who were initially dismissive, backed down eventually and granted some of the exemptions required.[61]

The state could not only hear about rural hardships and abusive *arendaşi*, it also saw how the administrative chain functioned, or malfunctioned. As a disgruntled peasant traveller observed, 'they complained to the Prefect and his administration that the Jewish *arendaş* should be made to lease them more land and nothing was done. They were all in cahoots with each other, so [the peasants] were going to lodge a complaint with the Ministry of the Interior, maybe they might help them.'[62]

Did the rumours and unguarded train-ride complaints turn out to be true upon official inspection? The reports of district administrators (*administratori de plasă*) corroborated some of the information thus received from surveillance brigades, qualified it, as well as rejected some of it as 'unfounded rumour' or 'pure invention'. Unsurprisingly, complaints about informal payments demanded by local authorities could neither be proved nor disproved.[63]

Further reports disclosed the corruption that still plagued the system: even when the Prefect took action and investigated the matter, his good intentions could easily be undermined by corrupt subordinates. This was the case with the conflict between the *arendaş* and the local peasants over land rental in the village of Cristeşti (Tutova commune, Iaşi county). As one peasant complained on the train: 'the Prefect together with the

---

[60] ANR, Fond Direcţia Generală a Poliţiei, Dosar 2/1909, folio 88 (recto).

[61] ANR, Fond Direcţia Generală a Poliţiei, Dosar 2/1909, folio 90 (recto).

[62] Arhivele Nationale, Fond Direcţia Generală a Poliţiei, Dosar 2/1909, folio 21 (verso).

[63] ANR, Fond Direcţia Generală a Poliţiei, Dosar 2/1909, folio 39 (recto)

Agricultural Inspector came into the village to persuade the *arendaş* to rent land for maize cultivation to the villagers. The district administrator (*administrator de plasă*) promised he would intercede with the *arendaş* on behalf of the inhabitants. After the Prefect left, the Administrator, who spent every day at the house of the *arendaş*, started telling people that the *arendaş* was master of his own estate and he could not force him to rent them land.'[64] A classic case of 'when the Prefect's away, the *arendaş* (in cahoots with the local authorities) will play.'

The authorities industriously collected information about the peasants and their discontent (from undercover agents, from newspaper articles— police files are full of cut-and-pasted newspaper clippings) and actually acted on it. A feedback loop seems to have come into being after the systemic shock of 1907. Newspaper reports and casual conversations between peasants in train carriages were taken on board and formed the basis of official investigations. The county prefect sent in his subordinates to look into the matter and report back on the veracity and accuracy of the initial rumour or alert. The system was anything but watertight. There was still rampant corruption and cliquish behaviour; there was also, in some cases, a hazy grasp of where places lay on the map (see annotations on police reports indicating that such and such a village did not exist in that county, or their name might have been changed in the meantime[65]).

HUNGARY

The longest stretch of the frontier between Romania and the Austro-Hungarian Empire fell in the Hungarian half of the Monarchy. As such reverberations of the 1907 peasant uprising in Romania were more likely to affect the Hungarian lands. The eastern reaches of Hungary stretching along this lengthy frontier were also, as pointed out in previous chapters, among the poorest and least-developed regions of the Monarchy. What was the grasp of the Hungarian authorities over this frontier territory and how did they react to news of the uprising across the border?

[64] Arhivele Naţionale, Fond Direcţia Generală a Poliţiei, Dosar 2/1909, folio 40 (recto and verso).
[65] ANR, Fond Direcţia Generală a Poliţiei, Dosar 2/1909, folio 30 (recto), folio 45 (recto), folio 46 (verso).

Infrastructure

Hungarian police infrastructure came into being following the splitting of the Monarchy into two in 1867. Hungary could draw on influential precedents such as the Bach system following the 1848–1849 civil war, or further back in time, Metternich's police system or, the template for the previous two, the Josephinian notion of a *Polizeistaat*. According to these models, the job of the state was to know as much about its own population as possible. In Hungary, where more than half the population was not ethnically Hungarian and, as such, intrinsically suspect of irredentist tendencies and where, also, with the rise of industrialization and the emancipation of the peasantry, the ranks of urban and rural proletariat increased, state representatives were acutely aware of the necessity for effective policing. The cultural activities of the non-Magyar nationalities and the socialist susceptibilities of the urban and rural proletariat represented the two-pronged nemesis of the Hungarian state.[66]

Throughout its existence from 1881 until 1918, the royal Hungarian gendarmerie retained its double subordination to both the Royal Hungarian War Ministry (*Honvédelmi Minisztérium*) and the Hungarian Ministry of the Interior (*Belügyminisztérium*), and was legislated into being as 'a militarily structured defence body' (*katonailag szervezett őrtestulet*).[67] And indeed the input of manpower and expertise from the Royal Hungarian War Ministry was considerable especially in the early days of the new institution. In all other respects (infrastructure and material supplies) the Interior Ministry was responsible.[68] Although by no means smooth or without teething problems (lack of manpower and poor quality of personnel were common ones), the development of the Hungarian *csendőrség* (rural police) proceeded steadily, the institution gaining in prestige and complexity by the turn of the century. The personnel received training for half a year (or three months if under the aegis of the Honvéd Ministry) and were supposed to have the three Rs, be fit and unmarried (although, in practice, some of the criteria of selection lapsed for lack of

---

[66] Csapó Csaba, *A Magyar Királyi csendőrség története 1881–1914*, Pro Pannonia, Pécs, 1999, p. 41.

[67] Parádi József, *A Magyar Királyi Csendőrség. Az első Magyar polgári, központosított, közbiztonsági őrtestület 1881–1945*, Szemere Bertalan Magyar Rendvédelem-történeti Tudományos Társaság, Budapest, 2012, p. 42 – henceforth *A Magyar Királyi Csendőrség*.

[68] Parádi, *A Magyar Királyi Csendőrség*, p. 47.

personnel).[69] The network of gendarmerie posts ramified to cover the entire country by the end of the nineteenth century and acquired specialized units such as the border guards (*határcsendőrség* or *határszéli csendőrség*), auxiliary units and, from 1902 onwards, detective units (*járásmesterek*).[70] By the beginning of the twentieth century the gendarmerie had become a much valued and fairly efficient institution of the Hungarian state but also much hated by the groups that constituted its prime suspects: politically active non-Magyar nationalities and workers/ poor peasants. The institution found fierce critics among the nationalities, who denounced the brutality of the institution, and among some Hungarian politicians such as Lájos Mocsáry, who viewed it as a tool of 'Hungarian absolutism'.[71]

With the consolidation of the modern border between the Habsburg Monarchy and, since 1878, independent Romania, the Hungarian gendarmerie evolved specialized border-defence structures, which came into being after the establishment of the frontier line 1891.[72] The strengthening of border defence continued into the early twentieth century, with increased numbers of border police posts and a redoubled function of not only border defence but also surveillance and intelligence collection (*'figyelő' és nyomozó szolgálat ellátása*). In this latter task detectives in civilian clothes were used against smugglers, spies and irredentists.[73]

The frontier line with Romania and Serbia evinced a much higher concentration of state 'feelers' than the rest of the country. The frontier had traditionally been viewed as a place of contamination with epidemics and, increasingly in the latter half of the nineteenth century, with dangerous anti-state ideas. It was the place where tariff wars were played out: between 1886 and 1891 the mutually debilitating customs conflict with Romania and, more notoriously, the 1906 Pig War with Serbia. As an interface with the neighbouring states it was also a vantage point for collecting intelligence on them at all levels: economic, military, social.

Most importantly from an operational point of view, the frontier was the place where the jurisdictions of several ministries overlapped most tightly (the Interior Ministry, the Ministry of Finance, the Ministry of

[69] Csapó, *A Magyar Királyi Csendőrség Története*, p. 25; Parádi, *A Magyar Királyi Csendőrség*, p. 46.
[70] Parádi, *A Magyar Királyi Csendőrség*, pp. 48–53.
[71] Csapó, *A Magyar Királyi Csendőrség Története*, pp. 40–41.
[72] Parádi, *A Magyar Királyi Csendőrség*, pp. 51–52.
[73] Csapó, *A Magyar Királyi Csendőrség Története*, pp. 123–124.

Agriculture, Industry and Commerce). The local institutions of these ministries were called upon to collaborate for more comprehensive intelligence collection. Thus in 1885 a secret circular of the Ministry of the Interior instructed all these ministries to gather information and provide daily reports on the state of the army, of officials, and mood of the population on the Romanian side of the border. All structures of the local administration together with the gendarmerie were expected to work together under the coordination of the prefect (*főispán*) of Szeben County.[74] The strength of the system lay not so much in the efficiency of one single institution but rather on cross-institutional collaboration and centralization of information.

Policing Strategy

The Hungarian state was fairly efficient at policing its population. Despite the atomization of the archive of the Hungarian Ministry of the Interior following the First World War, a mere look at splinters of this once unified archive shows the extent of policing and surveillance exerted on the Hungarian population in the last decades of the nineteenth century and the early teens of the twentieth century. Any activity that was deemed unpatriotic (*hazafiaellenes*) or directed against the Hungarian state (which was synonymous to the Hungarian nation and the interests of the great landowner oligarchy) was criminalized, closely kept tabs on and punished. If one refers to historical bibliography on the late Habsburg Monarchy and in particular on the Hungarian half of the Monarchy, one gets the impression that the dominant internal conflict, overriding all other concerns, took place along nationalist lines and pitted the Hungarian state against the non-Magyar nationalities. While this was undoubtedly an important dimension of political life in post-*Ausgleich* Hungary, it was by no means the only one and an exploration of the extant holdings of the Hungarian Ministry of the Interior points to another central preoccupation of the Hungarian state: the inroads socialism made among Hungarian workers and peasants. Socialism was the other great fear of the Hungarian authorities and this is reflected in the considerable number of reports and exchanges between various levels of authority in the Hungarian state regarding this topic. While (non-Magyar) nationalism undermined the political power of the Hungarian magnates, socialism threatened the economic base on which their power was predicated.

---

[74] Botond Nagy, 'Rendvédelem a Magyar-Román Határon a 19. Század Második Feléleben', *Acta Siculica* 2007, pp. 437–453 – p. 448.

Consequently, both of them were considered arch-enemies of the Hungarian state and as such copiously policed.

What did Hungarian police reports keep tabs on? They closely followed the spread of socialism among the population, kept an eye on socialist activities, on legal and illegal assemblies, on peasant associations and their activities, on conflict (overt or imminent) between peasants and landlords, on strikes (urban and rural) and 'acts of terrorism', on local grievances and complaints, on conflict resolution and deals struck between peasants and landowners. This information was extracted via intelligence networks that connected local authorities (*főszolgabíró, rendőrkapitány*)[75] with the regional authorities (county mayors) and further on with the relevant ministries: the Interior Ministry worked hand-in-hand with the Ministry of Agriculture, which in turn liaised with the Ministry of Commerce, the Imperial Ministry of Foreign Affairs and the Emperor's Chancellery (*Kabinettkanzlei*). Annual reports were sent to county mayors accounting for socialist activity (or lack thereof, as the case may be) and disturbances. There were also local reports from this or that town or village, which described public assemblies in scrupulous detail: how many people attended, of what nationality, the content of speeches and discussions.[76] Less frequently, detectives were sent in and they fed back reports on various suspicious subjects and situations.[77]

The great impetus for Hungarian authorities to start policing the countryside came in the wake of large-scale rural unrest in the 1890s in particular in the counties of Békés, Csanád and Csongrád, which were known as the 'Storm Corner'.[78] The post-emancipation Hungarian peasantry was increasingly proletarianized and, with the advent of the Socialist Democratic Party on the Hungarian political scene, increasingly courted and co-opted by the socialist movement. 'The party organizers', noted a police report, 'realizing that their movement cannot acquire any importance in an agricultural state like Hungary so long as it is confined to factory and industrial workers, aim to also bring farm labourers into the movement'.[79] In a country where 68.6% of the population was

[75] ANR, Arhiva CC al PCR, PCR archive, Fond 50/6612, p. 31/verso.

[76] ANR, Arhiva CC al PCR, PCR archive, Fond 50/6607, p. 5/verso.

[77] ANR, Arhiva CC al PCR, PCR archive, Fond 50/6601, p.2; Fond 50/6663, pp. 94, 104–105.

[78] Warriner, *Contrasts in Emerging Societies*, p. 107.

[79] Warriner, *Contrasts in Emerging Societies*, p. 108.

employed in agriculture,[80] the socialists had to take into account the predicament of the rural population if they were to make any political headway. Representing peasant interest was a do-or-die matter for the
Hungarian socialists.

As a result of the political organization of the peasantry by the socialists
a wave of strikes swept through the Hungarian countryside in the last
years of the nineteenth century, with the most widespread strike encom-
passing all Alföld communities in the summer of 1897. It was the shock of
this that led the Hungarian authorities to introduce stricter means of
policing the population as well as a well-developed strategy of conflict
prevention and management. Punishments were meted out generously:
fines and days of imprisonment on the basis of Industrial Act no. 159.[81]

Hungarian authorities' scripted behaviour left nothing to chance when
it came to conflict management. An impressive amount of detailed directives circulated among the various levels of authority and covered all con-
tingencies. Particularly in the case of rural strikes, which threatened to
plunge striking workers and inflexible landlords into dire economic difficulties, which in turn would produce more social unrest, plans A, B and C
were considered by the authorities and all possible outcomes of the conflict were taken into account and provision was made for them. The measures followed a gradient from peaceful talks with the two parties and
mediation, to the provision of contingents of reserve agricultural workers
brought from elsewhere if negotiations broke down or were so protracted
that the crop risked going to waste, and finally brute force was by no
means shied away from: the army was called in whenever the previous,
peaceable measures failed.

The most cost-effective measure was of course mediation. Theoretically,
it was easier to defuse a conflict in its early stages than to deal with a poten-
tially dangerous standoff. Ministerial circulars insisted on impartiality
when dealing with the conflicting parties and equal rigour in judging the
complaints of either side as well as observing workers' legal rights.[82]
However, the conflict was to be resolved in accordance with existing laws
and in Hungary the law was decidedly on the side of the great landowner.
The 1898 law, also known as the 'Slave law', cropped up in all these com-

[80] Warriner, *Contrasts in Emerging Societies*, p. 110.
[81] ANR, Arhiva CC al PCR, PCR archive, Fond no. 50, Brassó gendarmerie telegram to
the Minister of the Interior, 26 March 1907, p. 4.
[82] ANR, Arhiva CC al PCR, Fond 50/6612, p. 34 (verso).

munications. Should mediation bring no results, the authorities' first duty was to attend to the legally protected interests of the employers. This was plan B, and was envisaged down to the smallest detail: replacement workers were to be used.[83]

The operation that was put in place to secure them impresses through thoroughness and detail. In May 1904, the Hungarian Minister of Agriculture circulated a set of confidential instructions to all the mayors and deputy sheriffs (*alispán*) demanding that they all provide him with grassroots information on harvest conditions:

> No later than 15 June you should report to me on the following: 1. If the lawful landowners have hired harvesters or not. Whether or not contracts were fulfilled without problems 2. If the conclusion of contracts occurred according to custom, were there hopes that the hiring process won't encounter problems? 3. If contracts have not been concluded and there are no hopes of them being concluded without problems, then how many landowners are without workhands and how many workers are missing? 4. Should signs of a strike movement be detected in your territory, you should report on the availability and whereabouts of harvest machines 6. Are there in your territory workers who in the first days of July would be willing to go to other regions to replace the striking harvesters? How long would it take them to gather at the nearest train station? In which district? What are the exact names of the judge and head of police?[84]

The local authorities were to keep a record of all workers and immediately inform superior authorities of the availability of reserve workers and be in charge of their dispatch wherever needed. The Minister, the directives insisted, was to be apprised at all times of how many replacement workers were available.[85] The actual substitution of striking local workers with extraneous work hands was to take place with due consideration to the economic interests of the community the replacement workers originated from and in consultation with the local landowners (so that the movement of the workforce to another region did not end up destabilizing the region that provided the replacements). The employers, moreover, were urged to conclude contracts according to the law in order to receive administrative assistance in case of a strike and should associate themselves

---

[83] ANR, Arhiva CC al PCR, Fond 50/6612, p. 30 (verso).
[84] ANR, Arhiva CC al PCR, Fond 50/6612, p. 29 (recto and verso).
[85] ANR, Arhiva CC al PCR, Fond 50/6612, p. 29 (verso).

to make up for a possible shortage of work tools (scythes and forks) in case the strike took wider proportions. The district authorities (judge, mayor and chief of police) must report immediately, by telegraph or telephone, on any telltale signs of an impending strike movement and any incident that could possibly have relevance to this.[86] Should the necessary replacement workers not be available locally, the Minister was to be notified immediately and a comprehensive report on the situation was to be submitted in order to secure ministerial assistance. Three types of information were to be provided: (1) number of required workers, (2) written agreement of the employer to foot the bill, and (3) the train station to which they were to be sent.[87] The whole process of strike management should be conducted 'with caution, determination, vigor and tact [...] and with as little disturbance, hesitation and disruption as possible'.[88]

Judging by the amount of detail these top-down instructions contained, one could describe Hungary as the very opposite of a *laissez-faire* state. Nothing was left to chance, there was a directive for every possible case that might arise. The whole thing has something logical-mathematical about it: if A, then B, if non-A, then C. What also stands out from these instructions and, as we shall see further on, from other similar provisions, is the importance given to the time factor. All information requested, all reports and notifications from the territory were to be effected 'immediately', 'forthwith', with the greatest urgency. Time, as the Hungarian authorities will have learnt from the spread of rural unrest in 1897, was crucial in conflict management and made the difference between small isolated flares and general conflagration.

Three years later in June 1907 the same concern and punctilious preparation of harvest-time peace-keeping measures is to be found in a report sent by the Hungarian Minister Agriculture, Daranyi, to Emperor Franz Joseph, apprising the latter of the measures taken for securing the smooth unfolding of harvest works. The Minister acknowledged the recurrence of agrarian movements in the past few years and acted on input from regional authorities (*ersten Beamten der Munizipien*) and from agricultural associations (*landwirtschaftlichen Vereine*). These had warned him that there were signs that the harvest would not take place without problems. Consequently, the Minister saw fit to take a number of preventive

---

[86] ANR, Arhiva CC al PCR, Fond 50/6612, p. 30 (recto and verso).
[87] ANR, Arhiva CC al PCR, Fond 50/6612, p. 31 (recto).
[88] ANR, Arhiva CC al PCR, Fond 50/6612, p. 31 (verso).

measures to cover every possible situation that might arise: (1) 12,000 reserve workers were secured from the woodland regions of northeastern Hungary (Máramarossziget, Ungvár, Bersterczebánya and Székelyföld) and entrusted to the care and protection of stud farms (*Gestütsdomänen*); (2) he ordered 300 harvest machines from the machine factory of the Hungarian railways society (these were to be provided, upon request, to employers within 24 hours); (3) instructions were issued to regional authorities to proceed with caution and tact, but also with energy and determination; (4) conflict mediation should be engaged in within the legal limits of contract stipulations (whoever breaks the contract should be punished according to the law); (5) district judges (*Berzirks-Oberstuhlrichter*) were instructed to provide the Minister with daily telegraphic reports on the course of the harvest; (6) for better coordination and information circulation, the Ministry of Agriculture liaised directly with the Ministry of the Interior; (7) every matter relative to the harvest was to be attended to with exceptional celerity by telegraph or telephone.[89]

When all of the above measures failed, there was the infallible plan C: police and army force. The authorities frequently resorted to the rural police (*csendőrség*), which was a staple for maintaining order during agricultural works. Military troops were used as a last resort, more often than not during the more serious riots such as the 1894 one in Hódmezővásárhely or for breaking the wave of industrial strikes across Hungary during 1895.[90] Requests for army backup seemed to have been issued on a regular basis, although not always approved by the military authorities, be they the *Honvédministerium* in Budapest or the *Kriegsministerium* in Vienna. Thus a request addressed to the Honvéd ministry by the Economic Association of Sáros county—*Sárosmegyei Gazdasági Egyesület*—(northern Hungary, currently in Slovakia), to the effect that troops in active service be deployed in case of rural strikes was rejected by the Hungarian military authorities.[91] A similar request was issued by the Hungarian Minister of the Interior to the War Ministry in Vienna in April 1907 and was repeated in June of the same year. As strikes were expected, just like in the previous years, to break out in many places during agricultural works, the Hungarian authorities requested the reinforcement of their police manpower with

---

[89] HHStA, Kabinettkanzlei, Karton 20, 1907, Akt 1957.
[90] Warriner, *Contrasts in Emerging Societies*, p. 108.
[91] *Gazdasági Lapok*, 28 April 1907, p. 327: 'Hirek: Az aratás és a katonaság.'

military troops, so that for every policeman deployed to keep order during harvest time, there would be a replacement from among the regular troops. The initial request for 1,785 infantrymen subsequently decreased to 1,400 when the situation seemed to have improved slightly. The additional troops were to be used as and when needed.[92] The Viennese War Ministry rejected the 'proposed system of distribution of individual infantry men to gendarmerie posts' whilst professing willingness to 'send in tactical units if there was actual danger and only as many as it was strictly necessary to the task in hand and only for the duration which was strictly necessary to provide assistance'.[93] In the above answer, one can detect the impatience of the imperial military authorities who must have resented being at the beck and call of the Hungarian civilian authorities and in particular the prospect of having their troops integrated and subordinated to the Hungarian gendarmerie.

Reactions to the Romanian Uprising

What do you do when the house next door is on fire? This was basically the situation the Hungarian state was in when the Romanian peasant uprising of spring 1907 extended country wide. First reactions were dictated by self-preservation: reinforcing frontier defence and keeping tabs on their own population. Both sets of measures were not exceptional or unprecedented; they had been rehearsed for years: policing the Romanian frontier and closing it down to traffic was practised during the tariff war of 1886–1891; collecting information on relations and conditions across the border was not anything new either; the late 1880s and the 1890s saw intense nationalist activity within and without the Hungarian borders and consequently enhanced Hungarian police supervision and institutional vigilance. They were also the years when the Hungarian establishment stepped up efforts at Magyarization and came down all the more fiercely on anything so much as smacking of irredentism (which was basically any non-Magyar cultural activity). Collecting information inside the Hungarian borders on the mood of the population and any signs of impending conflict was common practice for all Hungarian state institutions. Year in, year

---

[92] Romanian Central National Archives, Arhiva CC al PCR, Fond 50/6663, pp. 109–115: 'Katonai karhatalom csendör őrökre'//'Hadügyminister. Katonai karhatalom a csendőrőrsökre'.

[93] ANR, Arhiva CC al PCR, Fond 50/6663, p. 107: FZM Schönaich to Graf Andrássy, Minister des Innern, 12 July 1907.

out, urban and rural strikes broke out across Hungary; the authorities expected them and were ready for them, as seen above, with plans A, B and C, of action. During 1907, the Hungarian state machinery was set in motion once again and dealt with the crisis across the border in the same way it would have dealt with an internal crisis.

In a telegram dated 1 April 1907 the Austrian Ministry of the Interior pointed out to their Hungarian counterpart that 'the Romanian authorities would be very grateful if the competent Hungarian authorities were to temporarily reinforce the defence of the frontier', given that the border guards on the Romanian side were being used in the repression of the uprising. To which the Hungarian Interior Ministry replied that 'they had already reinforced the border upon receipt of the first news of the Romanian uprising'.[94]

Input from the three main border crossing points—Orsova on the Danube, near the Iron Gates; Brassó across the Carpathians, where they turn westwards; and Besztercze in north-eastern Transylvania—kept the Hungarian Ministry of the Interior informed of border traffic, stream of refugees and the situation in the immediate proximity of the border. Where did the border authorities get their information from? From a combination of sources: refugees' accounts of the course of the uprising, Hungarian and Romanian newspapers, public rumour (*közszájon forgó hírek*), own sources such as Romanian-speaking detectives sent across the border to assess the seriousness of the situation, and information from the Austro-Hungarian legation in Bucharest. The sources were not always reliable as the Brassó chief of police pointed out in one of his telegrams to the Ministry: 'It is impossible to obtain genuine information even from Romanian officials, who themselves get their information to a great extent from the newspapers.'[95] For all the uncertainty regarding news reliability, the snippets of information they reported were fairly accurate on the whole: that the uprising started in Moldavia was spreading apace down south, that local troops were insufficient and additional army troops had been called in to make up the numbers, that there had been instances of disobedience among peasant recruits as 'they refused to fight against their

---

[94] Egyed Ákos, 'Az 1907-es romániai parasztfelkelés visszhangja a magyar sajtóban' in Ion Cicală et al., *Adalékok az 1907-es parasztfelkelés történetéhez*, Tudományos könyvkiádó, Bukarest, 1957, p. 72.

[95] ANR, Arhiva CC al PCR, Fond 50/6659, pp. 3;

Ion Cicală (Ed.) *Adalékok az 1907–es parasztfelkelés történetéhez*, Appendices: Magyar kir. VII. Sz. Csendőrkerületi parancsnakság, Brassó, 1907 év márczius hó 25-én.

parents and relatives', and that the government had resigned and a new one had been formed under the presidency of Sturdza.[96]

The most reliable information the border guards collected was that sourced by their own employees. The Orsova border police sent in a Romanian-speaking agent (*román ajku rendőrbiztos*), under strict instructions to cross the border to Turnu-Severin and speak to the local prefect, whom he knew personally, and sound him out for information. 'The police lieutenant witnessed great panic and confusion in town, could not find the prefect and had to confine himself to collecting information from what he himself saw and heard.' The image composed through his eyes and those of fellow travelling refugees was that of a town guarded by the local garrison and army troops deployed to neighbouring villages, which had been attacked by rebellious peasants; at the main railway stations (Vârciorova and Turnu-Severin) groups of 30 to 40 peasants were dotted around in the fields and in the streets, whispering and talking among themselves, while everywhere patrols maintained order. Hosts of called-up reservists were dismissed without justification. According to Romanian refugees, this was because there was no need for them; according to Jewish refugees, it was due to their unreliability because the young recruits were peasants' sons and sided with the rebels. Rumours circulated about poor army discipline, especially when it came to fulfilling orders to shoot.[97]

These were gleanings extracted from hearsay and own experience but epistemic doubt remained as to what was really happening in Romania as a whole given the great difficulties in obtaining reliable information: 'telegraph networks in Romania are so damaged and it is so difficult to get hold of newspapers that the general reception and speedy communication of news is virtually impossible. All signs point to the fact that the neighbour's house is on fire. But it is impossible to tell how long it will last and how extensive it is, based on the data available. At any rate the peasantry in the whole country are in open revolt, with great outbursts of violence here and there.' The same complaint about newspaper suppression was voiced by the Brassó border guards, who pointed out that 'Romanian newspapers were under censorship and in Predeal, the Romanian border

---

[96] Cicală (Ed.) *Adalékok az 1907 – es parasztfelkelés történetéhez*, Appendices: Magyar kir. VII. Sz. Csendőrkerületi parancsnakság, Brassó, 1907 év márczius hó 25-én.

[97] Cicală (Ed.) *Adalékok az 1907 – es parasztfelkelés történetéhez*, Appendices: Magyar kir. Határszéli rendőrkapitány, Orsova, 1907 évi márczius hó, 27-én.

town on the other side of Brassó, newspaper sales had been discontinued since the 20th of March.' This, they supposed, was meant to prevent the population from finding out about the uprising.[98] The *főispán* of Brassó suggested as a solution to news unreliability that the Austro-Hungarian legation in Bucharest liaised directly with them 'given the big scale of the Romanian uprising and the fact that newspaper coverage was wholly unreliable'. Could the legation be instructed to send directly to the border authorities any information regarding any matters of concern for border safety and also report on numbers of refugees to be expected?[99] A year later, in March 1908, the Besztercze border police was still industriously collecting information on the state of affairs across the frontier. According to rumour picked up by the border guards at the mountain passes of Gyimes and Gyergótölgyes, a new peasant uprising was brewing in Romania, similar to the one that broke out the previous year, only much better organized and much more powerful. Romanian authorities, the report went further, dismissed such rumours as exaggerated; various travellers, however, confirmed them.[100]

What fears and reactions were triggered by the stream of information that seeped through to the Hungarian authorities in 1907? Was contamination a valid scenario for the Hungarian gendarmerie and border county authorities? What precautionary measures were called for and eventually taken? The Orsova border police feared for the frontier counties of Krassó-Szörény and Hunyad, whose Romanian population were deemed 'likely to rebel against the landlords, loot and kill', all the more so, stressed the chief of border police, as in the last years the population had been 'artificially infected with political strife by nationalist instigators', so that his concern seemed fully justified that the flames were likely to extend to this 'contaminated territory'.[101] By contrast, in response to a request from the Ministry of the Interior, the Brassó *főispán* reassured the higher authorities about the mood of the Romanian population in their county: 'at the moment the

---

[98] Cicală (Ed.) *Adalékok az 1907 – es parasztfelkelés történetéhez*, Appendices: Magyar kir. VII. Sz. Csendőrkerületi parancsnakság, Brassó, 1907 év márczius hó 25-én.

[99] Cicală (Ed.) *Adalékok az 1907 – es parasztfelkelés történetéhez*, Appendices: Brassóvármegye főispánja, Brassó, 1907 márczius 28.

[100] ANR, Arhiva CC al PCR, Fond 50/ 6607, p. 9: A beszterczei határszéli rendőrkapitányságtól a Belügyminister Úrnak, 21 márczius 1908, Besztercze.

[101] Cicală (Ed.) *Adalékok az 1907 – es parasztfelkelés történetéhez*, Appendices: Magyar kir. Határszéli rendőrkapitány, Orsova, 1907 évi márczius hó, 27-én.

Romanian population are all quiet and there is no trace to be detected in their behaviour of tendencies that could occasion the least concern. [...] the only impact that the troubles in Romania have had on the town of Brassó so far has been the fact that several noble and well-off Romanian families have moved here'.[102]

Measures to reinforce the border were taken all along the frontier. Orsova pressed for military reinforcement from the imperial military command on the Danube island of Ada-Kaleh, who together with the local Orsova gendarmerie should work towards securing the border.[103] The Brassó *főispán* reassured that, for all the reported peace and quiet, precautionary measures had been taken and the developments across the border were being watched with vivid attention.[104] The Brassó gendarmerie instructed all subordinate posts to stay vigilant, take the necessary measures of precaution and immediately relay all intelligence they received.[105] This was all the more imperative due to the depletion of border defence on the Romanian side, as signalled by the Brassó gendarmerie: 'with few exceptions, the Romanian border guard troops stationed in Predeal have left for an unknown destination, equipped with ammunition and bayonets'.[106] Reinforcement troops, such as the Honvéd reserves (*póttartalékosok*), were, despite criticism of their poor training, viewed as vital help in case of a spillover of a Balkan conflict.[107]

The Hungarian authorities not only sought to keep the rebels out, but also their own peasants in. Seasonal workers were denied permission to travel to Romania in spring 1907, as becomes apparent in a telegram from Aehrenthal to the Hungarian Minister of the Interior: 'The administration

---

[102] Cicală (Ed.) *Adalékok az 1907 – es parasztfelkelés történetéhez*, Appendices: Brassóvármegye főispánja, Brassó, 1907 márczius 28.

[103] Cicală (Ed.) *Adalékok az 1907 – es parasztfelkelés történetéhez*, Appendices: Magyar kir. VII. Sz. Csendőrkerületi parancsnakság, Orsova, 1907 év márczius hó 25-én.

[104] Cicală (Ed.) *Adalékok az 1907 – es parasztfelkelés történetéhez*, Appendices: Brassóvármegye főispánja, Brassó, 1907 márczius 28.

[105] Cicală (Ed.) *Adalékok az 1907 – es parasztfelkelés történetéhez*, Appendices: Magyar kir. VII. Sz. Csendőrkerületi parancsnakság, Orsova, 1907 év márczius hó 25-én.

[106] Cicală (Ed.) *Adalékok az 1907 – es parasztfelkelés történetéhez*, Appendices: Magyar kir. VII. Sz. Csendőrkerületi parancsnakság, Brassó, 1907 év márczius hó 30-án.

[107] MOL, K 148 Elnöki Irattara 1907, letter from the Hungarian Honvéd Minister to Andrássy Gyula, Minister of the Interior, 23 March 1907.

of the Romanian Crown Domains has contracted seasonal workers from the villages of Kuvin, Kovaszincz, Mária-Radna and Baracska in Arad County to work on the Crown estate Segarcea near Craiova. The Hungarian authorities are denying them permission to travel. According to the Romanian Crown Domain administration, we are not talking here of emigration. The Legation are therefore requesting me to intercede with the Hungarian authorities in order to obtain the said permission to travel.'[108] As with other similar prophylactic measures, this too was not unprecedented with the Hungarian authorities. Long before the Romanian uprising they tried to limit the centrifugal tendencies of their rural work force, who chose to work abroad or emigrated.[109]

The imperial military authorities backed up the efforts of the Hungarian civilian authorities: as reported by Transylvanian newspapers, the main army corps in Transylvania and the Banat (the 12th Army Corps in Hermannstadt and the 7th Army Corps in Temesvár) received orders of mobilization. Smaller units in Nagyvárad and Szeged were also set at the ready for possible intervention.[110] Memoir literature testifies to the impact that these measures had on the mobilized Romanians from Hungary. Mihail Şerban, rector of the Agricultural Academy in Cluj after the First World War and a prominent Transylvanian nationalist leader, did his military service at the K.u.K. officer school in Szeged. In spring 1907 he was mobilized and spent 'three days and three nights at the Szeged railway station awaiting dispatch as part of intervention troops to put down the Romanian uprising'. Şerban's son mentioned this episode in his memoirs as a turning point in his father's life: 'This was the ultimate proof that the liberating Romanian soldier (*dorobanţ*), whom his father expected to cross the mountains, was starving in his own country. Later on he learnt that they used cannons against the peasantry.' It was a sobering experience that

---

[108] MOL., K 149 B Reservált Iratok, 11. Tétel, 1907, p. 57: Aehrenthal to Hungarian Interior Minister, 21 March 1907.

[109] Covasna National Archives, RO_BJANCV_F_9_1907/2035, RO_BJANCV_F_9_1907/5027, RO_BJANCV_F_9_1908/1278. I am most grateful to Dr. Botond Nagy for providing me with this archival information; see also MOL, K 149 B Reservált Iratok, 11. Tétel, 1907, pp. 6 and 11, for references to authorities' concern with large-scale emigration.

[110] Lájos Vajda, *1907. A Nagy Parasztfelkelés erdélyi visszhangja*, Politikai Könyvkiadó, Bukarest, 1977, pp. 190–191.

sparked off his lifelong interest in agriculture and economics, which he went on to pursue at German universities.[111]

Military mobilization in Hungary during spring 1907 has been attributed two functions:[112] (1) domestic order keeping (i.e. making sure the Hungarian peasantry did not follow the Romanian example) and (2) possible military intervention should the Romanians ask for help or the situation get so much out of hand that foreign intervention becomes a must. Judging by the reluctance of imperial military authorities to commit troops to help with Hungarian rural strikes, it seems, however, more probable that the partial mobilization ordered in spring 1907 was primarily aimed at border defence and possible foreign intervention.

How much of an influence did the peasant uprising in Romania have on the Hungarian peasantry and the episodes of violence that flared up in the Hungarian countryside in 1907? Peasant strikes were reported in southeastern Hungary in spring 1907 but also in summer of the same year, only some of them taking place at the same time as the peasant uprising in Romania. Most of them occurred in counties that did have a majority of Romanian population but were *not* immediately contiguous with the Romanian frontier: Szolnok-Doboka, Bihar, Temes-Torontal, Szatmár, Máramaros counties. A few of these counties (Szolnok-Doboka, Hunyad, Máramaros, Torda-Arányos) had the lowest rates of literacy in dualist Hungary. In Szolnok-Doboka county, peasants set fire to a notary's house, the latter just about escaping their murderous rage; in another village the local judge was killed; in Torda county, the local judge and notary were attacked by irate peasants and were saved by the timely intervention of armed gendarmes. Violence was thus not only visited upon landowners and lessees (*bérlők*), merchants and local authorities were equally targets.[113]

---

[111] Alexandru Şerban, 'Amintiri peste generaţii', unpublished manuscript, pp. 81–82. (A digital copy was kindly provided by Dr. Ioan Ciupea, researcher at the History Museum of Transylvania, Cluj, Romania): 'Această perioadă de stagiu militar a adus marea turnură în viaţa tatii, căci a fost mobilizat în gara Seghedin – timp de trei zile şi trei nopţi – pentru a fi trimis ca trupă de intervenţie în vederea înăbuşirii răscoalei ţărăneşti, declanşată la Flămânzi (jud. Botoşani) şi extinsă în întreaga ţară (1907). Era dovada că dorobanţul eliberator aşteptat de tatăl său şi de el însuşi, să treacă peste Carpaţi, murea de foame la el acasă. Aflase apoi curând că se trăsese cu turnurile în ţăranii răsculaţi. N-au fost necesare trupe de intervenţie străine, pentru că răscoala a fost înăbuşită cu mijloace proprii, dar tânărul Mihai Şerban şi-a reorientat gândurile de viitor, abordând în ţările de limbă germană, tot ce era de studiat în legătură cu agricultura, cu socialul, cu juridicul şi cu economicul.'

[112] Vajda, *1907. A Nagy Parasztfelkelés erdélyi visszhangja*, pp. 190–191.

[113] Vajda, *1907. A Nagy Parasztfelkelés erdélyi visszhangja*, pp. 195, 216.

There was plenty of local rural discontent on the Hungarian side of the border. The flares of Hungarian rural violence remained just that, mere flares, owing to effective policing. The detective system, which came into being in 1902, was used to the full. Detectives were sent in to collect information from the counties of Szolnok-Doboka, Hunyad, Arad and Máramaros. Acting on intelligence from their own sources and from gendarmerie reports, the local authorities had the gendarmerie troops reinforced in places deemed at risk of rural violence.[114] Use of weapons by the gendarmerie and reinforcement by *honvéd* troops were fairly frequent occurrences.[115] According to Iuliu Maniu, Romanian MP in the Hungarian Parliament at the time, in Panád, a village near Blaj (Balázsfalva), the clashes between *honvéd* troops and rebellious peasants resulted in six dead, 15 seriously wounded and 30 lightly wounded. Official figures regarding casualties were lower.[116] Violence and violent repression were present also in the Székely inhabited regions of Transylvania: in Kézdivásárhely clashes between the police and workers (*cselédek*) resulted in several dead.[117]

Rumours of a planned general uprising in Transylvania coursed in parallel to the peasant uprising in Romania. A note published in the *Bukowinaer Gebirgsjournal* on 20 March 1907 alerted that: 'a serious and reliable source has reported to us that a brochure is circulating under the greatest of secrecy among village notaries in Hungary and Transylvania, which contains plans for a general popular uprising. At the same time notaries are receiving weapons and ammunition to be distributed to the population.'[118] The published note was brought to the attention of the Imperial War Ministry, who proceeded to inform the Hungarian Honvéd Ministry, who in turn relayed the information to Wekerle, the Hungarian Prime Minster, who finally acquainted Andrássy, the Hungarian Minister of the Interior.[119] No other information is available on the outcome of this alert.

Although sporadic official reports, such as those from Szolnok-Doboka county, did make connections between local protest movements and the

---

[114] Egyed Ákos, 'Az 1907-es romániai parasztfelkelés visszhangja a magyar sajtóban' in Cicală et al., *Adalékok az 1907-es parasztfelkelés történetéhez*, pp. 76–77, p. 80.

[115] Vajda, *1907. A Nagy Parasztfelkelés erdélyi visszhangja*, pp. 195, 217.

[116] *Budapesti Napló*, 1907, augusztus 29, 30 – quoted in Lájos Vajda, *1907. A Nagy Parasztfelkelés erdélyi visszhangja*, p. 255.

[117] Székely Hírlap, 1907. Október 9. – quoted in Vajda, *1907. A Nagy Parasztfelkelés erdélyi visszhangja*, p. 217.

[118] MOL, K 149 B Reservált Iratok, 2. Tétel, 1907, p. 265.

[119] MOL, K 149 B Reservált Iratok, 2. Tétel, 1907, p. 264.

Romanian peasant uprising,[120] most of the quoted official reports assessed the mood of the population and the necessity for increased measures of protection without making explicit reference to any contamination from the uprising in the neighbouring country. It seems that the connection between domestic and cross-border unrest was spelt out by the Hungarian press, but there is no evidence of the uprising actually crossing the border.[121] This reinforces the idea that contiguity in itself does not lead to contamination and coincidence of timing/synchrony does not necessarily presuppose a causal relation. Contamination almost comes across as a feat of imagination in a society obsessed with the notion of contamination and given to interpreting social conflict in terms of contamination. This, as we saw in previous chapters, holds true of internal contiguities in Romania during the uprising (with counties that remained peaceful despite their vicinity to rebellious ones) as it holds true of the Russian vicinity (the Romanian peasant uprising did not break out through contamination from the Russian troubles across the border).

Austria

If Hungary defended the longest stretch of the Habsburg imperial frontier with Romania, Austria shared only a small portion of this frontier but received the bulk of the refugees. According to the information provided by the K.K. *Landespräsident* of Bukovina, Oktavian Regner von Bleyleben, between 18 and 23 March 1907, '2,500 refugees came from Romania to Suczawa and Itzkany and several hundred more to Synoutz',[122] having fled Romanian towns such as Mihăileni, Botoșani and Dorohoi, and the border town of Burdujeni, which had been attacked by rebellious peasants. As far as Bleyleben knew, although there had been much devastation of Jewish shops, houses and businesses, there had been no dead among the town population; the only dead were the result of clashes between the peasants and the army.[123] The Bukovinian *Landespräsident* was confident

---

[120] Ion Cicală et al., *Munkás és parasztmozgalmak Erdélyben 1905–1907*, Tudomanyos Könyvkiadó, Bukarest, 1962, p. 287.

[121] This of course needs to be taken with an inevitable pinch of salt given the state of the archives at the moment, with huge holdings pertaining to the Royal Hungarian Ministry of the Interior still off-limits for researchers.

[122] PAAA, Berlin, R 9652 Rumänien Allgemeine Angelegenheiten 1906–1907, Der K.K. Landespräsident im Herzotume Bukowina, Czernowitz, 23 March 1907, pp. 1–2.

[123] PAAA, Berlin, R 9652 Rumänien Allgemeine Angelegenheiten 1906–1907, Der K.K. Landespräsident im Herzotume Bukowina, Czernowitz, 23 March 1907, p. 2.

that the troubles were not going to spread over the border into Bukovina, but he did allow for this possibility and took precautionary measures in the form of a reinforcemȃnt of the border through gendarmerie forces.[124] Similar reassurances that peace would not be disturbed in Bukovina were also given by the Austrian Minister of the Interior, Freiherr von Bienerth.[125]

According to the German consul in Vienna, the imperial officials there 'felt very uneasy at the ongoing peasant troubles in Romania, which were in part taking place close to the Austrian border, because of the big number of destitute refugees who deluged the border regions and also because they did not exclude the possibility that the dangerous movement might spread over to Bukovina'. Given that the necessary measures were taken immediately in order to stave off any potential danger, the German consul concluded that there was no reason for concern, all the more so as 'the standard of life of the Romanian peasant population in Bukovina was different from that of Moldavia.'[126]

Extant documents produced by the lower ranks of the Bukovinian administration testify to fairly effective policing and population control in this Austrian borderland. From reports on electoral assemblies of the Social Democrats, to alerts about peasant antisemitism, to exchanges with the Ministry of the Interior, Ministry of Justice and Ministry of Agriculture regarding the peasant condition and attempts to ameliorate it, these documents show that the Bukovinian government paid attention to what happened on the ground and were bent on strengthening security measures.[127] In 1905 an independent urban police for Czernowitz came into being, based on an 1853 precedent and following the model of urban police forces in cities like Vienna, Prague and Trieste. This new structure complemented the existing Bukovinian police structures, which were subordinated to the Ministry of the Interior and whose personnel had been increased several times at the end of the nineteenth century (in 1891, 1892 and 1895). These police increments were considered by the Ministry of the Interior as insufficient 'given the exposed situation of the provincial

[124] PAAA, Berlin, R 9652 Rumänien Allgemeine Angelegenheiten 1906–1907, Der K.K. Landespräsident im Herzotume Bukowina, Czernowitz, 23 March 1907, pp. 2–3.

[125] PAAA, Berlin, R 9653, Rumänien Allgemeine Angelegenheiten April–December 1907, Report no. 117, Vienna, 4 April 1907, pp. 2–3.

[126] PAAA, Berlin, R 9652 Rumänien Allgemeine Angelegenheiten 1906–1907, Report no. 106, Vienna 23 March 1907, pp. 1–2.

[127] ANR, Fond Guvernământul Bucovinei, Ministerul de Interne, Mapa 86/2; Mapa 78/fasciculul 6.

capital Czernowitz in the easternmost part of the Monarchy and given the political, national and confessional relations that dominated the region'.[128]

The Austrian gendarmerie in Bukovina did not have the bad reputation of the Romanian or Hungarian gendarmes. This was because they were not beyond accountability. Their policing activities could be, and were, criticized and looked into by higher authorities. Thus, a parliamentary interpellation to the Ministry of the Interior about the abuses of the local gendarmerie in Sereth triggered a thorough investigation into the legality of the gendarmerie's actions in a poaching case. The investigation is emblematic in two ways: first, as proof that complaints against the gendarmerie were taken seriously and explanations were asked for and, second, as the case was brought to the Interior Minister's attention in Parliament, it shows that the peasant on the ground did wield some agency and their grievances did reach the highest places, that is, that parliamentary representation was responsive to peasant needs.[129]

Peasant antisemitism was kept tabs on by the Bukovinian authorities and rumours of impending violence against Jews were taken seriously and reported on at length. Such was the case of rumours circulating in the village communities of Storonetz-Putilla and Radautzi in late April and early May 1907. The news gave rise to profuse exchange of correspondence between the local and the regional authorities and triggered prevention measures. The head of the local gendarmerie detailed on his inquiries among the peasants and traced the course of hearsay among them: threats and ominous preparations (blacksmith making iron bars allegedly to arm peasants against Jews) were made, fear spread among the local Jewish population and also among some the local Christian intelligentsia, who proceeded to send their women away, others left with their entire families. 'It is noteworthy', remarked the gendarmerie commander, 'that the peasants of the area openly admit to having knowledge of agitation against the Jews. When asked where they know this from, they reply "it is known in the entire village" or "a Jew told me and I told other people". Of course, no one owns up to wanting to take part in the unrest'.[130] Information of

---

[128] ANR, Fond Guvernământul Bucovinei, Ministerul de Interne, Mapa 81, dosar 1, Allerunterthänigster Vortrag des treugehorsamsten Ministers des Innern Arthur Grafen Bylandt-Rheidt, Wien am 12. Mai 1905, pp. 26–27.

[129] ANR, Fond Guvernământul Bucovinei, Ministerul de Interne, Mapa 78 – fasc. 6, pp. 26–32.

[130] ANR, Fond Guvernământul Bucovinei, Ministerul de Interne, Mapa 86/2, Report to the K.K. Landesgendarmeriekommando by the gendarmerie commander Lt. May, 29 April 1907, p. 48.

impending unrest and violence was collected from other sources as well. A Uniate priest recounted to the commander his encounter with a Ruthenian peasant in the village of Kisselitza: 'the Greek-Catholic priest Strepko from Storonetz-Putilla drove through Kisselitza, where a Ruthene peasant stopped him and told him the following: "Your Grace, we peasants trust you because we know you will not betray us. Something's brewing and we might need a few bombs. Can you tell us where we could get them without danger of being discovered?"'[131]

In stark contrast to the attitude to peasant unrest in Romania, the hypothesis of foreign contamination was discarded out of hand and the brewing conflict was explained in terms of local social tensions:

> It is therefore evident that there has arisen an antisemitic movement among the peasants. This was not kindled by foreign elements but rather has its starting point in the mountains and is led by disgruntled, impoverished farmers who were once landowners (*von unzufriedenen und herabgekommenen eistigen Grundwirte geführt werden*).[132]

The response was to deploy additional gendarmes in the villages that showed signs of unrest and keep alert should the need for more arise.[133] These reports show the vagaries of information management in case of a looming crisis: the first signs of unrest did not seem to point to a major social movement and, although looked into, they were initially dismissed. Subsequent alerts from the local authorities, however, were taken on board and, although the unrest was still referred to as 'alleged', these alerts were acted on by reinforcing gendarmerie numbers.

Was there a connection between this simmering unrest in Bukovina and the concomitant peasant uprising in Romania? There was, and this was reflected in the gendarmerie reports, which kept abreast of the rumours in the villages. As one such report pointed out on 27 April 1907, 'for a few days now there have been circulating in the village of

---

[131] ANR, Fond Guvernământul Bucovinei, Ministerul de Interne, Mapa 86/2, Report to the K.K. Landesgendarmeriekommando by the gendarmerie commander Lt. May, 29 April 1907, p. 48.

[132] ANR, Fond Guvernământul Bucovinei, Ministerul de Interne, Mapa 86/2, Report to the K.K. Landesgendarmeriekommando by the gendarmerie commander Lt. May, 29 April 1907, p. 48/verso.

[133] ANR, Fond Guvernământul Bucovinei, Ministerul de Interne, Mapa 86/2, Report to the K.K. Landesgendarmeriekommando by the gendarmerie commander Lt. May, 29 April 1907, p. 49; Report by the K.K. Bezirkshauptmannschaft Radautz, 29. April 1907, p. 52.

Seletin rumours, which were spread out from an unknown source and which caused much concern among the local Jews, that in the near future there will take place in this village a battle similar to the one in Romania (*eine Schlacht auf gleiche Art wie in Rumänien*), which will aim to kill the local Jews, burn down their houses and in this way pass the land of the Jews into the hands of the *Huzulen*.'[134] Those who spread out the rumours were arrested and handed over to the district tribunal (*k.k. Bezirksgerichte*).

Military intervention was not resorted to despite requests to this effect from the panicked local Jewish population. The gendarmerie did not exclude such a possibility but it did not figure at the top of their list of preventive measures. They preferred instead to make full use of the available gendarmerie forces and only if the situation became unmanageable to call in the military:

> I ordered the immediate transfer of 20 gendarmes to Storonetz-Putilla and refrained, for the time being, from asking for military assistance. At the same time, I made provisions that, should military assistance become necessary at a later date, troops could be made available within three hours in Wiznitz.
>
> In a telegram I received on 2 May this year, district commissar Jech reported that the reinforcement of the gendarmerie had such a calming influence on the population that no incidents occurred and military assistance was not necessary.
>
> Today I sent instructions by telegraph to district commissar Jech that he should personally talk to village leaders and calm them down, as well as advise the Jewish population not to panic and to refrain from any provocations, to close down pubs on Sunday, and that the gendarmerie should make themselves conspicuous through frequent patrols and any incidents should be nipped in the bud.
>
> I also directed Jech to ask for new reinforcements, should the existing gendarmerie troops turn out to be insufficient and I stressed that, according to regulations, military assistance should never be resorted to for mere pacification of the population, but only when the available means of order keeping are not sufficient anymore. Finally, I instructed Jech to place telegraph lines under strong supervision.[135]

---

[134] ANR, Fond Guvernământul Bucovinei, Ministerul de Interne, Mapa 86/2, Report to the K.K. Bezirkshauptmannschaft from the Seletin gendarmerie post, 27. April 1907, p. 56.

[135] ANR, Fond Guvernământul Bucovinei, Ministerul de Interne, Mapa 86/2, pp. 57–58: report dated 3 May 1907 from the K.K. Landesregierung in Czernowitz to the Austrian Minister of the Interior in Vienna.

These measures calmed down the village community, who proceeded to send a deputation of 120 peasants from Storonetz-Putilla and Sergie under the leadership of the archpriest (*Erzpriester*) Orest Kozak, who gave reassurance that no violence would take place.[136]

The authorities remained alert to rumour of peasant unrest in Bukovina. A 1908 dispatch from the Ministry of the Interior to the *Landespräsident* in Czernowitz asked for more information on a newspaper note that warned of imminent peasant violence in Bukovina: 'The Viennese newspaper *Die Zeit*, evening edition, of 9 September 1908, carries a telegram from Czernowitz according to which the peasant population in Bukovina is in ferment, which is likely to lead to peasant disturbances. I request your Excellency to communicate to me as soon as possible your opinion on this and what measures have been taken in this respect.'[137]

The said newspaper couched their alert in the following terms:

> Looming Peasant Disturbances in Bukovina.
> Czernowitz, 8 September. For a while now the peasant population in Bukovina has been in ferment. Peasants organize secret meetings in the villages and they agitate intensively. It is feared that these secretive counsels and agitation are the harbinger of peasant disturbances, similar to those in Romania. The movement is a purely social one and has no political background.[138]

Antisemitism in Bukovina came back on the political and administrative agenda in the following years as a direct result of the expansion of franchise and attempts by radical leaders of ethnic parties to recruit the voting peasant population into their political camp. Brochures were disseminated among the village population that singled out Jews as not only the religious but also the economic archenemies of the peasants and portrayed them as a major village pest. Such hate-mongering did not go unnoticed: it triggered interpellations in the Austrian Parliament and a string of

[136] ANR, Fond Guvernământul Bucovinei, Ministerul de Interne, Mapa 86/2: report dated 3 May 1907 from the K.K. Landesregierung in Czernowitz to the Austrian Minister of the Interior in Vienna, p. 58/verso.

[137] ANR, Fond Guvernământul Bucovinei, Ministerul de Interne, Mapa 86/2, report dated 11 September 1908 from the Präsidium des k.k. Ministeriums des Innern to the Landespräsident in Czernowitz, p. 64.

[138] Arhivele Naţionale Centrale Bucureşti, Fond Guvernământul Bucovinei, Ministerul de Interne, Mapa 86/2, Newspaper cutting, Abendblatt „Die Zeit" vom 9. Sepmtember 1908, p. 65.

correspondence between Bukovinian and central imperial authorities assessing the impact of these brochures on the local peasant population. Those who distributed the inflammatory brochures were brought to court and fined.[139] Although the conclusion that Bukovinian authorities reached was that the impact of the brochures was negligible and that, after all, they only incited 'an economic battle' against the Jews, the official commitment remained to maintain order and prevent any damage to the person and property of the Jews. As the Bukovinian *Landespräsident* put it in a 1909 report to the Austrian Minister of the Interior:

> I instructed the district gendarmerie in Kimpolung and Suczawa to make use of all legal means to deter any illegal acts of a potential antisemitic movement and, in case the security of person and property is endangered, to take appropriate action and to notify me of all of their steps in this respect. I would like to stress that I continue, just like before, to give full attention to the antisemitic agitation which has appeared of late and which is taking increasingly more radical forms and in all cases of illegal activity of this nature which are brought to my knowledge I will initiate immediate investigation and take the appropriate measures.[140]

Tsarist Bessarabia

Infrastructure

Maurice Bompard, the French Ambassador to Russia between 1902 and 1909, remarked in his memoirs: 'In Russia there is no administration in the true sense of the word; there is only police, and what a police that is!'[141] This could also be applied to the Tsarist province of Bessarabia, where law and order were maintained via the time-honoured system of *ispravniks*, who were in charge of the eight administrative regions into which the province was divided: Orhei, Khotyn (Hotin), Beltsi (Bălți), Bender (Tighina), Soroca, Kishinev (Chișinău), Izmail and Akkerman.

---

[139] ANR, Fond Guvernământul Bucovinei, Ministerul de Interne, Mapa 86/2, Präsidium des k.k. Ministerium des Innern, Einsichtsakt des Justiz-Ministeriums, mit einem Berichte der O.St. A. in Lemberg, betreffend die Straffälle wegen der judenfeindlichen Bewegung in den Bezirken Suczawa und Kimpolung, p. 115.

[140] ANR, Fond Guvernământul Bucovinei, Ministerul de Interne, Mapa 86/2, Report dated 18 January 1909 from the Landespräsident in Czernowitz to the Austrian Minister of the Interior, pp. 107–108.

[141] Maurice Bompard, *Mon Ambassade en Russie, 1903–1908*, Paris, Librairie Plon, 1937, p. 259.

Ispravniks were the eyes and ears of the regional imperial authorities: they headed the local police, were in charge of keeping order, supervising administrative tasks (road and bridge maintenance, for instance), placed themselves at the disposal of troops that passed through their territory, kept tabs on harvest works and grain production, attended to complaints and suits, punished those who broke the law. According to an 1816 directive given by the Bessarabian governor A.C. Catacazi, the *ispravniks* together with other local authorities had to visit their territories once every three months, acquaint themselves with the state of affairs and report back. Inspectors were appointed to make sure that they did so.[142] As seen through the eyes of American agricultural expert Louis Guy Michael in 1910:

> The rural isprovnik is a man of varied activities. In addition to supervision of the village policemen in his district, he is a sort of sheriff to keep the inhabitants within legal bounds. He is also a secret service agent of the government to ferret out violations of the laws of the Crown.[143]

In the countryside at the village level police duties were delegated to *dvorniks* (Rom. *vornici*), who mediated conflicts, investigated crimes, kept tabs on the local population and on the comings and goings of outsiders, and reported back grievances to the *ispravnik*.[144]

This was in theory the make-up of the Bessarabian police system. In practice, the police force was efficient but followed its own laws and was riddled with corruption. Prince S.D. Urusov, the governor of Bessarabia between 1903 and 1904, despaired of ever being able to eradicate corruption from the provincial police system. The Bessarabian police—explained the governor—'consists of several persons who never take bribes, of many persons who take bribes that the local custom recognizes as legitimate; and finally of a small proportion of bribe takers who are always and everywhere regarded as corrupt'.[145] He showed how this was structurally engrained. The underpaid and overworked police could not make ends meet on their

---

[142] Valentin Tomuleț, *Basarabia în epoca modernă (1812–1918), (Instituții, Regulamente, Termeni)*, Chișinău, 2012, pp. 358–359.

[143] Louis Guy Michael, *More Corn for Bessarabia. Russian Experience 1910–1917*, Michigan State University Press, 1983, p. 56.

[144] Tomuleț, *Basarabia*, pp. 676–677.

[145] S. D. Urusov, *Memoirs of a Russian Governor*, Transl. by Herman Rosenthal, London&New York, Harper and Brothers Publishers, 1908, p. 30.

salaries so they had of necessity to resort to other sources of income. Restrictive legislation against the Jews provided both the context and the willing bestowers of bribes:

> In accordance with the temporary regulations of 1882 the Jews could not lease lands. The lands of the Bessarabian estates leased by Jews was the first source of income to the police. [...] The lessee, thus holding the property illegally, would gladly pay fifty kopecks per desyatin of land rather than have trouble with the authorities and be dragged into court.[146]

The second source of police income derived from a practice that was common to both Bessarabia and neighbouring Romania: the interdiction of Jews to live in the countryside. Temporary permission was granted 'for commercial and other reasons' but it was the local police who decided when their time had come to an end and could discretionarily order their removal with perfect impunity:

> [The policeman's] actions are legal; that is his interpretation of the law; and in fact the question, from the standpoint of the law, is always debateable. Furthermore, its solution always depends upon inquiry made by the self-same police. It is, therefore, profitable to pay the police in order to peacefully wind up one's business in the village.[147]

Finally, the frontier police boosted their incomes with bribes from Jewish merchants who traded across the border and for whom 'it is more profitable to pay three rubles to the police official than to apply for a fifteen-ruble passport at the provincial administrative bureau. This applies to all whom the official does not recognize as merchants.'[148]

Urusov admitted that, despite his best efforts, bribery remained a widespread practice in Bessarabia. This was due to administrative shortcomings: 'the village authorities frequently conceal these facts from the police, the minor police officials from the district police, and the district police from the Governor.'[149] The main reason for the ongoing corruption was, however, the very legal framework that excluded the Jewish population

---

[146] Urusov, *Memoirs of a Russian Governor*, p. 28.
[147] Urusov, *Memoirs of a Russian Governor*, p. 29.
[148] Urusov, *Memoirs of a Russian Governor*, p. 30.
[149] Urusov, *Memoirs of a Russian Governor*, p. 29.

from basic rights and subjected them to the whims and abuse of local administration: 'I do not believe that this evil can be rooted out as long as a portion of the population is deprived of the natural rights of existence that are enjoyed by the rest of the population.'[150]

Okhrana 'Feelers' in Romania

The Tsarist secret police extended the scope of its surveillance operations to Romania, which had become a haven for refugee Narodniki in the final quarter of the nineteenth century, some of them originating from Bessarabia.[151] In an 1891 diplomatic report, which was aimed at informing the newly appointed Tsarist consul, *Hofmeister* Fonton, about the state of affairs in Romania, the presence of the Okhrana on Romanian territory was spelt out clearly: 'This country has long been a refuge for dangerous political personalities, who have been expelled from various European states. This led us to strengthen our border control and also to set up a secret police agency in Romania. Your Excellency will become acquainted with its activity upon taking over your post.'[152] Okhrana had agents in Bucharest—A.A. Motiilev and Zamanova/Gheorghiu Melasii—the former having lived and operated in Romania for the best part of 30 years, according to 1905 Okhrana internal correspondence, that is, since before Romania's acquisition of state independence. Motiilev provided services for the Tsarist gendarmerie and military and was instrumental in setting up a border guard security agency.[153]

In addition to secret police input, the Tsarist consul in Romania, von Giers, reported regularly to the Ministry of the Foreign Affairs conveying rumours and reports he received from the territory. Such was the 1906 report received from Sinaia on meetings between Romanian nationalists and representatives of the autonomy movement in Bessarabia, or the great

---

[150] Urusov, *Memoirs of a Russian Governor*, p. 31.

[151] Flavius Solomon, Adrian-Bogdan Ceobanu, Andrei Cușco, Grigorii Șkundin (Eds.), *Rapoarte diplomatice ruse din România (1888–1898)/ДИПЛОМАТИЧЕСКИЕ ДОКУМЕНТЫ РОССИЙСКИХ ПРЕДСТАВИТЛЕЙ В РУМЫНИИ (1888–1898)*, Editura Universității Alexandru Ioan Cuza, Iași, 2014, p. 258, footnotes 24, 25.

[152] Flavius Solomon, Adrian-Bogdan Ceobanu, Andrei Cușco, Grigorii Șkundin (Eds.), *Rapoarte diplomatice ruse din România (1888–1898)/ДИПЛОМАТИЧЕСКИЕ ДОКУМЕНТЫ РОССИЙСКИХ ПРЕДСТАВИТЛЕЙ В РУМЫНИИ (1888–1898)*, p. 256.

[153] Okhrana Archives, Hoover Institution Archives, Stanford University, reels 11 and 12. Many thanks to Ron Basich for digital copies of this material.

impression made in Romania by the publication of the memoirs of Kniaz Urusov, the former governor of Bessarabia.[154]

Reactions to the Romanian Uprising

The Tsarist Ministry of the Interior did not initially deem the Romanian peasant troubles menacing enough to take any special measures along the frontier. A note, dated 15 March 1907, from the Press Bureau (*Reci*) of the Kishinev Police indicated: 'in the Ministry of the Interior they are of the view that the news which was received directly to the Ministry from Romania leads one to believe that the movement is not likely to cross the Russian-Romanian border.'[155] Notwithstanding this, the provincial authorities (*ispravniks* and heads of the local *zemstva*) scanned the border for any signs of contamination and, although satisfied that the conflict had not rippled across the border, took precautionary measures:

(1) reinforced border supervision by means of gendarmerie officers;
(2) the police was requested to limit the number of permits and issue them only with the greatest of care;
(3) an infantry guard was deployed along the Prut River and cavalry guards made their way there too;
(4) increased police and *zemstva* supervision of the districts along the border;
(5) a convention was established between three border guard brigades and the police for potential collaboration; and
(6) a permanent government liaison officer (*membru permanent al asistenței guberniale*) was appointed in all border districts.[156]

The Governor gave reassurance that there were enough troops in the province but their deployment seemed to him premature: 'the late coming of spring and the great quantity of snow are preventing the start of field-work and, probably, also any peasant claims.'[157] By 16 March the Ministry of the Interior had received secret telegrams of the Tsarist Ambassador

---

[154] ANR, Arhivă Microfilme, Fond Xerografii Rusia, Pachet XVII, nr. Act. 2, Anul 1905–1909, Report dated 3 October 1906 from Sinaia, pp. 40–43; Report no. 53 dated 8 July 1907, pp. 44–45 – Many thanks to Andrei Cușco for providing me with a copy of these documents.

[155] Gheorghe Matei, *Răsunetul internațional al răscoalei țăranilor din 1907*, Editura de Stat pentru Literatură Politică, București, 1957, p. 113.

[156] Matei, *Răsunetul internațional al răscoalei țăranilor din 1907*, p. 117.

[157] Matei, *Răsunetul internațional al răscoalei țăranilor din 1907*, p. 117.

in Bucharest from the Ministry of Foreign Affairs and highlighted the 'necessity for taking precautionary measures along the frontier'.[158]

The only incident reported from the Bessarabian border regions was an attempt by the peasants of Mingeri, in southwestern Bessarabia, to occupy land. According to the Director of the Police Department, this was thwarted by the local *ispravnik* and order was soon re-established: 'the information circulating in newspapers about this is all a concoction and what happened there had nothing to do with the unrest in Romania, which has since moved on somewhere else; these are just exaggerations of the leftist press.'[159] In addition to the set of measures taken by the Governor to secure the border, orders were issued to the gendarmerie officers on the border to prevent Professor Constantin Stere from the University of Iaşi to enter Bessarabia, given information received to the effect that he had close connections with Kishinev revolutionaries and that he was behind the peasant agitation in Romania.[160]

Just as in the case of the Bukovinian peasantry, some of whom were rumoured to have crossed over into Romania and joined the uprising, information circulated to similar effect about some of the Bessarabians. In a report dated 19 March 1907, the gendarmerie commander in charge of the Izmail border crossing relayed news received from the town of Tulcea in south-eastern Romania, that Russian fishermen from Izmail together with Romanian ones requested the county prefect to waive the fees levelled by the state on putting up thatch fences for fishing purposes. The gendarmerie commander reckoned that their demand must have been complied with under pressure of the current uprising.[161]

The available information points to the fact that the Bessarabian Police reacted promptly and efficiently to news of the Romanian uprising, took precautionary measures to prevent contamination and, most importantly, learned from their neighbours' traumatic experience. Thus in May 1907 a Kishinev Police employee, whose task was to study the agrarian question, was asked to provide a comprehensive report on the causes of the recently subsided peasant uprising in Romania.[162]

* * *

[158] Matei, *Răsunetul internaţional al răscoalei ţăranilor din 1907*, pp. 117–118.
[159] Matei, *Răsunetul internaţional al răscoalei ţăranilor din 1907*, p. 120.
[160] Matei, *Răsunetul internaţional al răscoalei ţăranilor din 1907*, p. 121.
[161] Matei, *Răsunetul internaţional al răscoalei ţăranilor din 1907*, p. 123.
[162] Matei, *Răsunetul internaţional al răscoalei ţăranilor din 1907*, p. 137.

The policing systems around the triple frontier differed dramatically from one another in their makeup and overall efficiency. By far the most scant and dysfunctional was that of the young Romanian Kingdom, which was embedded into an inchoate administrative framework that was highly politicized and as such debilitating and inefficient. The most grievous drawback of the Romanian police was its inability, for a complex of reasons, to react promptly and in good time to inceptive social unrest. Worse yet, local administrative neglect reflected similar mismanagement at the higher levels of authority: communication was disjointed and crucial information was ignored. Across the triple frontier in the imperial borderlands, Hungarian Transylvania, Austrian Bukovina and Tsarist Bessarabia, a higher degree of responsiveness characterized the local police structures. By far the best organized was the Hungarian rural police, with its multiple-scenario plans of action and intervention in case of rural unrest. In Austrian Bukovina, where rural unrest usually went hand in hand with outbursts of antisemitism, the channels of communication worked fairly well and a system of complaint and redress was safely in place. The timely response of the Tsarist police in Bessarabia to the Romanian peasant uprising as well as their liaising with the central imperial authorities shows that, for all its everyday corruption, when push came to shove, the Tsarist police were adept at keeping order.

BIBLIOGRAPHY

Miklós Bánffy, *Transylvanian Trilogy*, vol. 1: 'They Were Counted', Trans. Patrick Thursfield and Kathy Bánffy-Jelen, Arcadia Books, London, 1999

Maurice Bompard, *Mon Ambassade en Russie, 1903–1908*, Librairie Plon, Paris, 1937

Ion Cicală et al., *Adalékok az 1907-es parasztfelkelés történetéhez*, Tudományos könyvkiádó, Bukarest, 1957

Ion Cicală et al., *Munkás és parasztmozgalmak Erdélyben 1905–1907*, Tudomanyos Könyvkiadó, Bukarest, 1962

G.D. Creangă, *Grundbesitzverteilung und Bauernfrage in Rumänien*, Erster Teil, Leipzig, Verlag von Duncker und Humbolt, 1907

Sorin Cristescu (Ed.), *Carol I. Corespondența personală (1878–1912)*, București, Triton, 2005

Csapó Csaba, *A Magyar Királyi csendőrség története 1881–1914*, Pro Pannonia, Pécs, 1999

Rudolf Dinu, and Adrian-Bogdan Ceobanu (Eds.), *Gheorghe Rosetti-Solescu. Corespondență diplomatică personală și oficială (1895–1911). Petersburg*, Editura Unversității Alexandru Ioan Cuza, Iași, 2016

P.G. Eidelberg, *The Great Rumanian Peasant Revolt of 1907: Origins of a Modern Jacquerie*, Leiden, Brill, 1974

Keith Hitchins, *A Concise History of Romania*, CUP, Cambridge and New York, 2014

Jandarmeria română: 161 de ani de istorie în slujba legii, ordinii și siguranței publice, Editura Ministerului Administrației și Internelor, http://www.editura. mai.gov.ro/documente/biblioteca/2011/JANDARMERIA.pdf (Accessed on 25 August 2015)

Charles and Barbara Jelavich, *The Establishment of the Balkan National States, 1804–1920*, University of Washington Press, Seattle and London, 2000

C. Jormescu and I. Popa-Burcă, *Harta agronomică a României*, București, Inst. de arte grafice "Carol Göbl", 1907

N.V. Leonescu, *Anul 1907. Răscoala țăranilor*, Atelierele grafice "Lumina Moldovei", Iași, 1924

Gheorghe Matei, *Răsunetul internațional al răscoalei țăranilor din 1907*, Editura de Stat pentru Literatură Politică, București, 1957

Louis Guy Michael, *More Corn for Bessarabia. Russian Experience 1910–1917*, Michigan State University Press, 1983

Botond Nagy, 'Rendvédelem a Magyar-Román Határon a 19. Század Második Feléleben', *Acta Siculica* 2007, pp. 437–453

Andrei Oțetea and Ion Popescu-Puțuri (Eds), *Documente privind marea răscoală a țăranilor din 1907*, București, Editura Academiei Republicii Socialiste România, 1977

József Parádi, and A Magyar Királyi Csendőrség. *Az első Magyar polgári, központosított, közbiztonsági őrtestület 1881–1945*, Szemere Bertalan Magyar Rendvédelem-történeti Tudományos Társaság, Budapest, 2012

Ion Popescu-Puțuri et al., *Documente privind marea răscoală a țăranilor din 1907*, Vol. V, Editura Academiei Republicii Socialiste România, București, 1987

Liviu Rebreanu, *The Uprising*, Trans. P. Crandjean and S. Hartauer, Peter Owen Ltd., London, 1965

Henry L. Roberts, *Rumania. Political Problems of an Agrarian State*, Yale University Press, New Haven, 1951

Flavius Solomon, Adrian-Bogdan Ceobanu, Andrei Cușco, and Grigorii Șkundin (Eds.), *Rapoarte diplomatice ruse din România (1888–1898)/ ДИПЛОМАТИЧЕСКИЕ ДОКУМЕНТЫ РОССИЙСКИХ ПРЕДСТАВИТЛЕЙ В РУМЫНИИ (1888–1898)*, Editura Universității Alexandru Ioan Cuza, Iași, 2014

Alin Spânu, *Istoria serviciilor de informații/contrainformații românești în perioada 1919–1945*, Iași, Demiurg, 2010

Ioan Șerbănescu (Ed.), *Evreii din România in secolul XX. 1900–1920. Fast și Nefast într-un răstimp istoric. Documente și mărturii*, Vol. I, Editura Hasefer, București, 2003

Charles Tilly, *Politics of Collective Action*, CUP, Cambridge, 2003

Valentin Tomuleţ, *Basarabia în epoca modernă (1812–1918), (Instituţii, Regulamente, Termeni)*, Chişinău, 2012

Lájos Vajda, *1907, A Nagy Parasztfelkelés erdélyi visszhangja*, Politikai Könyvkiadó, Bukarest, 1977

S. D. Urusov, *Memoirs of a Russian Governor*, Trans. Herman Rosenthal, Harper and Brothers Publishers, London and New York, 1908

Doreen Warriner (Ed.), *Contrasts in Emerging Societies. Readings in the Social and Economic History of South-Eastern Europe in the Nineteenth Century*, Indiana University Press, Bloomington, 1965

CHAPTER 6

Paper Worlds

The authorities around the triple frontier received news of the Romanian peasant uprising from newspapers as well as from their own contacts and correspondents. Newspapers played a vital role in the transmission of information and were a constant reference point for all parties involved. Newspapers got their news from other newspapers; the gendarmerie got their news from their own informants and from newspapers; the Romanian government found out about the uprising from the newspapers. The peasants themselves got wind of the uprising elsewhere through people who had read the newspapers. Information circulated through other channels as well but newspapers remained the most important medium of information dissemination and the most closely policed.

Newspaper coverage of events was as problematic then as it is now. Source unreliability, reporting inaccuracy, political bias, distortion in quest of sensationalism and bigger sales can easily be held against newspaper stories. In 1907 writers all around the frontier complained about it while the besieged Romanian government tried to suppress newspaper circulation, intercept news vendors, and censor newspapers in an attempt to prevent news of the uprising spreading and contaminating other hitherto quiet regions of the country. Editors of newspapers across the border, on the contrary, welcomed the stream of news from Romania, but struggled to cope with the baffling amount of contradictory rumour and information. As the Bukovinian *Czernowitzer Allgemeine Zeitung* remarked,

© The Author(s) 2018

I. Marin, *Peasant Violence and Antisemitism in Early Twentieth-Century Eastern Europe*,
https://doi.org/10.1007/978-3-319-76069-8_6

It is a difficult and thankless task to work through the deluge of news arrived from Romania. It is difficult because, in addition to it being almost impossible to distinguish chaff from wheat, falsehood from truth, it requires a lot of willpower to read through endless variations on the same horrific news; it is a thankless task because it presupposes Sisyphus-like work in order to extract a clear picture of the situation out of the chaos of reports.[1]

How did information about the Romanian peasant uprising reach the pages of foreign newspapers? More often than not indirectly, with the journalists cobbling together bits of information from local Romanian newspapers, from other foreign newspapers and from their own unnamed sources and correspondents, more often than not citing international papers on what was happening close by.

As we shall see in this chapter, newspaper coverage ranged from *Schadenfreude*, smug finger pointing and antisemitism, to thoughtful, apprehensive analyses of the crisis and its wider implications for the region. What follows is a bird's-eye view of press coverage of the uprising around the triple frontier with Austria-Hungary and Tsarist Russia in an attempt not so much to ascertain whether the various papers got things right or whether they succeeded in their 'Sisyphus-like toil' of extracting a clear picture out of the helter-skelter of information about the crisis, as to use the neighbouring agrarian crisis as an x-ray of local concerns, fears and preconceived ideas. As such, the foreign newspaper coverage of the Romanian uprising is more revealing about the issues and political hobbyhorses of the countries it originated from than about the country and events reported on.

THE HUNGARIAN PRESS

Pesti Napló, the main Hungarian liberal newspaper of the day and the brain-child of prestigious personalities such as József Eötvös and Ferenc Déak, featured news about the Romanian uprising almost one month into the uprising, with title-page coverage dating from 22 March onwards. They drew their information from a combination of disparate sources, once or twice removed from the horse's mouth. They quoted other newspapers such as Romanian *Dimineața*, the Romanian press agency *Agence*

---

[1] *Czernowitzer Allgemeine Zeitung*, 28 March, 1907, p. 1: 'Die Agrarunruhen in Rumänien'.

Roumaine, the Viennese *Allgemeine Zeitung, Kölnische Zeitung*, and local Hungarian newspapers such as *Aradi Közlöny*; they also obtained accounts from their own, unnamed correspondents in Bucharest, Czernowitz, Iaşi and Berlin, who themselves sometimes got their knowledge from the newspapers too. In Czernovitz the *Pesti Napló* correspondent read the Viennese *Allgemeine Zeitung* quoting Romanian *Adevărul* on what was happening just a stone's throw away across the border in the market town of Târgu Frumos. For more official information they quoted border-town authorities such as the Izkany gendarmerie and the head of the Suceava County on the seriousness of the agrarian unrest in Romania. First-hand reports by Jewish refugees coming from Romania to Austrian Bukovina were also included to spice up the already gory accounts of anarchy and devastation. Thus, information passed, as a matter of course, through several filters and diffused on several levels, not necessarily intersecting, before it reached the pages of the Hungarian liberal daily.

The first news broadcast by *Pesti Napló* replicated the initial assumption that had delayed the reaction of Romanian authorities to the first tidings of trouble: this was a peasant pogrom against the Jews,[2] which was nothing new in that part of the world. In both Romanian Moldavia and Tsarist Bessarabia there had been antisemitic episodes throughout the last decades of the nineteenth century and, especially grim, at the turn of the century. In metonymic fashion, the mere mention of places like Kishinev in Bessarabia could be, and was, used as a threat against Jews elsewhere in the Tsarist Empire.[3] Expectations were shaped by previous news of social violence, which took the form of pogroms. From their own correspondents in Bucharest reading the Iaşi daily *Dimineaţa*, *Pesti Napló* readers found out that Prime Minister Cantacuzino held the Botoşani Prefect Văsescu responsible for the escalation of the conflict for not informing him in good time while Văsescu himself reportedly answered 'The Romanians were not in any danger. [...] I value one Christian citizen more than a million Jews.'[4]

The newspaper's view of the uprising soon shifted as more news trickled in, showing that the peasants were indiscriminately destructive. The uprising was not antisemitic, but economic in character: 'The peasant

[2] *Pesti Napló*, 1907 március 20, 68 szám, page 6: 20 March 1907: 'Zavargás Romániában'.

[3] Klaus Richter, 'Kišinev or Linkuva? Rumors and threats against Jews in Lithuania in 1903' in *Revista Română de Studii Baltice şi Nordice*, 2011, Issue 3 (1), pp. 117–130.

[4] *Pesti Napló*, 1907 március 20, 68 szám, page 6.

uprising,' noted the newspaper on 21 March, 'gradually takes on the character of a rural revolution. The peasants devastate, without discrimination, the property of Jew and Gentile alike. More than two hundred mansions and estates were plundered and in the big towns Jewish shops were destroyed'.[5]

News from Czernowitz, the capital town of Bukovina, and from frontier towns such as Itzkany, Sereth and Suceava depicted an angst-ridden picture of spreading violence and impending danger. From the Austrian side of the border, the uprising in Romania was seen to be growing in proportion, with border towns being devastated and fire dancing on the horizon, followed by streams of refugees, mainly women and children, thronging the Austrian twin towns across the border. The refugees told stories of destruction at the hands of irate peasants, of unreliable troops siding with the rebels and joining in the looting. Echoing these testimonies, Benno Straucher, the representative of the Jewish community in Bukovina and an MP in the Austrian Parliament, claimed in his letter to the Foreign Ministry that 'the [Romanian] army and the police were in cahoots with the rebels.'[6] More worryingly still, rumours began to circulate that Bukovinian peasants were crossing the border and taking part in the uprising:

> Czernowitz, 22 March. *Allgemeine Zeitung*: reports are coming in that the rebellious peasants in the region of Sereth cross over into Suceava and return with Bukovinian peasants to the Romanian counties. There are a lot of stolen goods along the Austrian frontier. The Austrian border guards are turning away many Romanian peasants. The political authorities have ordered that Bukovinian peasants can only leave their villages if they can prove the purpose of their journey.[7]

This news was several times disproved and confirmed in subsequent issues of the newspaper depending on the source quoted. Information derived from Romanian governmental sources, such as the news agency *Agence Roumaine*, sought to downplay the extent of the troubles and to convey instead the impression that the Romanian authorities were in control of the situation and fully reliant on their troops, which they were not.[8]

---

[5] *Pesti Napló*, 1907 március 21, 69 szám.
[6] *Pesti Napló*, 1907 március 21, 69 szám; *Pesti Napló*, 22 március 1907.
[7] *Pesti Napló*, 23 március 1907.
[8] *Pesti Napló*, 22 március 1907, pp. 4–5.

Jewish networks promptly sprang into action and sought to provide relief and succour to the refugees or, alternatively, to intercede with the authorities, Romanian and Austro-Hungarian. The *Alliance Israélite* in Vienna, upon receiving calls for help from the Jewish refugees in Bukovina, sent in one of their representatives to Czernowitz to assess the situation. The president of the Zionist association in Berlin turned to King Carol for help on behalf of the refugees in Bucharest: 'Jews stream into Bucharest by the thousands. There is famine and the city council won't give them shelter.'[9]

The frontier between Moldavia and Bukovina suddenly became of utmost strategic importance for both Austrian and Romanian authorities. On both sides attempts were made to secure the border. Reports from Bucharest pointed out that 'the Romanian government makes every effort to restore peace in the counties along the border and rumours that the army and gendarmerie took part in the devastation are totally unfounded' and reassured that newspapers greatly exaggerated the news, that there was some rebellion in Moldavian villages but that was readily suppressed and peace reigned in the principal towns of the province.[10]

On the Austrian side of the border, the authorities worried that their border guards and gendarmerie might prove insufficient in case of an overspill of the conflict: 'The government ordered that local infantry troops be ready to be deployed as border reinforcement [...] At Czernowitz train station, military trains have been prepared for shipment of troops. [...] they do not exclude the possibility that the Austrian government will eventually have to mobilize armed forces for border defence.'[11]

As the uprising snowballed further south and the Romanian authorities could no longer paint a respectable face on it, they resorted to news suppression. By 26 March the *Pesti Napló* editors were complaining that 'there was hardly any news from the Romanian countryside because censorship was withholding telegrams.'[12] As we saw in the previous chapter, the Hungarian border authorities pointed out the same dearth of news and newspapers due to tight censorship. This served two purposes: it stopped news circulating internally and contaminating other parts of the country, and it reduced the trickle of information across the borders,

---

[9] *Pesti Napló*, 21 március 1907; *Pesti Napló*, 22 március 1907, pp. 4–5.
[10] *Pesti Napló*, 23 március 1907; *Pesti Napló*, 22 március 1907, pp. 4–5.
[11] *Pesti Napló*, 23 március 1907; *Pesti Napló*, március 23, p. 4.
[12] *Pesti Napló*, 26 március 1907: '*A román parasztlázadás*'.

which made things easier for Romanian diplomacy when it came to conveying a picture of control and efficiency.

What did Hungarian newspapers make of the incoming stream of news? Did they feel threatened? Did they draw any lessons from it? One would imagine that a great-landowner-dominated country such as Hungary, itself reliant, admittedly to a much lesser extent, on the system of land lease, would empathize with the Romanian landed elites and thoroughly disapprove of the barbarism of the peasant rebels. Hungarian reactions were in fact the very opposite of this. Their attitudes were filtered through the prism of Magyarization debates, which constituted a rankling issue in the tug-of-war between Magyar elites and representatives of the non-Magyar nationalities, Romanians included.

After ascertaining that the violent events across the border were not a pogrom, *Pesti Napló* journalists set about exploring the causes of the uprising and providing explanations for the plight of the Romanian peasantry. While expressing the horror of the civilized at the gruesome deeds of the peasants, they nevertheless did not hold them responsible but viewed them as victims of their leaders: 'Never was a people more debased and degraded than the Romanian people at the hands of its own leaders!' was the leitmotif of *Pesti Napló*'s analysis of events, which was a searing indictment of the Romanian political elite across the border in the fledgling Romanian Kingdom and, as we shall see further on, by extrapolation, an indictment of the Romanian national leaders in Hungary as well.

Pesti Napló assessed that the immediate cause of the uprising was economic, but this in itself was to be traced back to a fundamental ill of Romanian society: the lack of genuine culture and the elites' unwillingness to spread it among their own population:

> If human solidarity is shocked and turns to the victims of the Romanian horrors with deep commiseration, spare some compassion also for the unhappy people who do not rise to the height of human feeling because their leaders do not allow them, like other peoples are allowed, to become part of the human community. What is happening in Romania is not only a pogrom, not only a rural revolution, but also the terrifying sign of a people's poisoned soul. [This is] a state in which people are denied access to culture and in which the leaders' power is based on the blind submission of an ignorant, uncultured people.[13]

---

[13] *Pesti Napló*, 22 március 1907, p. 1.

With more than a tinge of *Schadenfreude*, the journalists of *Pesti Napló* quickly turned the discussion to their own concerns and political hobby-horse, the problem of Magyarization: lo and behold, the famous culture-state that so much criticized us Hungarians. See Romanian culture at work: horror everywhere and news that repels the civilized world! Everywhere you can see its crimes: the state of dire spiritual and economic poverty in which the Romanian peasantry finds itself. Plundered towns, burnt down houses, marauders wading in blood. 'Let us remember the recent memoranda of the heads of the Romanian Greek-Catholic Church in Hungary, in which they attacked our schools with undisguised cynicism. They opposed the schools that would have lifted the Romanian people to a higher human level. The memoranda and these attacks aimed to keep the people of Romanian nationality away from the magic circle of knowledge and civilization. For deprived of knowledge, they would remain like a herd of cattle and blindly follow the bell.'[14]

To buttress their argument and render more effective their double criticism of both the Romanian elite in the Romanian Kingdom and that in Hungary, *Pesti Napló* harked back to the still rankling memories of civil war during the 1848–1849 revolution, when, unable to reach a satisfying compromise for all nationalities of Hungary, Hungarian revolutionaries saw most of the non-Magyar nationalities turn against them in a civil war punctuated by atrocities on all sides:

> Nowhere has the recent Romanian uprising had a deeper echo than here in Hungary. We know the savagery of Romanian rebel warfare. We remember their dire ways. In the Transylvanian mountains to this day the memory is still alive of 60 years ago, when, led by their leaders and oblivious of the spirit of humanity, the Wallach peasantry wallowed in an orgy of human blood. It is terrible that the Wallach people have not yet been delivered from the grip of those who oppress them.[15]

In the eyes of *Pesti Napló* journalists, Romanian elites across the border and those of Hungary were birds of a feather. The former were guilty of 'cultural crookery' (*kulturszélhámosság*), that is, superficially adopting European ways and mores, whilst grossly mishandling and neglecting their own people, keeping them in ignorance and poverty: 'Their leaders are the

[14] *Pesti Napló*, 22 március 1907, p. 1.
[15] *Pesti Napló*, 22 március 1907, p. 1.

worst of robbers because they rob their own people, the poor, oppressed peasantry, of their human soul.' The latter (the Romanian national leaders of Hungary) displayed the same inclination as their peers across the border: 'they want to keep our Romanian-speaking people away from knowledge, literacy, civilization [...] they make sure that culture is not spread among their flock, [who] would gain human dignity by means of Hungarian culture. You can well understand that those who oppose humanity and human solidarity look down haughtily on this culture.'[16] No mention, of course, of Hungarian authorities suppressing the spread of culture in any other language but Hungarian.

Equally scalding in their criticism of Romanian culture were the editors of the conservative daily *Pesti Hírlap*. The newspaper covered the uprising more generically than *Pesti Napló*, following the main storyline and dwelling on some of the more egregious pieces of news.

Pesti Hírlap found in the Romanian peasant uprising the ultimate argument for rejecting the claims of the Romanian national leaders in Hungary for state-funded means of promoting their own, Romanian culture. The context in which this exchange of poisonous darts was taking place was the recently passed Education Law of Count Apponnyi: 'For weeks now the nationality MPs have been trying to demonstrate to Hungarians the rightfulness of Wallach culture. And now interestingly enough we are receiving telegrams from Bucharest revealing to us what that Wallach culture is which they want to spread to Hungary.'[17]

Just like their colleagues from *Pesti Napló*, *Pesti Hírlap* associated the reported savagery of rebellious Romanian peasants with traumatic episodes of Hungarian history: 'Behold Romanian culture, whose blessings Hungary repeatedly enjoyed during the uprising of Horea and Closca[18] and the 1848 days of terror.'[19] The uprising in Romania thus conjured up painful memories for Hungarian nationalists, for whom, as *Pesti Hírlap* put it, the mere mention of Romanian rebelliousness made them clench their fists and set their blood boiling.[20]

---

[16] *Pesti Napló*, 22 március 1907, p. 1.

[17] *Pesti Hírlap*, március 21, p. 1: '*Az oláhok vitézsége*'

[18] The reference is here to the Transylvanian peasant uprising of 1784, whose ringleaders were Romanian and who were pressing for the abolition of serfdom and political rights for the Romanians in Hungary.

[19] *Pesti Hírlap*, március 21, p. 1.

[20] *Pesti Hírlap*, március 21, p. 1.

No trace of fear or self-doubt comes out of the *Pesti Hírlap* articles. At no point do the editors voice any concern that the uprising might spread over to Hungary, that Hungarian peasants might be contaminated, that this was in some way a lesson to be learnt. One of the leading articles acknowledges land hunger as a common feature that both Hungarian and Romanian agriculture were confronted with and gave some thought to rural problems in Hungary: 'In Hungary it is not the Jewish lessees that take away land from the peasants, but it is rather the entailed and Church estates that prevent the peasant from acquiring or at least renting land.'[21] The author came up with a simple equation for explaining the different peasant behaviour in the two countries: 'Land hunger, which admittedly is great in Hungary as well, makes civilized people, such as the Hungarians, emigrate, whereas it makes uncivilized people, like the Wallachs, rebel, rob and kill.'[22] No mention was made, however, of Hungarians' own rural troubles of the 1890s, when the military were used to break up strikes and suppress protests in the central counties of Hungary. The basic rationale that *Pesti Hírlap* put forward, although erroneous and self-congratulatory in itself, did highlight a major safety valve of the Hungarian agricultural system, which the Romanian system lacked: emigration. This bled away rural discontent and prevented land frustration from accumulating to explosive proportions. As pointed out in a previous chapter, emigration was not an option in Romania, for reasons that the *Pesti Hírlap* editors could not possibly know: the legal stipulation that land distributed to the peasants could not be sold, mortgaged or otherwise alienated for 30 years, the lack of an emigration infrastructure and network as well as active governmental vigilance against foreign emigration agents. There were other reasons as well, which the Hungarian socialist newspaper *Népszava* pinpointed accurately, as we shall see further on in this chapter.

The whole discussion in *Pesti Hírlap* was framed in terms of a basic opposition between civilization and barbarism: Hungarian peasants were civilized, whilst their Romanian counterparts were not. Even the different treatment of Jews in the two countries followed the logic of the same dichotomy, according to the newspaper. Hungarian peasants were, on this occasion as well, cleverer and more civilized and did not allow themselves to be baited and set off against the Jews, so that the only pockets of anti-semitism in Hungary were to be found among the non-Magyar peasantry,

---

[21] *Pesti Hírlap*, március 21, p. 1.
[22] *Pesti Hírlap*, március 21, p. 1.

notably the Swabians and Romanians. Otherwise, Jews were thoroughly integrated within the Hungarian nation.[23] This argument served to counteract what *Pesti Hírlap* editors described as a smear campaign against Hungarians conducted by Romanians abroad while the Romanian uprising was used as a foil to highlight Hungary's own civilized credentials.

The most striking part of *Pesti Hírlap*'s analysis of the uprising was their appeal to the Romanian intelligentsia of Hungary, which showcased the contradictions implicit in the Hungarian hegemonic position and also the fundamentally irreconcilable views that divided the Hungarians from the non-Hungarians in the Austro-Hungarian Monarchy:

> We turn now to the Romanians in Hungary. Are you going to gravitate to a foreign state so devoid of culture, order and security and leave behind an orderly culture-state? What idle blindness must be that of someone who wishes to leave a big, strong and free state for the bonds of a savage state, in which life is uncertain if you are a landowner. We turn to the national Romanian intelligentsia with a petition: join us in common love, in common culture and let us strengthen our civilized (*rendezett*) Hungarian state. Look at the civilized West: only those states are strong which are monolingual, in which all the sons of the nation are bound together by a unique culture. We turn to those beautiful cultured Romanian ladies, who live in our beautiful houses and who sometimes are to be seen in the gallery of our Parliament: Become the guardian angels of Hungarian national culture! Become the apostles of social fusion! [...] Romanian barbarousness keeps us apart, because lack of culture always divides people, whereas civilization and a unique culture always brings people together.[24]

What comes out of this exhortation is the total impossibility of Hungarian nationalists' acceptance of the existence of another culture that was not Hungarian. Romanian peasants were deemed to be backward and uncivilized, but the solution was not to have them educated in their native language, but rather in Hungarian. In other words, only Hungarian was the language of culture and civilization and the alternative to it must always be illiteracy, lack of civilization and, ultimately, barbarity. This was actually how things turned out in Hungary, where the lowest rates of literacy were to be found in the eastern parts of the country, which were inhabited by a majority of Romanian population. This was not due to the

---

[23] *Pesti Hírlap*, március 21, p. 1.
[24] *Pesti Hírlap*, március 21, p. 1.

negative influence of the Romanian intelligentsia, as claimed by *Pesti Hírlap*, but ironically by the very policies of Magyarization, which were supposed to attract and enlighten people. As Iuliu Maniu, one of the leading Romanian national leaders in Hungary, once put it, the main effect of Magyarization on the Romanian community was that the Romanian peasants remained largely illiterate.

Like their liberal colleagues at *Pesti Napló*, the editors of *Pesti Hírlap* denounced the counterfeit character of culture in Romania, going one step further and substantiating their arguments with quotations from respected Romanian intellectuals. From Titu Maiorescu, former Romanian Minister of Public Works and a fierce critic of indiscriminate cultural imports, *Pesti Hírlap* took over the theory of forms without content, which they used to drive home their damning indictment of the Romanian state as a whole:

> Lies are the cardinal sin of Romanian culture: lies in their aspirations, lies in their politics, in poetry, in grammar, in all its manifestations. Would you like to know who said this? Mr. Titu Maiorescu, former Minister of Public Works. And he did know Romanian culture. Another lie is that Romania is a civilized state. The whole of the Balkan peninsula is full of such lies, and of operetta-kings.
>
> In the great cities of the civilized world rich princes are getting bored. They are relatives of the rulers. They want to play at being kings. And if the princely offspring cry long enough, the wealthy mother Klementina or grandfather Wilhelm will buy them a throne in the Balkan Peninsula. This is how the offspring of the Battenbergs, Hohenzollerns and Koburgs ended up there [...] And down there they play the game of 'national kingdoms'. The European reader often reads about this or that "national dynasty" dying. Now it is the turn of the Romanian 'national state'.
>
> Good old Carmen Sylva quietly wrote her poetry in Bucharest and a handful of good fellows brought over from the Budapest university, the *Babeş*-es and their companions, built a university and a parliament [for the Romanian state], in one word, they created the facade of a culture-state. Only the culture-state and the cultured people behind it were missing.[25]

The conclusion *Pesti Hírlap* reached was that the peasant uprising in Romania was not an antisemitic pogrom of Russian inspiration but rather the expression of a much greater ill, which they called by its Romanian

---

[25] *Pesti Hírlap*, 29 March, 'Robirea terranului', p. 4.

name *robirea terranului*, or peasant servitude. This had, in their view, historical roots and set apart the fate of the Romanian peasant from that of the Hungarian peasant. For extra punch, *Pesti Hírlap* resorted again to a quotation from Romanian sources:

> The present peasant uprising is not so much a Jewish pogrom as the rebellion of the oppressed and backward Romanian peasantry against their rulers.
>
> The leaders of the Romanians in Hungary and in Romania are guilty of not taking care of their people, who are kept like animals and exploited. Because the Romanian herd-like multitudes are left to their own devices, they rise up against the Romanian boyars in poverty and illiteracy.
>
> Here in Hungary, just like over there [in Romania], the Romanian peasant is a nomadic cultivator. But here he can obtain land, and the free Hungarian state and cultural nation supply him aplenty with bread and good manners, while over there in Romania, in his own house, conditions are worse. The law released him from serfdom, but his rulers are still keeping him subjugated.
>
> In 1595 the Wallachian Prince Mihály introduced a law called 'Asedamentul' (Settlement Law), which placed the Romanian peasantry on the same level as cattle. The Romanian writer Balcescu complained: 'Mihály was the very first prince who legislated that all land-cultivating peasants who lived on estates were to become "allodial Romanians", that is, they would be serfs tied to the land. The prince was forced to it by the aristocracy. The feudal system has endured in our country ever since. [...] Not only were peasants sold with land but their names were listed in the sale documents, as they couldn't be sold without the land. [...] The landowner has ever since been able to force the peasant to work for him as much as he liked.'
>
> It is because of this enserfment of the peasant that this agrarian revolution has broken out.
>
> They cannot make a civilized culture-state out of their own country but they would nevertheless like to destroy the civilized Hungarian state: such is the Romanian politics of mendacity.[26]

No mention, however, that in Transylvania under Hungarian rule at roughly the same time, the Romanian peasantry were enserfed and subject to discriminatory legislation, nor any actual historical analysis of how the late-sixteenth-century legislation of Prince Mihály came to affect peasant–owner relations at the beginning of the twentieth century.

[26] *Pesti Hírlap*, 29 March, p. 4.

At the opposite end of the journalistic spectrum, the Budapest socialist daily *Népszava* viewed the uprising in Romania as a reminder of how close Hungary itself was to the brink of the precipice. Their analysis of the causes of the uprising does not differ from the conclusions reached by the other two newspapers, although it is put across more forcefully and in more vivid language. The Romanian state, argued *Népszava*, was to blame for the uprising. The boyars, and not the *arendași* trusts, were to blame for it for the former preferred to rent land to the Jews rather than to the peasants: the Jews were better payers and handy scapegoats.[27]

Unlike *Pesti Napló* and *Pesti Hírlap*, the socialist newspaper believed there were ominous systemic similarities between Hungary and Romania and that the Hungarian peasantry was just as likely to start a general uprising as their Romanian counterpart. While the first two newspapers insisted that such an uprising could never happen in Hungary for reasons of superior civilization, *Népszava* warned that the uprising had not taken place in Hungary *yet* (*nálunk* még *nincs*)[28], but that given the right conditions Hungary too was ripe for an uprising.

In Romania the peasants are killing Jewish and Gentile landlord alike. In Hungary labour organizations are being suppressed at the request of Gentile and Jewish landlords and statistics are invoked to complain that the people are emigrating. Why make this connection between the two? Why draw a parallel? Not because they are events which happen to be occurring at the same time but because they are mutually enlightening. In Romania there is an uprising because there are no labour organizations to suppress and no reason to complain about emigration. In Hungary, on the other hand, there is no uprising because there are labour organizations and there is emigration.

Ten or fifteen years ago Hungary and Romania were dangerously similar. There was famine on the thousand-hold estates of Romanian landowners and Hungarian *boyars* alike, the gendarme's bayonet glistened before the eyes of the rebels in both Romanian and Hungarian villages in order to protect the oppressors' dominion. Hungary just like Romania was constantly on the brink of uprising. In Romania the uprising broke out and the Congo-river white Saracens of Hungary did not learn from the example set by the murderous red-and-black flag and the repression of the uprising [...] The Hungarian people found a bloodless way out of their predicament and that way led to Fiume. [...].

[27] *Népszava*, 23 March, p. 4.
[28] *Népszava*, 24 March, 'Véres Tanulságok', p. 1.

Sudden migration took young men to mines and factories [...] this, because of a lack of workhands, increased wages and not only prevented a bloody uprising but also prevented, and still does, the formation of labour organizations in agriculture.

The destitute population beyond the Transylvanian mountains do not have a Fiume. Transport from Romania to America takes longer and emigration is more expensive. The trade in 'emigration seduction' and boat tickets is not as good business in Romania as it is in Hungary. [...] In Romania there are no emigration agents and no emigration in the Hungarian sense of the word. [...] In Romania there are no labour organizations that would refashion the murderous struggle of raised scythes into a bloodless revolutionary and economic war.

[...] Whether you like it or not, the truth is that the Hungarian boyars are artificially increasing the chances of a bloody uprising through their purposeful actions against the labourers. The endeavours to stave off emigration will put a stop to the draining away of poor people. The dissolution of labour organizations will result in a rebellious spirit taking over the economic struggle. [...].

Should the clampdown on organized labour continue, there are two possible outcomes: either the destruction of labour organizations and the end of emigration, or organized labour will grow stronger by fighting and emigration will take its course. In the latter case, there would be introduced the universal franchise law and social, political, economic, wage-related problems will be improved. ... In the former case, the country would grow rebellious, an uprising would be in the offing and both landowner and capitalist would pay much more dearly. This road – the great landowners know it – leads to Romania.'[29]

Népszava attacked the self-sufficiency of the Hungarian establishment, who rejected out of hand the possibility of contamination:

Over there in Romania the rebellious peasants, the exploited slaves of the land, are wading in blood. They are illiterate, unorganized, wretched pariahs. They are wading in the blood of Jews and Gentiles, they are burning down their houses, wrecking their wine barrels, robbing money and machinery without any confessional discrimination. And, out of these saddening, gory events, the Hungarian nationalists have drawn the proud conclusion: "Look", they said to the Romanians of Hungary, "here is the famous Romania that you are aspiring to! Look how different Hungary is from it! Here the people have it so good that they would never rebel, burn, rob and kill!"[30]

[29] *Népszava*, 22 March, pp. 1, 2.
[30] *Népszava*, 24 March, p. 1.

The outlook of the Hungarian ruling classes amounted, according to *Népszava*, to a complacent illusion that all was well among the lower classes of Hungary and the only problem was incitement by 'heartless agitators', who were better put in jail so that the old system could go on unchanged.

Népszava identified two main causes for the Romanian uprising. The first was the exploitative system of land rental. *Népszava*'s assessment of it is among the most lucid judgments contemporaries passed on the land tenure system of 1907 Romania:

> First of all, given the great number of big estates, a growing number of peasants do not have enough land and are forced to proletarianize. Additionally, the boyars, Romania's strongmen (*bőrkabátosai*), do not allow the peasants to make a decent living from wage labour on the great estates; they instead rent out their land to Jews and foreign newcomers with no regard for the interests of their co-national peasantry. The Jews and the newcomers pay the boyar better and they pay on time. This however is only possible because they push down wages to abysmal levels. The boyars themselves could pay better wages if they cultivated their own land themselves on a scientific, intensive basis and in this case the land would bring them at least as much income as the *arendaşi* pay him. But the boyars like the easy life without labour and tiredness. They don't care that the *arendaşi* get rich at the expense of the boyars' co-national peasants. To hell with the peasant and national feeling; let there be profit only, with no other concern. This is how the Romanian peasant has become an enserfed pariah (*földhöz ragadt pária*) thanks to his co-national boyars.[31]

The second cause of the uprising that *Népszava* pinpointed has a *pro-domo-sua* ring to it: Romanian peasants' lack of organization. Unlike the Hungarian peasants, the Romanians had not been touched by socialism and as such did not know that organized labour was a much more powerful weapon than fire and raised scythes and that the great revolution against capitalism must be thoroughly prepared. 'This is why the Romanian peasant lashes out without organization or a plan in savage, murderous uprising.'[32]

---

[31] *Népszava*, 24 March, p. 1.
[32] *Népszava*, 24 March, p. 1.

Reiterating their explanation as to why there was no general uprising in Hungary yet, *Népszava* concluded that there were two reasons for the different outcome: (1) because the Hungarian peasants 'knew the road to America very well' and (2) because in Hungary socialists were preparing a better, more organized, more modern revolution. Although trying hard, the exploiters had not yet succeeded in staving off either of the two tendencies (towards emigration and towards socialist revolution). 'That's why there is no uprising here yet. If they do succeed,' warned *Népszava*, 'then there will soon come the time of fuming castles, robbed boyars and bayonets instead of sowing. But we believe that they will not succeed. We put our faith not in God, but in our own fellow Hungarian workers'.[33]

A Magyar-Zsidó Szemle (Hungarian-Jewish Review), one of the leading Jewish journals in Hungary, traced the origins of the Romanian uprising to the self-destructive short-sightedness on the part of the Romanian authorities and political elites. Their brief note on the full-scale uprising across the border pointed to official condoning of violence against the Jews in Romania and the false reassurance deriving thereof:

> The first news was not terrible: they said that the God-given people besieged, looted and burned towns, the Jew-inhabited towns. The prefects were reassured that the bloody deeds were directed against the town merchants [...] it [soon] became crystal clear that 'the people' did not engage in hairsplitting, did not look to see if the blood spilt was red or blue; they only looked to see who was the owner of the land.[34]

Although understandably making their argument from a *pro-domo-sua* position, the authors of the article moved beyond an exclusively Jewish standpoint and put forward a John-Donne-esque rationale for the escalation of violence in the neighbouring country: the Romanian authorities and landlords failed to see for whom the bell tolled. This may, at first sight, come across as a rather trite philosophical explanation (or an instance of poetic justice), but upon closer inspection it reveals a basic truth about social violence: what the state-condoned antisemitism resulted in was a weakening of ordinary people's sense of morality. 'The people', pointed out the authors, 'will never understand to kill and rob only in those places where they are encouraged to. The great boyar landowners filled up the

[33] *Népszava*, 24 March, pp. 1–2.
[34] *Magyar-Zsidó Szemle* 24. évf. 2. sz. (1907. április), p. 115: http://epa.oszk. hu/01800/01891/00006/pdf/mzssz_1907_02_115-117.pdf Accessed 4.01.2018).

ears of the whole world with protestations about the sanctity of life and property, but the people did not listen to them. Why, if it is allowed to steal from the poor man, is it not allowed to steal from the rich man? An estate is an estate, no matter who the owner is'.[35] In other words, if you give green light to violence, you foster a social environment propitious to violence, and violence once unleashed takes its own unpredictable course. The 'ethical foundation of society' once destroyed, the sky is the limit and no one can channel the flood of violence. The peasants did not stop to ask 'what kind or religion the landlord belonged to who was standing in their way. The people who have been thus frequently incited to violence don't listen to the priests or to the officials sent from the capital on government instructions. Why is it that what yesterday counted as a virtue, today is a sin? All over the world, antisemitism as a governing principle has borne the same fruit – it has led to a demoralization of the people. The persecution of the Jews orchestrated by the ruling elite has cut deeper and bloodier wounds in the mighty body of the Russian empire than the Japanese swords ever did, because it upset the moral foundation, it destroyed the power built on it.'[36] This final parallel to the Russian case invites the speculation whether antisemitic practices and especially officially sanctioned antisemitic violence represented the thin end of the revolutionary wedge that convulsed Russia in the teens of the twentieth century. Rather than allowing for a little steam to blow off from time to time to relieve huge social and economic pressures, could it be that this amounted to allowing the revolutionary elements to cut their teeth on the Jews and then move on, with redoubled confidence, to the next social or political enemy?

By far the most balanced coverage in the Hungarian press came from *Pester Lloyd*. The same sense of deceptive appearances and deceived expectations underlay the tone of its articles, although in the case of *Pester Lloyd*, unlike *Pesti Napló* and *Pesti Hírlap*, there was no apparent *Schadenfreude* but rather genuine disabusement with what had appeared to be a bastion of order (*das zuverlässigste Element der Ordnung auf dem Balkan*)[37] in an otherwise unreliable and disorderly Balkan Peninsula:

> The world is taken by surprise by this violence. For a few years now one has become accustomed to viewing Romania as one of the most progressive and civilized countries of the Balkan region and the clever and humane leadership

[35] *Magyar-Zsidó Szemle*, 24. évf. 2. sz. (1907. április), p. 116.
[36] Magyar-Zsidó Szemle, 24. évf. 2. sz. (1907. április), p. 116.
[37] *Pester Lloyd*, 26 March, 1907, p. 1.

of King Carol reinforced this impression. Now it becomes clear that wild barbarism is hidden under the thinnest of veneers and these events will not be easily swept under the carpet.[38]

Pester Lloyd presented the revolutionary situation in Romania as the outcome of a vicious circle of antisemitism (the refusal to bestow citizenship and citizen rights on the Jewish population), land tenure restrictions (Jews could not own land, but they could rent it) and a squandering landowning aristocracy, who preferred to rent out their land to big capitalists, who in turn would exploit the peasantry.[39] The editors went on to draw lessons from the Romanian uprising, towards which 'Austria-Hungary could not remain indifferent either politically or economically.' In an assessment echoing the point made by the editors of *Magyar-Zsidó Szemle*, *Pester Lloyd* pointed out that the misguided political agitation against the Jews in Romania was a warning to any 'wanton street politician' that antisemitic baiting could easily degenerate into general social unrest.[40]

As the uprising extended to the south and took on an increasingly anarchic character, *Pester Lloyd* came to doubt whether Romania could avoid dissolution as a state. The prospect of this, as well as the causes of the devastating upheaval, was, according to the newspaper editors, of the utmost importance to the European powers that took a direct interest in the region. The editors thus feared not so much that the Romanian unrest could spread over to Hungary, but rather that it could be replicated in fellow-Balkan states such as Serbia and Bulgaria.[41] In this they were wrong, as at least the agrarian unrest was more likely to spread to Hungary, with which Romania shared commonalities of land tenure, than to Serbia and Bulgaria, which had a completely different structure of land ownership and were less combustible from an agrarian point of view.

Romanian Newspapers in Hungary

Depending on the sources on which they drew, Romanian newspapers in Hungary ranged in their attitude to the troubles across the border from concern and criticism of the Romanian land-tenure system, to a sense of

---

[38] *Pester Lloyd*, 21 March, 1907, p. 2.
[39] *Pester Lloyd*, 26 March, 1907, p. 1.
[40] *Pester Lloyd*, 26 March, 1907, p. 1.
[41] *Pester Lloyd*, 27 March, 1907, p. 2.

superiority and condescension, comparative reflections on Hungarian land relations, and, in some cases, full-blown antisemitism.

In northern Transylvania, *Gazeta Bistriței* reproduced whole articles by A.C. Cuza from *Neamul românesc* and *Apărarea Națională* and perpetuated the Iași professor's brand of virulent antisemitism, which portrayed Romanian Jews as exploiters, spoliators and the culprits for everything gone wrong in Romania.[42]

The Cluj newspaper *Răvașul* voiced unadulterated disappointment at the violent contrast that the uprising created with the 1906 royal jubilee festivities and the gulf between the image projected by the Romanian authorities and the squalid reality on the ground. The disappointment of *Răvașul* editors also came from the sobering awareness that the idealized kingdom of Romania, on which they had pinned so many hopes, failed to live up to nationalist expectations:

> We have got to admit that this news pains us greatly. No sooner had the royal jubilee year come to an end, no sooner had the paeans and eulogies from the royal exhibition ceased to ring out, no sooner had decorations stopped being given out [...] than all of these festive memories were buried along with human bodies and drenched in blood! The contrast has come so suddenly and so soon that we cannot but feel it too, and maybe we of all people feel it all the more as in these moments we were expecting to see and hear something completely different from across the mountains.[43]

Unlike *Gazeta Bistriței*, *Răvașul* rejected the instigation thesis as well as A.C. Cuza's antisemitic scapegoating: 'We believe that it was not instigations from the enemies without, who are numerous enough, nor from the enemies "within", as depicted by Mr. A.C. Cuza in *Neamul românesc*, but rather the accumulated pain caused by the wickedness of some and, even worse, by the indifference of others, that caused this deplorable destruction, which the sooner is mended and removed, the better for everybody.'[44]

In Arad the local Hungarian newspaper *Aradi Közlöny* asked Romanian notabilities to comment on the latest events in Romania. The interviewees—Vasile Goldiş, MP in the Hungarian Parliament, Ioan Beleş, notary

---

[42] Bistrița-Năsăud National Archives, *Revista Bistriței*, 'La chestiunea răscoalelor țărănești', No. 17, 11 mai/28 aprilie, 1907, pp. 1–2; No. 18, 18/5 mai 1907, pp. 2–3.

[43] *Răvașul*, 22 March, 1907, p. 206.

[44] *Răvașul*, 22 March, 1907, p. 207.

public, and Ioan Russu-Şirianu, former MP—were 'prominent leaders of the Romanian community in Arad and not only were familiar with the realities of the Romanian Kingdom but had also frequently travelled to Moldavia, where now the flames of the uprising were scorching estates and villages'.[45] All three agreed that the uprising in Romania was 'an agrarian revolution', stemming from the ruthless exploitation of the peasantry, and not a manifestation of antisemitism. Goldiş took the opportunity to caution Hungarian statesmen over the risks implicit in leaving unsolved the land-hunger problem, which was common to both Romania and Hungary:

> From the latest regrettable rebellion of the [Romanian] peasantry even the least initiated of people can plainly see that this is an exclusively economic action and not an antisemitic one. This could serve as a memento to Hungarian statesmen, who would do well to pay attention to the events in Romania, for here in Hungary, too, discontent is great in many places. The great landowners and the Hungarian state lease out their estates, which are then subleased to the peasantry for double or treble the price. Land hunger and discontent are great in Romania as they are here, but because in Hungary relations are more consolidated and public security is sturdier, an uprising can be more easily repressed. To give one example of the unbearable situation here in Hungary, which carries the germ of danger, I'll be referring to the predicament of the population of the Maros river valley. Here state forests have been leased out to the big *arendaşi*, instead of being passed on to the peasants. It's true that the people can't get together in associations and cover the rent for lack of corresponding income, but with state intervention and under the leadership of our foresters and public servants, the state could get its rent and the population would be happy and content. But now the peasant only sees that the *arendaş* is getting rich and he himself lives in poverty, so he is discontent and grumbles against the state, which does not take good care of him.[46]

Goldiş highlighted another dangerous commonality: the accusation of agitation, which was easily resorted to and with which both the Romanian and the Hungarian government were ready to dismiss any forms of protest, thereby losing sight of the actual root of the problem and thus not standing a chance of solving it: 'In vain do Romanian officials invoke the activity of agitators, just as [Hungarian officials] would do here as well. Where there

[45] *Aradi Közlöny*, 21 March 1907, quoted in *1907 in Arad*, pp. 66–67.
[46] *Aradi Közlöny*, 21 March 1907, quoted in *1907 in Arad*, pp. 68–69.

is no ground for agitation, there is no agitator either. Burning tinder will never set iron bars on fire, but will set alight dry wood.'[47]

Just like Goldiş, the other two interviewees stressed the systemic nature of rural oppression and conflict in Romania. Ioan Russu-Şirianu, who was on friendly terms with the socialist professor Constantin Stere from Iaşi University, echoed the latter's criticism of the *arendaşi* system, which gave rise to capitalist monopolies that functioned as a stranglehold on the peasant population:

> For years I lived in Romania and travelled across Moldavia and, on the basis not only of the received telegrams but also of my own experience, I can affirm that the present-day uprising in Romania is an economic action of the peasantry just like the uprising around Bucharest was in 1888. [...] The situation of the peasantry is extremely sad. They rent state land from arendaşi and not only pay three times a *falca* – which is bigger than a Hungarian hold – but also are forced to do manual labour and provide produce in kind; there are also cases where they pay 200 lei for a *falca* which the arendaş gets from the state with 20–25 lei. In 5 counties of Moldavia 85% of the land is in the hands of the Fischer family, which, as a veritable trust, dictates wages and rental prices. Under these circumstances there was no need for Russian agitators to start an uprising. The predicament of the peasantry was in itself enough of an instigation, the peasants only wanting that the state should lease them land at 25–50 lei per *falca* instead of giving it to the arendaşi, who do no work and yet get rich.'[48] Russu-Şirianu remembered Constantin Stere's warning a year before the uprising: 'he told me that, if the situation of the peasants was not improved, he feared an economic revolution would break out. His prophecy came true one year later.[49]

Ioan Beleş followed the same line of argument and struck on a paradox of Romanian agriculture, whereby the native peasants were trapped in an inescapable system of quasi-serfdom, while Szekely peasants from Transylvania earned good wages working in Romania as temporary land labourers or, in the case of Szekely women, as domestic servants.[50] One of the first measures taken in the aftermath of the uprising by the Romanian government was to prohibit the use of foreign workers.[51]

[47] *Aradi* Közlöny, 21 March 1907, quoted in 1907 in Arad, p. 68.
[48] *Aradi Közlöny*, 21 March 1907, quoted in *1907 in Arad*, p. 70.
[49] *Aradi Közlöny*, 21 March 1907, quoted in *1907 in Arad*, p. 71.
[50] *Aradi Közlöny*, 21 March 1907, quoted in *1907 in Arad*, p. 68.
[51] Covasna National Archives, RO_BJANCV_F_9_1907/5027.

Taking its information from their own sources as well as from Stere's *Viaţa românească*, the Arad Romanian newspaper *Tribuna* equally rejected the notion that the uprising was an antisemitic movement and voiced their criticism of the Romanian state and elite with an explicit sense of superiority: 'We won't make so bold as to give advice to the [Romanian] King's hard-tried councilors. We believe, however, that we can serve the cause of the peasantry, which is that of the nation as a whole, if, for the orientation of the great landowners, we sketched, albeit briefly, within the limits of an article, the way in which we, the landowners here, great or small, as well as the town and village intellectuals, treat our peasants.'[52] The *Tribuna* editors proceeded to expound on the political involvement of the Romanian peasantry in Hungary (which can't have been very great given the 6% male franchise in Hungary at the time!) and their participation in the national struggle ('300 peasants joined the Memorandum movement', dozens of peasants endured the winter's cold and political chicanery in order to vote for Romanian candidates) and traced the origins of this happy cooperation to Romanian landowners' concern for their co-national peasants, to schooling in Romanian and to the financial opportunities available thanks to national networks: banks, cooperatives, cultural foundations. 'In a nutshell', *Tribuna* summed up, 'there is a bond between [Romanian] landowners and peasants and a community of interest based on justice and love'—the very opposite conclusion to that which had been put forward by their political adversaries in the conservative *Pesti Hírlap* and the Liberal *Pesti Napló*, who claimed that the Romanian intelligentsia of Hungary prevented their flock from acquiring culture and civilization.

Tribuna set up Romanian landowners in Hungary as an example for and a contrast to those of Romania: 'At the agrarian congress held last autumn in Bucharest the current prefect of Ilfov county, Mr Alimănişteanu, pointed out that the great Romanian landowners do not lose very much sleep over their peasants' education [...] Mr. Constinescu had the courage to say in parliament that both parties have neglected the peasantry, while G. Panu noticed the same in the latest issue of his newspaper.'[53] This, as well as their case for a different situation of the peasantry in Hungary, echoed Parteniu Cosma's comparative analysis of the fate of the Romanian peasantry on either side of the border, which was mentioned in a previous chapter.

[52] *Tribuna*, 22 March (4 April) 1907, 'Plevna internă', p. 1.
[53] *Tribuna*, 22 March (4 April) 1907, 'Plevna internă', p. 2.

There was one point on which Romanian and Hungarian newspapers, irrespective of their political colour and deep-seated enmities, agreed. And that was Romania's oriental character. *Pesti Hírlap* had lumped it together with the 'operetta' kingdoms of the Balkans; the Romanian *Tribuna* hinted at the same when they denounced the 'Byzantine system of land tenure',[54] of which the Romanian peasantry bore the brunt; alternatively, the same newspaper viewed the latest peasant uprising as a continuation of the war of independence of 1877–1878: *Tribuna* metaphorically called the uprising an 'internal Plevna' (Plevna, or Pleven, being one of the places in Bulgaria where fierce fighting was conducted during the Russo–Turkish war) thus indicating that, having conquered their independence from the external Ottomans, Romanians now had to fight a new war against the internal oppressors.[55]

AUSTRIAN NEWSPAPERS

Taking its information from Bukovinian authorities and from Jewish contacts, the *Neue Freie Presse*, one of the most important Viennese newspapers, presented the rising as a pogrom of Russian contamination and of Romanian encouragement. They recognized the agrarian character of the movement but stressed its antisemitic character and dwelt on the gruelling experience of the Jewish refugees and the need to provide relief. Quoting Dr. Heinrich Lupul, a Bukovinian lawyer, the newspaper depicted the distressed situation of the Jewish refugees:

> Those who have not seen the refugee camps for Romanian Jews in Itzkany have no notion of their misfortune: men looking pale and gaunt, enfeebled by fear, brooding women with babies in their arms, children munching on stale bread that charitable people have pressed into their hand, sleeping on straw in Jewish synagogues, society headquarters and in the town hall, as private houses were not enough to give shelter to more than 2000 people.[56]

---

[54] *Tribuna*, 17 March, 1907, quoted in Marin Badea, Andrei Caciora, Nicolae Rosut, Eugen Gluck (Eds.), *Aradul și răscoala țăranilor din 1907: 70 [ani]*, Universitatea Cultural Științifică Arad, 1977, p. 58.

[55] *Tribuna*, 22 March, 1907, p. 1.

[56] *Neue Freie Presse*, 23 March, p. 5.

The causes of the uprising, as identified by *Neue Freie Presse*, were anti-semitism (the unfulfilled stipulations of the Treaty of Berlin and the limbo stage in which Romanian Jews found themselves), Russian influence (constant reminder of the Bessarabian pogroms and also of alleged involvement of Potemkin sailors in the Romanian uprising) and political strife as well as a Dickensian process of scapegoating. Harking back to Dickens' last novel *Our Mutual Friend*, the editors compared the situation of the Jewry in Romania to that of the Jewish usurer Riah, who was forced to serve as a front for Fledgeby, his ruthless Christian master: spoliation, in other words, was taking place through Jewish hands but for the benefit of the Christian master. Similarly, assessed *Neue Freie Presse*, the Romanian boyars, not unlike the absentee landlords of Ireland (the comparison is a frequent one), owned most of the land, yet lived abroad and rented their land to Jewish capitalists:

> The boyar owns the greatest part of the fertile land in the country, he orders his clothes from the most expensive tailors in Vienna and his wife wears Paquin[57] dresses from Paris. It is in the casinos of Monte Carlo that the high degree of civilization, which this type of landowners have appropriated very quickly, can be seen most frequently and can be observed at leisure. It is there that the gold, which was extracted from the land by the backbreaking toil of the peasants, is spent in the dissolute company of dubious ladies. Many of these boyars don't even live in the country, which would present the advantage that the money stayed in the country.[58]

In an assessment reminiscent of the coverage of *Magyar Zsidó Szemle*, the editors of *Neue Freie Presse* concluded that, having 'played all too often with the fire of confessional hatred', the Romanian authorities lost control of it and realized too late that 'rebellious peasants made no difference between christened and circumcised capital'.[59] The violence across the border was deplored not just in itself, but also for its contaminating effect: 'This is the situation in Romania in close proximity to the Austrian and Hungarian border, in the immediate vicinity of parts of the Monarchy

---

[57] Jeanne Paquin—French *haute-couture* designer of evening dresses at the end of the nineteenth, beginning of twentieth century.

[58] *Neue Freie Presse*, 27 March, p. 1.

[59] *Neue Freie Presse*, 27 March, p. 1.

where social combustibility (*gesellschaftlicher Brennstoff*) is not lacking and to which a gust of wind could spread the fire.'[60]

While the *Neue Freie Presse* brought before its readers' eyes images of woe and suffering of Romanian Jews at the hands of peasant hordes with the blessing and under the incitement of profiteering Romanian elites, at the other end of the Viennese journalistic spectrum the humorous and by the end of the nineteenth century fully antisemitic paper *Kikeriki* turned this image on its head and claimed the very opposite was taking place along the Romanian-Austrian border. Their cartoon 'Romanian Jews in Safety' (see Figure 6.1) depicted the Jewish refugees to Austrian Bukovina as a grinning bunch of wealthy people watching with satisfaction the butchering of peasants at the hands of the Romanian army across the border and exclaiming 'Such a pogrom, we like much better!'[61] A few days earlier, *Kikeriki* had published a rhyme that encapsulated their undisguised antisemitic reading of the uprising in Romania: 'The Jew has driven once again a nation to ruin// as he always successfully does.//He first comes as a "friend"// roots everybody out and sucks them dry//then leaves the land// as a martyr.'[62]

In keeping with the paper's irreverent satirical agenda, *Kikeriki* poured scorn and laughter on all the parties involved in the uprising, saving some

---

[60] *Neue Freie Presse*, 27 March, p. 1.
[61] *Kikeriki*, 11 April, p. 2: 'Die rumänischen Juden in Sicherheit'
[62] *Kikeriki*, 7 April, p. 11:
'**Rumänien.**
Ein neues Memento
Hat wieder erricht't,
Der Jüd' in Rumänien,
Das deutlich g'nug spricht.
Daß der Antisemitismus
Gut wächst und gedeiht,
Hab'n getreulich gesorgt
Dort unt' „ünsere Lait".
Der Jüd' hat da wieder
Ein Volk ruiniert,
So wie er es stets
Mit Erfolg praktiziert.
Erst kommt er als „freund",
Wurzt und saugt alle aus,
Und zieht aus dem Land
Dann als „Märtyrer "h'naus.'

Fig. 6.1 'Die rumänischen Juden in Sicherheit/ Romanian Jews Keeping Safe', cartoon in the Austrian satirical newspaper *Kikeriki*

decidedly disdainful compassion for the backward and much mishandled Romanian peasant:

> The Romanian peasant scratches himself because the lice have become too itchy. Of course his scratching is most impolite, but what does a peasant know of manners! He doesn't even read the 'Liberal' press!
>   or
> Good news from Romania: 3,000 peasants have been shot, 8,000 have been imprisoned, the situation is much improved. Obviously the only thing that needs to be done is to keep on shooting and imprisoning for the situation to become great indeed.[63]

Fellow humourists from *Der Floh* used cartoon and satire to mock the degree of civilization in Romania as well as to jeer at Russian reactions as reported by the Viennese mainstream press. 'In this year the Kingdom of Rumania has entered in the sixteen-hundredth year of European witch-hunt' ran the caption to the front-page illustration *Der Floh* dedicated to the Romanian peasant uprising, harking back to pre-modern witch hunts and pogroms and thus suggesting that Romania itself had not yet entered the civilized twentieth century[64] (see Figure 6.2).

On the following page of *Der Floh*, a genuine bit of news from *Neue Freie Presse* occasioned a spoof on the notorious antisemitism of Russia's ruling circles. On 22 March the Viennese newspaper conveyed news from St Petersburg regarding Russian reactions to the Romanian peasant uprising: 'the Russian government takes great interest in the recent outbreak of an antisemitic agrarian movement in Romania. The Minister of the Interior instructed the governor of Bessarabia to take all necessary precautions so that the movement does not spill over into Russia.' *Der Floh*'s imaginary correspondent from Petersburg proceeded to provide additional information: 'and indeed, thanks to the energetic measures taken by the Russian authorities, they succeeded to prevent the antisemitic movement from crossing the border. The Jews who took refuge on Russian soil are everywhere received with open arms. Their stories of unspeakable horrors, which befell their co-religionists, have everywhere triggered indignation. Rumours of a diplomatic intervention of Russia in Romania on behalf of the oppressed Jews are however rather premature. In all of Russia, however, the collections for Jews have had wonderful

[63] *Kikeriki*, 7 April, p. 2.
[64] *Der Floh*, 24 March 1907, p. 1.

Fig. 6.2 Front-page cartoon in *Der Floh* with the caption 'Inn disem Jar ist daß Königereych Rumenien in daß sechszehnt Jarhundert evropeischer Hextrechnungt eyngetretten'

success. The Tsar himself donated 100,000 Rubles. A relief committee, headed by Krushewan, is tirelessly working towards the repatriation of the unhappy refugees'.[65]

Bukovinian Newspapers

The main Bukovinian German-language newspaper *Czernowitzer Allgemeine Zeitung* hit the nail on the head by pointing out that in Romania the peasant question was intertwined with the Jewish question. In addition to the pervasive impression created by the Romanian establishment that Jews were 'free game' (*Vogelfrei*), which was reinforced by numerous expulsions of Jews from Romania in the years running up to 1907, the Jew had also become a scapegoat in the tug-of-war between peasants and boyars. The boyars neglected the fate of the peasantry in endless political games aimed at staying in power or coming back to power; they also had no problem renting out their estates to Jewish capitalists, who would extract for them a maximum of rent at the expense of the peasantry.[66] Systemic antisemitism aggravated rural relations in Romania as well as contributing to the uprising getting out of hand, as the authorities failed to react promptly.[67]

Unlike the previous newspapers, *Czernowitzer Allgemeine Zeitung* relied mostly on information from its own sources given the geographical proximity of Czernowitz to northern Moldavia, where the peasant troubles initially broke out, and also its being on a direct train line to Iaşi and other Moldavian towns. One of the most vivid accounts of Romanian towns during the uprising came from a couple of its reporters, who ventured into Romania at the height of the troubles.

Trains coming from Romania into Itzkany and Czernowitz are full to the brim and return all but empty back to their country, where 'all hell has broken loose', as they say in popular parlance. We are swimming against the current. In Czernowitz the people looked at us half jokingly, half compassionately, when they heard us talk of our planned journey to Romania; in Itzkany, when we asked for tickets to Iaşi, the ticket vendor gave us a stunned look. To Iaşi

[65] *Der Floh*, 24 March 1907, p. 2.
[66] *Czernowitzer Allgemeine Zeitung*, 22 March 1907, p. 3; 24 March 1907, p. 1.
[67] *Czernowitzer Allgemeine Zeitung*, 19 March 1907, p. 1.

of all places, where, as one reads in the newspapers, the rebellious peasants are planning to lay siege and plunder? We set out anyway and are the better for it. We get to feel what to us at least is one of the more convenient consequences of the uprising: in the empty night train we can sleep very well until we get to Itzkany, which is impossible to do under normal circumstances, which as well-seasoned travellers we can testify to.[68]

Itzkany, one of the border towns of Bukovina, was the first port of call for the stream of Jewish refugees from Romania. Here the *Czernowitz Allgemeine Zeitung* reporters saw the predicament of the refugees at first hand: 'In the waiting room of the train station pitiful looking figures are huddling on benches and chairs, all cramped and clutching their belongings fitfully in their sleep. Romanian Jews – refugees waiting for the train which will take them as far as possible from their inhospitable country, or those who no longer found a place in the emigrant shelters.'[69] A quick trip to the emigrant shelter, where they were showered with tales of woe, left them numbed by the recounted suffering and relieved to escape the crowded, oppressive place.

Once on Romanian territory they made their first incursion into the town of Pașcani, the main railway hub of the region. They discovered a small place, scarcely deserving the name of a town, studded with military and hardly accessible because of the heavy mud along the unpaved streets. The Austrian journalists went on to depict an unflattering image of Romanian troops, with antisemitic officers and lackadaisical soldiers, who according to local gossip only half-heartedly intervened to stop attacks against the Jews or 'watched with undisguised envy how their "brethren" filled up their pockets'.[70] The question of the troops' reliability came up repeatedly during their journey. In Pașcani the waggon driver told them that the troops were being changed every couple of days for fear that they might start fraternizing with the rebels. Further down south in Roman, a town under military occupation and with an enforced blackout, a Jewish banker and good acquaintance of the reporters appraised that order was much better kept since they replaced the local troops with troops from other regions of the country. 'Do you think the troops are reliable?', one reporter asked him.

[68] *Czernowitzer Allgemeine Zeitung*, 26 March 1907, p. 1.
[69] *Czernowitzer Allgemeine Zeitung*, 26 March 1907, p. 1.
[70] *Czernowitzer Allgemeine Zeitung*, 26 March 1907, p. 1.

The answer to this question is not easy. One cannot definitely say yes or no. You should not compare our military with the Austrian or German troops. The Romanian soldier is docile, frugal, courageous and obedient. Here there have scarcely been any cases of refusing to obey orders. But you should not forget that 90% of the soldiers are peasants' sons and also that at least half the troops currently mobilized are made up of reservists. And among the reservists there are also people who had robbed and plundered and now they have to fight against the rebels. [...] [The authorities] are not afraid that the troops will rebel; this is out of the question. But there is a danger that they might refuse to shoot and one can imagine what the moral effects of such an incident could be. However courageous the Romanian soldier may be, he is not, however, imbued with a military spirit that only a tradition of hundreds of years and strict discipline has produced in Western armies. The [Romanian] soldier remains a uniformed, weapon-bearing peasant and he cannot help sympathizing with his rebellious brethren.[71]

The trip to Iași frustrated the Bukovinian journalists' eager expectations for spectacular social violence. Once in town, they made their way through a surprisingly quiet place, with hardly any soldiers about. With peasants massed at the gates of the town and troops deployed ready to meet them, the peaceful atmosphere turned out be the calm before the storm. The smooth journey across town provided, however, a different kind of surprise, which tied in with the civilization debate informing foreign press articles about the uprising and testifies to the popularity of the phrase 'Half Asia' in Austro-Hungarian journalistic discourse:

In the town itself there's nothing to see. We therefore decide to head out to the 'Barrier', where the troops are ready for attack standing face to face with the peasants. After long haggling a waggon driver agrees to take us there. A most interesting journey! We cross the 'European' Iași. A thoroughly modern town. Beautiful buildings, elegant clubs, artistically valuable monuments, exquisite great buildings, in particular churches. After we pass a dilapidated half-crumbling building – the old prefecture, which now houses the main post office – we go down a hill and we are in ... Half-Asia.

The Jewish street. Wretched, crumbling huts, knee-deep animal droppings, through which our two strong horses wade with great difficulty, pigs, geese, chickens all over the street, gaunt, careworn and emaciated people,

---

[71] *Czernowitzer Allgemeine Zeitung*, 27 March 1907, p. 3.

Ghetto-figures. And through it all, the electric tramway trundles along.
How closely together have the East and West come here![72]

Throughout their coverage, *Czernowitzer Allgemeine Zeitung* based
their judgment of the causes of the uprising on the pervasive assumption
that the Romanian peasants had been incited from various quarters and
that Russian troubles had constituted a precedent and a model. Although
they recognized peasants' economic misery and the aggravating combination of overbidding for land contracts and the boyars' indifference, the
Bukovinian newspaper made constant reference to agitation and incitement as one of the main motors of the uprising. 'One cannot help notic-
ing the similarities between the Romanian peasant movement and the
Russian agrarian revolution. The similarity stems from the fact that
Romanian peasants have been instigated by Russian emissaries',[73] decreed
the newspaper upon first receiving news of the uprising. One day later
they noted that Romanian *agents provocateurs* had joined the Russian
instigators in stoking up peasant discontent.[74] 'Lipovans who emigrated
from Russia have spread the rumour among the Romanian peasants that
in Russia they are dividing all land among peasants. This is how the conviction came into being among Romanian peasants that they can achieve
the same in Romania if they rebel.'[75] Within the Romanian establishment
antisemitic agitation was rife, with respectable personalities such as
Professor Nicolae Iorga holding the Jews to be a national pest and urging
for their eradication from Romanian society.[76] Further information
regarding incitement among the peasants came to *Czernowitzer
Allgemeine Zeitung* from an unnamed 'high-ranking, thoroughly knowl-
edgeable Romanian official', who attributed the peasant uprising to
instigation:

the outbreak of the peasant revolt did not come as so much of a surprise as
it appeared to. It is no secret that the movement has been in the making for
a long time. For years the peasants have been prepared by social democratic
agitators, who lead the popular banks and who put it into peasants' heads
that if they invested their little money in the popular banks, they would

[72] *Czernowitzer Allgemeine Zeitung*, 26 March 1907, p. 2.
[73] *Czernowitzer Allgemeine Zeitung*, 19 March 1907, p. 3.
[74] *Czernowitzer Allgemeine Zeitung*, 20 March 1907, p. 1.
[75] *Czernowitzer Allgemeine Zeitung*, 20 March 1907, p. 2.
[76] *Czernowitzer Allgemeine Zeitung*, 22 March 1907, p. 3.

acquire land. The agitators' instigation work was favoured by the poor administration, which is also to blame for the rapid spread of the uprising.[77]

Agitation among the peasants was not only detected in Romania but also at home in Bukovina. Romanian-language newspapers such as *Voința poporului* and the teachers' newspaper *Lehrerzeitung* pinned the blame for the peasant uprising in Romania on the Jews as did, according to *Czernowitzer Allgemeine Zeitung*, the Ruthene teachers of Luzan, who reportedly called up a meeting to explain the Romanian events to the local peasants. Such attempts to fan the flames of local antisemitism were laughable, said *Czernowitzer Allgemeine Zeitung*, as they showed a gross misreading of the actual cause of the uprising: Jews as well as Christian *arendași* and landowners were equally targeted by the peasants and it would be as absurd to blame the whole Jewry for the doings of the Jewish *arendași* as it would to blame the whole of Christianity for the misdeeds of the Christian landowners.[78]

The Romanian peasant uprising broke out at a feverish time in the Austrian half of the Monarchy: universal male suffrage had been freshly introduced at the end of 1906 and all political, ethnic and confessional groups were caught up in the unprecedented fever of upcoming elections. This inevitably made for the political instrumentalization of news seeping through from Romania into Bukovina. The uprising became a lesson to be learnt and a caveat for each and every ethnic group of the Habsburg province. For each of them the lesson was different and spoke to their immediate domestic concerns and fears, and political agenda.

Voința Poporului, the Romanian-language Bukovinian newspaper with which *Czernowitzer Allgemeine Zeitung* took issue over the issue of antisemitism, represented one of the several Romanian political factions in Bukovina and practiced an electoral kind of antisemitism in that their anti-Jewish discourse was more a function of electoral competition than a clearly formulated ideological stance:

Romanian newspapers are bringing us the sad news that almost 50,000 peasants from Iași, Dorohoi, Botoșani and Suceava counties have left their homes, wives and children and are roaming the country in huge groups of

---

[77] *Czernowitzer Allgemeine Zeitung*, 28 March 1907, p. 1.
[78] *Czernowitzer Allgemeine Zeitung*, 27 March 1907, p. 1.

hundreds and thousands burning and destroying the mansions and estates of the Jewish *arendaşi*, laying waste market towns and ruthlessly beating back the Jews, who have overrun Moldavian market towns like locusts. The peasants are asking for land. They are asking that the state should divide the land for rental to peasants and village associations and stop leasing it out to the Jews, who are now masters of almost all estates in Moldavia. These *arendaşi* not only rent the land at a ludicrous price but they also sublease it to peasants at a tenfold price and seek by all means to turn the peasants into perpetual slaves.' [...] In addition to the division of estates, the peasants are asking that Jews be denied the right to settle in villages. No one knows how far the uprising will go, but one thing is clear, that Jewish greed has once again brought so much misfortune onto a country.[79]

The frequent comparison with the state of the autochthonous peasantry cropped up in *Voinţa Poporului* as well. The editors of the newspaper fell into the category of those who saw clear similarities of fate between the peasantry on either side of the border:

As regards the Bukovinian peasantry, they don't fare much better than their brethren in Moldavia. Here, too, the peasantry is dirt poor and has no other choice than to emigrate to America. Here, too, all estates, belonging to both church and boyars, have ended up in the hands of foreign *arendaşi*, who are mercilessly fleecing the peasantry.

Our arendaşi pay for a *falce* no more than 20–30 crowns and rent it to poor peasants for 100 up to 160 crowns. They don't even receive peasants as day labourers because the *arendaşi*, and in particular the Jews, bring workers over from Galicia. Here, too, the peasants are crying out. Give us our rights, down with the leeches sucking the blood of the peasants![80]

Voinţa Poporului was justified in drawing a parallel, albeit a simplistic one, between Bukovina and Romania in point of land lease and land fragmentation. As we have seen in a previous chapter, Bukovinian agriculture suffered from all of the transitional dysfunctionalities that Austro-Hungarian agriculture experienced in its passage to capitalist relations. In the same simplistic, populist way, *Voinţa Poporului* highlighted one of the safety valves of the Bukovinian agricultural system, that is, migration. Their electioneering showed through when they moved on to criticize

---

[79] *Voinţa Poporului. Organ poporal independent*, Cernăuţi, 24 martie 1907, p. 1.
[80] *Voinţa Poporului. Organ poporal independent*, Cernăuţi, 24 martie 1907, p. 1.

political freedom in Bukovina in a glaring misreading of both the political situation in Romania and that of Bukovina:

> here the situation is even worse than it is in Moldavia. Here Jews are robbing us not only of our work and wealth, but also of our political rights. To this purpose, Jewish supporters have gathered money and paid Moldavian rascals to deceive the peasantry during elections. The Jews know full well why they spend their money on elections, why they insist on deceiving the peasantry. Only then does their *Geschäft* pay off, for the deputies elected with Jewish money only serve Jewish interests and not those of the peasants.[81]

Voința Poporului reacted primarily against Jewish electoral campaigns in those districts of Bukovina inhabited by a majority of Romanian population. They also lashed out against other Romanian political factions in Bukovina, who followed a moderate line and sought to form political alliances with Jewish parties. To reinforce their electoral point, they seemed happy to ignore that in Romania the political situation of the peasantry was much worse than in Bukovina, given that restricted and indirect franchise made genuine peasant representation virtually impossible. In perfect self-contradiction, two weeks later the same newspaper was deploring the plight of the peasantry in Romania:

> The misfortune which has befallen our brethren in Romania should be a lesson for our peasants, who should beware and make sure they don't end up in as bad a situation. [...] The Romanian peasants elect their deputies the way we used to elect our *Wahlmänner* here, and are all the worse for it because the *Wahlmänner* always support the rich and powerful so that the peasants have no one in parliament to stand up for them. They put up with it for a while, until their patience came to an end but they were, alas, shot, beaten and tortured. Lest our peasants should come to the same bitter end, they should listen to our advice for we give them good advice and wish them prosperity and progress.[82]

The typicality of the antisemitism practised by *Voința Poporului* becomes most apparent when juxtaposed with the eerily similar ideas purveyed in humoristic fashion by the Viennese *Kikeriki*: Jews ruining whole countries and peoples with their nefarious activities, or Jews grossly

---

[81] *Voința Poporului. Organ poporal independent*, Cernăuți, 24 martie 1907, pp. 1–2.
[82] *Voința Poporului. Organ poporal independent*, Cernăuți, 7 aprilie 1907, p. 3.

exaggerating the violence of the Romanian peasantry while the latter bore the brunt of repression:

> In Itzkany, on the Romanian border, the place is teeming with 'representatives' of the Jewish press in Berlin, Vienna, Budapest and Czernowitz. The telegraph is working incessantly to spread out to the world the most preposterous lies about the 'terrible revolution', which is said to exceed in barbarism and cruelty the mass killings under Nero and Tamerlane. As far as we know, *no Jewish blood has been shed*, whilst the poor exploited peasants, who are still slaves in the land liberated with their own blood, are being crushed by bullets.[83]

This might well have been a caption to the *Kikeriki* cartoon 'The Romanian Jews in Safety'.

Continuing the theme of 'preposterous lies', *Voința Poporului* deemed it necessary to counteract what they viewed as an international campaign against the Romanian state by highlighting the achievements of the said state, despite its shortcomings:

> As the foreign press is spreading the most preposterous lies against the Romanian Kingdom because of the peasant uprising against the unprecedented oppression of the Jewish, Greek and Bulgarian *arendași*, we consider it appropriate to publish a few authentic pieces of information regarding the great progress made by Dobrogea under Romanian rule. There are, of course, many things in need of reform in the young Kingdom before it reaches the cultural and economic standing of Western European countries.[84]

In an oversimplified account of Dobrogea's transition from Ottoman to Romanian rule, the editors of *Voința Poporului* deplored the state of the province under imperial rule and sang the praises of Romania and the great improvements it brought about in its new province in 28 years of rule. They called this 'the cultural mission of the Romanian Kingdom in the Orient'. In doing so, they showed how disconnected they were from Romania's structural problems as a fledgling state, they swept under the carpet the state's responsibility for the exploitation of the peasantry

[83] *Voința Poporului. Organ poporal independent*, Cernăuți, 31 martie 1907, p. 14.
[84] *Voința Poporului. Organ poporal independent*, Cernăuți, 31 martie 1907, p. 2.

effected through the *arendași* system and, most strikingly, they selected for their Romanian paean the one province that had only just been acquired and as such evinced none of the pernicious features of land tenure that the rest of the state struggled under. If anything, the example of Dobrogea deconstructed their argument and showed not so much that the Romanian state brought civilization to the new province, as the other way round: that the new province brought with it a fairer system of land tenure, which was proved also by the comparatively low levels of social violence during the uprising.

Partaking in the same electoral fever, but from the other end of the political and ethnic spectrum, the *Bukovinaer Post* reported on the Romanian uprising as instructive for the deeply divided Jewish community in Bukovina:

> You Jews who sow the seeds of division among your own people, who wage a battle against your own co-religionists, against your own national brethren – you should consider that only the harmonious union of all forces can ward off evil and peril, which have not disappeared and are still lurking. The events in Romania, close to the border of Bukovina, are a gruesome *Mene tekel* for our Jews. You should understand this right. All personal issues and all hurt feelings should be suppressed and put aside among the Jews, given the gravity of present-day events. He who conquers himself is the strongest of victors. This self-conquest has become a Jewish necessity. [...] Common danger has always been a binding medium and this danger is now crying out to us from Romania so loudly, pitiably and ruthlessly, that we too must hear it here.[85]

Electoral didacticism did not, however, lead to oversimplification or blindness to the true causes of the uprising or to the land situation in Bukovina. Just like *Voința Poporului*, the editors of *Bukovinaer Post* engaged with the topic of land fragmentation and emigration in Bukovina, but they did so as part of a much more thorough and mature analysis of the land-tenure system. *Bukovinaer Post* alerted to the degradation of peasant land ownership in Bukovina by increasing fragmentation and indebtedness and called for politicians to stop 'chasing phantoms' and give due consideration to the fate of the impoverished peasant. As for Romania,

---

[85] *Bukovinaer Post*, 21 March 1907, p. 2: 'Judenhetze in Rumänien'

Bukovinaer Post provided an excellent analysis of the continuation of serf-dom by new means—the *arendaşi* system, and criticized the source of Romanian land injustice, the legal system:

> this legislation serves only to ensure that the peasant scrapes the bare minimum living off his land, that he is tied to this land, and all the rich income goes to the privileged classes. Therein lies the art of Romanian lawgivers. They know all about ornamental legislation. They did this impeccably with the Jews as well. The legal form is always highly polished and presentable. The social content and oriental environment are, by contrast, grim. Under the beautiful forms lies the greed without scruples of a ruling class who can hide their vested interests very well and have no compunction in delivering the lives of hundreds of families to the wrath of the peasants.[86]

TSARIST PRESS

Drug was one of the two newspapers that the infamous Pavel Krushewan published in Bessarabia in the 1890s and early teens of the twentieth century. The other was *Bessarabets*, which had notoriously instigated against Jews and paved the way for the 1903 Kishinev pogrom. Fathered by the same deeply antisemitic mind, *Drug* used the peasant troubles in 1907 Romania to drive its Jew-hating agenda and turned events around so that the conclusion was invariably the same: the Jews were to blame for everything. The type and nature of sources the newspaper relied on reinforced the primacy of this tendentious reading. Firstly, it is quite striking for a newspaper that was produced in Kishinev, which was virtually a stone throw away from the Romanian border, that its editors based their judgments on reports carried in other newspapers, which were more often than not geographically much more removed from the events than Bessarabian *Drug* (Vienna, Berlin, Hamburg, Kiev, Silesia). Secondly, despite the ideological variety of newspapers quoted in its pages, *Drug* did not use them for a more rounded view of events but as sources of pro and con arguments that amounted to the same foregone antisemitic conclusion.

Such was the tendentiousness of the publication that the basic explanation of the causes of the Romanian peasant uprising was unabashedly

---

[86] *Bukovinaer Post*, 24 March 1907, pp. 1–2.

self-contradictory. The uprising, as seen by *Drug* editors, seems to have been a wholly Jewish affair: it was the Jews' fault that the peasants were so mercilessly exploited but it was also Jews who incited the peasants to rebel. As the newspaper took stock of the causes that led to the uprising, the editors wondered at Romanian public opinion, who blamed 'Potemkinists and Russian fugitives who found friendly reception with the Romanian government' and 'talked about an agrarian-anarchistic movement', neglecting what to them seemed to be the central factor in the uprising: the Jews. 'In Moldavia, the movement was antisemitic.' Here 'the Jewish and land questions are directly and closely interconnected: for almost thirty years Jews have been taking land on lease in Romania', which was part and parcel of an 'economically and morally favourable attitude to capital at the expense of the welfare of the peasantry [...] A sort of epidemic is raging among Romanian landowners in that they only lease their land out to Jews because they appear to be better and regular payers'. *Drug* found it 'instructive to point out that the main feature of the agrarian question in Moldavia was the battle between two Jewish millionaire [leaseholder] families, the Fischers and the Justers'. These succeeded one another every ten years in renting the great latifundia of Moldavia and outbid one another in the process so that rent and subrent went higher and higher. The stiff costs 'did not affect the income of the leaseholders because they were immediately shifted onto the peasants'. *Drug* was well informed regarding the exploitative practices of the leaseholders: reintroduction of labour dues, total dependence of peasants on the leaseholder, the injunction to cultivate the leaseholder's fields first, the extremely low wages, and the practice of forcing peasants to accept payment in overpriced produce from the leaseholders' shops.[87]

Quoting the daily *Kievlianin* (1864–1919), a conservative Russian-language newspaper that appeared in Kiev, *Drug* claimed that revolutionary activity in Romania was not antisemitic since the propagandists were fugitives from Russia and themselves mostly Jewish, but 'when the riots broke out, the agitators in Moldavia lost control of the situation and the peasants started going after the Jews.'[88] These allegedly Jewish agitators, the *Drug* editors continued the argument in a later

---

[87] *Drug*, No. 82, 28 March/10 April 1907, p. 1: 'Zagranichnaia Zhizni'.
[88] *Drug*, No. 82, 28 March/10 April 1907, p. 1: 'Zagranichnaia Zhizni'.

issue, turned the peasants against the landowners, instigated them to confiscate the land and divide it among themselves and convinced the peasants that nothing bad would happen to them as the troops would not shoot.[89] This rationale came in handy when trying to account for the uprising in Wallachia, where there were almost no Jewish leaseholders.

In *Drug*'s coverage of the Romanian uprising, there is a very fine line between source criticism, which is what every respectable publication does, and tendentious reading, in that sensible information comes to buttress antisemitic claims. The editors thus pointed out the exaggerations and inflated figures that circulated in the Romanian press at the time: 'Romanian newspapers claim peasants gathered in huge groups of thirty thousand and headed for Iaşi and troops were powerless against them. In reality, the crowds of peasants did not exceed 100 to 2,000.' This, as contemporary official documents corroborate, was a sensible enough assessment to make. The newspaper did not leave it there, however. It went on to attach malign intention to the exaggerations and traced it invariably to Jewish origins. Such news, ratiocinated the *Drug* editors, must have come from Jewish newspapers, which reported 'incredible brutalities' such as 'peasants smashing Jews' heads against house walls and cobble stones'.[90] Moreover, the majority of news about the uprising received from foreign newspapers was filtered through 'filthy Jewish witnesses', who pinned the blame on the local administration and accused them of organizing pogroms.[91] Among the newspapers considered guilty of exaggerating the extent of the troubles in Romania were the Liberal foreign press such as *Frankfurter Zeitung*, *Berliner Tageblatt* and, *Drug*'s pet hatred, the Viennese *Neue Freie Presse*.[92] There may have been some devastation of property, as the *Drug* editors were ready to concede, but this was only in response to Jewish self-defence.[93] Several weeks later, they reported with satisfaction that the majority of Jews who had fled Moldavia had returned only to find out that 'the horrors reported by some newspapers of devastated towns were not true.

[89] *Drug*, No. 85, 31 March/13 April, p. 1: 'K Bezporiadkami v Rumiinii'.

[90] *Drug*, No. 71, 16/29 March 1907, p. 2: 'Bezporiadki v Ruminii'.

[91] *Drug*, No. 70, 15/28 March 1907, p. 2: 'Zagranichnaia Zhizni'.

[92] *Drug*, No. 82, 28 March/10 April 1907, p. 1: 'Zagranichnaia Khronika'.

[93] *Drug*, No. 71, 16/29 March 1907, p. 2: 'Bezporiadki v Ruminii'.

They were confined to a few Jewish houses, but in general neither small nor big towns had much to suffer.'[94]

The general drift of *Drug* coverage was that of downplaying the extent and violence of the events, rejecting the notion that Jews were victimized. This was evident in the choice of words used to refer to the Jewish population who fled Moldavia: these were constantly referred to as *begletsov* (fugitives, runaways, escapees) rather than *bezhenets* (refugees).[95] *Begletsov* was also the term the newspaper used in reference to Russian revolutionaries and the former Potemkin sailors who had taken refuge in Romania after the 1905 rebellion.[96] Testimonies from *Silezkoi Gazetii* were quoted to buttress this idea: their correspondent visited Iași and ascertained that all was peaceful and quiet, 'life followed its course as usual and no one thought of any revolution [...] The peasants had no intention to invade the town.'[97] This was not the only testimony to the effect that peace and quiet reigned where newspapers had reported savagery. Even some Jewish sources corroborated this impression.[98] However, the point of quoting the *Silezkoi Gazetii* was to deny any persecution of the Jews. The Iași prefect, with whom the *Silezkoi Gazetii* correspondent spoke, insisted that 'there is no such thing as an oppression of the Jews in Romania. There is no lawlessness or persecution of the Jews as claimed by the press and agents of "Alliance Israélite". [...] Romanian Jews have no grounds to complain about their fate. The peasant in Moldavia has, on the contrary, plenty of reasons to be displeased with the Jews because of their shameless dealings. The hostility of the Romanian people towards the Jews does not have religious but economic causes and, unsurprisingly, in moments of popular indignation, besides the culprits are harmed also the innocent.'[99] Downplaying the scale of the uprising also satisfied Russian national pride

---

[94] *Drug*, No. 85, 31 March/13 April, p. 1: 'K Bezporiadkami v Rumiinii'.

[95] *Drug*, No. 70, 15/28 March 1907, p. 2: 'Zagranichnaia Zhizni'.

[96] Drug, No. 82, 28 March/10 April 1907: 'Zagranichnaia Zhizni'.

[97] *Drug*, No. 81, 27 March/9 April 1907, p. 2: 'Zagranichnaia Khronika: Rumiinia – Pravda o bezporiadnakh'.

[98] Central Archives for the History of the Jewish People in Jerusalem, RM 165, Report no. 451, Czernowitz 23 March 1907, p. 1; Report no. 452, Vienna 31 March 1907, p. 3. Many thanks to Elisabeth Weber for pointing out this reference to me and for kindly providing me with a digital copy of the material.

[99] *Drug*, No. 81, 27 March/9 April 1907, p. 2: 'Zagranichnaia Khronika: Rumiinia – Pravda o bezporiadnakh'.

as, before the Romanian uprising, the Russians had dominated the negative headlines of the foreign press under similar accusations. Thus *Drug* latched onto to an article published in the *Hamburger Anzeiger*, which noted that the 'tendentious distortion of truth' in the liberal foreign press was similar to the exaggerations about Russian developments. The overt goal of the foreign press, concluded *Drug*, was to conduct an anti-Romanian campaign, which was led by the Viennese *Neue Freie Presse*.[100]

Coincidentally or not, *Drug* published in its 17/30 March issue a letter to the peasants of Bessarabia from Emilian A. Melenchiuk, Bessarabian MP in the second Russian Duma, who responded to numerous letters and telegrams which he had received from the peasants regarding the land question. The MP reassured the Bessarabian peasant population that he would do his best to put their demands before the president of the Duma and explicitly linked the resolution of the land question with the Jewish question. To further reinforce his point, he quoted the declaration of the Interior Minister Stolypin before the Duma in which he committed to 'defend the rights and interests' of the peasantry'.[101]

At the opposite end of the Bessarabian journalistic spectrum in contrast to Krushewan's publication there were the well-informed views of *Bessarabskaia Zhizni*, a social democrat publication, with connections among Bessarabian socialist emigrees in Romania and, as such, with access to good sources of information on the socio-economic relations of the neighbouring country.

The editors of *Bessarabskaia Zhizni* picked up on the helter-skelter of rumours, which circulated in the Romanian press and among Romanian officials, about the putative culprits for the Romanian peasant uprising. With each new contribution the newspaper covered one more instance of a wild goose chase: the Liberals, the Russians, Bessarabian students, Stolypin himself were, according to the Romanian authorities, to blame for inciting the peasants to rebel. These, as the editors argued, were preposterous notions and amounted to pinning the blame on others and thus deflecting responsibility for the elites' mismanagement. The views espoused by the newspaper were informed by reports from a correspondent in Romania identified by his initials as I.V.M.:

---

[100] *Drug*, No. 82, 28 March/10 April 1907, p. 1: 'Zagranichnaia Khronika'.
[101] *Drug*, No. 73, 18/31 March 1907, p. 2: 'Mestnaia Khronika. Pismo deputata ot krestian Bessarabskoi gubernii E.A. Melenchuka.'

The culprits for the peasant movement are the ruling circles, who are made up of nabobs, who do not understand the needs of the hungry and do not know what the needs of the village are. They seek the causes of the movement and say that the spark has come from Moscow, or from the Russian government, or from Stolypin himself, who allegedly wished to start this fire to show to the Duma that agrarian troubles could start even under constitutional governments, that even there the army shot their rebellious brothers and fathers.[102]

This exculpatory attitude on the part of Romanian officials put the correspondent of *Bessarabskaia Zhizni* in mind of the similar tendency among Russian authorities of exporting blame as captured by the phrase 'The English lady is muddying the waters' (*Anglichanka mutit*),[103] which went back to Pushkin and stemmed from the antagonism between the Tsarist Empire and the British Empire.

For the newspaper correspondent the uprising in Romania was a purely agrarian upheaval that had nothing to do with pogroms and peasant animosity against Jews:

> Many short-sighted politicians were overjoyed: the movement was antisemitic. They couldn't have been more wrong. [The peasants] soon started to destroy the properties of ministers, MPs, landowners, all the exploiters of the labouring masses. The peasants are not to blame for the pogroms organised in Botoşani, Târgul Frumos and Vaslui. It was the urban rabble and the worst elements from among the peasants such as the Lipovans who were to blame.[104]

The peasants, concluded the correspondent, were not antisemites; they got on perfectly well with the village Jews.[105]

If Romanian peasants were not after the Jews, who or what were they after? Basing his conclusions on testimonies of peasant deputies who went to the capital to make their claims known to the government and those given by arrested peasants under interrogation, the newspaper correspondent emphasized his conviction that the true cause of the uprising was

---

[102] *Bessarabskaia Zhizni*, No. 60, 1907, 'The Peasant Movement in Romania'.
[103] *Bessarabskaia Zhizni*, No. 60, 1907, 'The Peasant Movement in Romania'.
[104] *Bessarabskaia Zhizni*, No. 60, 1907, 'The Peasant Movement in Romania'.
[105] *Bessarabskaia Zhizni*, No. 60, 1907, 'The Peasant Movement in Romania'.

twofold: endemic land hunger and the merciless exploitation of the peasants by the ruling elites. He built a strong case in support of these assumptions and deployed detailed and well-informed evidence regarding contractual terms, payments and peasant debt. Of particular interest is the reported intention of peasants to emigrate and the perception that Bessarabia was a better place for Romanian peasants:

> From each village peasant deputies left for Bucharest asking for the agrarian question to be solved in the interest of the peasants and of the country. [...] Many of these deputies said they would not back down nor go back to work unless they received land; [they said] they were ready to leave their 'native' country and cross over into Bessarabia, where the Duma would give them land, or go to another country, for instance to Transylvania or to Canada.[106]

Romanian elites were accused of gross neglect of the agrarian question and the Hohenzollern King of Romania and his Prussian bureaucracy were blamed for the perpetuation of the peasant plight. The correspondent of *Bessarabskaia Zhizni* expressed disdain for the Romanian electoral system, which was presented as inefficient and unrepresentative of peasant interest. The Bessarabian newspaper was not the only Russian-language source that took issue with Romania's electoral system (as we shall see in the next chapter, the Tsarist consul in Iași objected to it too). Romania, therefore, was in their view living proof that constitutional and representative government was by no means a political panacea, which conclusion in itself fed into the feverish debates over the form of government to be adopted in the Tsarist Empire at the time.

Novoe Vremya, the main Russian central newspaper, put forth an antisemitic explanation for the peasant uprising in Romania: 'Telegrams to the effect that anti-Jewish unrest turned into agrarian unrest are inaccurate. As a matter of fact, it was agrarian unrest that turned anti-Jewish.'[107] The reason for this, according to the editors, was Jewish monopolization of land in the context of the Jews enjoying full citizen's rights in Romania. *Novoe Vremya* found it instructive to read about the Jewish question in Romania as this resonated with current debates in the Tsarist Empire

---

[106] *Bessarabskaia Zhizni*, No. 60, 1907, 'The Peasant Movement in Romania'.
[107] *Novoe Vremya*, 13/26 March 1907, 'Antievreiskie bezporiadki Rumîinii', p. 5.

about a possible emancipation of the Jews. To this end they dedicated a series of articles to the Jews of Romania based on the views of the Romanian Foreign Minister Jean Lahovary. In his 1902 tract *La Question Israélite en Roumanie* Lahovary presented the situation of the Romanian Jews as favourable: infrequent outbursts against Jews were, he argued, infrequent and no harm came to them personally but only to their property. All but political rights were granted to them and, in Moldavia, the entire commerce and industry was in their hands, while the Romanian population did all the hard work. Far from accepting that the Jewish community in Romania was victimized, Lahovary depicted them as a menacing mass of aliens, who were not interested in assimilating and threatened to outnumber the autochthonous population, sucking their energy and grabbing all land.[108]

With a certain sense of superiority, the Russian newspaper also highlighted the tardiness of Romanian authorities' response to the first news of the uprising and deemed the growing unrest a consequence of poor policing: the authorities failed to take energetic measures from the very beginning; had this happened, the uprising would never have got out of hand.[109]

*   *   *

The press around the triple frontier refracted the incoming stream of news from embattled Romania according to their political orientation with regard to the issues of the day in their respective countries and each had their version of the Romanian peasant uprising to report on. The antisemitic press felt vindicated in their rantings against the Jews, who were portrayed as spoliators of the peasantry; the socialist press saw the roots of the problem in the economic predicament of the peasantry and their inability to organize; nationalist publications pointed to the failure of the Romanian elites to genuinely include the peasantry into their nation and care for them; the moderate, liberal press voiced disappointment and concern at the implosion of social order in what had hitherto looked like one of the most orderly and reliable states in the Balkan region.

---

[108] *Novoe Vremya*, 16 March 1907, 'Evrei v Rumïinii (I)', p. 2.
[109] *Novoe Vremya*, 13/26 March 1907, 'Antievreiskie bezporiadki Rumïinii', p. 5.

BIBLIOGRAPHY

Aradi Közlöny
Bessarabskaia Zhizni
Bukovinaer Post
Czernowitzer Allgemeine Zeitung
Drug
Der Floh
Kikeriki
Magyar-Zsidó Szemle
Népszava
Neue Freie Presse
Novoe Vremya
Pester Lloyd
Pesti Hírlap
Pesti Napló
Răvaşul
Tribuna
Voinţa Poporului. Organ poporal independent
Marin Badea, Andrei Caciora, Nicolae Rosut, Eugen Gluck (Eds.), *Aradul şi răscoala ţăranilor din 1907: 70 [ani]*, Universitatea Cultural Ştiinţifică Arad, 1977

CHAPTER 7

Diplomacy of the Uprising

Austro–Hungarian Diplomacy

Information Networks

The Austro-Hungarian government received news of the uprising via their consulates in the main Romanian towns: Turnu-Severin, Giurgiu, Brăila, Galați, Focșani and Iași. The information was then centralized in Bucharest by the general consul and forwarded for the attention of the Ministry of Foreign Affairs in Vienna. The consulates relayed news not just on the uprising proper but also on the state of affairs locally and any situation that might affect commercial or business relations. These were the eyes and ears of the Austro-Hungarian Empire on Romanian territory and were at times more efficient and more in the know than the Romanian authorities themselves. Consular reports afford the twenty-first-century reader an alternative view on Romania's agrarian crisis. These reports combined information from the regional level with high-level discussions with Romanian statesmen and with King Carol himself, offering a broad picture of the causes, course and consequences of the uprising at the end of several weeks of raging troubles.

Fear of Contamination

Was there ever any concern among the Austro-Hungarian authorities that the uprising might cross the border into Transylvania and Bukovina?

© The Author(s) 2018
I. Marin, *Peasant Violence and Antisemitism in Early Twentieth-Century Eastern Europe*,
https://doi.org/10.1007/978-3-319-76069-8_7

There was indeed concern, redoubled by precaution, but never downright fear of impending contamination. The uprising did not last long enough for the Austro-Hungarian authorities to consider it a threat and also domestic social and ethnic relations firmed them up in their belief that the Romanian troubles could not replicate within the border provinces of the Monarchy. During a discussion with the German Consul in Vienna on 3 April 1907, Aehrenthal, the Austro-Hungarian Minister of Foreign Affairs, accounted for this belief as follows:

> There was never any serious fear of an outburst of unrest in Transylvania because the reliable Szeklers and Saxons who live there constitute a counter-weight to the Transylvanian Romanians. He had, however, been concerned as regards Romanians in Bukovina, particularly because, as the troubles in Moldavia had leaped across and contaminated parts of Wallachia, a leap over the Austrian border did not seem unlikely. The (Austrian) Minister of the Interior Freiherr Bienerth is, nevertheless, fully confident that there won't be any troubles in Bukovina.[1]

Aehrenthal was, however, fearful of a different type of contamination and this came out in correspondence regarding the arrest of former Potemkin sailors by the Romanian authorities. In July 1905 following the famous rebellion on the battleship Potemkin, the ship and the mutinous crew ended up in Constanţa, the main harbour on the Romanian Black Sea coast. The ship was eventually returned to the Tsarist authorities. The crew remained in the host country after the Romanian authorities refused to extradite them. The bulk of former Potemkin sailors went to work in the railway workshops in Paşcani, eastern Romania, and on the oilrigs in the Prahova valley in the south. A combination of a spite-the-Russians attitude and a dire need for a qualified workforce for industrial enterprises persuaded the Romanian authorities that holding on to the Potemkin rebels was a good idea, despite endemic fears of anarchist contamination. In spring 1907 the Potemkinists became prime suspects for the Romanian authorities, who, despite acknowledging the economic predicament of the peasantry, were nevertheless convinced that what sparked off the uprising was the work of instigators.[2]

---

[1] PAAA, Berlin, R 9653, Rumänien Allgemeine Angelegenheiten April–December 1907, Report no. 117, Vienna, 4 April 1907, pp. 1–3.

[2] Andrei Oţetea; Ion Popescu-Puţuri (eds), *Documente privind marea răscoală a ţăranilor din 1907* (henceforth quoted as *Documente*), Bucureşti, Editura Academiei Republicii Socialiste România, 1977-., vol. 2, p. 356; *Documente*, vol. 3, p. 140–141, 251.

The Austro-Hungarian consul in Bucharest reported to Aehrenthal on the arrest of 70 Russian sailors:

Yesterday evening Mr. Sturdza told me about the Prahova prefect's already executed order of arrest of around 70 Russian sailors from the 'Kniaz Potemkin'. The Prime Minister is doubtful if this was a wise measure to take as there are 300 more sailors from the mentioned ship in the country, who might want to take revenge. Mr. Sturdza is convinced that the peasant movement was planned and fostered by anarchist agitators and, to his mind, the European anarchists contributed to the outbreak of the troubles just as much as Russian revolutionists.[3]

The contamination hypothesis appears to have carried weight not just with the Romanian authorities but also with the Austro-Hungarian ones. Aehrenthal's reaction to the prospect of Romanians allowing the Potemkinists to emigrate over the Austro-Hungarian border showed the same conviction that their otherwise peaceful population could only be incited to violence by anarchists. Thus, in a letter dated 9 April 1907 Aehrenthal communicated to Hungarian Prime Minister Wekerle:

As the revolutionary activities of these elements could have a dangerous influence on social relations in the frontier territories bordering on Romania, I considered it useful to communicate to the Romanian Prime Minister, via our imperial consul, that I took an active interest in the news of the Romanian energetic measures taken against the Russian revolutionaries. At the same time I gave Prince Schönburg the task that, in case there is an intention to deport the arrested sailors, or even the remaining ones, *he should find the right manner in which to persuade them not send these highly dangerous individuals over our border.*[4]

Ten days later Sturdza was sending off a request to Aehrenthal for permission for the former Potemkin sailors to transit through to America. 'Mr Sturdza', ran the missive from Schönburg to Aehrenthal, 'intends to get rid of the Russian sailors from the Potemkin who are currently living in the oil region of Prahova. Their number is around 100 (at most) and,

---

[3] MOL, K 26 Miniszterelnök, 'Abschrift eines Telegrammes des k.u.k. Gesandten in Bukarest vom 5. April 1907, No. 33', 1907, p. 67.

[4] MOL, K 26 Miniszterelnök, 'K.u.K. Ministerium des kaiserl. Und königl. Hauses und des Aeussern/Aerenthal – Seiner Excellenz dem Herrn königlich ungarischen Minister-Präsidenten Dr. Alexander Wekerle', Wien am 9. April 1907, pp. 125–127 – emphasis added.

given the intrigues they have spread throughout the country, they cannot be kept there anymore. These 100 sailors are allowed to emigrate to America and they agreed to it. And it will be a matter of us and Germany giving permission for the transit journey. A German harbour would have a definite advantage over Galatz, Brăila or Constanța as in the latter case there is no direct sailing route to America and the sailors could leave the ship at an intermediate harbour. Mr. Sturdza explains that he would only like to ask our permission for a transit journey just as was granted, on the basis of the existing agreement, in the case of other anarchists; [this is] the sort of permission that has often been granted by us. Mr. Sturdza is going to talk about getting such permission also with my German colleague'.[5]

1907 Romania Seen through Austro-Hungarian Eyes

Months before the uprising, the Iași consulate reported to the Austro-Hungarian general consul in Bucharest on the poor state of the Romanian peasantry. In a report of 27 November 1906 they laid down the main features of the Romanian state as a predominantly agrarian state and cautioned that the fate of the peasantry, who formed the great majority of the population, was inevitably interwoven with that of the state itself. The report echoed misgivings that, despite the 1864 emancipation of the peasantry under Prince Cuza, the condition of land workers not only did not improve as expected, on the contrary, it was worse than before. 'The impression one gets when entering a Romanian village is difficult to describe. Here and there is the odd clay hut; the majority of the inhabitants live in holes in the ground, whose roofs, which look like tents and are made of all sorts of wickerwork, lead one to think, when looking at them from a distance, that they are burial mounds. In the underground space live both family and livestock.'[6] The poor diet, rampant alcoholism and numerous religious fasts contributed—continued the report—to the spread of illnesses such as malaria, typhus, syphilis and pellagra, which for lack of adequate medical care resulted in a high mortality rate. 'In some districts and in particular in Moldavia population numbers are decreasing

---

[5] HHStA, Karton 9: Ges. Bukarest, Berichte 1907–1908, 19. April 1907, no. 20: B, 'Eine Bitte des Herrn Sturdza betreffend Durchlieferung russischer Matrosen des Kniaz Potemkin die nach Amerika auswandern'

[6] HHStA, Wien, Karton 7, 7 March 1907, No. 9, Abschrift eines an das hohe k.u.k. Ministerium des Aeussern erstatteten Berichtes vom 27 Nov. 1906 Nr. 72 res, des k.u.k. Consulates in Jassy.

visibly, so that there are not enough autochthonous work hands to till the fields and every year thousands of foreign seasonal workers must be brought in to reinforce the local work force, who are not numerous or strong enough. Other countries that resort to this method do so in order to make up for the dearth of work hands, which were absorbed by the industry at the expense of agriculture. In Romania, which possesses hardly any industry and is an agrarian state *par excellence*, the necessity of such a measure is an alarming symptom.'[7] The governments that came and went were all well aware of the predicament of the peasantry and sought to ameliorate it but, rather than addressing the problem head on, they resorted to palliatives, which often had the opposite effect. 'Although the necessity of change is generally acknowledged, the hotly conducted party politics of the ruling classes is however motivated by reasons that have nothing to do with state interests.'[8]

Weeks before any news reached foreign newspapers and local authorities across the border, the Austro-Hungarian consul in Bucharest, Prinz Schönburg, was reporting to Aehrenthal that he had it 'from reliable sources that in Moldavia there is a ferment of peasant unrest brewing up. The condition of the peasantry there has for a long time been known to be a wretched one: alcoholism, exploitation by Jews and great leaseholders, lack of schools, indolence of the authorities. All of these elements conspire to the physical and moral ruin of the peasants in Moldavia and also those in some parts of Wallachia.'[9] The peasants of Moldavia had, of late, been taking justice into their own hands against the exploitation of landowners and leaseholders. 'These incidents have not so far been of a serious nature, but the government is all the same concerned that socialist-revolutionary ideas could seep in from across the Russian border and prefects have apparently been issued with strict instructions to prevent a repeat of such incidents.'[10]

---

[7] HHStA, Wien, Karton 7, 7 March 1907, No. 9, Abschrift eines an das hohe k.u.k. Ministerium des Aeussern erstatteten Berichtes vom 27 Nov. 1906 Nr. 72 res, des k.u.k. Consulates in Jassy.

[8] HHStA, Wien, Karton 7, 7 March 1907, No. 9, Abschrift eines an das hohe k.u.k. Ministerium des Aeussern erstatteten Berichtes vom 27 Nov. 1906 Nr. 72 res, des k.u.k. Consulates in Jassy.

[9] HHStA, Wien, Karton 39, PA, XVIII, Bericht no. 9, F, Bucharest, 7 March 1907, pp. 101–102.

[10] HHStA, Wien, Karton 39, PA, XVIII, Bericht no. 9, F, Bucharest, 7 March 1907, p. 102.

As the uprising eventually broke out, the Austro-Hungarian consul in Bucharest Prince Schönburg explained to Foreign Minister Aehrenthal the existential threat posed by the peasant uprising as primarily a consequence of internal problems, although he did not discard the contamination potential of the region (Russian revolutionary influence, spread of anarchist ideas from the West, contamination with Balkan unrest from the south). The low moral and religious level of the peasantry was, according to Schönburg, a consequence of the dearth of schools and preoccupation of teachers with politics rather than tuition, whereas Orthodox bishops shunned their responsibilities to their flock and were useless when it came to pacifying them, and priests were 'to quote my Russian colleague, nothing but anarchists (*ce sont des anarchistes*)'. Further isolating the peasantry from the workings of the state was the lack of a proper system of justice that peasants could resort to. Because of high legal fees, 'the poorer peasants don't even think about taking their grievances to court' and 'in penal cases the jurors are too lenient even with murder and arson'. 'He who claims that the Romanian peasant has a good life is talking of exceptions only, which may even be numerous, but the majority of peasants are victims of rampant pellagra, the poverty disease as they call it here, as it stems from a diet based exclusively on maize, and of poor housing conditions. The holes in the ground, which the local landowners and *arendași* offer as accommodation to the seasonal immigrant workers from Hungary, Slavonia and Bukovina, represent in some regions the usual "worker dwelling". In apologetic response to the complaints we lodged, the authorities claimed that the Romanian peasants feel at home in these holes in the ground.' Moreover, 'in Romania there is no cadastral system. Carp wanted to introduce one. Apparently the costs were too high [15 million]. The consequence of this lack is that in case of boundary conflict the peasant can't defend his right and little wonder that he is convinced that everybody is trying to cheat him!' Add to this chronic land hunger, frequent and politicized change of administrative personnel, cronyism and demagoguery and the picture of Romania's misfortunes is complete. 'Domestic conditions', concluded the consul, 'are more than sufficient to account for the outbreak of the uprising'.[11]

On 3 April 1907, as the uprising was gradually burning out, Schönburg submitted another report on the state of Romanian agriculture, this time relying on data provided by the new Romanian Finance Minister

---

[11] HHStA, Wien, Karton 39, PA, XVIII, Rumaenien Ber Weisungen Varia, pp. 149–150.

Costinescu. The analysis is lucid and unsparing: everybody recognizes that agricultural misery is one of the main causes of the peasant movement.

> The system of great land rental is most widespread in Moldavia. The great *arendaş* entirely replaces the landowner and the latter's activity is confined to cashing in the rent, which in recent years has reached an enormous height. In his turn, the *arendaş* must oppress and (the expression is not too harsh) downright swindle the peasant in order to collect the high rent, which especially for a few years now no longer corresponds to land yield. The way in which this occurs is in places – I'm taking my data from Romanian sources – downright perfidious. If he doesn't want to die of hunger the peasant has no other alternative than complying with the conditions set by the cartelized great *arendaşi*. [...] In Moldavia the great *arendaş* subrents land to the peasant at a price which is the double of what it used to be; in Wallachia this is done by the administrator of the great landowner. Here the peasant has to work the land of the great landowner and receives in exchange for this some poor-quality land which he can work for himself. Of course he has to work the land of the landowner first, so that often the peasant doesn't have any time to work his own. [...] There are also all sorts of other dues that the peasant is liable to as a result of these relations. They can only be described as corvée.[12]

What stands out in this report is the acknowledgment of the oppressive effect of Romanian agricultural legislation, which very few contemporary commentators picked up on, despite its overwhelming importance for the predicament of the Romanian peasantry. Existing legislation amounted to a hamstringing of the Romanian peasant, who was thus caught up in a check-mate situation whereby he could in no way take advantage of his emancipation and the land he was given:

> P.S. In the report above I have failed to mention one important circumstance. By legislating the inalienability of peasant land in the past few decades the Romanian lawgivers have created (albeit with the best of intentions) a situation whereby the peasant cannot easily increase his land possessions. And as the plot that is on average given to one peasant decreases naturally with every hereditary subdivision, the peasant is forced to resort to working for the great *arendaş*, or (in Wallachia) for the great landowner. There are certainly numerous exceptions, the above circumstances are however the rule.[13]

[12] MOL, K 26 Miniszterelnök, Prinz Schönburg an Freiherrn von Aehrenthal, Bericht nr. 15 C., Bukarest, 3. April 1907, p. 117.
[13] MOL, K 26 Miniszterelnök, Prinz Schönburg an Freiherrn von Aehrenthal, Bericht nr. 15 C., Bukarest, 3. April 1907, p. 118.

Should the Austro-Hungarian Army Intervene?

As to the course of the uprising and especially the much discussed question of army discipline, Schönburg relayed his impressions based on a discussion with King Carol that, 'while there may have been instances of insubordination in the army at the beginning of the uprising, these were not to blame so much on the soldiers and officers as on the high command at the War Ministry, which was at the time in the hands of the Conservative government.'[14] Once General Averescu, the War Minister under the new Liberal government, took charge of the army, the situation improved and, according to King Carol himself, the short-notice general mobilization, which was completed in a matter of days, made a great impression on the Bulgarian consul in Bucharest.[15]

The last days of March 1907 were critical for Romania in Schönburg's view. In a telegram to Aehrenthal dated 24 March he described the desperate situation of the Romanian authorities, who battled with chronic shortage of troops and ever pressing demands from foreign consulates for protection of their citizens. 'I am receiving a steady stream of urgent telegrams from our co-nationals who live here asking us for protection and intercession. However, great apathy reigns here. Whenever I try to intervene, they [the authorities] reply that the entire country is teetering on the brink of disaster and they don't have enough means at their disposal, although 100,000 men are already under arms, of whom two thirds are in Moldavia and one third in Wallachia.'[16] A day later, following an incendiary telegram from the consular office in Giurgiu on the Danube, Schönburg turned to Foreign Minister Lahovary and urged him to secure the necessary protection for the Giurgiu consulate and for the Austro-Hungarian community there. Lahovary reportedly gave the exasperated answer: '"What can I do, all available troops are already deployed, I cannot conjure any more up out of thin air." This was followed by a discussion on the telephone between him and the War Minister, the latter giving assurance that fresh troops would be sent off to Giurgiu.'[17]

[14] HHStA, Wien, Karton 39, PA, XVIII, 30 May 1907, report no 30, A-B, from Schoenburg to Aerenthal, pp. 250–251.

[15] HHStA, Wien, Karton 39, PA, XVIII, 30 May 1907, report no 30, A-B, from Schoenburg to Aerenthal, p. 251.

[16] Abschrift eines Telegrames des k.u.k. Gesandten in Bukarest vom 24. Maerz, 1907, MOL, K. 26 Miniszterelnök, p. 66.

[17] HHStA, Wien, Karton 39, PA, XVIII, Varia, Bericht, Bukarest 4 April 1907.

It was in the context of the Conservative government meltdown that the possibility of asking for foreign military help was contemplated. 'One of the personalities here has recently alluded, in private conversation, to the possibility that, given the partly unreliable troops, foreign military help could be asked for against the rebellious peasants.'[18] A later telegram disclosed the name of the prominent Romanian statesman, who broached the topic with Schönburg:

> Mr Take Ionescu described the situation as exceptionally critical and went so far as to tell me that he did not exclude the possibility that 'our military help might be necessary'.[19] By contrast, Lahovary,[20] the new Romanian Minister of Foreign Affairs, made it clear that foreign military intervention was totally out of the question.[21]

Lahovary voiced one side of what was essentially divided opinion among Romanian politicians regarding the wisdom and expedience of foreign intervention. He represented the voice of proud Romanian nationalism, which could not begin to conceive foreign troops marching into an independent kingdom and restoring order. This would have been the height of national humiliation, especially if one considers that Romania had acquired its state independence a mere 30 years before and had been striving ever since to project an image of modernity, stability and reliability. Military success had been a vital ingredient in 1878 in the Romanian claim for independent statehood. Their brave military stance during the Russo-Turkish war of 1877–1878, despite all the shortcomings inherent in a fledgling army, gave them a say in the final peace negotiations and consolidated the perception that Romanian independence was gained on the battlefield. To resort a quarter of a century later to foreign military help to suppress domestic disturbances would have been tantamount to internationally acknowledging military failure and as such state failure.

Virgil C. Arion, a member of the Conservative Party, criticized some of his party colleagues for toying with the idea of foreign intervention:

---

[18] Abschrift eines Telegrames des k.u.k. Gesandten in Bukarest vom 24. Maerz, 1907, MOL, K. 26 Miniszterelnök, p. 64.

[19] HHStA, Wien, Karton 39, PA, XVIII, Varia, Bericht, Bukarest 4 April 1907, p. 14.

[20] Ion Lahovari (1844–1915) was interim Minister of Foreign Affairs between 9 February 1907 and 11 March 1907.

[21] HHStA, Wien, Karton 39, PA, XVIII, Varia, Bericht, Bukarest 4 April 1907, p. 14, verso.

Ever since the peasant uprising broke out I have heard many people around me talk of the possibility of foreign troops entering the country. This prospect is viewed by some not as the greatest misfortune that could befall Romania but as redemption for the country. There are some who even regret not having called the Austrian army as early as three weeks ago. And all this time the Romanian army that was sent out to put down the uprising has behaved admirably with patience and unparalleled discipline and courage. And you wonder: have some people lost their sense of national duty to such an extent that, hard hit as they may be in their material interests, they no longer realize what a humiliation it would be if Romania were to be occupied and the uprising were to be put down by foreign armies? Be that as it may, one ought not to speak lightly of foreign occupation. And even less so today, when the unparalleled military spirit of our troops has proved the extent of their patriotism. More than ever it has become apparent that the army gives the people a national conscience. In a society like ours, in which the intellectual elite of the country thinks, speaks, lives and feels in foreign languages, the only hub of intense national life remains the army. At this moment it is the repository of our culture and freedom and when the transient dissidence between army and peasantry, which was brought about by a spate of madness, has passed, the army will continue to be the only place where the peasant can learn solidarity, national pride and national love.[22]

Although tentative thoughts of bringing in foreign military help were conveyed to Vienna, no further discussion of such a scenario is recorded in extant official documents. This may well have been because such a request was never formally issued and, with the change of government, the coming of a firmer, more ruthless military command and the consequent repression rendered unnecessary such an option. The Romanians got a grip on their country at the eleventh hour and the worst-case scenario never materialized.

Have They Learnt Their Lesson?

As the uprising eventually ground to a halt and order was re-established with great violence and after great violence, Schönburg expressed his

---

[22] ANR, Arhiva CC al PCR, Colecție nr. 50, Unitate de păstrare nr. 10,256, p. 32: newspaper cutting from *Adevărul*, 24 Mai 1912, 'Răscoalele țărănești. Represiunea, armatele străine și partidul agrar. Cum judecă d. Virgil Arion atitudinea și acțiunea partidului conservator'.

doubt, which echoed that of some Romanian politicians, that the Romanian political class had learnt its lesson from the terrible experience. As the worst of the uprising lasted only 14 days, he wondered if this was too short a time to make a lasting impression on them. 'Will Romania persist in their frivolous party politics, which is dictated only by personal interests, or are they finally going to dedicate themselves to the task which serves national interests?'[23] Yet more laws was *not* what Romania needed, insisted Schönburg, but the raising of the cultural and economic level of the peasantry, better administration and justice system. 'Here the problems and mistakes that have been made seem to be well known. The leaders of political parties, however, have failed to show the necessary strength to break with the old ways and wholeheartedly proceed to the much-needed healing of social relations and assistance. […] The elimination of relations which for years have been embedded in society cannot of course take place overnight, but one would have thought that the last weeks were enough to make the two parties try to develop a definite [reform] programme.'[24] The same Take Ionescu, who had earlier hinted at a possible Austro-Hungarian military intervention, reinforced Schönburg's impression that the uprising, for all its violence, left the Romanian political class unruffled and further set in their ways:

> Mr Take Ionescu, who every summer takes long journeys to Germany, France or England, told me he 'was ashamed' to show his face abroad this year. 'Not because our peasants have been killing and plundering, but because the effect of these sad events seems to be such a limited one here. *Je ne vois pas jusqu'ici l'effet du coup de fouet que nous avons reçu.*' [I cannot so far see any effect of the blow we have received]. Mr. Ionescu likened his compatriots to the Greeks, who one month after their defeat in the war against the Turks seemed to have forgotten the bitter lesson and were back to their old shenanigans.[25]

And, indeed, once the country was pacified and the danger was gone that had made Conservatives and Liberals huddle together in fear, the old political quarrels began again. Reform projects proposed by the Liberals

[23] HHStA, Wien, Karton 39, PA, XVIII, Bericht B, 18 April 1907, p. 163.
[24] HHStA, Wien, Karton 39, PA, XVIII, Bericht no. 24, H, Bukarest, 3. Mai 1907, pp. 217/verso, 220, 221.
[25] HHStA, Wien, Karton 39, PA, XVIII, Bericht no. 48 B, 17 Mai 1907, p. 232 (recto, verso).

tripped up on the opposition of the Conservatives. What improved the lot of the peasantry from the Liberal point of view was perceived as an existential threat by the Conservatives, what one party held to be just and right was reviled and rejected out of hand by the other. Such was for instance the issue of transferring pastureland from the great landowners to the peasants—a necessary measure meant to ensure the economic independence of the peasants, which the Conservatives interpreted as a hidden attempt at expropriation. This comes across in the diplomatic reports from Bucharest to Vienna in the months following the uprising. What stands out in particular is the great inflexibility of the Conservatives, and in particular of their doyen, the great landowner P.P. Carp. In a discussion with the Prince, Carp spelt out his intransigent position in the following terms, as reported by Schönburg:

> Mr Carp went on to tell me that the Prince said to him: 'You must concede that something must change for the peasants! To which Carp replied: "What the peasant asks for is too much and he will always want more. I cannot and will not give him that. However, I am ready to concede that something must change for the peasant, but not what he demands but what *I* consider to be useful and good for him. I am fully aware that this mode of treating the peasants, which I consider the only right way, might lead to renewed peasant unrest. In my opinion, there will be peasant unrest in any case, although on a smaller scale than earlier this year. One mustn't take this to heart too much. These are growing pains, which every young state must go through."'[26]

Carp remained true to his Conservative short-sightedness and insensitivity to peasant suffering, despite his otherwise sharp mind and great personal charisma. During the uprising his conservative colleague Take Ionescu dismissed the great violence that had been used against the rebellious peasants in similarly callous terms: 'I don't care if innocents have suffered. I feel no compunction. There was a war and wars are not fought with flowers (*la guerre ne se fait pas avec des fleurs*).'[27]

The King himself was aware of this political deadlock and of the predicament of the peasantry, which had led to the uprising in the first place.

---

[26] HHStA, Wien, Karton 39, PA, XVIII, Bericht no. 58 C, Bucarest 11 December 1907, p. 457.

[27] 'Discours de M. Take Ionescu a Iassi', *La Roumanie*, Mardi 10 (23) Avril 1907, HHStA, Karton 9: Ges. Bukarest, Berichte 1907–1908, 3. Mai 1907, Report number 27.

The agrarian question seemed all but unsolvable to him as he indicated to Schönburg during an audience in December 1907: 'His Majesty remarked that, unless one knows the social relations here very well, one cannot begin to conceive the difficulty posed by the negotiations over the agrarian question. There is no correspondent for it, not even in Hungary, where agrarian relations are in a certain respect very similar to those in Romania.'[28] The positions of the two political parties were polar opposite and irreconcilable: '[the Liberals] want to create a "free peasant class"; [the Conservatives] on the contrary want to continue to exploit the peasants as wage labourers'.[29] Both factions came in for royal criticism. The King complained that the Liberal draft reform projects were 'in part so bad that he could never give his approval to them'. This was due to a very poor knowledge of land relations and of the needs of the peasantry.[30] The Conservatives, on the other hand, worried the King with their already mentioned inflexibility ('the cession of the necessary pastureland to the peasant communities is seen by the great landowners as expropriation, whereas in reality it is no such thing'[31]) and with their threat to organize massive street demonstrations against the Liberal reform projects.[32]

Tsarist Diplomacy

Mikhail Nikolaevich Giers, the Russian ambassador in Bucharest, was the main source of information for the Tsarist authorities on the Romanian peasant uprising. He liaised with the Russian consuls in Iași, Galați and Sulina, with the authorities in Bessarabia, and with the Tsarist Ministry for

[28] HHStA, Wien, Karton 39, PA, XVIII, 11 December 1907 Bukarest, report from Schoenburg to Aehrenthal, 'Audience with the King and the latter's concerns regarding agrarian reform and political life in Romania', p. 6/verso, p. 7/recto.
[29] HHStA, Wien, Karton 39, PA, XVIII, 11 December 1907 Bukarest, report from Schoenburg to Aehrenthal, 'Audience with the King and the latter's concerns regarding agrarian reform and political life in Romania', p. 7/verso.
[30] HHStA, Wien, Karton 39, PA, XVIII, 11 December 1907 Bukarest, report from Schoenburg to Aehrenthal, 'Audience with the King and the latter's concerns regarding agrarian reform and political life in Romania', p. 1/recto, verso.
[31] HHStA, Wien, Karton 39, PA, XVIII, 11 December 1907 Bukarest, report from Schoenburg to Aehrenthal, 'Audience with the King and the latter's concerns regarding agrarian reform and political life in Romania', p. 5/verso.
[32] HHStA, Wien, Karton 39, PA, XVIII, 11 December 1907 Bukarest, report from Schoenburg to Aehrenthal, 'Audience with the King and the latter's concerns regarding agrarian reform and political life in Romania', p. 3/recto.

Foreign Affairs in St Petersburg. As unrest was reported from Wallachia as well as from Moldavia, Giers urged that, 'given the epidemic character [of the agrarian troubles in Romania], extraordinary measures of precaution were necessary lest they should spread to Bessarabia',[33] while the Iași consul sent urgent requests to Romanian prefects for the protection of the property of Russian subjects in Moldavia.[34] Orders were issued from the Tsarist Ministry of Foreign Affairs to the governor of the Kherson *gubernia*, where a small number of Moldavians lived, for a full report on the situation in the province. Within a day, the Kherson governor reported that the Romanian agrarian troubles had had no impact on their province and as such no special measures should be taken in that respect. He did, however, ask for 100 Cossacks to maintain order in the troublesome central region of the province, where there had been disturbances in 1905.[35] All information thus gathered was forwarded to the Ministry of Foreign Affairs in St Petersburg, who in turn fed it to the Ministry of the Interior.

A lengthy report from Brunner, the Russian consul in Iași, put the peasant uprising into perspective for the Russian Ambassador and recapitulated the course of events as they had come to his acquaintance since 6 March: looting and arson, killing and rape in Moldavia; huge damages; 300,000 reservists called up; rumours of peasant uprisings in Bukovina; the situation degenerating further as the uprising spread to Wallachia where the movement, for lack of Jewish *arendași*, shifted against Romanian landowners.[36] In a mirror image of the contempt and disenchantment voiced by newspapers across the Austro-Hungarian border, the Russian consul reflected on the contrast between the image the Romanian authorities had tried to project internationally and the reality of violence and savagery revealed by the uprising:

> soon there will be no place untouched by the above-mentioned destruction and violence against peaceful inhabitants irrespective of religion or nationality. And all of this is happening after the noisy jubilee celebrations of the Bucharest exhibition and after an amazing crop. What a terrible wake-up call

---

[33] Gheorghe Matei, *Răsunetul internațional al răscoalei țăranilor din 1907*, Editura de Stat pentru Literatură Politică, București, 1957, p. 112.

[34] Matei, *Răsunetul internațional al răscoalei țăranilor din 1907*, p. 116

[35] Matei, *Răsunetul internațional al răscoalei țăranilor din 1907*, p. 119.

[36] Copy of the report from the Russian General Imperial Consul in Iași, the State Councillor Brunner, to the Russian Imperial Ambassador in Romania, Hoffmeister Giers, 11 March 1907, no. 176 in Matei, *Răsunetul internațional al răscoalei țăranilor din 1907*, pp. 126–127.

for Romanian society, who was caught unawares apparently, and for the ruling circles, who foresaw none of this and who, not so long ago, were proclaiming Romania as the most trustworthy bastion of West European civilization on the frontier of the Asiatic Orient. And so sturdy was this bastion that within months it sank into the most savage vandalism in a situation bordering on anarchy.[37]

The comparison with the state of the peasantry in Russia inevitably came up. Brunner saw similarities but was of the opinion that the Romanian peasantry had different claims to those of their Russian counterparts:

The Moldavian peasantry and also that of Western Romania have rebelled and are unequivocally demanding land. Unlike our domestic troubles, which are of a similar nature, the Romanian peasants are asking for land not to own but to work, in other words, to take on lease. There is therefore a fundamental difference between the conception of our peasants and that of the Romanian peasants as regards the agrarian question, although there is a certain ideological connection between them which is the result of the sudden awakening of the peasantry to their own economic predicament.[38]

Brunner was only partly accurate in his assessment of Romanian peasants' demands. The uprising indeed started with claims for better land contracts and for more land to be available for peasants to take on lease at affordable prices and particularly in Moldavia this was certainly the case at the beginning of the agrarian troubles. This was also the view held by Romanian officials in Moldavia.[39] As the uprising snowballed into a countrywide phenomenon, the peasants went the whole hog and dropped their initial, moderate claims and asked for a radical redistribution of all land. The similarities of peasant claims and peasant behaviour, complete with the myth of the students as revolutionaries, made the 1907 peasant revolt in Romania an almost carbon-copy of peasant unrest in Russia in 1905.[40]

---

[37] Copy of the report from the Russian General Imperial Consul in Iași, the State Councillor Brunner, to the Russian Imperial Ambassador in Romania, Hoffmeister Giers, 11 March 1907, no. 176 in Matei, *Răsunetul internațional al răscoalei țăranilor din 1907*, p. 127.

[38] Copy of the report from the Russian General Imperial Consul in Iași, the State Councillor Brunner, to the Russian Imperial Ambassador in Romania, Hoffmeister Giers, 11 March 1907, no. 176 in Matei, *Răsunetul internațional al răscoalei țăranilor din 1907*, p. 127.

[39] P.G. Eidelberg, *The Great Rumanian Peasant Revolt of 1907: Origins of a Modern Jacquerie*, Leiden, Brill, 1974, pp. 220–221.

[40] HHStA, Russland 1905, Karton 125 PA X, Beilage and Bericht No. 26 D, St Petersburg, 23. April/6. Mai 1905.

The constant comparison with Russia and the invocation of Russian influence touched a raw nerve with the Tsarist official, who waxed defensive and shifted the blame onto the West. It was not Russian revolutionaries—Brunner contended—that led to an awakening of the Romanian peasantry. 'It was not us who concocted the well-known social doctrines, which were imported wholesale from Western Europe together with the much vaunted, but also superficial West European civilization which has been adopted by our neighbours. Why is it that, now that the country is going through harrowing trials, which are however inevitable in the evolution of humankind, the Romanian press often blames our country for introducing into Romania the harmful seeds of popular disturbance under the flag of the anti-Jewish movement? Their conclusion is the following: all that is good and pleasant comes from Europe; all that is bad and unpleasant comes from Russia. This is unjust and illogical.'[41]

The Tsarist consul in Iași criticized the failure of the Romanian constitutional system and insisted that Western European imports (in this case, institutional imports) were useless in improving the condition of the peasantry:

> And indeed, despite the fact that a constitutional system has existed in Romania for the past 50 years, the great majority of the Romanian people is languishing in the darkest of ignorance. And this is not difficult to prove given the unprecedentedly high percentage of illiteracy, which according to the latest official data stands at an extraordinary 82%. Therefore, as can be seen, the constitutional regime has brought very doubtful benefits to the Romanian people and, when one considers that no less than five sixths of the population belongs to the peasant class, one can see why the Romanian peasant's methods of tilling the land are very undeveloped.[42]

Brunner went through the by now classic list of ills that the Romanian system of land tenure suffered from in an attempt to show that the uprising had not occurred by contamination from Russia but rather through sheer self-combustion: extensive rather than intensive cultivation predominated,

---

[41] Copy of the report from the Russian General Imperial Consul in Iași, the State Councillor Brunner, to the Russian Imperial Ambassador in Romania, Hoffmeister Giers, 11 March 1907, no. 176 in Matei, *Răsunetul internațional al răscoalei țăranilor din 1907*, p. 128.

[42] Copy of the report from the Russian General Imperial Consul in Iași, the State Councillor Brunner, to the Russian Imperial Ambassador in Romania, Hoffmeister Giers, 11 March 1907, no. 176 in Matei, *Răsunetul internațional al răscoalei țăranilor din 1907*, p. 128.

land fragmentation was soaring and, as a consequence, the system of land lease was what the peasant had to fall back on to feed his family; 'the majority of great landowners'—pointed out the consul—'prefer a leisurely life and are thus happy to rent out land to in particular Jewish capitalists, who hold out all the guarantees of a secure income'; big agrarian trusts have come into being as a result [...] and land has become the object of the most obscene commercial speculation, whilst the poor peasant is trapped in a state of complete dependence on these foreign businessmen.'[43]Against this background of economic exploitation of the peasantry—Brunner argued further—it was not Russian emissaries that struck the spark of the uprising but rather autochthonous 'hot defenders of the Romanian ploughman such as Cuza and Stere, who are Professors at the University of Iaşi, and Professor Iorga from University of Bucharest. [...] Romania too has its *kadets*, its *trudoviks* and also, albeit not yet numerous, its Socialists as well.'[44]

Brunner's attempt to fend off the blame that had been laid at Russia's door in Romanian public discourse was a leitmotif of Tsarist diplomacy in Romania. This went back to the charged atmosphere that dominated Russian–Romanian relations following the Treaty of Berlin of 1878, when the southern districts of Bessarabia, which had been reattached to the Principality of Moldavia since the Crimean War, were annexed once again by the Russian allies in the wake of the Russo-Turkish war of 1877–1878. This whipped up a frenzy of anti-Russian feeling among the Romanian elites and turned the Russians into pet scapegoats for all things gone wrong in Romania. Thus, as the Tsarist Consul in Bucharest, Mikhail A. Khitrowo, pointed out, during the 1888 peasant uprising in southern Romania wild rumours coursed to the effect that:

in some places the peasants were asking for money, which reportedly had been provided by Russia to be distributed to them, or that Prince Cuza had donated it, 5000 for each commune. In other places the rumour ran among the peasants that the Russians would soon arrive to save them and defend them against the much-hated German government. [...] in the Collectivist

---

[43] Copy of the report from the Russian General Imperial Consul in Iaşi, the State Councillor Brunner, to the Russian Imperial Ambassador in Romania, Hoffmeister Giers, 11 March 1907, no. 176 in Matei, *Răsunetul internaţional al răscoalei ţăranilor din 1907*, p. 129.

[44] Copy of the report from the Russian General Imperial Consul in Iaşi, the State Councillor Brunner, to the Russian Imperial Ambassador in Romania, Hoffmeister Giers, 11 March 1907, no. 176 in Matei, *Răsunetul internaţional al răscoalei ţăranilor din 1907*, p. 129.

press[45] there appeared concocted articles about the presence of Russian secret agents in the country, who instigated the peasants to rebellion, about Russian icon peddlers, who roused whole regions to rebel, about Lipovans and Skoptsy,[46] who agitated in Russia's favour, and about Russian rubles, which I allegedly had distributed in Bucharest pubs by means of various agents.[47]

Khitrowo dismissed these accusations by dwelling on the situation of the Romanian peasantry, which, he insisted, was bad enough to fuel the uprising without any need for Russian stoking. If anything, such fantastic rumours proved, in the Consul's view, the very opposite of what Romanian politicians claimed. They proved that Russia was perceived by the common people not as a threat but as a saviour and benefactor.

All of these rumours dispersed among the rebellious population and coming from God knows where, the rumours about the money donated by Russia, about the coming of the Russians to liberate them from the hated German government – aren't they an indication of the love that ordinary Romanians cherish for Orthodox Russia? And, indeed, despite all our enemies' intrigues and propaganda, in the eyes of ordinary Romanians the Russian Tsar has to this day remained the almighty protector and master, who to this day can change their rulers according to his will. And this is only natural given that, in the mind of the people, the best years of prosperity and of measures taken for the benefit of the people are connected to the times when the Russians were in Romania.[48]

Khitrowo was a staunch believer in Russia's sacred mission of protecting the Orthodox peoples in the Balkans and in the peasants' allegiance to the Tsar.[49] And he was not alone in his opinion that the Romanian

---

[45] The Romanian Liberal press, which was overtly anti-Russian.

[46] A Russian Raskolnik sect, who practiced castration and abstention from alcohol in pursuit of redemption. They were persecuted in Russia and some crossed over into Romania.

[47] Flavius Solomon, Adrian-Bogdan Ceobanu, Andrei Cușco, Grigorii Șkundin (Eds.), *Rapoarte diplomatice ruse din România (1888–1898)/ ДИПЛОМАТИЧЕСКИЕ ДОКУМЕНТЫ РОССИЙСКИХ ПРЕДСТАВИТЛЕЙ В РУМЫНИИ (1888–1898)*, Editura Universității Alexandru Ioan Cuza, Iași, 2014, p. 140.

[48] Flavius Solomon, Adrian-Bogdan Ceobanu, Andrei Cușco, Grigorii Șkundin (Eds.), *Rapoarte diplomatice ruse din România (1888–1898)/ДИПЛОМАТИЧЕСКИЕ ДОКУМЕНТЫ РОССИЙСКИХ ПРЕДСТАВИТЛЕЙ В РУМЫНИИ (1888–1898)*, p. 144.

[49] See the introduction by Flavius Solomon and Andrei Cușco to *Rapoarte diplomatice ruse din România (1888–1898)/ДИПЛОМАТИЧЕСКИЕ ДОКУМЕНТЫ РОССИЙСКИХ ПРЕДСТАВИТЛЕЙ В РУМЫНИИ (1888–1898)*, pp. 28–29.

peasantry had pro-Russian leanings. The Tsarist consul A. Giers reiterated it ten years later on the occasion of King Carol I's visit to St Petersburg in 1898 and following a discussion with the Romanian officers in King Carol's retinue. According to Giers,

> in a bout of sincerity the commander of a [Romanian] cavalry detachment said to me: 'I've got to admit that there were fears among our higher military echelons regarding the behavior of the army in case of a possible or, as they assured us, inevitable confrontation with Russia. We could rely on our officers to a greater or lesser extent, but in the case of the rank and file the expectations were grim; we knew full well that, should it come to a war against the Russians, the soldiers <u>were going to defect en masse</u>.'[50]

According to Russian diplomacy, Romanian scapegoating of the Russians was not a justified fear, but rather a very handy rhetorical weapon, much used and abused as political ammunition. In a report of 1895 *Hofmeister* Fonton, the Russian consul in Bucharest, alerted to the fact that:

> the socialist press [in Romania] continues its campaign against Russia, ceaselessly publishing sensationalist news about alleged Russian agents overrunning Dobrogea, about Russian officers who come and take photographs and familiarize themselves with the surroundings, about the concentration of Russian troops in Bessarabia and so on. [...] There have been speculations of late in the press and in public opinion about the coming of a European war and the alteration of Romania's foreign policy. It is noteworthy that these rumours were launched almost simultaneously in the Conservative and Liberal camps and were exploited by both in pursuit of their political goals.[51]

One of the most revealing foreign diplomatic analyses of the economic situation in Romania and implicitly of the causes that led to the peasant uprising came from the Tsarist vice-consul in Sulina, a port town on the Danube where the river flows into the Black Sea. The report is singular in

---

[50] Flavius Solomon, Adrian-Bogdan Ceobanu, Andrei Cușco, Grigorii Șkundin (Eds.), *Rapoarte diplomatice ruse din România (1888–1898)*/ДИПЛОМАТИЧЕСКИЕ ДОКУМЕНТЫ РОССИЙСКИХ ПРЕДСТАВИТЛЕЙ В РУМЫНИИ *(1888–1898)*, p. 446.

[51] Flavius Solomon, Adrian-Bogdan Ceobanu, Andrei Cușco, Grigorii Șkundin (Eds.), *Rapoarte diplomatice ruse din România (1888–1898)*/ДИПЛОМАТИЧЕСКИЕ ДОКУМЕНТЫ РОССИЙСКИХ ПРЕДСТАВИТЛЕЙ В РУМЫНИИ *(1888–1898)*, p. 355.

its wider-scope economic study bringing together both industry and agriculture. Whereas most analyses of the background to the peasant uprising confined themselves to pointing out the underdevelopment of Romanian industry and the lack of a professional alternative for proletarianized peasants, the Russian consul in Sulina stands on its head this image of the Romanian economy as dominated by agriculture and held back by an atrophied industry: instead he views agriculture as closely connected to developments in industry and following the same rules and rationales that the government employed in order to boost national industry. The report is thus a survey of trusts and cartels in Romania, with leaseholding trusts being only one such type of monopoly, sitting side by side with cartels in branches of industry producing sugar, paper, rope, nails and oil.

> In recent decades the Romanian government have been concerned about the comparatively weak development of the industry in the country, which is predominantly agricultural. They have therefore been pursuing protectionist policies, which through customs protection, patronage and preferential tariffs have accelerated and eased the formation of alien Romanian national cartels. The result of this process of cartelization has been the creation of trusts; the landlease trusts of Jewish leaseholders caused in the spring of this year an acute agrarian movement, which was antisemitic in character but also closely connected with purely economic causes. With its weak development of industry, Romania appears to be most suited to widespread cartelization, as especially in the sphere of mass production it is easier for big enterprises to form cartels than for small producers. [...] the cartel entrepreneurs have as their goal the elimination or weakening of free competition between individual companies.[52]

More Conservative than the Russians

Russia was not only a negative example and influence but could also be a positive one. Giers, the Tsarist ambassador in Bucharest, had occasion to ascertain this in the months following the uprising, when the Romanian government and opposition were locked in a struggle for reforms at each other's expense in an attempt to solve the thorny agrarian question. The Conservatives (in particular Take Ionescu) contemplated the setting

---

[52] ANR, Bucureşti, Fond Microfilm Rusia, Rola 36, Cadru 175: 13 January 1908 – report of the Russian Vice-Consul in Sulina forwarded by the Minister of Foreign Affairs to the Minister of the Interior.

up of a *Caisse rurale*, or rural bank, long before the uprising, and the initiative resurfaced on the governmental agenda with increased urgency afterwards. The Russian ambassador was consulted on the efficiency of a similar institution that had been set up in Tsarist Russia 30 years before, namely the *Banque des Paysans* (The Peasant Bank). King Carol himself sounded him out on the matter during an audience after having read a study by a Russian author regarding the peasant bank. Once contemplated, however, the Russian example was discarded, not because it was deemed ineffective and not reformist enough, quite the contrary, for being too radical and posing a threat to the well-being of the great landowners. 'Mr von Giers remarked also that Mr Carp considered the Russian institution as "too socialist" and even his Majesty the King inclines to think that the advantages secured by the state for the Russian peasants go too far.'[53] As the Austro-Hungarian ambassador pointed out, the Romanian boyars feared that the peasant communities could gain enough leverage to buy land and even oust them out of their own properties through this credit system. Giers, on the other hand, thought these fears were unfounded and explained that in order for this credit institution to be effective it would have to be placed under state control. This in itself clashed with the Romanian Conservatives' notion of a *Caisse rurale* as a private enterprise based on foreign capital. According to Schönburg, the Romanian boyars feared that state involvement would send the wrong message to the peasants, who would be led to think that the credit was a gift from the state, which they did not have to pay back. More importantly still, in a country where the state was virtually colonized by party politics, state control of the rural bank could have easily been misused as dangerous ammunition in the bitter political battle between Conservatives and Liberals, and was as such to be avoided at all costs.[54]

Peasant troubles recurred in the following year in Romania. Ambassador Giers apprised the Tsarist Foreign Minister of the tensions reported in the northern districts of Moldavia in March 1908, one year after the devastating uprising. This, the ambassador pointed out, coincided with the annual renewal of contracts between peasants and *arendași*. The peasants did not seem to have adjusted to the new rules and legislation that had been passed

---

[53] HHStA, Wien, Karton 39, PA, XVIII, Bericht no. 44 B, Sinaia, am 6. September 1907, from Schönburg to Aehrenthal, p. 325 (recto/verso).

[54] HHStA, Wien, Karton 39, PA, XVIII, Bericht no. 44 B, Sinaia, am 6. September 1907, from Schönburg to Aehrenthal, p. 325–328.

by the government in the meantime. The isolated flares of discontent did not connect into a major uprising, as they had done in the previous year. Giers pointed out, however, that the Romanian authorities had all the same taken the strictest precautionary measures to prevent a repeat of the 1907 uprising: '[the Romanian government] have organized emergency cavalry troops, which are sent in on military expeditions to all the places where rebellions are likely to break out for various reasons. It seems that the appearance of these troops makes a deep impression on the peasants.'[55]

BIBLIOGRAPHY

P.G. Eidelberg, *The Great Rumanian Peasant Revolt of 1907: Origins of a Modern Jacquerie*, Leiden, Brill, 1974

Gheorghe Matei, *Răsunetul internaţional al răscoalei ţăranilor din 1907*, Editura de Stat pentru Literatură Politică, Bucureşti, 1957

Andrei Oţetea and Ion Popescu-Puţuri (Eds.), *Documente privind marea răscoală a ţăranilor din 1907*, Editura Academiei Republicii Socialiste România, Bucureşti, 1977

Flavius Solomon, Adrian-Bogdan Ceobanu, Andrei Cuşco and Grigorii Şkundin (Eds.), *Rapoarte diplomatice ruse din România (1888–1898)*/ДИПЛОМАТИЧЕСКИЕ ДОКУМЕНТЫ РОССИЙСКИХ ПРЕДСТАВИТЛЕЙ В РУМЫНИИ *(1888–1898)*, Editura Universităţii Alexandru Ioan Cuza, Iaşi, 2014

---

[55] Telegram from the Russian Ambassador in Bucharest to the Minister of Foreign Affairs, 20 March 1908, no. 19, quoted in Gheorghe Matei, *Răsunetul internaţional al răscoalei ţăranilor din 1907*, p. 139.

CHAPTER 8

Conclusions

The research that went into the present book started with an interest in the issue of communication and cognition: how do people learn about violence elsewhere? How do people respond to what they learn? What is the dividing line between knowledge and rumour? How does information filter through internal and international borders? Does everybody understand the same thing? Are there multiple readings of the same event? Do people understand what they want to and not necessarily what is being conveyed? Is this a dialogue of the deaf? What does the threat of violence and contamination do to other national/ethnic/social groups? How do they react? This being the starting point, the book has ended up as a story of crisis management and mismanagement across a triple frontier at a time of great violence that combined antisemitism with rural unrest. When a major social explosion such as the Romanian peasant uprising of spring 1907 occurred on one side of the border, with ethnic kin on the other, the frontier behaved very much like a cell membrane: it was selectively permeable to news and to people; it refracted rumour and information through the prism of three different polities (Austrian, Hungarian, Tsarist) and conjured up different spectres ranging from fear of contamination and self-criticism to *Schadenfreude* and gloating superiority. The ripple effect revived old prejudices, social and political hobbyhorses, and became grist to the mill of internal controversies. Within Romania, where the uprising took place, rumour and news coursed in ways that showed the disconnection

© The Author(s) 2018
I. Marin, *Peasant Violence and Antisemitism in Early Twentieth-Century Eastern Europe*,
https://doi.org/10.1007/978-3-319-76069-8_8

between the majority of the population and the ruling elites as well as the instrumentalization of news for social and political purposes. The uprising was fuelled by genuine peasant grievances and rampant antisemitism, both of which were to be traced back to the exclusionary brand of state and nation building practiced in Romania at the time, which used and abused its peasants and Jews alike while debarring them from political life. The initial confusion as to the nature of the rural unrest (was it directed against the Jews or against the establishment?) showed the interconnection of the two questions (peasant and Jewish) in the Romanian Kingdom and how antisemitism functioned as a red herring that deflected attention from the real, economic causes of the uprising.

This book has been conceived as a transnational history but has also proposed to engage in *interstitial* history, which means looking at the process of information percolation, its contamination potential as well as its impact on shaping cross-border reactions to news of peasant and anti-semitic violence. I called it so after one of the most crucial spaces in living organisms, that is, the interstitium or interstitial space, a microscopic space between cells or capillaries, where vital exchanges of fluid, substance and information take place, and a process of selection happens between what goes into and out of a cell. The substance thus exchanged does not stay the same; it is transformed, metamorphosed to suit the new medium. This interstitial space and what happens within and across it is the lynchpin of life as understood in biology. In the second chapter I therefore extrapo-lated the biological concept of interstice to the sphere of social relations and used it to account for the unprecedented spread of the 1907 peasant uprising in Romania and the informational maelstrom on which it fed. In my understanding, this biological metaphor captures fundamental aspects of social psychology and information circulation: (1) the constant exchange of news and information is what binds people together and represents the very essence of social interactions; and (2) information is not circulated from one person to another, from one social group to another as one would a bowl of cereal, it is first filtered through peoples' minds and then passed on. People do communicate with one another but in this complex, negotiated way. One metabolizes information and uses it for one's own purposes. The imperial borderlands with which the book busies itself were themselves a type of interstice, an in-between space, which was heteroge-neous from an ethnic point of view and saw a constant flow of people and information.

In order to understand the transformation undergone by the flow of news and rumour surrounding the uprising, I chose to look at the social infrastructure, at the capillary network of villages and towns, the points of contact, the places of exchange, and the metabolization of news. The resulting image is admittedly no Google-Earth-type map of the exchanges that took place within and outside the villages and towns of Romania during spring 1907. This is due to the inevitable limitations of empirical data that the self-selecting nature of historical documents imposes on the researcher. The helter-skelter of documents that did survive the century provide, however, plenty of fascinating insight into the inner workings of the uprising. There was no single channel or thread that determined the spread of the rebellion, but rather a combination of interconnected factors: infrastructure (roads, railways), social and economic practices, administrative divisions as well as governmental mismanagement. Court case hearings, official correspondence between central and local authorities and peasant testimonies show how peasants received, processed and passed on information. Far from being a mere quirk of the uprising, rumours regarding real or imaginary figures, such as university students, the Tsar, the Queen, the Seven Emperors, served otherwise disempowered communities to take control of a fluid situation and steer it to their advantage by galvanizing and mobilizing to action. The power of folk mythologies to get people to act together in a synchronized manner should not be underestimated, especially in the case of a social class notorious for its reluctance to mobilize. As the British Consul to St Petersburg put it in 1905 in reference to peasant uprisings in Tambov, 'the peasant is hard to move, and once started is hard to stop, so that influence must be brought to bear upon him in good time, while, once his inertia is overcome, he is apt to go out of hand.'[1]

Rumour mills were not only common among the rural population but also among the elite. The rumours that circulated among the latter regarding the potential culprits for the peasant uprising and the alleged existence of a grand conspiracy to destabilize the young Romanian Kingdom were equally fanciful but, instead of having a galvanizing, mobilizing effect, as village rumours often had, they were essentially self-harming and self-defeating. The fears of the elite regarding Jews and foreigners created false enemies and hid the actual problems of the country behind a smokescreen

---

[1] The National Archives, London, Russia 1906, No. 9773: Agrarian Disorders, Consul-General Smith to Sir Edward Grey, March 1906, p. 240.

of self-complacent xenophobia, which went hand in hand with the elite's disparaging view of the peasants as lazy, immature and easily manipulated by outsiders. As many among the Romanian political elite were also great landowners, antisemitism and xenophobia were the result of an extra-punitive process whereby they protected their vested interests and deflected blame onto others. The paradox of this stance was apparent in both the case of Romanian Jews and that of the Potemkin defectors, whom the Romanian state was happy to receive in 1905, then proceeded to treat like a pest. Both the Jews and the Potemkinists were perceived as a threat, yet they were needed by the state. The Potemkinists gave a boost to Romanian industrial expertise, which was in sore need of skilled work force. They were, however, closely policed and were among the first to blame and to arrest when the peasant uprising started. The relationship between the Romanian state and the Jewish population was, admittedly, older and more complex, but in its broader outlines it boiled down to a similar dual-ity of hatred mixed with dependence. For a long time the Jewish commu-nity filled in a gap in the Romanian social structure contributing to commerce, finance and craftsmanship. With the creation of the modern Romanian state along ethnic-national lines, the Jews were excluded and deemed a foreign body; they came to be associated with the worst aspects of capitalist market relations and became a handy scapegoat for the Romanian political elite's frustrations and failure of statesmanship. There were, of course, Jews among the much hated leaseholders but the vital thing to remember is that there were just as many Christians among them too and that all of them, Jews and Christians alike, functioned as extractors on behalf of the great landowners.

Why did a major peasant uprising occur in Romania but not in the neighbouring, similarly economically underdeveloped, imperial border-lands? Why did it not spread among the ethnic kin in the neighbouring states? A comparison of land tenure around the triple frontier reveals fun-damental differences in the initial terms of land reforms, how these reforms were then implemented, the extent of peasant agency, the existence of modernization initiatives as well as the possibility of exiting the system through emigration. The Romanian land tenure system was singular in that land reform was not aimed at allowing the peasantry to become self-sufficient, but rather at ensuring cheap and captive labour for the great estates. This was best seen in the use of access to pastureland and wood-land, which were for the most part left in the hands of the great landown-ers, who used them to blackmail the peasants into onerous work contracts.

The pervasive system of unregulated land leaseholds turned Romania into a bonanza for greedy entrepreneurs, foreign and autochthonous alike, who, in collusion with the Romanian elites, made huge profits at the expense of the peasants. Around the frontier in the imperial borderlands, land-lease never reached the cancerous proportions it did in Romania, it could be modernizing in its overall effects or, at least, was kept in check by legislation that protected the interests of the peasantry. In the imperial borderlands, unlike in independent Romania, the peasantry benefited from the tug-of-war between provincial elites and imperial authorities, as was the case in Tsarist Bessarabia, or enjoyed the support of their co-national elites in Austria-Hungary. While peasant discontent existed in various degrees all around the triple frontier, Romania combined the highest rate of systemic pressure on its peasants with the lowest rate of emigration, which was actively discouraged by the government. This was instrumental in building up discontent to explosive levels.

The different degree of social combustibility around the triple frontier was, moreover, a function of the policing capability of the bordering states. This, as shown in Chapter 5, was very weak in a fledgling state like Romania and considerably more developed in the neighbouring imperial borderlands. Ever since the 1880s the Hungarian half of the Habsburg Monarchy was confronted with rural strikes and social unrest and, as a consequence, evolved elaborate and effective policing strategies that succeeded in keeping in check rural discontent and did not shy away from state violence. The Austrian half of the Monarchy had in place a good complaint-and-redress loop, which ensured that social ferment was not ignored nor was it allowed to get out of hand. A look at police reports and other official correspondence shows that imperial authorities feared contamination from neighbouring Romania, took precautionary measures to nip such a possibility in the bud and, especially the Austrian authorities in Bukovina, managed the stream of mostly Jewish refugees that fled Romania in fear of their lives. Tsarist Bessarabian police, although hopelessly corrupt, successfully liaised with the central authorities to secure the border with Romania. Input from the Russian ambassador in Bucharest as well as from their Okhrana agents stationed in Romania provided the Russians with a good indicator of the course of the Romanian peasant uprising. There is little evidence that shows any actual contamination or immediate transference of the conflict from Romania to the imperial borderlands, beyond some rumours circulating in the villages. Even when the spectre of a Romanian-like peasant uprising was raised, no such explosion ever materialized across the border. Here social ferment had its own localized sources and did not occur by imitation.

News of the uprising in Romania rippled through to the neighbouring countries in a cascade of information, which often had little to do with the actual events across the border and much more so with the political agendas and the hot debates animating internal affairs in each of the countries around the triple frontier. The flow of news was intertextual in its quality, with newspapers quoting a string of other newspapers, which were geographically remote, on events that were happening just a stone's throw away across the frontier. The refraction of the Romanian peasant uprising in the Hungarian, Austrian and Tsarist press also provided an x-ray of the young Romanian Kingdom's relationship with its neighbours, of historical enmities and current antagonisms. Most prominent among these were the tug-of-war between Romanian and Hungarian elites, who were at loggerheads in their respective nation-building projects and the enduring fear of Russian foul play among Romanian authorities paired up with the Tsarist defensive stance rejecting all such accusations. A wide range of conflicting emotions were stirred up in the heat of reporting depending on the political orientation of the newspaper: fear of contamination but also amused superiority, philosemitism and antisemitism, disappointment and genuine concern, but also finger-pointing and gloating, soul-searching and ominous awareness of similarities but also denial and smug complacency.

While public opinion was thus animated in its apprehension of the implosion of social order across the border, the diplomats stationed in Romania at the time sent out their own views on the situation to the imperial centres, Vienna and St Petersburg respectively. Their assessment of the course of the uprising and the causes of peasant discontent was based on input from their own contacts and informers but also on interactions with Romanian statesmen and with the King himself. A look at the timeline of, in particular, the Austro-Hungarian diplomatic reports reveals that weeks before the uprising proper these diplomats were more aware of the social ferment and taking it more seriously than the Romanian authorities did. The same Austro-Hungarian diplomatic correspondence shows that Conservative officials did toy with the notion of asking for Austro-Hungarian military help but this initiative was never put into practice as it would have amounted to national humiliation. Cross-border contamination constituted a possibility that Austro-Hungarian statesmen took into account and made provisions for but it seems that they feared less the spread of peasant troubles to the imperial borderlands and more the threat of anarchist, revolutionary contamination that the Potemkin sailors who were stationed in Romania posed. In similar fashion, Tsarist diplomacy called for caution and preventive measures to be taken along the border with Romania, but was reassured that the troubles would not cross the frontier and indeed they did not. Tsarist consuls in Romania smarted at the frequent pinning of the blame on Russia by Romanian public opinion and engaged in a *pro-domo-sua* argument showing that constitutionalism and parliamentarianism, especially the superficial ones that existed in Romania, were not a solution to the agrarian question. Much was made in Tsarist diplomatic correspondence of the Russo-philia of the Romanian peasants as reflected in the rumours about Russia and the Tsar circulating in the Romanian countryside and as evidenced by the Orthodoxy of the Romanian peasant. Tsarist Russia was not only a neighbour to fear, but also one with whom Romania had a lot in common in terms of peasant predicament and rural unrest. As such, Romanian statesmen looked to Russia when it came to finding solutions for the peasant question, in particular as regarded the setting up of peasant banks: the Russian model was, as it turned out, worthy of interest but eventually discarded as too radical.

The archival research that went into the present book has made apparent the fact that contamination through contiguity (geographical proximity and population contact) was, by and large, an illusion shared by all the authorities around the triple frontier and had little to do with how things actually took place on the ground. Ethnic kinship across the border did not mean that social conflict was therefore more easily transferrable. Nor did multi-ethnicity entail a higher potential for social combustibility. As Constantin Stere pointed out, in the maelstrom of the 1907 peasant uprising in Romania the newly acquired province of Dobrogea stayed relatively peaceful:

Note that Dobrogea, where the peasants have around nine hectares of land per family head, is the only province in the country that remained peaceful, despite its population being made up of various races and religions, which would have lent themselves more easily to domestic and foreign instigation.[2]

One might add that the relative peacefulness of the region was also despite its bordering on some of the most rebellious counties in Romania

[2] Constantin Stere, 'Cauzele mişcărilor agrare', *Publicistică*, Editura Universul, Chişinău, 2006, p. 240.

and despite its exposure to foreign influences through the flow of people coming into its harbours.

The authorities' fear of anarchism and contamination was often symptomatic of their denial about the true causes of social ferment and their attempt to deflect blame and responsibility onto outsiders. It was not inner or outer foreigners that stoked things up and inflamed social relations, although there were plenty of foreigners and outsiders among the exploiters. It was the system of laws and social and economic practices that strained social relations to breaking point and placed foreigners (but not only) in a position to extract maximum profit at the expense of the peasantry; the landed elites allowed them to do so and partook in the financial benefits of this economic system. Romanian statesmen practised a duplicitous game whereby they conflated national interest with their own economic interest.

In 1907 Romania the turn of the screw was the pervasive sense of injustice and the unfairness of rural relations in addition to grinding poverty. The peasants were endlessly and with impunity cheated and abused by the leaseholders in cahoots with the local authorities. There was no one they could turn to as justice and the law were only for the rich and powerful. None of the neighbouring imperial borderlands were peasant utopias. Indeed the Tsarist Empire was barely recovering from the social upheavals of the 1905 revolution; the Hungarian authorities were not afraid to open fire against rural protesters and were at a loss as to how to stem the tide of peasant emigration; the Austrian borderlands were confronted with land fragmentation and endemic peasant indebtedness and emigration. The major difference, however, was that in these imperial borderlands the terms of peasant emancipation were considerably more favourable to the peasants than they were in Romania, the recourse to the law was not impossible and, when all else failed, there was always the possibility of emigration. In other words, the imperial borderlands around the triple frontier were less socially combustible than the fledgling Romanian Kingdom. As the Romanian playwright and social critic I.L. Caragiale put it in his pamphlet on the 1907 peasant uprising: 'You can throw however many burning coals onto a pile of sand [and it still doesn't catch fire]... but in a gunpowder shed even the tiniest of sparks, which you can barely see in the dark, is one too many'.[3]

[3] I. L. Caragiale, *1907 Din primăvară până'n toamnă*, Capitolul II, www.ilcaragiale.eu/opere/articole/1907/capitolul2.html#.Wk4KEyTTWhD (accessed 4.01.2018).

PLUS ÇA CHANGE...

Karl Scheerer concluded his 1971 study of the Romanian peasant uprising remarking on the 'shockingly small direct consequences' that the uprising actually had 'despite the fact that it endangered the state as a whole and despite its figuring prominently in Romanian historiography.'[4] He went on to list the laws that were passed by the Romanian Parliament which were supposed to alleviate the fate of the peasantry: a law to regulate agricultural contracts, one that created a rural bank and one that placed limitations on leaseholder trusts.[5] In addition to these, there was a reorganization of administrative units and, most importantly, of the gendarmerie. Sceptical contemporaries warned that the new laws would remain dead letters and, especially the law against *arendași* trusts, would be circumvented just like similar regulations had been in the past.[6] Official documents and police informers' notes bear out these misgivings showing how little things changed for the peasantry after the uprising. Exploitation and mistreatment at the hands of the *arendași* and local authorities continued.[7] As late as 1913 the secret police picked up on discussions of the peasants' predicament: a lawyer from Ploiești remarked in private conversation that 'the peasants were very unhappy with the landowners and *arendași*, who refuse to divide the crop, which is still in the field, and give them their share of it. The district administrators do not obey the law, which says that if an *arendaș* fails to share the crop with the villagers, the administrator, accompanied by two assistants, should go out there and give the peasants their share. The administrators don't do their duty because they enjoy a lot of advantages from landowners and *arendași*, so they let the peasants suffer and complain'.[8] It was only the land reform of 1921 that dismantled the latifundia and gave peasants more land, although by then rural overpopulation made such a redistribution a drop in the ocean. The overhaul of the gendarmerie and a more careful supervision of

[4] Karl Scheerer, *Die Rumänische Bauernaufstände vom Frühjahr 1907*, Mainz, 1971, p. 123.

[5] Scheerer, *Die Rumänische Bauernaufstände*, p. 123.

[6] PAAA, Berlin, R 9653, Rumänien Allgemeine Angelegenheiten April–December 1907, Report no. 147, Bucharest, 3 December 1907, p. 7.

[7] Andrei Oțetea; Ion Popescu-Puțuri (eds), *Documente privind marea răscoală a țăranilor din 1907*, București, Editura Academiei Republicii Socialiste România, 1977, vol 2, pp. 587–588.

[8] ANR, Arhiva CC al PCR, 50/10256, p. 212.

peasant unrest were the only measures taken in the wake of the uprising that were actually applied and they prevented a repeat of the 1907 social meltdown.

The 1907 peasant uprising brought to light the fundamental antagonisms and social inequities informing Romanian society at the time but also, more importantly, as it occurred so soon after state formation and independence, it called into question the very foundations of the young Romanian state, its representativeness and the notion of national interest, given that the mercilessly exploited peasantry represented the overwhelming majority of the population. The details of the official handling of the uprising and its final repression paint a most unflattering picture of systemic corruption, self-interest and state violence, which far from being a mere episode in the state's development has to this day defined the rapport between Romanian political elites and ordinary people.[9]

BIBLIOGRAPHY

Cornel Ban, *Ruling Ideas. How Global Neoliberalism Goes Local*, Oxford University Press, 2016

I. L. Caragiale, *Din primăvară până'n toamnă*, Capitolul II, *1907*: www.ilcaragiale.eu/opere/articole/1907/capitolul2.html#.Wk4KEyTTWhD (Accessed 4.01.2018)

Andrei Oțetea and Ion Popescu-Puțuri (Eds.), *Documente privind marea răscoală a țăranilor din 1907*, Editura Academiei Republicii Socialiste România, București, 1977

Karl Scheerer, *Die Rumänische Bauernaufstände vom Frühjahr 1907*, Mainz, 1971

Constantin Stere, *Publicistică*, Editura Universul, Chișinău, 2006

---

[9] For the disconnect between Romanian political elites and ordinary people nowadays see also Cornel Ban, *Ruling Ideas. How Global Neoliberalism Goes Local*, Oxford University Press, 2016, p. 72.

Appendices

Example of a Typical Agricultural Contract in 1906 Romania

Source: G.D. Creangă, *Grundbesitzverteilung und Bauernfrage in Rumänien*, Erster Teil, Leipzig, Verlag von Duncker und Humbolt, 1907.

Ciocănești Commune

Agricultural Contract No. 7, 5 April 1906

Between us, the inhabitants of the Ciocănești commune and the estate owner, the following agricultural contract has been concluded:

1. As we the undersigned need land to cultivate for the year 1906, we have turned to the estate owner with the request that he should lend us land from the Ciocănești estate under the following conditions:

   a) of the land, which will be rented to us for the cultivation of maize, we take it upon ourselves to work two parts for the estate owner and one part for ourselves as follows: digging, sowing and weeding so that there are always 2–3 plants in each furrow; digging a second time and piling the soil up along the ridges, and this is to be done on request and without being paid for it. We will then harvest the maize, remove the leaves, load it onto carts, remove the stubble, stack it up and transport it to where we are directed.

© The Author(s) 2018
I. Marin, *Peasant Violence and Antisemitism in Early Twentieth-Century Eastern Europe*,
https://doi.org/10.1007/978-3-319-76069-8

It is only after we have completed all of these tasks and have obtained from the estate administrator a receipt to this effect that we are allowed to harvest our own maize.

The land given to us for our own use is to be cultivated according to the above rules too. The second digging must be done before 15 June at the latest, and we must inform the estate manager about it, so he can sow his rapeseed in between our rows of maize. Those who do not fulfil this condition on time are liable to pay the estate owner 10 Lei per ½ hectare as compensation for the costs incurred because of the late sowing. Also, those who neglect the first or the second digging are liable to pay 10 Lei per ½ hectare. In addition, the estate owner reserves the right to cultivate our land for his own purposes, without us being absolved of our duties.

b) For each strip of land which we sow with grain, barley, oats or millet, we are liable to work one *Pogon* (½ hectare) for the estate owner and one for ourselves, as follows: after ploughing the soil is to be harrowed with the harrow belonging to the estate administration, then sowing, harvesting, tying in sheaves, piling up, then transporting to the thrashing machine or to the barn. We are to give up the following quantities per ½ hectare of the harvest: for grain, barley or oats 100 litres, for millet 40 litres. The seeds must be cleaned and sieved well. In case we do not deliver the produce in kind, we must pay its value in money at the following prices: 2.5 Lei for 20 litre of grain, 1.6 Lei for 20 litre of barley, 1.20 Lei for 20 litre of oats and 1.50 Lei for 20 litre of millet.

2. We take it upon ourselves to each work four days with the hands and two days with the carts wherever the estate owner needs us, with no further remuneration. Equally without further remuneration, we must each cut six *prăjini* (1 *prăjină* = approx. 200 square meters) of thatch from the pond belonging to the estate administration and bind it in stacks and transport it to the mansion. This work is only to be done weather permitting. In case the weather is bad, no compensation will be claimed on the part of the estate owner.

3. The watch over the leased land is to be provided by the estate owner through his guards, for which we must pay for each *Pogon* of maize 20 litres of grain, for wheat, oats, barley or millet two sheaves each per

three stacks or 20 litres of produce for a *Pogon*. Or pay 2 Lei instead of 20 litres of maize and the above-mentioned prices for the other grains.

4. We, the inhabitants who received land to work from the estate Ciocăneşti are allowed to graze our cattle only on the pastureland on which the estate owner allows us to do so. The oxen, horses, cows, buffalo, foal and calves should be grazed in Lunca Colentinei whereas the sheep should be grazed in the forest, namely in those places indicated by the estate owner together with the other cattle approved of by the estate owner; the estate owner will under no circumstances allow more than two big animals (oxen, horses, buffalo etc.) and ten sheep per ½ hectare.

5. We take it upon ourselves to pay for the grazing either in cash or in labour as per the below-mentioned tariffs until 1 September 1906 at the latest, as follows: for every animal fit for yoking 15 Lei, for every cow, buffalo cow, calf or foal 10 Lei, for every sheep 2.5 Lei and for a lamb 1.25 Lei.

   The estate owner has the right to check, as often as he likes, the number of cattle on the pasture and, if he should find out that we have grazed cattle not according the indications or the cattle belonging to others, we are then under obligation to pay double the grazing fee.

6. The herding of the animals is done by shepherds paid by us and we are responsible for any damage inflicted to the estate by our animals.

7. All inhabitants who possess horses or oxen must each work three *Pogons* of wheat, barley, oats or millet during the summer 1906, for which work the fee will be waived for two animals, so that they will only have to pay 4 Lei per owner.

8. None of the undersigned is allowed to move on to harvesting their own maize before they have paid their grazing fee as well as completed all the other duties stipulated by this or another work contract.

9. We must fulfil all the works stipulated in this contract as directed by the estate employees and upon the first call, using our own implements and bringing our own food. In case we do not fulfil one of the duties or we come late to work, we must pay without objection all the compensation to the estate owner that he is legally entitled to.

10. The work we must do in exchange for grazing is calculated according to the following prices:

One hectare of rape—cut, bound and carted—15 Lei
One hectare of wheat, barley, oats, millet or peas—cut, bound, piled up
and carted—16 Lei
One hectare of rape—cut, bound and left in the field—10 Lei
One hectare of wheat, barley, oats, millet or peas—cut, bound, piled up
and left in the field—12 Lei
One hectare ploughing—10 Lei;
One hectare of harrowing with the harrow belonging to the estate 2 Lei;
One day's work with the cart between 1 June and 1 September 1 Leu.

Signed on behalf of the estate owner C. Pascu, Accountant
The Inspectorate of the Bucoveni District
The accuracy has been confirmed.
Signed District Inspector Georgescu
2 May 1907

G.D. Creangă's Explanatory Note:
'The cultivation of a hectare with maize costs in Ciocăneşti 54 Franks. The
peasant pays therefore in work for the hectare of land taken on lease from
the estate owner:

2 hectares ....108 Franks
2 carting days .... 8 Franks
4 days' work with the hands 6 Franks
11 ari (1 ar = 100 square meters) thatch cutting 2 Franks
Crop guarding ....2 Franks
Total 126 Franks

A peasant's hectare of land in Ciocăneşti produces on average 14 hec-
tolitres of maize, 1 hectolitre costing 8 Lei = 112 Franks. With 14 Lei per
hectare the peasant paid more rent than the actual worth of his maize
crop, and in addition he has also worked around 35 days without pay for
this hectare of land.'

ROMANIAN AGRICULTURAL STATISTICS

The percentage by which the small peasant property was overtaxed in comparison to the great property (over 500 ha):

1.	Argeş by 97%	17.	R-Sărat 38%
2.	Dorohoi 68%	18.	Teleorman 38%
3.	Putna 68%	19.	Fălciu 36%
4.	Olt 63%	20.	Neamţu 30%
5.	Tecuci 63%	21.	Dâmboviţa 29%
6.	Roman 63%	22.	Buzău 27%
7.	Covurlui 63%	23.	Brăila 27%
8.	Ialomiţa 58%	24.	Romanaţi 25%
9.	Muscel 55%	25.	Vlaşca 25%
10.	Mehedinţi 51%	26.	Tulcea 23%
11.	Gorj 51%	27.	Ilfov 21%
12.	Vâlcea 48%	28.	Dolj 18%
13.	Tutova 42%	29.	Botoşani 15%
14.	Iaşi 42%	30.	Vaslui 10%
15.	Prahova 40%	31.	Constanţa 8%
16.	Bacău 38%	32.	Suceava 6%

Average 43%
(Evaluation of peasant property as per 1905)
Source: G.D. Creangă, *Grundbesitzverteilung*, vol.1, p. 56.

	Place	Average size of land per peasant head of family (tax payer) in hectares
1.	Constanţa	8.47 ha
2.	Tulcea	7.05 ha
3.	Brăila	5.05 ha
4.	Ialomita	4.72 ha
5.	Iaşi	4.58 ha
6.	Botoşani	4.07 ha
7.	Ilfov	4.05 ha
8.	Covurlui	4.04 ha
9.	Vlaşca	3.97 ha
10.	Neamt	3.96 ha
11.	Teleorman	3.87 ha
12.	Suceava	3.80 ha
13.	Tecuci	3.54 ha
14.	Fălciu	3.53 ha
15.	Dolj	3.51 ha
16.	Roman	3.45 ha
17.	Romanaţi	3.40 ha
18.	Dorohoi	3.30 ha

	Place	Average size of land per peasant head of family (tax payer) in hectares
19.	Vâlcea	3.28 ha
20.	Olt	3.24 ha
21.	R-Sărat	3.22 ha
22.	Vaslui	3.16 ha
23.	Tutova	3.15 ha
24.	Buzău	2.98 ha
25.	Mehedinţi	2.96 ha
26.	Bacău	2.87 ha
27.	Putna	2.70 ha
28.	Dâmboviţa	2.70 ha
29.	Argeş	2.66 ha
30.	Gorj	2.35 ha
31.	Prahova	2.24 ha
32.	Muscel	1.95 ha

Average: 3.42 ha
Source: G.D. Creangă, *Grundbesitzverteilung*, vol.1, p.121

		Ranking of counties according to extent of leaseholds	Percentage of leased surface from the total surface of property over 50 ha (%)	Percentage of large property over 100 ha (%)	Ranking of counties according to the size of their large property
1.	Botoşani		76.98	67.65	3
2.	Iaşi		73.22	52.62	13
3.	Ialomiţa		70.92	68.97	2
4.	Prahova		70.26	47.79	17
5.	Dorohoi		68.56	66.25	4
6.	Vlaşca		67.41	60.15	7
7.	Fălciu		67.30	53.69	11
8.	Brăila		66.70	75.85	1
9 .	Ilfov		66.39	57.58	8
10.	Dâmboviţa		63.35	36.03	26
11.	Neamţ		61.93	40.11	21
12.	Teleorman		60.09	62.28	6
13.	Covurlui		57.37	47.96	16
14.	Dolj		56.42	46.26	18
15.	Putna		56.19	40.94	20
16.	Vaslui		54.30	54.20	10
17.	Tutova		53.74	56.67	9
18.	R-Sărat		53.28	64.63	5
19.	Tecuci		52.71	50.48	15
20.	Muscel		51.86	27.85	29
21.	Romanaţi		51.09	38.76	22
22.	Argeş		49.15	34.53	27

Ranking of counties according to extent of leaseholds	Percentage of leased surface from the total surface of property over 50 ha (%)	Percentage of large property over 100 ha (%)	Ranking of counties according to the size of their large property
23. Olt	48.89	45.83	19
24. Mehedinți	48.01	38.61	23
25. Suceava	47.57	36.23	25
26. Buzău	46.92	50.50	14
27. Bacău	44.34	38.44	24
28. Roman	40.15	53.36	12
29. Constanța	33.35	31.02	28
30. Vâlcea	31.67	6.26	31
31. Gorj	23.32	18.68	30
31. Tulcea	14.30	6.14	32
On average	56.88	48.69	–

The leased surfaced varies between: 70–77% in 4 counties
60–70% in 8 counties
50–60% in 9 counties
40–50% in 7 counties
30–40% in 2 counties
10–30% in 2 counties
of the total cultivable surface (of property over 50 ha) of a county

Source: G.D. Creangă, *Grundbesitzverteilung*, vol.1, p. 138.
The largest surfaces leased out are to be found in the following counties:

Ialomița .... 291,765 ha or 70.92%
Teleorman .... 149,318 ha or 60.09%
Ilfov .... 145,924 ha or 66.36%
Vlașca .... 127,715 ha or 67.41%
Botoșani .... 123,742 ha or 76.98%
of the cultivable total surface of property over 50 ha.

The smallest surfaces leased out are to be found in the counties:

Tulcea .... 2,986 ha or 14.30%
Vâlcea .... 4,422 ha or 31.67%
Gorj .... 9,431 ha or 23.31%
of the cultivable total surface of property over 50 ha.

Source: G.D. Creangă, *Grundbesitzverteilung*, vol.1, p. 140.

Land taken on lease by the Fischer brothers

Districts		Cultivable surface in hectares		Annual Lease in Lei	
		1903/1904	1905	1903	1905
1.	Botoșani	39,099	32,260	624,689	545,876
2.	Brăila	5,278	4,900	120,000	126,046
3.	Dorohoi	35,284	37,459	653,078	781,614
4.	Ialomița	18,050	16,574	526,770	451,000
5.	Iași	18,201	23,049	311,871	434,775
6.	Putna	9,504	11,125	242,268	453,814
7.	Romanați	1,700	–	62,956	–
8.	Suceava	7,891	14,004	196,484	207,102
9.	Vaslui	3,417	4,562	65,000	101,050
10.	Tecuci	–	4,991	–	116,800
11.	Fălciu	–	10,030	–	199,535
12.	Dâmbovița	–	445	–	23,731
	In total	138,424	159,399	2,803,116	3,441,343

Source: G.D. Creanga, *Grundbesitzverteilung*, vol.1, p. 150

The owners of the estates leased out to the Fischer brothers' trust

Type of owner	Cultivable surface in hectares	Land rent in Lei	Average rent per hectare in Lei
State	16,574	451,000	27.20
School Treasury (Schulkassa)	1,285	35,872	27.90
Charity	13,500	174,284	12.90
Insurance Company	3,906	92,233	23.60
Private persons	124,134	2,687,954	21.60
Total	159,399	3,441,343	21.60

OVERVIEW OF THE AUSTRO-HUNGARIAN DIPLOMATIC CORRESPONDENCE SENT TO VIENNA FROM THE CONSULATES IN ROMANIA

Source: HHStA, Wien, Karton 9

Iași, 17 March: the peasant unrest in the county and the war of attrition waged by the insufficient troops, coming and going, against the peasants, who devastated, withdrew, waited patiently until the troops were gone, then were at it again. The report recorded the antisemitic agitation fanned by Professor Xenopol and his students from the University of Iasi and engaged in an explanation of peasant misery.[1]

Bucharest, 21 March: peasant unrest in Moldavia continues. There's not enough army and a new decree has been given to call up reservists. The atmosphere in Bucharest is one of concern and sympathy for the peasants. Peasants are exploited by arendași trusts, the most prominent of whom, the Fischer brothers, are Austrian citizens.[2]

Galați, 22 March: peasant protests have broken out in Vladimirești. There is a sawmill strike and the conference of Professor Iorga was postponed.[3]

Iași, 22 March: there is a lack of clarity as to the nature of the movement. Teachers are suspected of agitation. Prefect Văsescu is much to blame for the escalation of conflict. The army is disorganized, with troops sent here and there erratically, with no plan. The consul finds himself deluged with requests for help from Austro-Hungarian citizens living in the county.

Giurgiu, 23 March: peasant troubles break out in southern Wallachia. The mood of the officers is very low and troops are deemed unreliable.

Giurgiu 24 March: the peasant movement in Vlașca takes on greater proportions; troops are repelled by the peasants; the mayor and other notables flee to Ruschuk; there is panic in town and

[1] HHStA, Wien, Karton 9, Iași consulate report, 17 March 1907, Grebowski to Aerenthal.
[2] HHStA, Wien, Karton 9, Bucharest, 21 March 1907.
[3] HHStA, Wien, Karton 9, Galați, 22 March 1907.

news circulates of plundered estates. The peasants, opines the consul, have no justification for rebelling here. They are of a passive nature and have no hardships and they enjoy comparative well-being. The peasants are led by townspeople. Full anarchy reigns in the countryside; the peasants make no difference between Romanian and Jew. Episode of army insubordination whereby one of the commanding lieutenants is lynched by the peasants. A town guard is formed.

Giurgiu 25 March: the situation is very fluid. The troops are tired and unreliable. There are fears about the rabble in town. The consulate is reaching out to Austro-Hungarian ships on the Danube for refuge. The Turkish consul has left town because he was denied military protection.

Brăila 25 March: the owner of the firm Fratelli B. Mendl, who leased an estate from *Banca Agricolă*, informed the consul that the peasants asked for new contracts and better conditions, then moved on to devastate the estate; could the consulate arrange the payment of damages?

Brăila 26 March: the peasants want to have old contracts cancelled and demand that the estate be rented out to them.

Brăila 27 March: all inhabitants of the town are relieved that peasants and arendași have reached an agreement

Giurgiu 27 March: Stănești and other villages are shelled by the army in retaliation for the savage murder of a lieutenant at the hands of the rebels. Dead count 28 peasants.

Galați 27 March: the Danube k.k. steamship company puts their ship Neptune at the disposal of the Giurgiu consulate for the protection of Austro-Hungarian citizens. Peasants gather before the hospital asking for the bodies of the killed peasants. The army is necessary to keep peace as disturbances are feared to break out during the burial. The consul looks forward to the coming of the new prefect, who has a much better hold on the people. Austro-Hungarian citizens send their wives and children abroad.

Giurgiu 28 March: lots of arrests are made from among peasants but also townspeople. The consul thinks the condition of the peasants was not that bad, that they had two years of good crops and revolted because of administrative and legal misdemeanor.

Brăila 28 March: more arendaşi make concessions. Manifestos are spread out by the authorities that order has been re-established everywhere and any rebellion will be suppressed by use of weapons.

Turnu-Severin 29 March: all possible measures have been taken by authorities to prevent the spread of the uprising: the town is ringed with a military cordon; the prefect has set up an armed civil guard. The majority of Austro-Hungarian citizens in the county have fled either to Turnu-Severin or across the Hungarian border.

Brăila 29 March: fresh reservist troops have come in; watch posts have been set up 10 km around the town; the new prefect sent from Bucharest has arrived.

Giurgiu 31 March: the pacification of the county has been achieved; troops take possession even of the most remote villages; the arendaşi are starting to come back to their estates; intimidated peasants are bringing back what they stole and hand over the ringleaders to the army; the local press is still circulating exaggerated rumours.

Brăila 2 April: in the town of Brăila and its surroundings peace is reigning under the protection of 4,000-strong troops. The new prefect sends people of confidence (*Vertrauensmänner*) out into the villages to explain to the peasants the contents of the government manifesto sentence by sentence.

Index[1]

[1] Note: Page numbers followed by 'n' refer to notes.

© The Author(s) 2018
I. Marin, *Peasant Violence and Antisemitism in Early
Twentieth-Century Eastern Europe*,
https://doi.org/10.1007/978-3-319-76069-8

297